Emerging Legal Certainty: Empirical Studies on the Globalization of Law

Oñati International Series in Law and Society

TITLES

Totalitarian and Post-Totalitarian Law
Edited by Adam Podgorecki and Vittorio Olgiati

Foreign Courts: Civil Litigation in Foreign Legal Cultures
Edited by Volkmar Gessner

Family Law and Family Policy in the New Europe
Edited by Jacek Kurczewski and Mavis Maclean

Procedural Justice
Edited by Klaus F. Röhl and Stefan Machura

Oñati International Series
in Law and Society

Emerging Legal Certainty: Empirical Studies on the Globalization of Law

Edited by Volkmar Gessner
and Ali Cem Budak

A Series published for
THE OÑATI INTERNATIONAL INSTITUTE
FOR THE SOCIOLOGY OF LAW

Ashgate

DARTMOUTH
Aldershot UK • Brookfield USA • Singapore • Sydney

Published by
Dartmouth Publishing Company Limited
Ashgate Publishing Limited
Gower House
Croft Road
Aldershot
Hants GU11 3HR
England

Ashgate Publishing Company
Old Post Road
Brookfield
Vermont 05036
USA

British Library Cataloguing in Publication Data
Emerging legal certainty : empirical studies on the globalization of law. – (ONATI international series in law and society)
1.Legal certainty 2.International law 3.Law – Cross-cultural studies 4.Sociological jurisprudence
I.Gessner, Volkmar II.Budak, Ali Cem
340.1'15

Library of Congress Cataloging-in-Publication Data
Emerging legal certainty : empirical studies on the globalization of law / edited by Volkmar Gessner and Ali Cem Budak.
p. cm. — (Oñati international series in law and society)
Includes bibliographical references and index.
ISBN 1-84014-420-3 (hbk.). — ISBN 1-84014-423-8 (pbk.)
1. Law—International unification. I. Gessner, Volkmar.
II. Budak, Ali Cem. III. Series.
K605.E46 1998
340—dc21 98-9493
CIP

ISBN 1-84014-420-3 (Hbk)
ISBN 1-84014-423-8 (Pbk)

Printed in Great Britain by Galliards, Great Yarmouth

Summary of Contents

Part Three Law and the New World Order

Part Four Conclusions

Table of Contents

Acknowledgements

This research has been carried out at the Zentrum für Europäische Rechtspolitik (Centre for European Law and Politics) at the University of Bremen, Germany. Two major grants were provided by the Volkswagenstiftung within its programme, 'Law and Behaviour'. It is mainly this foundation's generous support of sociolegal research which keeps empirical studies in the field of the sociology of law alive in an environment more conducive to doctrinal legal research in Germany. We are also grateful to the International Institute for the Sociology of Law in Oñati in the Spanish Basque country, which has hosted two meetings of the project, the general editors of the Oñati series, William Felstiner and Eve Darian-Smith, and our anonymous referees. We thank the Isvaran Consultancy of Madras, India, namely Balkrishna Isvaran, for their cooperation in various parts of the research and in the production of the book.

Introduction

VOLKMAR GESSNER AND ALI CEM BUDAK

I

This book deals with empirical aspects of what political scientists in their correct understanding of global diversity call patterns of globalization. It builds on social scientific reflections and discussions on globalization processes which converge on the observation that the world is shrinking in terms of economic exchanges, mobility and speed of communication. It follows those approaches in sociology and economics which emphasize the role of institutions as part of societal patterns. It also takes into account those enormous efforts of legal science, of state legislators, of international organizations and of legal practitioners which have carefully prepared and facilitated these developments. And just like most globalization studies, it is interested in the behaviours and strategies of global actors.

Notwithstanding the fact that we base our approaches on established knowledge,[1] we are aware of what separates us from mainstream research in global studies. Legal research in preparing instruments of legal unification and harmonization does not use empirical methods in order to determine the degree to which its legal tools accomplish their goals. We do not take for granted the effectiveness of legal arrangements made for cross-border exchanges and try to determine their use in daily practice. Political science approaches in explaining globalization processes mainly deal with the role of the nation-state, international organizations and regimes; if legal structures are taken into account at all, it is those of public international law. Our focus is not on state actors but on individual and business actors and horizontal relationships between them regulated by contract, tort and family law. Sociology of law mainly started dealing with aspects of globalization by discussing legal professions, arbitrators and accountants in their global strategies of what is perceived as 'law production', whereas we concentrate

1 See Röhl and Magen, "Die Rolle des Rechts im Prozess der Globalisierung", *Zeitschrift für Rechtssoziologie* 17 (1996), 1–57, (including a detailed bibliography).

not on law production by these intermediaries but on the mobilization and enforcement of law by the legal subjects, the parties to cross-border legal negotiations and disputes, their problems in an inhospitable global environment and the support they get from professions and institutions in pursuing their claims. And, most important, we consider state law and state institutions as being highly relevant: all global actors are located in some nation-state which provides to a smaller or larger degree legal regulations and support institutions for global exchanges. Even in the relatively anomic world society there is not a single area which is not to some degree legally structured and patterned before individuals, small firms, transnational enterprises, lawyers or arbitrators take the first steps in pursuing their private interests or professional goals. Autonomous creation of rules and institutions, which is also being studied in the course of our project, depends very much on what (national, international or supranational) legislators, administrations or courts have done before.

This concept, common to all contributions to this book, needs to be briefly explained. The book stems from a common research project conducted at the Centre for European Legal Policy at the University of Bremen, Germany, by a group of lawyers and sociologists of law from different countries. The project started by studying international cases in the domestic courts of Bremen, Hamburg, Bremerhaven (all in Germany), New York and Milan, leading to a first book publication.[2] Making use of rather traditional approaches of the sociology of law, we started by studying the types of international cases taken to domestic courts, the characteristics of the parties, the procedures in court, the application of foreign law and of international conventions, the success rates of domestic and foreign parties, and many other similar aspects.

In the course of these observations and the collecting of data, however, we learned that we had not just added another type of conflict (the cross-border conflict) to the research agenda of the sociology of law, but had entered a new social environment. Cross-border legal behaviour is not only embedded in more than one legal culture, but is part of a new type of global legal culture. This new setting is mainly characterized by a different role of the state as regulator, mediator and guarantor of legal certainty. There seems to lack what Max Weber called 'formal rationality' and Douglass

2 Volkmar Gessner, ed., *Foreign Courts – Civil Litigation in Foreign Legal Cultures* (Aldershot: Dartmouth, 1996).

North calls 'institutions' as the prerequisites of a flourishing economy. But world trade increases by the moment and has reached levels completely unexpected a few decades ago. What is the rationality of global interactions and which institutions support global exchanges?

There is intellectual assistance from political scientists in order to better understand this dilemma of social order in the global society – but there is no consensus. Most authors seem to agree that the international system is undergoing a rapid transformation and that the role of the state is decreasing, or at least is being redefined. But others argue that states remain the only guarantors of a global order.

The assumption of a decreasing role of the state and state law is traditionally supported by institutionalist approaches which point to the increasing number and importance of international organizations. The United Nations and its substructures, the European Union, the World Bank, the World Trade Organization and the International Monetary Fund, create rules for inter-state, inter-trade and intercultural exchanges or establish a consensual framework for policy options that undermines the state apparatus. Some areas are regulated by international regimes which leave little room for state intervention and national policy making. More recently, the thesis of a decreasing role of the state has been based on observations of, for example, the autonomy of financial markets, the autonomous strategies of multinational firms, the mobility of investment capitals and the mobility of service industries. State borders are becoming irrelevant for these exchanges. There are few border controls or customs, and taxation is difficult to apply. To a certain degree, legal services also are affected by the reduction of state control.

These latter observations seem to support the pluralist or structural–functional approaches, long prevalent in social science, which kept their eyes averted from state institutions. Government was not taken seriously as an independent actor but was viewed primarily as an arena within which economic interest groups or social movements contended or allied with one another in order to shape the making of public policy decisions. If state agencies were the object of study, the point was mostly made that they were captured by interest groups. Neo-Marxists understood the capitalist state as an instrument of class rule and an arena for class struggle, ruling out, by definition, autonomous state action. Globalization processes occurring outside the constitutional framework of nation-states seem to provide ample evidence for these approaches. Some 35 000 multinational firms dominate and structure the global market, and thousands of interest groups and non-governmental organizations influence global media networks.

Legal sociologists add examples of mega-law firms, accountants and international arbitrators who produce law for the global society. Legislators as producers of law are not even mentioned.[3] In this line of thought, it is even argued that the very concept of law has gone through a radical change in the international arena:

> The distinction between law and non-law is based on a hierarchy of legal rules where the higher rule legitimates the lower one. ... The difference between a highly globalized economy and a weakly globalized politics is pressing for the emergence of a global law that has no legislation, no political constitution and no politically ordered hierarchy of norms ... This makes it necessary to rethink the traditional doctrine of sources of law. When the frame of the rule hierarchy, with constitutionally legitimated political legislation at its top, breaks under the pressure of globalization, than the new frame which replaces it can only be heterarchical. It decentres political law-making, moves it away from its privileged place at the top of the norm hierarchy and puts it on an equal footing with other types of social law-making.[4]

Quite another picture is painted by the realists who emphasize the autonomous role of the state in domestic as well as international affairs. Within national societies, state bureaucracy and state law are considered crucially important and relatively independent of societal influences and pressures. In the international setting, realists insist that, in spite of globalization, the core of international politics and of the regulation of global economic exchanges remains in the hands of national governments. This perspective is shared by legal science, which points to the consensual character to be found in all operations of international organizations and of international conventions which have to be negotiated, signed and ratified in every single case in order to become effective.

At the political level, these two different theoretical positions concerning the role of state and non-state actors in the process of globalization correspond to two different ideological approaches.

3 See studies collected in Gunther Teubner, ed., *Global Law without a State* (Aldershot: Dartmouth, 1997).

4 Gunther Teubner, "Foreword: Legal Regimes of Global Non-state Actors", in Teubner, *Global Law without a State*, pp. xiii–xvii, at p. xiv.

Proponents of the globalization created by non-state actors call for deregulation, as withdrawal of the state from protection of national markets or regulation of the financial system, whereas supporters of the irreplaceable role of the nation-state advocate regulatory state intervention against global destruction of natural resources or loss of local cultural identities, and so on. Supporters of these two ideological positions are properly identified by Santos as *adaptive audience* and *transformative audience* of the current changes in the world system. However, both adaptive and transformative audiences are ideal-typical groups. In fact, many social actors (individuals, groups, classes, organizations) participate in both audiences, 'according to time or issue, moving back and forth between the two without pledging irreversible or exclusive allegiance with one or the other'.[5] For, while some features of globalization give rise to positive expectations and support a predominantly adaptive position, others lead to negative expectations and a predominantly transformative approach.

This is also true for current global changes in the legal field. In some areas, typically identified with *lex mercatoria*, non-state actors play the central role, while in other areas, such as regional integration of national economies, just the opposite can be observed. In some areas, such as environmental protection and human rights, both the community of nation-states and non-state actors are active.[6] Thus, recently, intermediate positions have been elaborated which see states as sharing a transnational space with other actors who pursue egoistic concerns but also contribute to the creation, maintenance and change of the rules of global interaction. According to this approach, the international arena is a set of interlinked civil societies, transnationally active only to a degree accepted and permitted by the states involved. This gives local and foreign actors an interest in the way states support global issues or regulate transactions and contacts such as economic exchange and travel. The globalization of law then mainly consists of those legal

5 Santos uses within some broader context the terms "paradigmatic" and "subparadigmatic" interpretations (or "readings") of the current changes in the world system. See Boaventura de S. Santos, *Toward a New Common Sense – Law, Science and Politics in the Paradigmatic Transition* (New York, London: Routledge, 1995), 250–62.

6 Cf. the table "The transnationalization of the legal field", ibid., 275.

initiatives which – under societal pressure or not – aim at fostering inter-societal exchanges. In addition to (or instead of) constitutional lawmaking for global interaction, some local and foreign actors create their own global structures which then may operate entirely autonomously from state law. Peterson formulates this approach in the following way:

> Thinking in terms of interconnected civil societies illuminates the need states and societal actors have for each other. States, if they are to avoid fossilization of their own apparatus and the country they rule, need dynamism created by an active and participatory civil society... At the same time, however, societal actors need states. Though political philosophers and visionaries have looked for alternate institutions, a state or something rather like it appears necessary to provide minimal security, guarantee property rights and help enforce contracts – all three of which are necessary to the good functioning of civil society and the activities of its members. Transnational contacts and transactions, which assume reasonably secure self-organizing partners on both sides, thus rest on a base provided by the states in whose territory any of the-participants are located. Furthermore, state attitudes affect the extent and pace of transnational activity. The flourishing of such activity among societal groups after 1945 depended heavily on Western, particularly United States, decisions to foster it.[7]

Similarly, Hirst and Thompson argue that, although the capabilities of the nation-state have weakened considerably, especially in the macroeconomic management by international markets and the new communication media, its unique position as the only possessor of democratic authority over the population remains intact, and therefore the nation-state is still the only legitimate institution in terms of creating the conditions for effective international governance. Such effective international governance is of value for the non-state actors as well:

> Most players in the international economy have an interest in financial stability, including the major companies, for whom the reduction in uncertainty is of obvious advantage in their planning of investment, and in their production and marketing strategies. ... Companies cannot create such conditions themselves, even if they are transnational. ... A

7 M. J. Peterson, "Transnational Activity, International Society and World Politics", *Millennium* 21 (1992), 371–88, at 386.

> world composed of diverse political forces, governing agencies and organizations at both national and international levels will need an interlocking network of public powers that regulate and guide action in a relatively consistent way... our model for such power remains the *Rechtsstaat*. ... The state may no longer be 'sovereign' in [the] old sense, ... but it will define the scope of legitimate authority and legitimate action in its roles as constitutional arbitrator and law-maker.[8]

II

Empirical studies mostly support intermediate theoretical positions. The research we have undertaken in the field of transnational legal activities shows quite the same mix of state and non-state structures which Peterson and Hirst/Thompson describe. Our areas under scrutiny were cross-border debt enforcement, cross-border insurance matters, cross-border banking, cross-border social security claims, cross-border contract and tort claims, and cross-border child-support claims.

These areas of global legal interaction provide some examples of complete state control, some of autonomous globalization and some mixed models. We also observe dramatic changes in some of these areas, either in the direction of increasing state control or in the direction of decreasing state control:

Patterns of Legal Globalization

State | **Mixed** | **Autonomous**

← - reinsurance

debt enforcement

child support - - - - - - - - - - - - →

← - - - - - - - - - - - - - - - banking

social security

contract and tort

8 See Paul Hirst and Grahame Thompson, *Globalization in Question – The International Economy and the Possibilities of Governance* (Cambridge: Polity Press, 1996), 171–94, at 192–3.

This diversity which we observed in the forms of legal globalization is in contrast to theoretical approaches which attempt to explain the process of the globalization of law with a standard definition applicable to all areas of legal interaction.[9]

As already mentioned, our focus is the horizontal relationship between the actors in cross-border legal interactions. Our perspective for the empirical research (that is, the first two parts of the book) was that of an individual or a businessman who seeks to enforce his or her rights across the national borders. That is, our actors enter the play as claimants. In this respect, it was necessary to make a distinction between 'small people's claims' and business interactions. It is self-evident that small people have more difficulties in enforcing their rights in cross-border interactions. Considering the legal cultural differences and the additional costs involved in cross-border law enforcement, Galanter's one-shotters must be even more disadvantaged when compared with the repeat players in the international arena. As a result, the small people need to be supported by state or non-state structures in order to be able to enforce their rights in a foreign legal system (see Chapters 6 to 8). The repeat players of international business are in a better position to help themselves, because they are able to build their own institutional infrastructure (see Chapters 4 and 5) or afford the law enforcement offered by the international service providers (see Chapters 1 to 3) to bridge the distance between separate national legal orders.

Starting with the most general aspect of business interactions, Ali Cem Budak's contribution deals neither with a particular business sector nor with 'glocalized' support structures, but it provides the results of empirical research on 'cross-border debt collection'. The survey was carried out in two selected jurisdictions, Germany and Turkey, and concerns the role of law firms and commercial debt-collection agencies. In view of the fact that the rules of procedure for enforcement of foreign judgments – contained in national law or in international agreements – are seldom used in practice, largely owing to a number of practical difficulties which must be overcome by the creditor, the author discusses the role of alternative/private law enforcement mechanisms, provided inter alia by commercial debt-collection agencies.

9 See, for example, Röhl and Magen, "Die Rolle des Rechts im Prozess der Globalisierung", where the authors listed 10 theses applicable to "the role of law in the globalization process" in general.

Hasan Nerad's comments on Budak's contribution report the results of a court survey made in Turkey concerning international cases in the first-instance commercial courts and gives insights into international lawyering in the area of debt recovery, depending on participant observation.

Turning to specific business actors, Klaus Frick, in Chapter 4, refers to cross-border payments in international banking. On the basis of empirical research, including interviews and a questionnaire issued to practitioners, the author traces the potential of conflicts on one side and the counteracting structures on the other from the actors' point of view. One result of the survey is the special meaning of the infrastructure established by the banks' heavy dependence on technical developments during the last decades, such as the eurocheque, the credit card system and the S.W.I.F.T. organization. Further, Frick discusses the objections raised by the EU Commission to banking activities in connection with cross-border payments. The Commission's approach presents an exemplary attempt to cut bank autonomy which may disadvantage the consumer. The author also discusses the initiatives of banks which result from the threatening legislative measures of the EU Commission.

Chapter 3, by Christine Stammel is, like Frick's study, based on a particular sector of global players, and it deals with the changing dispute behaviour in the London reinsurance market during the last 10 to 15 years. Because of its considerable share of international business, the London reinsurance market represents an inviting field for the study of legal behaviour of a limited number of actors within one specific field of international business. Until recently, reinsurance was known for not carrying out legal battles in public, if there were legal battles at all. Disputes were negotiated and remained in the privacy of arbitration. However, Stammel's research – consisting of interviews conducted with City solicitors who are engaged in reinsurance law – proved that reinsurance can no longer be called a non-litigious area. With the increasing importance of the London Commercial Court for the litigation of reinsurance matters, a hitherto autonomous area of global legal interaction seems to be moving towards becoming an area which is governed by state law.

Whereas Frick and Stammel discuss the role of internationally functioning infrastructures created by a business sector, Vittorio Olgiati deals with the role of Milan, Italy and the Chamber of Commerce in Milan, which provide a network of services supporting international legal interactions between various businesses. Chapter 5 discusses the Milan case as an example of 'glocalization' of international business and the structure and function of the Chamber of Commerce in Milan, emphasizing its role in building an infrastructural network that is based on the mix of skills, information and culture that characterizes Milan as a meeting place of the 'universe' of business activities: Universitas Mercatorum.

In Chapter 6, dealing with small people as global actors, Kirstin Grotheer studies cross-border maintenance claims of children. There are several bilateral and multilateral treaties which aim at a simplified and speedy processing of cross-border maintenance claims, yet, because of the especially weak position of the claimants, the application of these treaties faces important difficulties. In Germany, an interesting organization of a private law nature, the German Institute for Guardianship Cases, provides the maintenance creditors full support, concerning both outgoing and incoming child-maintenance claims in the country. The author discusses the role played by that Institute in the enforcement of cross-border maintenance claims, referring to the results of her own survey, including inter alia an analysis which was made of the file records of the same Institute.

Pierre Guibentif's contribution (Chapter 7) is also concerned with the small people, in this case the migrant workers, and reports the results of the author's research in Portugal which surveyed several public departments as well as private associations dealing with international social security and family matters. The data which were collected show that the various international agreements in these areas of cross-border legal interactions work relatively well, conditioned mainly by personal relations among officials strengthened by regular contacts among administrations of the involved countries, and between these and international organizations. Cross-border social security matters are disposed of by filling in forms prepared for that purpose by the EU. The device of the culturally neutral form may represent the future of global governance.

Andreas Petzold provides, in Chapter 8, the results of a survey on the role of state authorities and commercial services in supporting both individuals and businesses who lack information and experience about a foreign legal system. The study evaluates the answers, which were collected from German embassies, consulates and chambers of industry and commerce abroad, concerning an inquiry requesting legal advice for a fictitious debt-recovery case of a relatively small claim. The author discusses and compares the efficiency of state and commercial support structures with regard to their ability to supply information and provide assistance in cross-border legal interactions.

III

Independently of the position we have chosen for our areas of legal interaction on the scale of different (state v. non-state) globalization patterns, it is interesting to note that globalization of legal structures is much more effective at the levels of roles and institutions than at the level of programmes (rules). Globally active institutions such as courts, international law firms, consulates, chambers of commerce, debt-collection firms and central authorities have often developed structures and behaviours which are adequate for international cases, whereas statutes, international conventions or even some *lex mercatoria* rules are not providing sufficient legal certainty for the contingencies of global exchanges.

In search of examples of globalization of law in various areas of cross-border legal interaction, the research group expected to find non-state-produced sets of rules as suggested by the *lex mercatoria* discussion. In the end, numerous non-state organizations and structured behavioural patterns were found, but almost nothing was observed which can be defined as autonomous lawmaking. If the global legal order is a mixture of state and non-state components, non-state components of global legal order provide the institutional infrastructure of cross-border legal interactions. This observation is further developed in the third part of the book in the theoretical context of the globalization debate. The reference point is always the role of the nation-state and the national legal systems in the new world order, as compared to the non-state enforcement mechanisms regulating cross-border legal interactions.

McGrew's contribution (Chapter 9) provides a critical overview of the existing literature on globalization in order to establish a more rigorous understanding of the concept and the arguments and evidence which underpin it. Using the concept of 'historical forms of globalization', the author evaluates some of the key empirical evidence and counter-evidence regarding the intensification of globalization and assesses its implications for the late twentieth century nation-state. Thus the chapter situates the discussion of global legal interaction in the context of a broader discussion within political science about state sovereignty and state autonomy.

McGrew's critical introduction is followed by a legal theoretical discussion by Banakar, who investigates in Chapter 10 the relation between the rule of law, legality and legitimacy in cross-border legal interactions. In both classical and modern legal theory, the concept of law has been predicated on the concept of legitimacy, which in turn implies the acceptance of legal rules by citizens of the nation-state. Notions of 'citizenship' and 'nation-state' do not have their parallels at the global level; hence the legitimacy of international law making and law enforcement (by the state actors or by the support structures created by business actors) becomes problematic. In this context, the legitimacy of *lex mercatoria* and the activities of the international arbitration courts are questioned.

In the first concluding chapter, Neyer discusses our results from the point of view of a political scientist. Globalization may be understood as a socioeconomic process that raises the need for a new mixture of parallel 'transnational private' and 'national public' legal regulations. According to Neyer, in order to maintain the postwar level of support and to offer the same protection to its citizens, the territorial state needs to adopt an understanding of its transnational functions and to develop, not only cross-border support structures for 'small people', but also mechanisms for coping with the externalities of the decisions taken by transnational private actors. In making this argument, Neyer's study brings together some of the theoretical findings of recent research in international relations theory, international political economy and – last but not least – the contributions collected in this volume.

Volkmar Gessner then draws theoretical conclusions regarding the problem of legal certainty in the world society. In the closing chapter he discusses the empirical and theoretical results so far achieved in his current project and argues that, whereas the national societies integrate legal expectations on the levels of programmes and roles, the world society seems to integrate them on the lower levels of roles and persons. Thus, as required by most approaches in political science, the role of the state has to be redefined in the course of the globalization of law. The nation-state remains relevant insofar as this new legal cultural environment is taken into account.

IV

Our examples of cross-border legal interaction represent a wide variety in terms of geographical area of research. Some of the studies concern one or several national legal systems of different legal–cultural characteristics (Budak/Nerad: Germany and Turkey;

Grotheer: Germany in relation to neighbouring countries such as the area of the former Czechoslovakia, the Netherlands, Austria and Switzerland, as well as the USA and the EU in general; Guibentif: Portugal in relation to other EU member states), some studies deal with 'glocalized' centres of international business (Stammel: London; Olgiati: Milan); and others have a broader European or global ambit of research (Frick, Petzold). This wide geographical distribution was chosen just in case our positions on the globe still matter.

References

Gessner, Volkmar, ed. 1996. *Foreign Courts – Civil Litigation in Foreign Legal Cultures*. Aldershot: Dartmouth.

Hirst, Paul and Grahame Thompson. 1996. *Globalization in Question – The International Economy and the Possibilities of Governance*. Cambridge: Polity Press.

Peterson, M.J. 1992. Transnational Activity, International Society and World Politics. *Millennium* 21.

Röhl, Klaus F. and Stefan Magen. 1996. Die Rolle des Rechts im Prozess der Globalisierung. *Zeitschrift für Rechtssoziologie* 17.

Santos, Boaventura de S. 1995. *Toward a New Common Sense – Law, Science and Politics in the Paradigmatic Transition*. New York, London: Routledge.

Teubner, Gunther, ed. 1997. *Global Law without a State*. Aldershot: Dartmouth.

Part One
Business Interactions

1 Cross-border Debt Collection: Examples of Turkey and Germany

ALI CEM BUDAK

Introduction[1]

The literature on international economic relations, written by economists, political scientists or jurists, refers to the law of the international economy as a separate topic of discussion.[2] In this context reference is often made to the liberalization of international trade (elimination of tariff and non-tariff barriers, anti-dumping laws and so on), trade law applicable to international business

1 This chapter contains the summary of the initial results of comparative empirical research conducted in Germany, Turkey and England. For the detailed account of the research results see by the same author *Making Foreign People Pay – Law and Practice of Cross-Border Debt Collection with Special Reference to German, English and Turkish Law* (Aldershot: Dartmouth, forthcoming in 1998).

2 For example, S. Tamer Cavusgil, "Globalization of Markets and Its Impact on Domestic Institutions", Martin Shapiro, "The Globalization of Law" and Jost Delbrück, "Globalization of Law, Politics, and Markets – Implications for Domestic Law – A European Perspective" in *Indiana Journal of Global Legal Studies* 1 no.1 (1993), 9–36; Monir H. Tayeb, *The Global Business Environment – An Introduction* (London: SAGE, 1992); several contributions in Richard Stubbs and Geoffrey R. D. Underhill, *Political Economy and the Changing Global Order* (London: Macmillan, 1994); D.M. Day and Bernardette Griffin, *The Law of International Trade*, 2nd edn (London, Dublin, Edinburgh: Butterworths, 1993); Jürgen Bellers, "Nationale und internationale Normierungen auf dem Gebiet grenzüberschreitender Wirtschaftsbeziehungen", *Jahresschrift für Rechtspolitologie* (1993); Klaus Dieter Wolf, ed., *Internationale Verrechtlichung* (Pfaffenweiler: Centaurus, 1993), 127–46.

transactions (international sale of goods, cross-border payment and security methods, and so on), the 'protective law' (intellectual property protection, labour law, the protection of consumers – product liability, standards – protection of the environment, and so on) and resolution of disputes in international transactions (international litigation and arbitration). One important area of the law of international economy which has not been discussed in detail in the literature is cross-border recovery of debts arising from international economic interaction.

'Cross-border debt recovery' or 'debt collection' is distinguished from international litigation in that a debtor may refrain from paying the debt across the borders, even if there exists no (genuine) dispute between the parties taking part in the legal relation. International involvement in economic relations means increase of risks as well as increase in benefits,[3] one important element of such additional risks being non-payment of debts: the debtor may simply feel himself out of reach of the creditor beyond the borders.

It may fairly be assumed that international legal transactions are secured against the risk of non-payment better than domestic legal transactions. At the inception of a continuous cross-border relationship, credit reference agencies are used to investigate the credit rating of the foreign businesses. Partly because of the difficulty of communicating in foreign languages, it is the custom to use written documents, at least fax and telex, instead of the telephone. International collection and security methods which are standard in almost all countries ensure payment, to a large extent thanks to the intermediary role of credit institutions; these include bills of exchange, letters of credit, bank guarantees, factoring and forfaiting. Credit insurance facilities, including export credit insurance from government agencies, are used regularly: for example, NCM Credit Insurance in the United Kingdom, HERMES insurance in Germany, Türk Eximbank insurance in Turkey.[4] Real and personal securities, such as associated/parent company guarantees and retention of title agreements are used. In the case of investment credits, security types provided by national laws of the debtor are widely used by foreign creditors. The business community is

3 Asterios G. Kefalas, *Global Business Strategy – A systems approach* (Cincinnati, Ohio: South-Western Publishing, 1990), 9–13 ("The Internationalization/Globalization Process").

4 Generally see Clive M. Schmitthoff, *Export Trade – The Law and Practice of International Trade*, 9th edn (London: Stevens, 1990).

widely aware of these debt collection/security methods and makes use of them.[5]

Without going into the details of international collection and security methods, suffice it to mention some typical cases where these methods are not available or are not enforceable by the creditor. Firstly, standard collection and security methods are used mostly in commercial transactions. In cases where debt does not arise from a 'transaction', for example, in tort cases (a traffic accident during a holiday abroad), the creditor can neither obtain a security nor impose on the debtor a payment method such as letters of credit or bills of exchange. This is the case for most 'involuntary creditors', such as employees demanding redundancy payment from their ex-employers in a foreign country, children having maintenance claims against their parents living abroad or consumers of imported medicaments containing harmful substances. Secondly, even in contract cases, a contracting party with a weaker economic position cannot always benefit from international collection and security methods. This is the situation, for example, with a consumer who pays a mail order company abroad but who does not receive the goods which he has ordered. Last but not least, not every security included in international contracts is enforceable. The reason may be differences in national laws (as with losing enforceability of German retention of title clauses in standard contract terms in many foreign countries where the retention of title clause must be signed separately) or practical difficulties (such as costs of transporting back the goods exported under a retention of title clause).

In a case where debts arising from cross-border transactions are not paid, and a peaceful solution cannot be reached between the debtor and the creditor – such as an extension of time for payments – the creditor has two alternatives. He can go through the 'judicial methods' of debt collection available before the national courts or he can use what may be called 'extrajudicial methods of debt collection'. In the former alternative he can either sue the debtor in the foreign country where the latter lives or he can sue the same person in his own country of residence and can enforce the judgment which he has obtained from the domestic court in the debtor's country – or, to put it more correctly – in the country where the debtor has his assets. As an alternative to the judicial

5 For the results of a survey concerning the collection and security methods used by export firms in Istanbul, see *Making Foreign People Pay*, Chapters 14–15.

debt collection methods, 'extrajudicial methods of debt collection' are provided inter alia by commercial debt collection agencies in many countries, which make contact and deal with the debtor professionally and collect the debt, as far as is possible, out of court.

Accordingly, this chapter is organized as follows. Firstly, judicial methods of cross-border debt collection are discussed, supported by statistical and other numerical data collected from Germany and Turkey. Secondly, the difficulties of the judicial methods which encumber the creditors using national courts in this matter are described. In this second part, the results of a recent EU-wide lawyers' survey which was made at the Zentrum für europäische Rechtspolitik at the University of Bremen, Germany have been widely used. Next, we turn to some modern sociolegal developments in the area of debt recovery, which may be called the 'routinization' and 'privatization' of debt collection. Here again numerical data are given for the type of work provided by the courts in the area of debt collection, borrowed from judicial statistics and sociolegal literature. Following this discussion, under the heading of 'Extrajudicial methods of cross-border debt collection', the results are presented of a survey which was conducted in Germany among the commercial debt collection agencies which are involved in cross-border debt collection business. Finally, the role of international law firms in debt collection is considered, illustrated by interviews with two advocates in Turkey and with reference to the earlier discussion of 'routinization' and 'privatization'.

Judicial Methods of Cross-border Debt Collection

Going to Court in the Home Country

A creditor who has sued his overseas debtors in his own country of residence can enforce the judgment which he has obtained from the domestic court in the country where the debtor has his assets. Such enforcement of foreign judgments is possible in most legal systems provided that competent courts of the country where the judgment is sought to be enforced declares the (foreign) judgment enforceable with a separate decision of its own (that is, with an *exequatur* order). In cases where reciprocity exists between the country of origin of the judgment and the country where the judgment is sought to be enforced, an *exequatur* order is normally made without re-examining the merits of the original case which has been already heard by the foreign court.[6]

Thus, where the contractual reciprocity for enforcement of foreign judgments exists, such as between the EU member states, most of which are also members of the 1968 Brussels Convention[7] on reciprocal enforcement of foreign judgments, cross-border enforcement of domestic judgments is possible under a simplified procedure. Where no international agreement on the reciprocal enforcement of judgments exists, many national courts are again not unwilling to enforce foreign judgments. In Turkey, the General Assembly of Civil Chambers of the Court of Cassation held in 1990[8] that the mere existence of an enforcement (*exequatur*) procedure in the German Code of Civil Procedure (§§ 722–3) which is in its nature similar ('parallel') to the enforcement of foreign judgments procedure in the Turkish Act on International Private and Procedural Law (IPPL) suffices to satisfy the reciprocity requirement between Germany and Turkey.[9]

6 For detailed information about the procedures for "enforcement of foreign judgments" in international conventions and in domestic private international law provisions of various countries, see *Handbuch des internationalen Zivilverfahrensrechts* (ed: Max-Planck-Institute für ausländisches und internationales Privatrecht), Bd. III/1 by Dieter Martiny and III/2 by Dieter Martiny, Jan Peter Waehler and Martin K. Wolff (Tübingen: Mohr, 1984).

7 Exceptions are the new member states, Austria, Finland and Sweden. (Finland and Sweden are, however, parties to the Lugano Convention aiming to cover relations between EU and EFTA countries, which is almost identical to the Brussels Convention.)

8 General Assembly of the Civil Chambers of the Court of Cassation ("HGK") 13.6.1990, no. 13/3-347, *Yargitay Kararlari Dergisi* 1990, 1282–6, reproduced in Baki Kuru, *Hukuk Muhakemleri Usulü*, vol. 4 (Istanbul: Yetkin, 1991), 4379–80.

9 To the same effect, in the German literature concerning execution of Turkish judgments, see, for example, Hilmar Krüger, "Das türkische IPR-Gesetz von 1982", *Praxis des Internationalen Privat- und Verfahrensrechts* vol. 2 (1982), 252, at 258, footnote 65. The information which was recently reported in the German *Anwaltsblatt* no. 3 (1994), 98–104 to the effect that "in spite of the international agreements [?], German court decisions were not recognised in Turkey", was not correct. (Cf. Thomas Schnorr, "Einzelanwälte und kleine Anwaltsfirmen im internationalen Rechtsverkehr – Eine empirische Untersuchung", *Anwalts blatt* 44, no. 3 (1994), 98, at 103.)

In addition, interviews which the author had with practitioners (judges, attorneys, civil execution officers, officers from the Ministry of Justice) in Turkey and in Germany indicate that many of the matters described in the literature as legal complications in international debt recovery (for example, various regulated national statutes of limitations, domestic security rights having no effect abroad, currency restrictions and so on) are indeed not so important in practice. Accordingly, it might be expected that the enforcement of foreign judgments is a part of the daily work of courts of first instance, especially in those countries where foreign trade is of great economic importance. However, this is not the case. The statutory execution of judgments procedures in the two countries, Turkey and Germany,[10] are seldom used in practice.

Statistical data available in Germany show that the use of the judicial 'enforcement of foreign judgments' procedures which are provided by the Federal Code of Civil Procedure and bilateral or multilateral international agreements on the reciprocal recognition and execution of judgments are rarely used. According to the official statistics which have been published by the Federal Statistical Office in Germany, the total number of cases decided at the German first instance courts (not including ex-GDR states) for enforcement of foreign judgments between 1969 and 1981 is only 22,504. The great majority of these cases (21,393) are based on international agreements on reciprocal recognition and enforcement of judgments;[11] each year, about 100 people make use of the procedure for the execution of foreign judgments provided by the Federal Code of Civil Procedure. To give a comparison, the annual number of concluded cases in German (not including ex-GDR states) first instance civil and commercial courts is currently about 2,250,000.[12]

10 For the first-hand data concerning the frequency of the enforcement of foreign judgments proceedings in England, see *Making Foreign People Pay*, Chapter 6.

11 See Erik Jayme and Rainer Hausmann, eds, *Internationales Privat- und Verfahrensrecht* (Textausgabe), 7th edn (Munich: Beck, 1994), 346–436.

12 See data provided annually by Statistisches Bundesamt, *Gerichte und Staatsanwaltschaften* (Rechtspflege, Fachserie 10, Reihe 2; booklets dated 1990–93), (Wiesbaden: Kohlhammer) concerning the workload of *Landgerichte*, *Amtsgerichte*, *Familiengerichte* and *Arbeitsgerichte*.

The number of foreign judgments in Turkey executed under the procedure for the statutory execution of judgments is also relatively small. The annual number of (second instance) cases held by the 11th Chamber of the Court of Cassation, that is, the chamber handling commercial matters, concerning execution of a foreign judgment is not more than 10.[13] A recent survey made in Izmir, the second largest export harbour and one of the largest tourism centres of the country, showed that in 1993 not one single action had been brought in the first instance commercial courts of the district seeking the execution of a foreign judgment in Turkey.[14]

Going to Court Abroad

The relatively small number of cases for the execution of foreign judgments in commercial matters may suggest that foreign claimants prefer to sue in the debtor's country. Judicial statistics in the two jurisdictions[15] do not provide information on the nationality of the parties in court proceedings. In an attempt to find out the frequency of foreign parties being involved in commercial cases in Turkey, the practice of the Court of Cassation again provides some insight. All Court of Cassation judgments rendered by the 11th (commercial matters) Chamber of the Court of Cassation in June 1995 – that is, between 3 June 1995 and 3 July 1995 – have been studied.[16] The number of international cases (that is, those cases in which at least one of the parties is a foreign corporation or

13 Turkish Court of Cassation, Judge 2.

14 Hasan Nerad, Selma Baktir, Esin Taylan and Sevilay Eroglu, *Izmir Asliye Ticaret Mahkemelerinde Görülen Davalar ve Hasimsiz Isler Konusunda Arastirma Raporu*, Dokuz Eylül Üniversitesi Iktisadi ve Idari Bilimler Fakültesi (not published, 1995). See Hasan Nerad, in Chapter 2 of the present volume.

15 For first-hand data concerning England, see *Making Foreign People Pay*, Chapter 6.

16 Such a sampling is of representative value. The Turkish judicial system provides only two court instances, namely first instance district courts and the Court of Cassation in Ankara. There is no third instance between the two where an appeal on the matters of fact or law is possible. In addition, no leave is needed to appeal at the Court of Cassation. In practice, an appeal is lodged ritually against most of the first instance judgments, even if no convincing ground of appeal exists.

individual) was 36 out of a total of 1,039 cases: that is to say, 3.5 per cent of commercial cases were 'international'.

For the purposes of comparison, the monetary volume of commerce in domestic and international transactions within a particular country may be taken as a common factor which has an influence on the number of domestic and international court cases in the commercial courts of the same country. As a criterion for defining the share of international trade in the national economy, political economists use the concept of 'foreign trade share' (*Außenhandelsquote*).[17] Foreign trade share is the 'ratio of total trade turnover (exports and imports) to national income'[18] which may be mathematically formulated as (import + export)/2 × 100/GDP. In 1993, the foreign trade share of Turkey was 17 per cent.[19] The 3.5 per cent share of international commercial cases suggests that cross-border commercial disputes come less frequently to the courts than national commercial disputes.

International commercial cases before Turkish courts were concentrated on a small number of issues. Most numerous were the transport cases: 16 of the 36 international cases (43 per cent) were either directly or indirectly (disputes between the export insurer and the insured or the third party sued for damages) related to the carriage of goods by sea or by land. These cases were followed by cases concerning patents, trade marks and unfair competition: nine cases (24 per cent). In domestic commercial cases the same types of disputes are less frequent: the disputes arising from transport and (all kinds of) insurance contracts were represented respectively by five and 29 cases among the 525 contested claims before the commercial courts in Izmir in 1993; that is, they only amounted to 6 per cent of the cases. Similarly, the number of (domestic) cases concerning trade marks and unfair competition before the same courts was seven, only 1.3 per cent.[20] Parties having commercial cross-border legal relations with Turkey other than those referred

17 See Jürgen Neyer, *Spiel ohne Grenzen – Weltwirtschafliche Strukturveränderungen und das Ende des sozial kompetenten Staates* (Marburg: Tectum, 1996), 27.

18 See Wilhelm Schäfer, "Außenhandelsquote" in *Wirtschaftswörterbuch*, vol. 2, 3rd edn (Munich: Verlag Franz Vahlen, 1991).

19 In 1988, the same ratio was 18 per cent. International Monetary Fund, *International Financial Statistics* (Washington, DC: IMF, December 1995); author's calculation using values for export and import of goods and international service transactions and GDP.

20 Nerad *et al. Izmir Asliye Ticaret Mahkemekrinde Görülen Isler*, 3.

to above seem to be less litigious. Disputes before the Turkish courts arising from foreign investments and foreign bank loans, for example, must be few in number.

A recent empirical study made in Germany shows that the proportion of 'international cases' (cases in which one party has its domicile outside Germany) in the caseload of the Bremen and Hamburg courts in 1988 was 2.8 per cent, that is 320 out of 12,029 cases.[21] Of these international cases 65 per cent (209 cases) were initiated by foreigners.[22] Owing to the fact that Hamburg and Bremen are traditional import/export cities, international commercial cases may be overrepresented in these court districts, as compared to the average for Germany as a whole.[23] Therefore the 'foreign trade share' criterion which was used for Turkey can be applied here more cautiously. In any case, in 1988, when the cases of the Gessner survey were taken to court, the foreign trade share in Germany was 27 per cent,[24] with the share of international commercial cases in these two districts remaining at 10 per cent. With reference to subject matters, international cases before German first instance courts were again concentrated on a small number of issues: 83 (41.2 per cent) of the cases were related to contract of sales, 51 (25.3 per cent) were related to sea or land transport, and 24 (11.9 per cent) concerned contracts for work.[25]

21 Cases regarding execution of foreign judgments and other cases on enforcement matters are included.

22 Volkmar Gessner, "International Cases in German First Instance Courts", in *Foreign Courts – Civil Litigation in Foreign Legal Cultures*, ed. Volkmar Gessner (Aldershot: Dartmouth, 1996): 149–207, Tables 2 and 5 in pp. 155 and 161.

23 Ibid.

24 In 1994, the same ratio was 29 per cent: International Monetary Fund, *International Financial Statistics*; author's calculation using values for export and import of goods and international service transactions and GDP. (The ratios found are different from those of Neyer, who used only export and import of goods, but not international services in the formula. Cf. Neyer, *Spiel ohne Grenzen*, p. 172.)

25 Ibid., 164.

Difficulties Impeding Access to the Judicial Methods

The reason for little use of judicial methods in cross-border debt collection may be either legal complications or some practical difficulties discouraging the creditors from suing before national courts.

Since the post-Second World War period, parallel to the growth of international trade, growing efforts have been made by the community of nation-states to improve the capacity of the national courts for solving international disputes. These efforts can be seen both at the national level, in the form of developments in domestic private international laws,[26] and at the international level, in the form of numerous international conventions on private international law[27] and unification of laws.[28] Such efforts not only avoided legal complications of cross-border litigation by and large, but also

26 An interesting example of this is the development in the English rules of international jurisdiction; c.f. jurisdiction rules in common law with provisions of Rules of Supreme Court, Order 11 and Civil Jurisdiction and Judgments Act 1982: Volker Triebel, Stephen Hodgson, Wolfgang Kellenter and Georg Müller, *Englisches Handels- und Wirtschaftsrecht*, 2nd edn (Heidelberg: Verlag Recht und Wirtschaft, 1995), 373–90. See also, for example, new Turkish (1982) and Swiss (1987) acts on private international law for their liberal attitudes to the application of foreign law and the enforcement of foreign judicial decisions: e.g., Art. 5 of the former and Art. 194 of the latter, which respectively narrow the possibility of application of the *ordre public* barrier against the choice of law contracts and adopt the liberal rules of enforcement of foreign arbitral awards of the 1958 UN Convention as provisions of domestic private international law.

27 For example, the European Convention on Information on Foreign Law 1968, the Hague Convention on the Service Abroad of Judicial and Extra Judicial Documents in Civil and Commercial Matters 1965, the Hague Conventions on enforcement of foreign maintenance orders dated 1958 and 1973, and the Brussels Convention on Jurisdiction and the Enforcement of Civil and Commercial Judgments 1968.

28 For example, the UN Convention on the International Sale of Goods 1980, the Convention on the Carriage of Goods by Road 1956. See René David, "The International Unification of Private Law", *International Encyclopedia of Comparative Law*, Vol.II, Chapter 5 (Tübingen: Mohr/The Hague, Paris: Mouton/New York:

created a reciprocal comity between different national courts. A well known English judge, Lord Diplock, summarized the latter development with the words 'judicial chauvinism has been replaced by judicial comity'.[29]

There exist, as is stated above, no special legal complications in German and Turkish law which make enforcement of foreign judgments difficult. Again the information gathered here from international law firms and commercial debt collectors through interviews and questionnaires suggests that matters which are mentioned in the literature[30] as legal complications in international debt recovery (such as variously regulated national statutes of limitations, losing the effect of domestic security rights abroad, currency restrictions and so on) are not important in practice. Similarly, no complaints were to be heard in our interviews that Turkish or German courts discriminate against foreign parties.[31] The answers given by European law firms to a ZERP questionnaire on 'Costs of Judicial Barriers for Consumers in the Single Market'[32] (hereafter

Oceana, 1971); Gerhard Kegel, *Internationales Privatrecht*, 7th edn (Munich: Beck, 1995), 60–99.

29 Cf. the *Abidin Daver* (H.L.(e.)), [1984] 1 A.C. 398, at p. 411.

30 See, for example, Horst Piggert, "Das Auslandsinkasso", *Teilzahlungswirtschaft* 15 no.1 (1968), 15 et seq.; Reinhard Böhner, "Forderungseinziehung gegen Unternehmen in der EG", *Schimmelpfeng-Review* 24 (1979), 69 et seq.; Albert Windolp, "Das Auslandsinkasso in den Ländern der EWG und EFTA", *Teilzahlungswirtschaft* 16 2 (1969), 56 et seq.; ibid, "Das Auslandsinkasso im Ausland", *Schimmelpfeng-Review* 18 (1976), 38 et seq. and ibid., "Das Inkasso nach deutschem und ausländischem Recht", in *Aktuelle Beiträge über das Inkasso im In- und Ausland*, 2nd edn (Frankfurt/M.: Schimmelpfeng, 1977); Hubert Timmermann, "Die Zwangsvollstreckung im Ausland ist schwierig", *Teilzahlungswirtschaft* 20 2 (1969), 56 et seq.

31 A series of interviews with international law firms in London confirmed this. See *Making Foreign People Pay*, Chapter 5.

32 See Hanno von Freyhold and Enzo L. Vial, "Report on the Cost of Judicial Proceedings in the European Union", in *Cost of Judicial Barriers for Consumers in the Single Market – A Report for the European Commission (Directorate General XXIV)*, ed. Hanno von Freyhold, Volkmar Gessner, Enzo L. Vial and Helmut Wagner (Bremen: Zentrum für Europäische Rechtspolitik an der Universität Bremen (ZERP), October/November 1995), 15–127.

'ZERP survey') proved again that no such discrimination against foreigners can be found anywhere in the courts in Europe.[33]

The more important reasons for little access of foreigners to the judicial methods of debt collection are what may be called practical or legal bureaucratic difficulties. Among such difficulties are the following.

- The creditor must know about the address and the location of the assets of the debtor, whether the proceedings can be served on the latter and whether the judgment obtained will be successfully enforced abroad. Such information may be very difficult or too expensive[34] to obtain abroad, especially where no satisfactory system for registration of addresses exists in the relevant foreign country, as is the case for England and Turkey.
- Variously regulated substantive and procedural law rules, different court languages and, last but not least, differences in legal cultures[35] make it almost impossible for a lawyer to proceed in a foreign country, even if such practice (by foreign lawyers) is allowed by the rules of procedure of the forum.

  Notwithstanding the liberalization of the legal market in the European Union,[36] for example, none of the lawyers, or even the court officers whom the research team asked in connection with the ZERP survey, could anticipate an application for recognition and enforcement of judgments being made in one of the EU member states by a (foreign) lawyer from another member state. As a result, the plaintiff who commences an action or who seeks to enforce a domestic judgment abroad must usually hire more than one lawyer: that is, a lawyer in the home country and a 'correspondent' lawyer abroad where the action is going to be brought or, as the case may be, where the domestic judgment is going to be enforced. This causes a substantial rise in costs, if not a duplication.

33 Similarly, see Schnorr, "Einzelanwälte und kleine Anwaltsfirmen im internationalen Rechtsverkehr", p. 103.

34 Costs of tracing the debtor's assets are not strictly a part of court costs and therefore they are not directly recoverable from the losing party at the end of the proceedings.

35 Schinobu K. Garrigues, "Collecting Beyond Our Borders", *Collector* July (1995), 12 et seq.

36 Council Directive 77/249, *OJL* 78, 26.03.1977 (amended: *OJL* 291, 24.05.1979 and *OJL* 302, 12.06.1985); ECJ Case no 107/83: *Ordre des Avocats au Barreau de Paris* v. *Klopp* [1984] *ECR* 2971.

- Despite the widespread application of relevant bilateral[37] and multilateral conventions,[38] service of documents and taking evidence abroad cost substantially more time and money as compared to the case in domestic proceedings. It was reported in the ZERP survey, for example, that cross-border service of process between EU member states costs about ECU50 and may reach ECU250 in the United Kingdom.[39]
- Different rules of procedure applicable to taking evidence in various countries may be inconvenient for the foreign parties who are not familiar with the procedure of the forum. For example, in a case before a United States court where a request to obtain evidence was made to a district court in Istanbul in 1993, the counsel for one of the parties was very dissatisfied with the assistance provided by the Turkish court in taking evidence, for they were not allowed to 'cross-examine' the expert witnesses. A correspondent Turkish lawyer who asked the author's legal advice said that her US colleagues wanted also to bring their own secretaries/stenographers to the court room in Istanbul, in order to tape-record or (if they were not allowed to use a tape-recorder) to write down the witness testimonies in full.
- Costs of translation of documents may reach substantial levels. The ZERP survey shows that costs of translation of a single page into the court language ranges between ECU50 (Luxembourg) and ECU22 (Italy and Belgium) in EU member states.
- In addition, whatever it costs, it may be in practice very difficult to obtain a reliable translation, especially of a document written in complicated legal language. Considering the grammatical structure of the Turkish language, which makes a word for word translation from English difficult, and the intricacies of its contents, a 'loan agreement' prepared by an American bank, for example, can only be rendered into good Turkish by an 'amateur' translator who is a lawyer.[40]
- Concerning small claims, national institutions supporting private individuals at the domestic level, that is, with *consumer advice* and *legal aid schemes*, cannot provide the same services efficiently for cross-

37 For example, see for Germany Jayme and Hausmann, "Internationales Privat- und Verfahrensrecht", pp.505–17.

38 For example, Hague Service Convention 1965 and Hague Evidence Convention 1970.

39 See Nerad, in Chapter 2 of the present volume.

40 Ibid.

> border claims. The reason with regard to the former is lack of sufficient information about foreign judicial systems and, as regards the latter, the fact that the individuals who cannot benefit from the legal aid, according to the level of their incomes, may indeed need such support where a cross-border claim which is more expensive is concerned.[41] The consumer associations from all EU member states which were asked by the research team in the ZERP survey stated unanimously that they would not be able to advise or otherwise assist a consumer in a cross-border consumer dispute. According to the same survey, commencing a cross-border lawsuit or cross-border enforcement of a domestic judgment is hardly feasible for any small claim which is less than ECU2,000. Such debt collection through 'judicial methods' costs in the debtors' country of residence an average of ECU2,489 (minimum ECU1,040, maximum ECU6,600) and in the creditors' country of residence an average of 2,437 (minimum ECU950, maximum ECU5,850). The duration of the proceedings would be an average of 23.5 months (minimum 13, maximum 48 months) and 29 months (minimum 12, maximum 29 months) in the debtors' and creditors' countries, respectively.

In the light of the above discussion, it would be fair to say that the efforts made by the nation-states to improve the capacity of the national courts to solve international disputes at the national level by means of private international law and at the international level by means of international conventions have not proved successful,[42] at least where cross-border debt collection is concerned, to a large extent because of the practical difficulties mentioned above.[43]

41 See EU Commission's Greenbook on Consumer Access to Justice of 16 November 1993, *COM(93) 576 final*, 77–8. Cf. *European Consumer Guide to the Single Market* (Luxembourg: Office for Official Publications of the European Communities, 1995), 31–45, 199–208.

42 See Volkmar Gessner and Angelika Schade, "Conflicts of Culture in Cross-border Legal Relations: The Conception of a Research Topic in Sociology of Law", *Theory, Culture & Society* 7 (1990), 253 et seq., pp. 261–3.

43 Considering the little use of national courts in international legal relations, the extent of the literature on international private and procedural law is astonishing. As Gessner puts it: 'Miles of book shelves deal with norms to be applied *if* an international case is taken into court. But the simple question *whether* this is done [...] is not asked' (Introduction to "Foreign Courts", note 22 *supra*).

One question to be answered is the following: does the little use of nation-state-produced enforcement systems amount to an anomy in the field of international debt collection, which could have resulted in an escape from cross-border transactions?[44] Or are there some other, autonomously created (non-state produced) sets of rules and enforcement systems which govern this area successfully and, as the case may be, which leave no need for the nation-states' intervention in their roles of lawmaker and/or law-enforcer?[45] Before we deal with these questions, some aspects of modern developments in enforcement of law in general, and debt collection in particular, must be considered.

Modern Developments in Debt Collection: 'Routinization' and 'Privatization'[46]

In the strict sense of the term, 'enforcement' or 'execution' is complementary to the court proceedings on the merits of the dispute between the parties. That is, the parties to a civil or commercial law dispute first 'go to court' to resolve the dispute and then, where the losing party fails to obey the judgment of the court, the

44 Generally, for the 'paralysing' effect of 'norm conflicts' preventing individuals from actively participating in social life, see Hans Peter Dreitzel, *Die gesellschaftlichen Leiden und das Leiden an der Gesellschaft*, 3rd edn (Stuttgart: Enke, 1980), 25–6. For an example of such a paralysing effect in the field of cross-border consumer behaviour, see the empirical data collected by the EU Commission in *EUROBAROMETER 43,0 of 17 May 1995*. EUROBAROMETER indicates that the consumers in the EU refrain from buying durable goods in member states other than their country of residence. That is, the Single Market share of purchases of durable consumer goods in the EU is only 3.2 per cent.

45 C.f. Volkmar Gessner and Angelika Schade, "Conflicts of Culture in Cross-border Legal Relations", p. 254. Gessner suggests that, 'if on the national level state produced norms (law) are dominant and autonomously created norms are complementary ... the reverse relationship [is true for] the international arena'; see his Introduction to Gessner, *Foreign Courts*, p. 7.

46 The term 'routinization' is borrowed from Robert A. Kagan, "The routinization of debt collection: An essay on social change and conflicts in the courts", *Law and Society Review* 18 (1984), 323.

enforcement of the judgment becomes necessary.[47] This picture of enforcement does not correspond to the reality of today, at least where enforcement for monetary obligations is concerned.

In practice, most of the court proceedings and enforcement procedures involving money claims in the industrialized countries appear to be routinized bureaucratic processes in which the debtor does not actively participate.[48] It has been reported that, in the High Court and county courts in England and Wales, an overwhelming majority of judgments are either default judgments or judgments on consent or admission of the defendant: for the years 1956–67, such judgments represented between 62 and 72 per cent of the total number of judgments in the county courts and about 90 per cent of the total number of judgments in the High Court.[49] There is evidence that the number and rate of contested trial court debt cases in the United States declined dramatically in the post-Second World War period. The percentage of contested contract cases in two US trial courts (for which published data exist) decreased from 20–25 per cent at the turn of the century to approximately 10 per cent in the postwar period.[50]

Similarly, the number of summary debt collection procedures in Germany which are mainly designed for the collection of undisputed money debts[51] is greater than the number of ordinary court

47 Many standard textbooks explain the function of the law of enforcement according to this pattern; for example, see Saim Üstündag, *Icra Hukukunun Esaslari*, 6th edn (Istanbul: Filiz, 1995), 2; Othmar Jauernig, *Zwangsvollstreckungs- und Konkursrecht*, 19th edn (Munich: C.H. Beck, 1990), 1.

48 See Michael Adler, "Alternativen zur Zwangsbeitreibung von Schulden", *Zeitschrift für Rechtssoziologie* 5 (1983), 41–9, p. 45.

49 See "Paynee Report", *Report of the Committee on the Enforcement of Judgment Debts* (London: HMSO, 1969 reprint 1977), §§ 61–4 and appendix 7, tables 4 and 5.

50 See the table in Kagan, "The routinization of debt collection", p. 334.

51 "The summary debt collection procedure in Germany (Mahnverfahren) is a court procedure *only* on the letter of the law. In the practice it appears to be a silent, mechanized, routine, administrative process", Günter Hörmann and Knut Holzscheck, "Schuldbeitreibung im Konsumentenkredit – Ergebnisse einer empirischen Studie", *Zeitschrift für Rechtssoziologie* 5 (1983), 26, at 39. See also, for example, Jürgen Schmid, *Elektronische*

proceedings at the civil and commercial courts of first instance. For the period 1982–91, the number of summary debt collection cases is 3.6 times higher than the number of all civil and commercial disputes in the ordinary first instance courts.[52]

These numbers demonstrate that 'the recovery of debts is very largely an administrative process' and the 'handling of undisputed claims' forms a large part of the everyday work of the courts.[53] The reason for this phenomenon must be seen inter alia in the standardization – and at the same time 'legal rationalization' – of credit transactions, including consumer credit transactions, by the business creditors (banks, finance companies, department stores, mail order companies and so on) with the involvement of legal specialists.[54] Thus standardized credit transactions cover virtually all contingencies in detail and leave little place for a future dispute on the merits of the legal relationship between the contracting parties to be settled by means of court proceedings. As a result of the expansion of the number and proportion of undisputed cases, the borderline between the two stages of judicial debt recovery process (litigation and enforcement) became indistinct for those (the majority of) debt collection cases where no actual dispute exists on the merits of the case.[55]

Datenverarbeitung im Mahnverfahren (Munich: V.Florentz, 1991), 29; Heinz Menne, *Das Mahnverfahren* (Neuwied: Luchterhand, 1979), 8–11.

52 Rechtspflege, Fachserie 10, Reihe 2: *Gerichte und Staatsanwaltschaften* 1991 (November 1994). Cf. the table in Georg Holch, "Mahnverfahren zwischen Schuldnerschutz und Entlastungsfunktion", *Zeitschrift für Rechtspolitik* 14 (1981), 281–5, at 281.

53 "Paynee Report", § 64.

54 See Kagan, "The routinization of debt collection", pp. 341–2.

55 Thus many professional books bear titles such as "Debt recovery on ..." or 'Commercial debt in ...', and so on, under which the enforcement and summary debt collection procedures are discussed together, within the same context. See, for example Richard Guy and Hugh Mercer, *Commercial Debt in Europe: Recovery and Remedies* (London: Longman, 1991); John K. Gatenby, *Gatenby's Recovery of Money*, 8th edn (London: Longman, 1993); Jürgen Capell, *Erfolgreich Mahnen – Handbuch für die Mahn- und Inkassopraxis* (Bonn: Rentop, 1989).

The routinization of the judicial debt collection procedures made them interchangeable with 'extrajudicial' or 'private' debt collection services provided by commercial organizations. The often repeated theory that the 'execution' involves an exercise of sovereign powers against individuals and therefore can be done exclusively by the national government through the competent execution officers[56] is only true for judicial execution procedures.[57] Besides the judicial debt recovery procedures (that is litigation plus enforcement of the judgment), there is a range of 'privatized' debt collection services at the business creditors' disposal.[58] Accordingly, the creditor may, for example, sell his receivables to a credit institution, either for the whole amount of receivables from the customers for a particular period of time (factoring) or for a number of individual debts of a mid- or long term maturity (forfaiting). Alternatively, he may retain the title on the debt, but may commission a commercial debt collection agency to collect the debt on his behalf.

The latter is especially of interest because of the similarity of its function to the judicial debt recovery. In Germany, debt collection through agencies has a tradition older than a hundred years,[59] and it is a serious competitor of the judicial debt recovery. Currently, the annual amount of debts collected by commercial debt collection agencies in Germany is three times higher than the amount collected by the court executors. In 1993, the annual amount of debts collected by 330 of 550 German debt collectors (members of the Federal Association of German Debt Collection Agencies) was

56 For example, see Haimo Schack, *Internationales Zivilverfahrensrecht* (Munich: C.H. Beck, 1991), 346–7; Stuart M. Duncan and Christopher I. Millar, "National report for the 'United Kingdom'", in *Enforcement of Money Judgments Abroad*, vol. 2, ed. Philip R. Weems (New York: Matthew Bender, Looseleaf, 1994), 17.

57 For a general discussion on the question, 'public versus private enforcement', see Richard A. Posner, *Economic Analysis of Law*, 4th edn (Boston, Toronto, London: Little, Brown & Company, 1992), §§ 22.1 and 22.2 (pp. 595 et seq).

58 See Eberhand Hoene, *Präventiver Kreditschutz und Zwangsvollstreckung durch Private* (Berlin: Duncker & Humblot, 1971).

59 See Bernhard R. Dietrich, *Inkasso-Unternehmungen* (Nuremberg: Hieronymus, 1986), 16–20.

DM6.2 billion,[60] whereas the amount collected by court executors in the same year was about DM2.2 billion.[61,62]

It has often been stated by sociologists of law[63] that the social control against the default (that is, the application of legal enforcement measures), unlike the case in crime, is not conducted by the state on its own initiative, but is caused by the creditors themselves. The use of commercial debt collection agencies represents a further stage where not only are the initiation and development of the debt recovery procedure caused by the creditor, but also the 'debt collector' is a private firm.

Although the debt collection methods used by the commercial debt collectors[64] may not include enforcement measures as such – or, to put it more correctly, debt collectors need involvement of official enforcement officers in order to utilize or apply judicial enforcement measures (such as attachment) – the persuasion tactics used by the same (warning letters, telephone calls, personal visits)

60 Data provided by the Federal Association of German Debt Collection Agencies, in *Frankfurter Allgemeine Zeitung*, 6.10.1992: "Die Inkasso-Branche profitiert von Recession".

61 To be precise DM2,194,606,058.48: information collected by the Deutsche Gerichtsvollzieher Zeitung from state administration of justice authorities, in "Übersicht über die Geschäftstätigkeit und den Personalbestand der Gerichtsvollzieher im Jahre 1993", *Deutsche Gerichtsvollzieher Zeitung*, no. 9 (1994), 143.

62 For the sake of fairness, it must be added that the amount collected by execution officers does not represent the whole amount of judgment debts collected through the judicial debt collection procedure, for attachment of earnings is made in Germany by civil courts without the execution officers being involved.

It must also be added, however, that the rate of increase in the business volume of commercial debt collectors is considerably greater than the increase in the workload of the court executors. In 1979, debts collected by debt collection agencies amounted to approximately DM900 million, whereas the debts collected by court executors amounted to DM1.1 billion; see Günter Hörmann, *Verbraucher und Schulden* (Baden-Baden: Nomos, 1987), 183–4.

63 For example, see Paul Rock, *Making People Pay*, London-Boston: Routledge & Kegan Paul, (1973), p. 6; Klaus F. Röhl, "Schuldbeitreibung als Kontrolle abweichenden Verhaltens", *Zeitschrift für Rechtssoziologie*, 5 (1983), p. 1,13.

64 See Dietrich, "Inkasso-Unternehmungen", pp. 73 et seq.

involve, albeit psychologically, a certain degree of pressure on the debtor.[65]

Considering the routinization of the debt collection process and special practical difficulties involved in the 'judicial' methods of cross-border debt collection which make going to court even less attractive in cross-border legal relations than in domestic legal relations, it may be supposed that privatized methods of debt collection are used more frequently in cross-border legal relations than in domestic legal relations. That is, one may suggest that debt collection methods autonomously created by the business community are utilized in order to compensate for lack of efficiently functioning nation-state produced enforcement systems in the international arena.

Surprisingly little is said in the literature on this topic. On the role of commercial debt collection agencies in cross-border collections in particular, virtually nothing has been written by jurists or sociologists of law.[66]

'Extrajudicial' Methods of Cross-border Debt Collection: the Example of German Debt Collection Agencies in Cross-border Debt Collection Business[67]

In a recent study analysing the economic efficiency of German debt collection agencies it is stated that cross-border debt collection by commercial debt collectors is assuming a growing importance in Europe as a result of growing trade volumes within the EU Common Market.[68]

65 See Rock, *Making People Pay*, Chapter 4 (pp. 77 et seq), critical.

66 There are a few articles on export factoring and forfaiting: for example, Friedrich Graf von Westphalen, "Rechtsprobleme des Factoring und des Fortfait von Exportforderungen", *Recht der internationalen Wirtschaft* no. 2 (1977), 80–6; Kurt F. Schär, "Die wirtschaftliche Funktionsweise des Factoring", in *Neue Vertragsformen der Wirtschaft: Leasing, Factoring, Franchising*, 2nd edn, ed. Ernst A. Kramer (Bern and Stuttgart: Paul Haupt, 1992), 275–8.

67 For cross-border debt collection by commercial agencies in England, see *Making Foreign People Pay*, Chapter 11.

68 Cora Stahrenberg, *Effektivität des externen Inkassos – Ein Beitrag zur Ausgliederung betrieblicher Funktionen* (Berlin: Duncker & Humblot, 1995), 200.

In the professional magazines for the branch of consumer credit and debt collection business, 'cross-border debt collection' appears occasionally as a separate topic of discussion.[69] The way the practitioners handle the theme suggests that the activities of debt collection agencies in the field of cross-border debt collection include the collection of commercial debts (Böhner) as well as consumer debts (Garrigues). The peculiarities of and difficulties experienced in cross-border debt collection can be perceived through reading these articles,[70] by means of which a 'Questionnaire on the Theme of Cross-Border Debt Collection'[71] was drawn up to be answered by German debt collection agencies (hereafter 'the Questionnaire').

The first draft of the Questionnaire was then corrected and finalized with the assistance of the Federal Association of German Debt Collection Agencies.[72] The same professional organization also pointed out that cross-border commercial debt collection is carried out in Germany only by a very small group of (three or four) debt collection agencies which may also work on the account of other (domestic) debt collectors. These debt collection agencies are affiliates or sister companies of international debt collection and credit reference agency concerns. Accordingly, the Questionnaire was distributed in August 1995 to 11 German debt collection agencies: to the four debt collection agencies named by the Federal Association and also to those debt collection agencies which, according to their size or international contacts, might also be involved in international debt collection.

69 See, for example, Horst Piggert, "Das Auslandsinkasso"; Albert Windolp, "Das Auslandsinkasso in den Ländern der EWG und EFTA"; Reinhard Böhner, "Forderungseinziehung gegen Unternehmen in der EG"; Garrigues, "Collecting Beyond Our Borders".

70 See also Albert Windolp, "Das Inkasso im Ausland" and "Das Inkasso nach deutschem und ausländischem Recht"; Hubert Timmermann, "Die Zwangsvollstreckung im Ausland ist schwierig".

71 The original is in German.

72 I thank Dr Carsten C. Ohle, the General Secretary of the Association, for his comments on the first draft of the questionnaire. I also thank Ulf Giebel, the Chairman of the Association for his support in putting me into contact with the German debt collectors, without this, the survey could hardly have been made in Germany, where debt collectors, because of concern about confidentiality, are unwilling to respond to such questionnaires.

During August–October 1995, seven answers were received, one simply indicating the firm does not make cross-border debt collection, one (which was one of the larger firms) apologizing 'on grounds of business administration' for not being able to answer the questionnaire and the other five returning the completed questionnaire form with a notice for anonymous processing of the provided data and information. All of the answering firms were larger debt collectors, three of them being largely involved in cross-border collection, that is, they either deal exclusively with cross-border debt collection or see this as being the main aim of their business. Considering the small number of German debt collectors which make cross-border collection, the answers received from the latter were not only informative but also representative.[73]

It is not possible with the available data to suggest the annual number of cross-border debt collection cases in Germany. Only two of the firms provided such numbers. In 1994, one of these firms handled about 7,100 cross-border cases and the other 6,300. Their business volumes have been growing during the last decade, the corresponding figures being 3,450 and 2,318 in 1985, and 6,200 and 4,601 in 1990, respectively.

In the overwhelming majority of the cross-border debt collections carried out by German agencies (approx. 80–90 per cent), the creditor is from Germany and the debtor is a foreign resident. The majority of foreign creditors who are being served by the German debt collection agencies are from continental Europe. The average amount of debt collected in cross-border cases tends to be – but is not necessarily – higher than that in domestic debt collections. Both consumers and commercial firms are among the debtors. It follows that, unlike judicial methods of debt collection, commercial cross-border debt collection is suitable also for small claims.

73 The debt collection market in Germany is highly concentrated. Although an estimated 550 debt collection agencies do business in Germany ("Mehr Insolvenzen, hohe Forderungsausfälle und geringe Zahlungsmoral" – from a speech by Ulf Giebel, Chairman of the Federal Associaton of German Debt Collecting Agencies, at the annual meeting of the Association in Berlin on 10 November 1994, reported in the *Frankfurter Allgemeine Zeitung*, 11 November 1994) a study on the income and cooperation tax statistics of the year 1986 showed that 12 firms represent approximately 80 per cent of the market's turnover in the country. See Stahrenberg, "Effektivität des externen Inkassos", pp. 120–22.

But for 'personal visits' to the debtor's home or workplace which cannot be made in some foreign countries, all debt collectors state that the methods used in cross-border debt collection are not different from those used in domestic cases. As stated above, court proceedings are also used. Cross-border debt collection is achieved, not necessarily by the German debt collectors themselves, but by German debt collection agencies cooperating with corresponding or sister debt collection agencies or lawyers in the relevant foreign country. As one of the firms stated:

> Only competent service provided on location can secure the client a return commensurate with the fees paid. Thus neither the debt collection agency nor the client has to deal with foreign legal systems, lawyers, enforcement difficulties etc. in each individual case, which would not be economical.

The information collected in the survey indicates that international cooperation is of great importance for the cross-border debt collection business. Without good organized business contacts abroad with sister or corresponding debt collection agencies and foreign lawyers, cross-border debt collection is neither commercially feasible nor professionally practicable. This explains why most of the transnationally organized credit reference agencies[74] also have debt collection departments[75] and sometimes a special department for cross-border collections.

International cooperation among debt collectors is also supported by international professional organizations, that is the American Collectors Association (ACA)[76] and the newly established Federation of European National Collection Associations (FENCA)[77] which

74 For example, Dun & Bradstreet (Schimmelpfeng), Credit Reform, Bürgel, LIC.

75 Generally, see Günter Döhler, "Aussergerichtliches Mahn- und Inkassowesen – Arbeitsteilung mit den Unternehmen", *Die Welt*, 21.12.1981.

76 ACA is also the publisher of a loose-leaf guide for cross-border collections including national reports: Shinobu K. Garrigues (ed.), *Guide to International Collections*, Minneapolis: American Collectors Association.

77 See "Europäische Inkasso-Branche schließt sich zusammen: Gleiche Richtlinien vom Nordkap bis Sizilien gefordert", *Bilanzbuchhalter* 10 (1993), 238.

aims inter alia to standardize its members' business practices and out-of-court resolution of conflicts among the members themselves or between these and their clients or the debtors.[78]

It is also noteworthy that cooperation with a German lawyer is never needed by a commercial debt collector for debt collection abroad. Even in most of the disputed cases, what a domestic law firm can offer for an outgoing debt collection case, that is, preparation of proceedings abroad for a foreign (corresponding) lawyer, can also be made by the debt collector himself. Accordingly, a creditor who chooses to go to a commercial debt collector instead of a lawyer may save money. According to the data collected in the ZERP survey, the legal fees for preparation of the foreign proceedings may reach substantial amounts, especially with respect to some Northern European countries: for a claim of ECU2,000 for example, ECU750 in the United Kingdom, ECU800 in Sweden and ECU1,300 in Finland.

Considering the barriers of legal and cultural differences, it may be assumed that the success rates in cross-border debt collection are lower than the success rates in domestic debt collection. This is not the case, however. Neither the foreign resident debtors owing to creditors in Germany nor the German resident debtors owing to foreign resident creditors are less cooperative than the debtors in domestic debt collection cases. The success rates in outgoing and incoming cross-border debt collection are not different from each other.

The questionnaire included questions regarding the costs of debt collection. For the purposes of comparison, the questions were formulated referring to different amounts of judgment and non-judgment debts to be collected from debtors in Turkey and in England, as well as from German debtors on account of creditors in Turkey or England. Three specialized firms provided information about their fees and costs. For example, if the debtor is in England, depending on the debt collection agency, a non-judgment debt in the amount of DM5,000 can be collected for a standard fee of DM100–300, plus a success fee of 18–30 per cent. If the debtor is in Turkey, the standard fee for the same amount will be DM150–200 and the success fee will be 25–30 per cent. Should the debtor be in Germany, the same amount of DM5,000 will be collected for a standard fee of DM300–315 plus a success fee of 5 per cent or DM30.

78 For international organizations of debt collection agencies, see *Making Foreign People Pay*, Chapter 15.

Considering the detailed figures provided by the answering firms, the following conclusions were drawn regarding the costs of commercial debt collection:

- Owing to the lack of a bilateral convention for reciprocal enforcement of judgments between Germany and Turkey and the lack of commercial debt collection agencies in Turkey (as a result of which the debt collection agency must always cooperate with lawyers), it was expected that debt collection – and particularly the collection of non-judgment debts – in Turkey would be more expensive for the German creditors than it would be in England. However, cross-border debt collection between Germany and Turkey is not more expensive than that between Germany and England.
- Notwithstanding the oligopolist nature of the cross-border debt collection market in Germany, fees charged vary considerably from debt collector to debt collector. Each debt collector uses different tariffs. The combination of costs and fees varies also from one firm to another: for example, one collector charges higher standard fees but lower success fees, the other the reverse.
- Both of the conclusions above confirm the commercial nature of the debt collection agencies. Debt collection, including cross-border debt collection, is a service industry like many others. In order to be sold, debt collection service must be priced reasonably; that is, the fees and costs charged must be commensurate with the service provided and each debt collector must take care not to price itself out of the market. This explains why a cross-border debt amounting to ECU2,000 cannot be economically collected by a law firm, but can be collected by a debt collector.

The Role of International Law Firms in Cross-border Debt Collection: the Example of Turkey[79]

The professional practices of international law firms again reflect the modern developments in debt collection towards routinization and privatization. Interviews conducted in two selected law firms in Turkey in October 1995 provide examples.[80]

79 For records of interviews with English and German law firms, see *Making Foreign People Pay*, Chapter 5.

80 Both interviews were conducted in Turkish. "Record sheets" were prepared, immediately after the interviews, from memory.

Law Firm 1: Traditional Lawyers

Law firm 1, one of the leading law firms of its kind, is run by four partners and appears in the 'recommended lawyers' list of the German and Austrian commercial attachés in Turkey. Some of the partners have an academic background. The clients of the firm are mostly exporters, export credit insurance companies and commercial debt collectors from Austria, Germany and Switzerland. They come into contact with their clients through the commercial attachés of the three countries or through their personal contacts.

Occasionally, the firm gives legal opinions on Turkish law, but its main field of expertise is litigation. The firm starts to handle the case, *when this is felt necessary*, with a telephone call to the debtor. Repeated warning letters are not written and negotiations are not made on the part of the client. Usually, the firm sues the debtor even without a prior warning. Instead, they commence a summary proceeding at the 'execution office' according to which the debtor will be served with a 'payment order':[81]

> The payment order is normally our first contact with the debtor. It serves the function of a warning letter. In this way, we obtain information also about the assets of the debtor. Sometimes they do not raise an objection in due time or they fail to make a statement of assets, in which case we can easily pressure them to pay.

One important difficulty which the firm experiences is locating the debtor: 'Today, for example, I have studied 32 files, and in eight of these 32 cases we cannot locate the debtor.' Sometimes they cannot proceed because they cannot find out where the debtor is. A usual practice used by some debtors to escape from creditors is to

81 The debtor can object to the payment order within seven days. If he does not raise an objection, the payment order becomes an enforcement title, equivalent to a final judgment. If he does object, he must also, within the same seven days, file a "statement of assets" with the execution office, declaring the particulars and location of his assets sufficient to satisfy the creditor and the particulars of his earnings and other financial means. Failure to make such a statement of assets is a "civil execution offence" punishable by imprisonment for a minimum of 10 days. Such punishment can be avoided by an application of the creditor or by the debtor paying the debt in full. (Turkish Code of Civil Execution and Bankruptcy, Arts 62 et seq, 74–7, 337 and 354.)

close the company or the partnership (which is also, in some cases, a judicial person under Turkish law) and to transfer the assets to another, mostly a newly established company. Another common trick is to change the address (the registered 'place of business') of the company or the partnership, without duly informing the creditors and the Commercial Registry. In such cases the firm uses all the legal remedies available to protect the rights of the creditor. For the first typical case referred to above it may be possible, under the substantive law, to make the new company or partnership responsible for the old debts incurred by the previous one.[82] As to the latter case where the debtor changes its address, the Ministry of Commerce and Industry has recently published a communiqué according to which the service made to the original (registered) address is deemed to be valid even if the firm has been moved to another address.[83]

The law firm seldom has recourse to the statutory enforcement of foreign judgments (*exequatur*) procedure:

> The enforcement of foreign judgments is not especially difficult. But it is time consuming. It is better to commence the proceedings in Turkey. A proceeding on the merits of the case itself takes not much longer than the exequatur proceeding.

The firm bills its clients on an hourly basis.[84] They are 'doing well' and they are very happy with their foreign clients who pay their fees regularly, unlike their Turkish clients who are seldom willing to pay in due time and especially before the proceeding has been completed successfully.

Law Firm 2: Debt Collectors

This firm, which has most of its clients in England, is run by two partners, both younger members of the profession in their early thirties. The firm entered the international legal market two years ago and it specializes in 'creditors' rights and debt recovery work'.

82 See Turkish Code of Obligations Art. 179, Turkish Commercial Code 151.

83 *Resmi Gazete* (Official Gazette), no.22373, 13 August 1995.

84 It has been reported that lawyers' fees of international law firms in Turkey range between $250–450 an hour for partners and $100–200 an hour for associates ("International Financial Law Review 1000, A Guide to the World's International Law Firms", p. 349)

The firm's most important clients are export insurers and commercial debt collectors from England. The clients coming from the former group are more numerous and they have larger amounts to be collected. Contacts with England are organized by an ex-officer of the British diplomatic service who has served many years in Turkey and who started to work for the firm after his return to England.

The firm offers both debt collection and consultancy services. It provides consultancy not only on legal matters but also about the business environment in Turkey in general and in particular cases. It advises clients, for example, on the creditworthiness of Turkish firms or private banks. Similarly, when drafting contracts for clients, it considers to a certain extent the commercial aspects of the contract as well as the legal framework.

The firm's approach to the debt recovery work is not different from that to the consultancy practice. Its style is summarized by the interviewee: 'We act in the first place *not* as a legal agent, but as a commercial agent.' Before it takes any steps for debt recovery, the firm contacts the debtor and, where necessary, initiates negotiations on the part of the creditor. The debtor is sometimes actually in financial difficulties, and offers a part payment or asks for an extension of time, which the firm is always prepared to discuss. This first (negotiation) step of the debt recovery process may be very fruitful, but it is blocked to a large extent where the client is itself a debt collection agency, that is, where the actual creditor is represented by another debt collector, as it is not possible to receive instructions from the original creditor.

The second step in the debt recovery process, following the (unsuccessful) negotiations, is an ex parte petition to the civil or commercial courts of first instance for a preliminary attachment order (that is, an order for attachment of the debtor's property for the protection of the creditor on the ground of prima facie evidence until an enforcement title has been obtained by the same). As a rule, the firm makes a second attempt for a settlement between the parties only after obtaining and executing such an order *and* commencing a summary debt collection proceeding at the 'execution office'. A third step to recover the debt may be to commence a full court proceeding in Turkey, which is very seldom done.

Similar to the law firm 1, law firm 2 rarely uses statutory procedure for the enforcement of foreign judgments. Until now, the firm has sought enforcement of a foreign judgment only in three cases, in two of them for reasons other than debt collection. The reason is the same: 'The enforcement of foreign judgments is not especially difficult, but it is time consuming. It is better to sue in Turkey.'

The interviewee said that the firm improved the legal position of its clients in their relations with Turkish parties by persuading them to change their usual business practices in connection with the Turkish markets. The export credit insurance companies in England, for example, used to cancel a British exporter's insurance policy relating to a Turkish importer in the case of a single default in payment on the part of the latter. Considering the business environment in Turkey, however, that reaction is said to be too harsh. Default in payment in due time is common in commercial sales in Turkey, which results sometimes in a chain of defaults in payment among a number of suppliers and purchasers. Such chain reactions are observed more often during times of economic crisis. In these difficult times it may not be possible to protect the liquidity of a firm for a period, but the fact that a firm is short of liquid assets does not necessarily (and does not usually) mean that it cannot survive the crisis or is no longer a safe trading partner. Accordingly, two major export credit insurers in England changed their practices for the Turkish market regarding the cancellation of insurance policies at the first default of the importer.

Similarly, the firm persuaded its clients to use negotiable instruments more often in their business transactions with Turkish parties. The interviewee said that negotiable instruments are not used in England as widely as in Turkey. Until recently, this had also been the case for transactions made with Turkish firms.[85] The firm advised its clients repeatedly of the advantages of receiving bills of exchange under Turkish law and persuaded them to accept and demand promissory notes more often in Turkey as a mode of payment or, as the case may be, as a security.

Contrary to law firm 1, law firm 2 finds that locating the unknown addresses of debtors is relative easy:

85 He explained the reason, stating – incorrectly – that bills of exchange under English law do not have the quality of negotiability. The actual difference between English and Turkish law in connection with negotiable instruments must be the existence of special summary procedures in Turkish civil procedure which enables the speedy collection of negotiable instruments, made especially easy for the creditor. See Code of Civil Execution and Bankruptcy, Arts 167 et seq and cf. Gatenby, "Gatenby's Recovery of Money", pp. 114–16.

> First of all we get information from telephone enquiries. Actually the enquiries do not give a subscriber's address but only the telephone number. But we know somebody in the telephone company who does that for us. If the debtor has a telephone number, we usually have no difficulty in finding him. Secondly, one usual practice in consumer credit sales is that the seller takes a photocopy of the first page of the buyer's passport, in the case where he is a foreigner. This is done especially where Turkish employees living abroad buy durable goods, furniture etc. If we have such a photocopy from the passport, we can search for the debtor in Turkey in his permanent domicile provided that the amount at stake is not too small for such an effort.

As a last resort the firm asks for assistance from a friend of one of the partners who has access to such information from official sources and who can find a person's address in a surprisingly short time. Until now, the firm has always managed to locate the addresses of the debtors in Turkey.

The firm bills its clients not on an hourly basis, as is the usual practice in the Turkish legal market for foreign clients,[86] but on a contingency basis; that is, 'no success – no fee'. The firm's billing practice is explained by the interviewee as follows:

> Some of our clients used not to proceed in Turkey at all, before they started to deal with us, because they found it too expensive. We entered the market with a bargain. At the outset we take only an amount equal to 4 per cent of the claim: 3 per cent for the court fees and 1 per cent for other initial expenditure such as translation costs. In cases where a preliminary attachment is necessary, we ask for an additional 15 per cent which will be deposited with the court as a security for costs. All other costs we pay ourselves and we ask for our legal fees only if we win the case or otherwise successfully collect the money.

It is worth noting that contingency fees absolutely dependent on the success of a case are not permitted in Turkey,[87] but it is standard business practice of British commercial debt collectors that fees are only charged for actual monies collected.[88] The firm is very proud of its success in debt collection for foreign creditors:

86 "International Financial Law Review 1000, A Guide to the World's International Law Firms", p. 349.

87 Lawyers Act 1969, Art. 69 II.

88 Helen Furniss and Kurt Obermeier, 'United Kingdom' (national

> In the first year of our practice in international debt collection we collected a total amount of $4 millions in Turkey for our foreign clients. Last year, even during the 'April crisis',[89] we collected 17.55 million pounds for a single client, which had had a total amount of 19 million outstanding from debtors in Turkey.

The firm's success is put down to its innovative practices according to which they concentrate on out of court debt collection. They do not work as lawyers, but mostly as if they were commercial debt collectors:

> Litigation is only a small part of our daily work. Only one of us, my partner, deals with court proceedings. All our associates and assistants concentrate on debt collection out of court – including summary proceedings – or other legal services. I am personally mostly busy with [he uses the English words] wheeling and dealing.

Conclusions

Notwithstanding the growth of a transnational economy without national boundaries, it is still too early to talk about a 'law without frontiers'[90] in the area of economic regulation. This is not because the community of nation-states, the traditional makers and enforcers of law, have not recognized the need for globalization of law. On the contrary, genuine efforts have been made, especially in the second half of this century, for harmonization or unification of national laws and for improving the access to justice in international legal interaction. The national courts, however, are simply not suitable for enforcing legal rights in cross-border legal relations. When the bureaucracy and costs inherent in the machinery of justice are doubled by the barriers created by legal/legal-cultural differences and practical difficulties in cross-border interactions,

report), in *Guide to International Collections* (Minneapolis: American Collectors Association loose-leaf).

89 At the beginning of February 1994, one US dollar was equal to TL13,000; by mid-April 1994, parity had risen by 300 per cent: one US dollar was then worth TL39,000.

90 "Law without Frontiers" is the title of a book by Edwin Godfrey on the professional rules applicable to "international lawyers" in various countries: Edwin Godfrey, ed., *Law without Frontiers* (London: Kluwer, 1995).

they put the national courts system beyond the reach of those who are in need of legal protection.

Judicial debt collection methods of today are largely routinized bureaucratic procedures, such as summary debt collection procedures, which take place outside the contested court proceedings. The judicial debt recovery procedures are now to a large extent interchangeable with what may be called 'privatized methods of debt collection' including modern financial services such as factoring, forfaiting and commercial debt collection.

Considering the fact that cross-border commercial disputes come less frequently to the courts than the national commercial disputes, the author assumes that the privatization of debt collection is a stronger trend in cross-border legal relations. Cross-border debt collection services provided by commercial debt collectors are a typical example of privatized debt collection. Debt collection agencies are run by non-lawyers. Debt collection, including cross-border debt collection, is a service industry like many others: in order to be sold, a debt collection service must be priced reasonably; that is, the fees and costs charged must be commensurate with the service provided. The results of the survey carried out among German cross-border debt collectors show that this is achieved to a large extent thanks to international cooperation organized by and between the debt collectors from different countries. Thus a cross-border debt amounting to ECU2,000 cannot be collected economically by a law firm, but it can be so collected by a debt collector.

Interviews with two international law firms in Turkey can be interpreted in the same context. The first firm is an example of a traditional attorney office which is being run by well educated 'gentlemen lawyers' who concentrate on international litigation. The second firm is one of the new 'entrepreneurial service providers' which provides an example of the 'banalization' and 'commercialization of the legal practice'.[91] The difficulties of the cross-border debt collection are overcome by the first law firm by means of legal remedies provided for protection of creditors' rights. The latter, on the other hand, solves the practical difficulties in this area again with 'practical' methods ('wheeling and dealing') which turn out more successful.

91 See Yves Dezalay, "The Big Bang and the Law: The Internationalization and Restructuration of the Legal Field", *Theory, Culture & Society* 7 (1990), 279–93.

References

Adler, Michael. 1983. Alternativen zur Zwangsbeitreibung von Schulden. *Zeitschrift für Rechtssoziologie* 5: 41–9.

Bellers, Jürgen. 1993. Nationale und internationale Normierungen auf dem Gebiet grenzüberschreitender Wirtschaftsbeziehungen. *Jahresschrift für Rechtspolitologie*: 127–46.

Birsel, Mahmut and Hasan Nerad. 1995. Turkey. In *Bank Security and Other Credit Enhancement Methods*, edited by Winnibold E. Moojen and Matthiew Ph. van Sint Truden. Amsterdam: Kluwer Law International.

Böhner, Reinhard. 1979. Forderungseinziehung gegen Unternehmen in der EG. *Schimmelpfeng-Review* 24: 69–70.

Budak, Ali Cem. 1998. *Making Foreign People Pay – Law and Practice of Cross-Border Debt Collection with Special Reference to German, English and Turkish Law*. Aldershot: Dartmouth.

Capell, Jürgen. 1989. *Erfolgreich Mahnen – Handbuch für die Mahn- und Inkassopraxis*. Bonn: Rentop.

Cavusgil, S. Tamer. 1993. Globalization of Markets and Its Impact on Domestic Institutions. *Indiana Journal of Global Legal Studies* 1, no. 1: 83–99.

David, René. 1971. The International Unification of Private Law. *International Encyclopedia of Comparative Law*, Vol. II, Ch. 5. Tübingen: Mohr/The Hague, Paris: Mouton/New York: Oceana.

Day, D.M. and Bernardette Griffin. 1993. *The Law of International Trade*. 2nd edn. London, Dublin, Edinburgh: Butterworths.

Delbrück, Jost. 1993. Globalization of Law, Politics, and Markets – Implications for Domestic Law – A European Perspective. *Indiana Journal of Global Legal Studies* 1, no. 1: 9–36.

Dezalay, Yves. 1990. The Big Bang and the Law: The Internationalization and Restructuration of the Legal Field. *Theory, Culture & Society* 7: 279–93.

Die Inkasso-Branche profitiert von Recession. 1992. *Frankfurter Allgemeine Zeitung*. 6 October.

Dietrich, Bernhard R. 1986. *Inkasso-Unternehmungen*. Nuremberg: Hieronymus.

Döhler, Günter. 1981. Aussergerichtliches Mahn- und Inkassowesen – Arbeitsteilung mit den Unternehmen. *Die Welt*, 21 December.

Dreitzel, Hans Peter. 1980. *Die gesellschaftlichen Leiden und das Leiden an der Gesellschaft*. 3rd edn. Stuttgart: Enke.

Duncan, Stuart M. and Christopher I. Millar. 1994. National report for the 'United Kingdom'. In *Enforcement of Money Judgments Abroad*, Vol. 2, edited by Philip R. Weems. New York: Matthew Bender, Looseleaf.

EU Commission's Greenbook on Consumer Access to Justice of 16 November 1993, *COM(93) 576 final.*

Europäische Inkasso-Branche schließt sich zusammen: Gleiche Richtlinien vom Nordkap bis Sizilien gefordert. 1993. *Bilanzbuchhalter* 10: 238.

European Consumer Guide to the Single Market. 1995. Luxembourg: Office for Official Publications of the European Communities.

Freyhold, Hanno von and Enzo L. Vial. 1995. Report on the Cost of Judicial Proceedings in the European Union. In *Cost of Judicial Barriers for Consumers in the Single Market – A Report for the European Commission (Directorate General XXIV)*, ed. Hanno von Freyhold, Volkmar Gessner, Enzo L. Vial and Helmut Wagner. Bremen: Zentrum für Europäische Rechtspolitik an der Universität Bremen (ZERP).

Garrigues, Schinobu K. 1995. Collecting Beyond Our Borders. *Collector* July: 12–20.

Gatenby, John K. 1993. *Gatenby's Recovery of Money.* 8th edn. London: Longman.

Gessner, Volkmar. 1996. International Cases in German First Instance Courts. In *Foreign Courts – Civil Litigation in Foreign Legal Cultures*, edited by Volkmar Gessner. Aldershot: Dartmouth.

Gessner, Volkmar and Angelika Schade. 1990. Conflicts of Culture in Cross-border Legal Relations: The Conception of a Research Topic in Sociology of Law. *Theory, Culture & Society* 7: 253–77.

Godfrey, Edwin, ed. 1995. *Law without Frontiers.* London: Kluwer.

Graf von Westphalen, Friedrich. 1977. Rechtsprobleme des Factoring und des Fortfait von Exportforderungen. *Recht der internationalen Wirtschaft* 23: 80–86.

Guy, Richard and Hugh Mercer. 1991. *Commercial Debt in Europe: Recovery and Remedies.* London: Longman.

Hoene, Eberhard. 1971. *Präventiver Kreditschutz und Zwangsvollstreckung durch Private.* Berlin: Duncker & Humblot.

Holch, Georg. 1981. Mahnverfahren zwischen Schuldnerschutz und Entlastungsfunktion. *Zeitschrift für Rechtspolitik* 14: 281–5.

Hörmann, Günter. 1987. *Verbraucher und Schulden.* Baden-Baden: Nomos.

Hörmann, Günter and Knut Holzscheck. 1983. Schuldbeitreibung im Konsumentenkredit – Ergebnisse einer empirischen Studie. *Zeitschrift für Rechtssoziologie* 5: 26–40.

Institut der Deutschen Wirtschaft, ed. 1994. *Zahlen zur wirtschaftlichen Entwicklung der Bundesrepublik Deutschland 1995.* Cologne: Deutscher Instituts-Verlag.

International Financial Law Review 1000. 1995. *A Guide to the World's International Law Firms.* Euromoney Publications.

Jauernig, Othmar. 1990. *Zwangsvollstreckungs- und Konkursrecht.* 19th edn. Munich: C.H. Beck.

Jayme, Erik and Rainer Hausmann, eds. 1994. *Internationales Privat- und Verfahrensrecht* (Textausgabe). 7th edn. Munich: C.H. Beck.

Kagan, Robert A. 1984. The routinization of debt collection: An essay on social change and conflicts in the courts. *Law and Society Review* 18: 323–71.

Kefalas, Asterios G. 1990. *Global Business Strategy – A systems approach.* Cincinnati, Ohio: South-Western Publishing.

Kegel, Gerhard. 1995. *Internationales Privatrecht.* 7th edn. Munich: C.H. Beck.

Krüger, Hilmar. 1982. Das türkische IPR-Gesetz von 1982. *Praxis des Internationalen Privat- und Verfahrensrechts* 2: 252–9.

Martiny, Dieter. 1984. *Handbuch des internationalen Zivilverfahrensrechts,* edited by Max-Planck-Institut für ausländisches und internationales Privatrecht. Vol. III/1. Tübingen: Mohr.

Martiny, Dieter, Jan Peter Waehler and Martin K. Wolff. 1984. *Handbuch des internationalen Zivilverfahrensrechts,* edited by Max-Planck-Institut für ausländisches und internationales Privatrecht. Vol. III/2. Tübingen: Mohr.

Mehr Insolvenzen, hohe Forderungsausfälle und geringe Zahlungsmoral. 1994. *Frankfurter Allgemeine Zeitung.* 11 November.

Menne, Heinz. 1979. *Das Mahnverfahren.* Neuwied: Luchterhand.

Nerad, Hasan, Selma Baktir, Esin Taylan and Sevilay Eroglu. 1995. Izmir Asliye Ticaret Mahkemelerinde Görülen Davalar ve Hasimsiz Isler Konusunda Arastirma Raporu (unpublished). Dokuz Eylül Üniversitesi Iktisadi ve Idari Bilimler Fakültesi.

Neyer, Jürgen. 1996. *Spiel ohne Grenzen – Weltwirtschafliche Strukturveränderungen und das Ende des sozial kompetenten Staates.* Marburg: Tectum.

Pekcanítez, Hakan. 1994. *Medeni Usul ve icra – iflas Hukukunda Yabancí Para Alacaklarínín Tahsili.* Ankara: Dokuz Eylül Üniversitesi Hukuk Fakültesi.

Piggert, Horst. 1968. Das Auslandsinkasso. *Teilzahlungswirtschaft* 15, no.1: 15–16.

Report of the Committee on the Enforcement of Judgment Debts, 1969. London: HMSO. Reprinted 1977.

Rock, Paul. *Making People Pay.* London, Boston: Routledge & Kegan Paul.

Röhl, Klaus F. 1983. Schuldbeitreibung als Kontrolle abweichenden Verhaltens. *Zeitschrift für Rechtssoziologie* 5: 1–49.

Schack, Haimo. 1991. *Internationales Zivilverfahrensrecht,* Munich: C.H. Beck.

Schäfer, Wilhelm. 1991. Außenhandelsquote. In *Wirtschaftswörterbuch*, Vol.2. 3rd edn. Munich: Verlag Franz Vahlen.

Schär, Kurt F. 1992. Die wirtschaftliche Funktionsweise des Factoring. In *Neue Vertragsformen der Wirtschaft: Leasing, Factoring, Franchising*. 2nd edn, edited by Ernst A. Kramer. Berne, Stuttgart: Paul Haupt.

Schmid, Jürgen. 1991. *Elektronische Datenverarbeitung im Mahnverfahren*. Munich: V. Florentz.

Schmitthoff, Clive M. 1990. *Export Trade – The Law and Practice of International Trade*. 9th edn. London: Stevens.

Schnorr, Thomas. 1994. Einzelanwälte und kleine Anwaltsfirmen im internationalen Rechtsverkehr – Eine empirische Untersuchung. *Anwaltsblatt* 44, no. 3: 98–104.

Shapiro, Martin. 1993. The Globalization of Law. *Indiana Journal of Global Legal Studies* 1, no. 1: 37–64.

Stahrenberg, Cora. 1995. *Effektivität des externen Inkassos – Ein Beitrag zur Ausgliederung betrieblicher Funktionen*. Berlin: Duncker & Humblot.

Statistisches Bundesamt. *Gerichte und Staatsanwaltschaften*. (Rechtspflege, Fachserie 10, Reihe 2; booklets dated 1990–1993.) Wiesbaden: Kohlhammer.

Stubbs, Richard and Geoffrey R.D. Underhill. 1994. *Political Economy and the Changing Global Order*. London: Macmillan.

Tayeb, Monir H. 1992. *The Global Business Environment – An Introduction*. London: Sage.

Timmermann, Hubert. 1969. Die Zwangsvollstreckung im Ausland ist schwierig. *Teilzahlungswirtschaft* 16, no. 2.

Triebel, Volker, Stephen Hodgson, Wolfgang Kellenter and Georg Müller. 1995. *Englisches Handels- und Wirtschaftsrecht*. 2nd edn. Heidelberg: Verlag Recht und Wirtschaft.

Übersicht über die Geschäftstätigkeit und den Personalbestand der Gerichtsvollzieher im Jahre 1993. 1994. *Deutsche Gerichtsvollzieher Zeitung* no.9: 143.

Üstündag, Saim. 1995. *Icra Hukukunun Esaslari*. 6th edn. Istanbul: Filiz.

Wagner, Rolf. 1995. Verfahrensrechtliche Probleme im Auslandsmahnverfahren. *Recht der Internationalen Wirtschaft* 41: 89–97.

Windolp, Albert. 1969. Das Inkasso in den Ländern der EWG und EFTA. *Teilzahlungswirtschaft* 16, no. 2: 56–60.

Windolp, Albert. 1976. Das Inkasso im Ausland. *Schimmelpfeng-Review* 18: 38–40.

Windolp, Albert. 1977. Das Inkasso nach deutschem und ausländischem Recht. In *Aktuelle Beiträge über das Inkasso im In- und Ausland*. 2nd edn. Frankfurt/M.: Schimmelpfeng.

Wolf, Klaus Dieter. ed. (1993). *Internationale Verrechtlichung*. Pfaffenweiler: Centaurus.

The Author

Ali Cem Budak. LL.B., M.A. (Istanbul), LL.M. (London), Dr. jur. (Bremen) is a research fellow at the University of Istanbul, Faculty of Laws, Department of Civil Procedure and Insolvency. His research areas concern comparative and legal–sociological aspects of civil procedure and insolvency. From August 1995 to March 1997 he was a member of the Bremen research group on 'Global Legal Interaction'.

Address: Istanbul Universitesi, Hukuk Fakultesi, Beyazit, 34452 Istanbul, Turkey.

Fax: 0090-212-546 74 35

E-mail: acbudak@ibm.net

Abstract

This chapter contains the summary of the initial results of comparative empirical research conducted in Germany, Turkey and England. This part of the research was made in two jurisdictions, Germany and Turkey, and concerns the role of law firms and commercial debt collection agencies. Judicial debt collection methods of today are largely routinized bureaucratic procedures which take place outside the contested court proceedings. Consequently, the judicial debt recovery procedures are now to a large extent interchangeable with what may be called 'privatized methods of debt collection' including modern financial services such as factoring, forfaiting and commercial debt collection. In view of the empirical evidence showing that cross-border commercial disputes come less frequently to the courts as compared with the national commercial disputes, the author argues that the privatization of debt collection is a stronger trend in cross-border legal relations.

2 Comments on Ali Cem Budak's Contribution: International Litigation and Arbitration in Turkey

HASAN NERAD

Introduction

It may be safely assumed that most of the obligations arising from international relations are performed to the mutual satisfaction of the parties involved. This assumption is based on the relatively small number of disputes as compared to the totality of the enormous number of transactions of an international nature, and no doubt this is equally true as far as domestic transactions are concerned. However, the importance of the disputes that do arise should not be underestimated. Large sums are usually involved, or the future of an investment may be at stake, with repercussions affecting the local economy. Speedy solutions of disputes in a manner that answers the requirements of justice and fast and satisfactory execution of court judgments and arbitral awards is a sine qua non of further development of global business relations.

What this chapter will endeavour to do is to examine some issues in the context of the above-mentioned considerations, first by making a few comments on Ali Cem Budak's chapter by giving examples from personal experience of some cases, and then putting forward results of a survey done in Izmir commercial courts. Remarks will be confined to certain aspects of Turkish law.

Remarks on Budak's Contribution

The author would like to refer briefly to examples from personal experience in international cases in support of Budak's views.

1. Should there not be an applicable bilateral or multilateral treaty providing for reciprocal enforcement of judgments, a foreign

judgment may only be enforced in Turkey if there is legal or de facto reciprocity concerning enforcement of judgments between the judgment country and Turkey. As Budak correctly says, the Turkish Court of Cassation takes a flexible attitude in this respect. The court, which is the highest judicial authority in civil law matters, finds the existence of an exequatur procedure in the laws of the foreign country involved sufficient for enforcement. In an unreported case, the Third Commercial Court of Istanbul ruled that 'English Courts are known to recognize and enforce foreign judgments, therefore a decision of the High Court of Justice, Queen's Bench Division, should be enforced in Turkey'.[1] When the decision was appealed on other grounds, the appeal was dismissed by the Court of Cassation.[2]

2. In a case brought in the Istanbul Commercial Court by a Turkish plaintiff against, inter alia, a Saudi Arabian defendant in 1988, service of the statement of claims to this defendant could have been achieved in 1993. The case is still pending, awaiting the service of the judgment of the court of first instance dated 1994 to the Saudi defendant to determine whether such defendant will appeal. The appeal procedure will probably take a similarly long time.
3. A professional translation bureau employed by a notary public translated a judgment of a Turkish court into English in such an incomprehensible way that the present author had to make a fresh translation of the whole text upon a request from a lawyer friend in London. This is by no means an isolated case showing language problems.
4. In an export transaction based on a letter of credit, goods were delivered to the buyer without the documents being handed over and the intermediary bank did not receive payment. The buyer informed the exporter that he was insolvent and offered to settle the account by paying 60 per cent of the amount due. The Italian counsel advised that an action would take at least three years and it would remain doubtful if the debt would be collected in spite of a favourable judgment; everything would depend on finding sufficient and attachable assets of the debtor company at the time of the execution of the judgment. The exporter consented to the offer despite enormous difficulties in Turkey arising from the harsh foreign exchange regulations then in force.

1 Decision Nr. E. 90/561, K. 92/1132, dated 25 November 1992.

2 19th Civil Chamber of Cassation, Nr. E. 93/5762, K. 94/5939 dated 9 June 1994, unreported.

5. Goods were carried by sea. Against the carrier, a Turkish company, a suit was brought before the arbitrator in London based on the arbitration clause in the contract of carriage; although the applicable law was Turkish Commercial Code, the arbitrator wanted to know whether the exporter would go bankrupt if it did not receive payment. This was not the case, and the arbitrator refused an award for reasons beyond the present author's comprehension.
6. A suit claiming damages because of breach of contract was brought by a Turkish party in Gothenburg, Sweden in 1988. I withdrew from the case in 1990 because I resigned my post in the plaintiff company and to the best of my knowledge, the case is still pending.
7. A Turkish contractor requested an injunction from a Turkish Commercial Court to prevent payment on a letter of guarantee given by a Turkish bank to foreign bank. The injunction was granted in 1988, although the Letter was called, no payment was made because of the injunction and the case is still pending.
8. Turkey is a party to the Convention on the Recognition and Enforcement of Foreign Arbitral Awards (New York Convention) done in New York in 1958,[3] effective 2 July 1992. Turkey also ratified the European Convention on International Commercial Arbitration done in Geneva in 1961, effective 23 September 1991.[4]

   Generally speaking, after the New York and Geneva Conventions have become effective, the court may refuse to enforce a foreign arbitral award made in one of the Convention states only on certain specified grounds. In cases of debt collection, relevant grounds of refusal would be the lack of an arbitration agreement between the parties, or where the party against whom enforcement is sought has not been notified of the arbitration proceedings or was not given the opportunity to be represented and heard, or the arbitral award violated the rules of the applicable law or exceeded the arbitration agreement or has not yet been finalized. It is clear that the Turkish court does not have jurisdiction on the merits of the dispute. However, just as in the execution of foreign judgments, Turkish courts tend to consider the substantive law issues as well. It is difficult to find this attitude compatible with the nature of international commercial arbitration.
9. In an arbitration case partly involving a monetary claim before an ad hoc arbitration tribunal in Geneva, the suit filed in 1988 reached the final stage in 1992 and caused enormous expenses.

3 Official Gazette 21 May 1991, 20877; 25 September 1991, 21001.
4 Official Gazette 21 May 1991, 20877; 23 September 1991, 21000.

10. The Turkish Civil Procedure Code (CPC), which is based on the Civil Procedure Code of the Neuchâtel Canton of Switzerland, contains provisions on arbitration in Turkey. Arbitration between two foreign or one foreign and one Turkish party are possible. However, arbitration with a foreign element and indeed between two parties of Turkish nationality under CPC have been rare. There are two main reasons for the lack of enthusiasm for Turkish arbitration. First, Article 529 of CPC allows six months for the arbitrators to make their award; this period can be extended by mutual consent of the parties. If arbitrators fail to give their decision within the foreseen period, the arbitration becomes null and void, and the parties face the high risk of going to the relevant court to solve the dispute, a result they wanted to avoid in the first place when they chose arbitration. Second, the arbitral award may be appealed pursuant to Article 533 of CPC. Although the grounds for appeal are specified and they pertain only to procedure, parties sometimes do not wish to prolong the proceedings with a stage of appeal and wish to avoid the probability of ending up in a court, although the Court of Cassation rather than a court of first instance would be involved.

The Arbitration Centre founded under the auspices of the Istanbul Chamber of Commerce in 1979, which is open to foreign parties as well as Turkish ones reportedly handled only 50 cases from 1979 until the end of 1995.[5]

A Survey in Izmir Commercial Courts

Izmir is the third largest city in Turkey, with a population of approximately two million in 1990. It is a major export and import harbour and port of entry for tourists with destinations to dozens of centres of tourism on the Aegean coast and inland. It was proposed to make a survey in the commercial courts of Izmir as a part of academic activities planned for 1994 to commemorate the fiftieth anniversary of the Faculty of Economics and Administrative Sciences of Dokuz Eylül University in Izmir. The survey was conducted by myself and three colleagues in the Department of Commercial Law in the faculty in 1994 from the archives of the three existing commercial courts on all their decisions rendered in

5 *Istanbul Ticaret* (Weekly Journal of Istanbul Chamber of Commerce), Nr. 1898, 2 February 1996, p. 8.

1993.[6] The files themselves were not examined. Substantive law issues involved were not taken into consideration. It was expected that we would find quite a few cases on carriage of goods by sea and land, disputes arising from agreements between tourists, tourism enterprises, carriers and tourism agencies with at least one foreign element. We were all surprised. Out of a total of 1,075 cases, there was only one which had a foreign party, a plaintiff suing a Turkish party for failing to pay a debt due. The plaintiff was a foreign corporation; however, it is deemed to be domiciled in Turkey pursuant to special legislation. Therefore the issue of *cautio judicatum solvi* did not arise.

One of the conclusions we reached was as follows:

> The most important result the survey revealed is not what it brought up so far as the suits filed were concerned but what suits did not materialize. Indeed, we have not come across any suit on maritime law, or with a foreign party or involving execution of a foreign judgment or enforcement of an arbitral award in the commercial courts of Izmir, the courts having sole jurisdiction on commercial matters in a city which is the hub of foreign trade and tourism activities. It is unthinkable that no dispute arose from relationships of important proportions that take place in Izmir every year, therefore we conclude that alternative methods of dispute resolution are employed, among which are arbitration and choice of jurisdiction of foreign courts. The reasons for such preferences should be further analysed.[7]

Conclusion

Budak's contribution gives valuable insights into cross-border legal problems. Even if parties prudently procure securities before extending credits in various ways,[8] they have to follow

6 The result was published in 1996. See Hasan Nerad, Selma Baktir, Esin Taylan and Sevilay Eroglu, "Izmir Asliye Ticaret Mahkemelerinde Görülen Davalar ve Hasimsiz Isler Hakkýnda Bir Arastirma", *Dokuz Eylül Üniversitesi Iktisadi ve Idari Bilimler Fakültesi Dergisis* 11, no. 2 (1996).

7 Conclusion Nr. 12 of the Survey. (Hasan Nerad, Selma Baktir, Esin Taylan and Sevilay Eroglu).

8 Mahmut Birsel and Hasan Nerad, "Turkey", in *Bank Security and Other Credit Enhancement Methods*, edited Winnibold E. Moojen

cumbersome, costly and inefficient ways to collect their claims. Alternative methods should be developed to further the globalization of commercial relations and achieve speedy legal results.

The Author

Hasan Nerad is a Professor of Commercial Law, School of Business, Dokuz Eylül University, Izmir, Turkey.

and Matthiew Ph. van Sint Truden (Amsterdam: Kluwer Law International, 1995), 416–30.

3 Back to the Courtroom? Developments in the London Reinsurance Market

CHRISTINE STAMMEL

Introduction

Cross-border Legal Interaction and 'Third Cultures'

Globalization has become a widely used term within the media business, as well as within financial and intellectual circles, underlying the widespread perception that modern communication technology has made the world a smaller place. McGrew offered a scientific definition in which globalization refers to the multiplicity of links and interconnections that transcend the nation-states (and by implication the societies) which make up the modern world system.[1] It defines a process through which events, decisions and activities in one part of the world can come to have significant consequences for individuals and communities in quite distant parts of the globe. Nowadays, goods, capital, people, knowledge, images, communications, crime and culture flow readily across territorial boundaries. Transnational networks, social movements and relationships are extensive in virtually all areas of human activity. Consequently, it may be argued that territorial boundaries are increasingly insignificant since social activity and relations no longer stop at those boundaries.

However, what may be true for social activities and economical transactions may not apply to the law and to the resulting rights. Legal sociological views might fruitfully complement what has so

1 Anthony McGrew, "A Global Society?" in *Modernity and Its Futures*, ed. Stuart Hall, David Held and Tony McGrew (Cambridge: Polity Press, 1992), 61–102, at 65.

far been produced in other disciplines, as legal sociological approaches point to structural elements without which neither intercultural communication nor economic exchange can be effectively realized.[2] There are indicators that certain areas of cross-border legal interactions have become involved in and subject to the development of 'third cultures', outside of and transcending nation-state-based legal cultures and barriers. A 'third culture' may be created by major actors who participate in global legal exchanges. One of the basic assumptions of a 'third legal culture' is that most of its exchanges remain outside the system of national courts and even outside national legal systems. Among the areas which globally have developed a particular autonomy from interference by governments and courts is the reinsurance business.

Until recently, reinsurance was known for not carrying out legal battles in public – if there were legal battles at all. Disputes were negotiated and remained in the privacy of arbitration. This study of the London reinsurance market consisting of interviews conducted with city solicitors who are engaged in reinsurance law proved that reinsurance can no longer be called a non-litigious area. Owing to its large share of international business, the London reinsurance market represents a field which invites the study of legal behaviour of actors handling cross-border legal interaction.

Subject-matter: Reinsurance

General

Reinsurance is an independent branch of the insurance industry. It is a method whereby an original insurer distributes its risks by giving the whole or some portion thereof to another insurer, with the object of reducing the amount of its possible loss.[3] The purpose of reinsurance could be said to be covered under the headings 'capacity, stabilization, confidence, catastrophe protection and spread of risks'.[4] As the direct insurers can reinsure part of certain risks they can therefore accept more of the original risk and increase their capacity. The result is growth within the insurance

2 Volkmar Gessner, Chapter 12 of the present volume.

3 C.E. Golding, *The Law and Practice of Reinsurance*, 5th edn (London: Witherby & Co. Ltd., 1987), 17.

4 G.C.A. Dickson and J.T. Steele, *Introduction to Insurance*, 2nd edn (London: Pitman, 1984), 178 et seq.

market as a whole and added prestige to the individual insurer. Just as the insured has no knowledge of when a claim will occur or what it will cost, similarly the direct insurer also lacks such knowledge.

Forms of Reinsurance

There are two methods of classifying the forms which reinsurance may take, and each of these methods has the same two broad subdivisions.[5] A reinsurance contract can be described as having been arranged in advance for use and when required; that is, as a treaty contract. Under a treaty contract the reinsurer agrees to accept in advance a certain class of risk for reinsurance in a portfolio that the ceding office will cede to him during the course of business. An example would be a motor policy or a household policy portfolio.

If the reinsurance contract contains a risk that has been individually negotiated between reinsurer and insurer as the risk arises, this contract is described as a facultative contract. An example would be the reinsurance of an aviation risk or an oil rig platform. Facultative reinsurance gives a great measure of control to a reinsurer over the quality of its risk which is not available under the treaty method.[6]

Material and Methodology

Literature on Legal Aspects of Reinsurance

A considerable volume of well established literature on legal aspects of reinsurance exists both in the United Kingdom and in Germany.[7] However, the fact that the sources of reinsurance law are governed above all by the contractual relationship between the parties of a reinsurance contract, as well as the fact that the preferred dispute resolution happens in the privacy of arbitration, makes

5 Dickson and Steele, *Introduction to Insurance*, pp. 181 et seq.

6 Golding, *The Law and Practice of Reinsurance*, ibid., p. 21.

7 Golding, *The Law and Practice of Reinsurance*, Chapter 2; J.S. Butler and R. Merkin, *Reinsurance Law* (London: Kluwer, 1986); Klaus Gerathewohl, *Rückversicherung – Grundlagen und Praxis*, vol. I (Karlsruhe: Verlag Versicherungswirtschaft e.V., 1976), 403–599; Andrea Schulte, *Rückversicherung in Deutschland und England: Unterschiede in Recht und Praxis* (Karlsruhe: Verlag Versicherungswirtschaft e.V., 1990).

difficult any qualified statement as to how conflicts are handled and how dispute resolution works. The law merchant literature sometimes refers to reinsurance, and notes that banks and insurances are in a special position with regard to their conflict resolution. It maintains that appearances that in international banking and insurance business there is no reason for commercial disputes might be deceptive. For resolving those disputes, however, internal measures have been taken whereby the access to such disputes by outsiders is limited.[8]

The limited access to information on reinsurance disputes, however, may not alone be the reason for so limited an interest in reinsurance disputes on a broader level. Thoughts of consumer protection might have been driving forces for sociolegal analysis with regard to primary insurance on broader terms. As long as insurance conflicts and legal battles relate to consumers, it appears that there is an incentive to study the legal behaviour of the primary insurers towards their clients, for example with respect to claims handling.[9] Legal interaction on a more equal footing between actors with business experience may appear less attractive for research because there might be the feeling that both actors are able to protect their own interests and need no outside interference.

Reinsurance has been rather shy about presenting its case to the public, even the insurance public.[10] As far as the continental reinsurance market is concerned, reinsurance has managed to stay out of the public eye. The London reinsurance market has made headlines by becoming increasingly litigious during the last decade.

Studying Dispute Behaviour in the Reinsurance Market

With respect to disputes, the first credo in the reinsurance industry used to be conflict avoidance. The reinsurance industry did not use standard contracts for avoiding conflicts. On the contrary, it must be stated that attempts towards standardization – whether they concern contract wording or only parts of the wording, as

8 Paul-Frank Weise, *Materielles Recht vor der internationalen Handelsschiedsgerichtsbarkeit* (Frankfurt/M.: Lang, 1989), 51–2.

9 Samantha J. Jones, *Compensating victims of mass accidents, A Socio-Legal Analysis* (Oxford: Centre for Socio-Legal Studies and Pembroke College, University of Oxford, 1992).

10 Klaus Gerathewohl, "The International Reinsurance Markets Today – Developments and Perspectives", *Versicherungswirtschaft* 14 (1987), 901.

with a standardized arbitration clause – had very limited success.[11] It was more a question of readiness to pay on the reinsurer's side which was the prevailing attitude until 10 to 15 years ago. Negotiations should take place if a dispute arises. Arbitration was deemed to be appropriate if a dispute could not be resolved within the previous negotiations. Again negotiations and, as a result, a settlement within arbitration proceedings were the favoured solution.

In the London reinsurance market, however, the courts – the Commercial Court in particular – have an important task in reinsurance disputes under certain circumstances. Generally, under English Law, they may become involved if (a) the law recognizes the dispute or claim as no fit subject for arbitration;[12] or (b) the parties have no arbitration agreement. In a case where there is an arbitration agreement, it seems that there is no choice between arbitration or litigation anyway. As a matter of contract term, the parties are bound to solve all disputes by arbitration. However, there are possible ways to bypass arbitration, if one party can persuade a court that its issuing court proceedings is merely an attempt to collect a debt and that there is no 'dispute'. It may further be that the defendant does not want to arbitrate either, so that the arbitration clause is conveniently ignored.

The courts may further become involved if (c) a third party, which cannot be bound by the agreement, is involved as plaintiff or defendant, as in the case of a broker; (d) one of the parties being involved in arbitration appeals against an arbitration award; or (e) an interlocutory order is sought.

Movements in the London reinsurance market have brought changes not only to the economic side but also to the handling of legal issues subsequently, ranging from the drafting of contracts to the dispute resolution culture.[13] To catch the 'changing winds' and

11 For different explanations of the failure, see Klaus Gerathewohl, *Rückversicherung Grundlagen und Praxis*, Vol. I, Chapter 7, p. 507; Andrea Schulte, *Rückversicherung in Deutschland und England: Unterschiede in Recht und Praxis*, pp.136–41.

12 Michael J. Mustill and Stewart C. Boyd, *The Law and Practice of Commercial Arbitration in England*, 2nd edn (London, Edinburgh: Butterworth, 1989), 149.

13 Even in insider books the "lack of attitude" in resolving a dispute compared to previous times is now frequently mentioned. See: J.S. Butler, *Reinsurance Practice and the Law* (London: Lloyd's of London Press Ltd, 1993), 25.5.1.

to convey the development to the reader will be a priority focus of this chapter.

This chapter contains some of the results of interviews carried out with solicitors of City law firms being involved in reinsurance disputes and work in reinsurance law during the period 16 January to 15 March 1995. With the help of lawyers' directories, the practitioners involved in reinsurance disputes in London were determined and approached regarding willingness to answer a questionnaire and to give a free format interview. In the case of consent to cooperate in the study, the questionnaire was mailed with the confirmation of the interview appointment. It must be stressed that agreement and the cooperation received were generously given by most law firms. Therefore it was possible to cover most of the relevant firms. A total of 29 interviews were conducted with lawyers and often more than one practitioner participated.

The data can claim to be exhaustive with respect to the topics covered in the questionnaire and the free format interview. Only interviews with the full range of information were included in the data base. In January and February 1996, follow-up interviews were conducted with solicitors who took a special interest in the continuation of the study. Also chambers known for their work in reinsurance were addressed for cooperation. This resulted in 10 free format interviews with barristers. Where considered appropriate, this chapter will refer to information obtained during a number of interviews conducted with broker houses and reinsurance consultants and talks with leading employees of reinsurance companies and insurance companies within the same period of time.[14]

The London Reinsurance Market

Reinsurance business in the UK is concentrated in the City of London. According to figures released by Lloyd's Market Planning Department in 1991,[15] the City accounted for 13 per cent of total reinsurance premium income making it the third largest provider in

14 Regrettably, a statement of confidentiality prevents the author from naming the participants in the study. However, I shall take the opportunity at this point to thank everyone for his or her time and cooperation. This chapter could not have been written without the information and support received.

15 1991 was the most recent year in which Lloyd's Market Planning Department provided figures.

reinsurance worldwide.[16] The entire London insurance market is the fourth biggest after the German market.[17]

However, the premium income is not the decisive reason for choosing the London market for the study presented and further research envisaged. The significance of the London market lies in a characteristic which distinguishes it from other reinsurance markets superior in premium income, such as the US market. No other reinsurance market maintains a comparable share of international business contacts and it is especially noted for the high proportion of its business originating abroad.[18] This role of London as an international centre of insurance has grown historically. Its origin was closely linked to marine and increasing world trade in which Great Britain had the leading role as the biggest maritime nation with a large merchant fleet. It comes as no surprise that the extent of the British empire led to a steady increase in the international significance of the British insurance industry. An additional aspect, still important today is the worldwide spread of the English language.

Market Participants

For the reasons mentioned above, primary insurers seek to cede the risks or part of the risks they have written. Every kind of primary insurer – even one dealing with motor or health insurance – seeks reinsurance cover. Reinsurance companies sell this reinsurance cover. It is necessary to distinguish between two kinds of reinsurance companies. A professional reinsurance company conducts reinsurance business exclusively; that is, such an enterprise carries out no primary insurance and subsequently has no direct dealings with the insured.[19] It may also occur that primary insurance companies take over reinsurance business. According to the volume of business two categories in such a case are to be distinguished.[20] The greater number of primary insurers take over

16 Toby Shelley, "Maintaining the City's global role", in *The London Underwriting Centre – One year on* (London: A Lloyd's List Special Supplement, 9–10 October 1994).

17 Horst K. Jannott, "Rückversicherung – Einige praktische Aspekte der Arbeit im Ausland", *Versicherungswirtschaft* 7 (1982), 376 et seq., at 382.

18 Ibid.

19 Christoph Pfeiffer, *Einführung in die Rückversicherung*, 4th edn (Wiesbaden: Gabler, 1994), 1.3.1.

20 Ibid., 1.3.2.

reinsurance business on an occasional basis. They do reinsurance business on a reciprocity basis with other primary insurance companies in order to distribute a certain risk. Besides them there are primary insurers which appear systematically in the reinsurance market and at some stage proceed to set up a previously integrated reinsurance department as an independent entity, which then acts like a professional reinsurer.

Lloyd's of London

Lloyd's of London, which has been the traditional London insurance institution from the late seventeenth century onwards and is active in all insurance business segments, acts as primary insurer as well as reinsurer. Actually, there is no difference from other insurance entities which sell and seek reinsurance cover at the same time.[21] However Lloyd's derives its special character from the fact that it is organized in so-called 'syndicates'. This is an assembly consisting of 'names' (underwriting members), private individuals, who are liable to pay for an underwritten risk, if a claim arises. The importance of Lloyd's for the London reinsurance market is mirrored by its involvement in reinsurance disputes either in the role of a ceding office or as a reinsurance syndicate. The interviewed lawyers stated that, in every second reinsurance file they open, Lloyd's is involved. This figure does not include the 'names' litigation'.[22]

Reinsurance Intermediaries

In insurance, intermediaries act either as brokers or as agents. As agents they are employees of the insurance company. As brokers they are self-employed and, according to English law, they act on behalf of the insured.[23] In reinsurance, a direct relationship between the professional reinsurers present in the London market and their

21 For further information on Lloyd's, see Anthony Brown, *Hazard Unlimited* (London: Lloyd's of London Press Ltd., 1987).

22 The term "names' litigation" refers to claims of "names" brought against their underwriting agents for negligent underwriting, a type of litigation which has become very prominent and publicly reported in recent years.

23 Edward Gumbel, "Neue Vertriebswege und das Beispiel des britischen Versicherungsmaklers", *Versicherungsrecht* 31 (1992), 1293–1300, at 1293.

clients is kept within modest limits compared to continental standards.[24] The vast majority of business originating abroad is exclusively attended by brokers. One may say that reinsurance placed in the London market is international and is mainly placed through brokers. The broker's task is to place the reinsurance cover that is sought by the ceding office. He will give a presentation to reinsurers that will contain the relevant information to assess the risk. He will then try to adjust the conditions under which the risk can be placed between the ceding office and the reinsurer by talking to and mediating between the parties until an agreement can be reached or until it becomes obvious that the parties will not close the deal. The broker will usually draft the 'slip' as well as the wording of the policy that is to follow the slip. A slip is a paper which documents the reinsurance contract in a short form. It may vary slightly in form or content, depending upon the nature of the risk ceded; however, it will contain the following elements:

- the identity of the reinsured,
- the nature of the risk,
- the limits of the indemnity and the reinsured's retention,
- the duration of the reinsurance,
- the premium.[25]

Reinsurance Placed through the London Market

All forms of reinsurance contracts are signed within the London market. However, the London market is known most for its 'excess of loss' reinsurance business.[26] These excess of loss contracts are a subdivision of non-proportional contracts and they may come in the form of excess of loss, catastrophe excess of loss or excess of loss ratio (stop loss ratio).[27] As mentioned before, these forms of reinsurance cover do have in common that the ceding office and the reinsurers do not share each loss in fixed proportions, and may not share some losses at all. The ceding office will bear all losses up to a certain figure (a so called 'retention') and the reinsurer will deal with the balance of any loss above this figure.

24 Ibid., at 1295.

25 Butler, *Reinsurance Practice and the Law*, 8.1.1.

26 Schulte, *Rückversicherung in Deutschland und England: Unterschiede in Recht und Praxis*, p. 216.

27 Dickson and Steele, *Introduction to Insurance*, pp. 185–6.

It is obvious that this kind of business bears a high amount of risk for the reinsurer. The underwriting of excess of loss policies has indeed turned out to cause trouble to reinsurance to an extent previously unknown.

The Legal Framework

With respect to the legal framework, a distinction may be made between regulatory, contractual issues and regulations that apply for reinsurance intermediaries such as brokers. Since this chapter examines the relationship of the reinsurance parties, it is not intended to deal with regulatory aspects and state control of reinsurance.[28]

Reinsurance Law

As a general remark it can be stated that reinsurance law very much dwells on the contractual relationship of the parties.[29] In English law, a special statute for reinsurance does not exist and even the extent to which the Marine Insurance Act (MIA) of 1906 is applicable to reinsurance is under dispute.[30]

Having said that, however, in English law the following inherent principles apply to insurance and reinsurance in like manner.[31]

1. There must be an insurable interest.
2. The contract is one of the utmost good faith (*uberrima fidei*). It calls for the disclosure by the reinsured to the reinsurer of every material fact relating to the risk to be reinsured.
3. The reinsurance contract is one of indemnity.
4. The subject matter of the contract must be in existence at the time the contract is made.

28 For an overview on the regulatory framework on reinsurance in Germany and the UK, see Andrea Schulte, *Rückversicherung in Deutschland und England: Unterschiede in Recht und Praxis*, pp. 103–27. On regulatory framework concerning brokers, compare Edward Gumbel, "Neue Vertriebswege und das Beispiel des britischen Versicherungsmaklers", pp. 1293–1300.

29 Pfeiffer, *Einführung in die Rückversicherung*, 1.4.1.

30 Schulte, *Rückversicherung in Deutschland und England: Unterschiede in Recht und Praxis*, p. 73.

31 Golding, *The Law and Practice of Reinsurance*, p. 8.

The lawyers gave the information that, on average, every second case will involve misrepresentation or non-disclosure. Misrepresentation means the making of a false statement with the intention of persuading someone to enter into a contract. It is a general contract law feature that a party having entered into a contract under those circumstances can seek to avoid the contract. Non-disclosure goes beyond the general duty not to deliver any false information to the other party. Two prominent cases on what information has to be revealed to the reinsurer have been decided by the courts: *Container Transport International Inc.* v. *Oceanus Mutual Underwriting Association (Bermuda) Ltd*[32] and *Pan Atlantic Insurance Company Limited* v. *Pine Top Insurance Company Limited*,[33] in which *CTI* v. *Oceanus* has partly been overruled.

The question arises to what extent the knowledge of facts ('material circumstances') may be assigned to intermediaries. This is a legal question of great relevance for the London market, where brokers mainly close the deals. The fact that London is a brokers' market as well as the fact that the quality of those intermediaries varies to a considerable degree might serve as explanation for the frequency of the problem. There are numerous hints in the literature on how the quality of brokers may vary and in which position of conflicts of interests they sometimes find themselves.[34] Those interviewed expressed a strong view that some brokers keep an eye on the volume of business, the turnover, and their premium above all. Although the information the brokers give to the reinsurer can only be as good as that they receive from the ceding office, the presentation of the risk leaves the way open to dress up a risk more attractively in order to find reinsurance cover for it.

The duties of the parties are a frequent issue as well. In 60 per cent of the cases questions such as whether the reinsurer is entitled to inspect the records of the reinsured and whether the reinsurer has to follow a settlement of the reinsured with the insured will give rise to disputes between the reinsurer and the reinsured.

32 [1984] 1 Lloyd's Rep 476.

33 [1992] 1 Lloyd's Rep 101 (QB Com. Court), [1993] 1 Lloyd's Rep 496 (CA).

34 For example, compare: J.S. Butler, *Reinsurance Practice and the Law*, 2.3; Christoph Pfeiffer, *Einführung in die Rückversicherung*, 1.3.3; Dirk Schmidt-Prange, "Katerstimmung in der Rückversicherung und wie es dazu kam", *Zeitschrift für das Versicherungswesen* 21/85 (1985), 572–4, at 574.

Liquidation and 'run-off'[35] themselves are not subject to disputes, but frequently may initiate disputes. Those interviewed made it clear that the suspicion of the other party being close to or in liquidation or run-off might be a reason to start proceedings. However, the initial assumption was not supported that, in a situation where an insurance or reinsurance company leaves or has left the market, it is likely that it will alter its dispute behaviour with respect to arbitration. This assumption was the basis for the question whether a run-off situation to any extent would harm the value of arbitration clauses, specifically whether interviewees experienced a stronger tendency for the parties to avoid arbitration in favour of legal proceedings. The majority of those interviewed did not support this assumption. Only nine out of 31 interviewed answered this question in the affirmative. Reasons included:

- no continuity of business relation for the future;
- therefore greater conflict of interests;
- a greater tendency to litigate in order to let third parties know that the one in run-off is serious about its position;
- the benefit of the discovery to a party in run-off;
- the need to revoke the question at stake in a larger number of contracts.

The Need for Precedents?

The completely consistent legal framework created through precedents is the key point in the attempt to explain the increasing appetite for disputes in reinsurance during the last decade. The facts that reinsurance was not shaken by major existence-threatening crises in previous times and that the majority of the few disputes were conducted in the privacy of arbitration have left the reinsurance business undersupplied with up-to-date precedents.

The lack of precedents became evident when the line of business in reinsurance changed and precedents were needed in order to assess the chances of success in trying a case. As Cornish (1994)

35 Run-off is a situation in which an insurance or reinsurance company has ceased underwriting, but the contract it is running must be dealt with. There are two possibilities for coping with this situation. Either the former company carries on working with a small staff; this will be done where other entities of the company are still working. The other and very common possibility is to give the claims handling to a run-off company.

states, although it is a painful experience for a reinsurer and its reinsured to end up in court, nevertheless the reinsurance market in general benefits, in that the decision is reported and written about and so the principle decided becomes widely known.[36] However, the question is how the need for precedents and the change in dispute resolution towards more litigation came about.

Factors Determining the Choice of Dispute Resolution Mechanisms

Various factors do influence the way a business community will go about resolving their disputes and together they set out the framework in which a business community is likely to act. It appears that these factors are also applicable in cases containing an international element.

Parties can be either corporations or individuals. They may be equipped with the same economic strength or one may well be inferior to the other, their encounter may be repetitive (repeat players) or they may do business or have contractual obligation towards each other only on one occasion. The assumption on the dispute behaviour of so-called 'global players' at the beginning of this chapter was that in general the global players, who are repeat players, will tend to resolve their disputes in a less formal and private manner than through courts. That is – of course – provided that the probability of their encountering each other again is quite likely. Where this is not guaranteed, as when one party leaves the market, the dispute behaviour is likely to change.

There has been a change in the characteristics of participants in the London reinsurance market. In the 1970s all kinds of participants entered the market in the hope of making money with reinsurance, including primary insurance companies that tried to establish reinsurance departments or subsidiaries.[37] The traditional 'club' of members was intruded upon by market participants who later have been described as innocent[38] or uninformed.[39]

36 Gordon Cornish, "English Reinsurance Law Developments During 1994", *Zeitschrift für Versicherungswesen* 21 (1994), 579–80, at 579.

37 Dirk Schmidt-Prange, "Katerstimmung in der Rückversicherung und wie es dazu kam", pp. 572–4, at 572.

38 Ibid., 573.

39 Klaus Gerathwohl, "The International Reinsurance Markets Today – Developments and Perspectives", pp. 901–9, at 902.

The volume of reinsurance business expanded rapidly. Lloyd's alone doubled its size during the 1980s, half of the business being reinsurance.[40] This growth of Lloyd's happened parallel to a general economic boom in the 1980s. One leading barrister in the names' litigation said:

> at that time Thatcherism tried to encourage a sort of mini capitalism. During that period Lloyd's went about to recruit new names and at the same time lowered the standard and qualifications for the assets those names had to bring in. Houses increased artificially in value and were taken in as security for the names' liability. Also a number of overseas names were recruited.

In this general expansion of the market, it was self-evident that the number of experienced underwriters could not increase in proportion to the market volume. One consequence of this was that some of the new companies started to employ older, frustrated underwriters who had underwriting experience but had no incentive to give much thought to developments beyond their programmed retirement in five to six years.[41]

A trigger for disputes, certainly, is economic loss, its dimension being the decisive factor in starting litigation. There was a series of catastrophes[42] which hit the market hard. The asbestos and pollution claims reached the reinsurance market. As Raphael (1994) describes, as the size of risks underwritten in the London market grew, these complex reinsurance policies, with their numerous intricate layers, tended to become more and more intertwined. Underwriters, influenced by Lloyd's insistence on security, began to reinsure one another's excess of loss risks in what became known as the London Excess of Loss Market or LMX. One result of this

40 Raphael, *The Ultimate Risk: The Inside Story of the Lloyd's Catastrophe* (London: Bantam Press, 1994), 313.

41 Schmidt-Prange, "Katerstimmung in der Rückversicherung und wie es dazu kam", pp. 572–4, at 573.

42 Raphael, "The Ultimate Risk: The Inside Story of the Lloyd's Catastrophe", pp. 173–4: the explosion of the Piper Alpha oil platform on 6 July 1988, Hurricane Hugo on 15 September 1989, Hurricane Gilbert, the *Exxon Valdez* oil spill, the San Fransisco earthquake, the Arco Bake fire, the Phillips petroleum explosion, Typhoon Mireille in Japan and three severe gales which struck Britain and northern Europe at the beginning of 1990.

incestuous pattern of trading was that the tiers of insurance became hopelessly confused.[43]

Internationality of Reinsurance Business in the London Market and its Influence on Legal Issues

Reinsurance is international in the sense that it is most successfully conducted by not confining it to one country. This certainly applies to professional reinsurers.[44] This is why nearly all reinsurance transactions of greater volume will contain a variety of international parties on the slip. Internationality on the side of risk takers with respect to the insurers and reinsurers has positive aspects as far as the risk spreading idea is concerned. However, internationality in insurance and reinsurance also means that the sources of definition of risks and the liability subsequent to it spread and in that way are likely to increase. It was a harsh experience that, with respect to liability of insurance, a foreign jurisdiction could throw overboard all previously known dimensions. This was the case with asbestos and pollution litigation in the US jurisdiction.

During the interviews with the City lawyers it became clear that the interviewed practitioners carefully monitor the developments in US liability and tort law and the reform it will undergo.[45] Furthermore, problems arise in connection with disputes owing to the fact the parties are international: this refers to cross-border cases, with all the attendant problems. It was found from the interviews that in fact more than two-thirds of the files opened by the lawyers were cross-border with respect to the parties or the facts of the case. In every fourth of these cross-border files a dispute about the applicable law arises, according to the lawyers interviewed.

43 Raphael, "The Ultimate Risk: The Inside Story of the Lloyd's Catastrophe", p. 176.

44 C.E. Golding, *The Law and Practice of Reinsurance*, p. 24; Horst K. Jannott, "Rückversicherung – Einige praktische Aspekte der Arbeit im Ausland", *Versicherungswirtschaft* 7/87 (1987), 376–86, at 386; Alois Alzheimer, "Probleme der internationalen Rückversicherung", *Versicherungswirtschaft* 12 (1971).

45 One lawyer expressed his view on the probability of a change in the American tort law and the lawyers as follows: "The political influence of American tort lawyers in the Congress has managed to leave the tort law unchanged and probably will do so in the future. It is well recognized in the market that the American jurisdiction in the liabilities cases will in the long run ruin the insurance industry."

This result might come as a surprise if one assumes that there should be provisions in the wording of reinsurance contracts concerning which law shall prevail in case of a dispute. In this context the fact must be stressed that documentation in place when reinsurance contracts are made obeys no hard rules – at least, this was so in the past. As mentioned above, the reinsurance contract – if the business is placed in the London market – is documented by a paper called a slip, which is supposed to be followed by a wording, but until this wording is issued, the slip represents the contract.

The solicitors interviewed stated that in the past the documentation in reinsurance was handled quite sloppily, as a consequence of which the solicitors find themselves in a position to give legal advice on a contract where no documentation of the reinsurance exists but the slip. The free format interview relating to the quality of drafting revealed both a conflict of interest and some professional tension between lawyers and brokers. It has to be said that some of those interviewed also work for brokers, sometimes in cases where the latter have to be defended against allegations of misrepresentation or non-disclosure.

However, the assistance of outside counsels in drafting, according to the interviewed lawyers, remains 'a touchy issue', as one interviewed put it. Drafting has for a long time been the brokers' domain and the idea that an outside counsel shall be of assistance in this matter – a perspective the lawyers would like to make them appreciate – has not really caught on.

Dealing with cross-border legal interaction where international parties are involved, the problem of cross-border disputes often lies in that, for one, a variety of laws may be applicable to the facts of the case and unification of law in that special field does not yet exist or will not prompt a satisfactory solution. Reinsurance here again may serve as a classic example, especially in connection with the underlying risk.[46] Since the applicable law is not mentioned on the slip, there is a relatively high percentage of cases where the question of applicable law has to be given some thought by the lawyers. The question of the applicable law as well as jurisdiction is by no means a theoretical problem.[47]

46 *Forsikringsaktieselkapet Vesta* v. *Butcher* [1989] AC; [1989] 1 Lloyd's Rep 331 (HL).

47 This summary originates from Stephenson Harwood, *Insurance and Reinsurance Group Newsletter*, December 1994. The footnotes within the text to explain certain expressions are the present author's.

It is to be borne in mind that the internationality of reinsurance is involved in every possible stage of the relationship of the parties of a reinsurance contract. This covers the risks of being exposed to interpretation of the national jurisdiction where they are generated: the parties involved coming from different jurisdictions and struggling with the applicable law and jurisdiction, and the enforcement of arbitration awards and court decisions within the various jurisdictions.

The Institutions in Reinsurance Conflict Resolution

It can be taken as a fact that more and more reinsurance disputes find their way to arbitration and also into the court system.[48] The recent edition of a special Lloyd's reinsurance law report, the *Lloyd's Reinsurance Law Report*,[49] which came out in January 1995 and is published quarterly, supports this suggestion in that the number of decisions made justifies a specialized publication.

The quality and contribution of the legal professions surrounding proceedings, whether arbitration or litigation, are essential factors if a venue is felt appropriate for resolving international disputes. International reinsurance parties do come to London for arbitration and litigation. They have recourse to the Commercial Court as a national court.

The Commercial Court

Reinsurance cases will almost always be heard before the Commercial Court in first instance because of the sums involved, although it has no exclusive jurisdiction over them. The Commercial Court as a subdivision of the High Court is a specialist court within the Queen's Bench Division and deals with large commercial cases.

The recruitment of Commercial Court judges certainly is one key factor explaining why the Commercial Court enjoys such a high reputation within the international trade community and the reinsurance market in particular. The commercial judges are recruited from senior Queen's Counsels who have practised at the Commercial Bar. They therefore have significant experience – including that of

48 Butler, *Reinsurance Practice and the Law*, 25.5.1.

49 Lloyd's Reinsurance Law Report (LRLP), quarterly, edited by M.M. Souza, Lloyd's of London Press.

reinsurance matters. Commercial business in London is dealt with at the Royal Courts of Justice, and in the provinces at the District Registries in Liverpool and Manchester, but the overwhelming majority of commercial cases are commenced in London.

The Commercial Court's work also includes appeals against the decision of independent arbitrators. In terms of time, arbitration work accounts for a small percentage of the Court's total business, but it involves a substantial number of cases and generates significant interlocutory work. All arbitration appeals must be commenced in the Commercial Court and, although a Commercial judge has a discretion to transfer such appeals to be heard by another judge or the High Court, appeals still account in numerical terms for at least a third of all hearings.

Legal–cultural differences faced by international parties when litigating before the Commercial Court

Foreign parties consider English law fair, and English courts impartial. Otherwise they would not have chosen the Commercial Court.

Still there are legal–cultural differences which are significant in cross-border disputes. Interestingly enough, these legal–cultural differences, according to the solicitors and barristers, become most apparent in procedural questions.

One of the major differences between litigation in England and in many other jurisdictions (including most European countries) is that English litigation normally involves a procedure known as 'discovery'.[50] This means that each party is required to serve on the other a list of all documents relevant to the actions which are or have been in its possession. The term 'document' includes anything upon which information is recorded, such as letters, memoranda, internal reports (or drafts of any of these), film, tape recordings or information held on computers. In major commercial cases, it is very common for parties to have to list thousands of relevant documents. Reinsurance as a business seems to generate more documentation than most. Indeed, the management of documents in a sensible and efficient manner by the client and by the lawyer can often be a decisive factor in succeeding in any such dispute.[51]

The solicitors stated that the discovery may cause major difficulties in understanding by the foreign client. Many of the continental

50 John O'Hare and Robert N. Hill, *Civil Litigation*, 7th edn (London: FT Law & Tax Publ., 1995), 375 et seq.

51 Butler, *Reinsurance Practice and the Law*, 25.6.1.1.

clients do find the disclosure of documents – whether or not these be in favour of the client concerned – *Ausforschungsbeweis*.[52] It may occur that clients will therefore not follow instructions of the solicitor to collect certain information and send it to the London forum. This again may put the solicitor in a difficult position, as he has an obligation towards the court to compile all information required and has to give an affidavit that required information and material if demanded but not delivered does not exist. It is for these reasons that many law firms have brochures for their commercial clients explaining the discovery process in detail and in the mother language.[53] This is despite the fact that the solicitors stated that communication problems with their foreign clients, especially in the reinsurance industry, do not exist. It is just that these legal–cultural differences in procedure can be better conveyed in the mother language of the client concerned. It was stressed during the interviews that the importance of discovery in preparing a settlement is of utmost importance. Tactical deliberations are very important, too.

In the area of evidence, again a legal–cultural difference between the common law system and other legal systems is striking and is likely to be one key factor in the Commercial Court being such an accepted forum for foreign parties in cross-border disputes. It has been said before that national courts often have difficulties in handling cases with a foreign element – let alone when foreign law has to be applied. The Commercial Court is not shy of handling such cases and the reason for this is twofold. First, the common law system runs on an adversarial basis: all information relating to the facts of the case have to be brought before the judge by the party. Second, the question of the applicable law according to English law is a question of fact. In practice, this means that the parties have to prove whether foreign law is applicable by the means of evidence and present it to the judge the way they think it applies to the case. If in an international dispute, for example, the forum clause says London, but no choice of law clause is made, the parties may in certain cases argue which law is applicable, and have indeed done so.[54] A foreign law expert may then be called in to give evidence as

52 Inadmissable inquiry.

53 See for example, Lovell White Durant, *La procédure de "Discovery" en matière judiciaire devant la High Court*, client brochure, London, 1990.

54 *Forsikringsaktieselkapet* v. *Butcher* [1989] AC, [1989] 1 Lloyd's Rep 331 (HL).

to the proper law and application to the case. This (costly) procedure is of course a different incentive really to apply the foreign law and, according to the solicitors, such a procedure is by no means infrequent.

Even more common, however, is the expert witness if evidence has to be given concerning a particular type of technology or how a particular market or industry normally works. Reinsurance is a complex and market-driven business.[55] Courts have needed in the past, and will continue to need, the assistance of market expertise. The following are illustrations of the ways in which experts may assist in the reinsurance context.[56]

1. The court may require assistance from an expert as to the meaning of a particular phrase in a reinsurance wording, which has no obvious or usual meaning but does have a generally accepted meaning in the market-place.
2. It may also be possible to call a broker to provide evidence as to the proper and reasonable practices in the broking industry if such issues are relevant to the particular case.
3. It will also be relevant, in cases of misrepresentation and non-disclosure, to call an expert underwriter to indicate whether particular facts which have been misrepresented or not disclosed are in fact material to a prudent underwriter.
4. It may, in certain circumstances, be necessary to call an expert accountant, perhaps to deal with certain accounting technicalities germane to the issues in question.

Normally, the expert witnesses will prepare reports which, like witness statements, are exchanged with the opponent on a specified date before trial.

In terms of number, one may be surprised that only a few cases which are tried end with a verdict. The vast majority of cases brought in the English courts (95 per cent) never go to a full trial. Generally, there are two ways in which a full trial can be avoided. The first is through obtaining a judgment prior to the full trial, for example through a 'summary judgment'. This is a speedy and cheap way based on documents, the 'affidavit(s)'. The summary judgment is only appropriate in situations where the plaintiff's claim is a strong one. The second way is for the parties to agree on an out-of-

55 Butler, *Reinsurance Practice and the Law*, 25.6.2.1.

56 Ibid., 25.6.2.2.

court settlement. Again, the interviewed solicitors and barristers stressed that the discovery contributes a great deal to the high rate of settlement.

Arbitration

The original idea of inserting arbitral clauses into reinsurance contracts was based on the experience that disputes rarely occurred and the expectation that disputes would not arise under those contracts in the future. If they ever should arise, the parties would resolve them with the assistance of arbitrators who are people with market experience, so to speak 'within one's own peers'. The absence of lawyers and judges was a declared favoured factor in this concept.[57] When cases became more complicated and legal issues more intricate, lawyers found their way into arbitration proceedings. Subsequently, arbitration proceedings increasingly resembled court proceedings.[58]

The concept – to conduct arbitration and not to go to court – worked in reinsurance for a considerable period of time, up to the recent past. Disputes between insurers and their reinsurers that related to the strict interpretation of policy conditions used to be relatively unknown. If they ever occurred, such disputes used to centre on adjustment of claims, and repudiation of the claim outright by the insurer due to non-disclosure, suspected fraudulent activity or similar reasons.

Now it has occurred to reinsurance that the genuine concept of arbitration as a dispute resolution mechanism has been overtaken by the fact that, in recent years, as the appetite for litigation has increased, the number of disputes has expanded at a considerable rate. In an attempt to resolve some of these disputes without the expense of going through a courtroom in the first place, efforts have been made to make increasing use of the processes of arbitration. During this increased use, arbitration in reinsurance changed its face. Costs and duration of proceedings have increased to an alarming degree.[59] It can be stated that arbitration turns out not to be a satisfactory

57 This was mentioned very frequently during the interviews. The Arbitration Act 1979 does not require any participation of lawyers.

58 As one practitioner conducting reinsurance seminars frankly put it: "Arbitrations were hijacked by the lawyers long ago and have been turning into mini-trials ever since."

59 Reform efforts on English arbitration law are in train. A full discussion of these efforts and the present stage is well beyond the

dispute resolution mechanism if it is used beyond a certain extent. This is at least the lawyers' view on arbitration in reinsurance.

Nevertheless, virtually all contracts of reinsurance will contain an arbitration clause. There are several different arbitration clauses that have been used. The basic feature that they all have in common is that they will make provision that any disputes between the parties to the agreement will be referred to an arbitration tribunal. Usually, since the 1970s, a standard arbitration clause has been widely used in the market. It provided for a panel of three arbitrators. It will frequently be found that the arbitrator appointed by each party will be a market man: a recognized person with insurance experience.[60] The third arbitrator, acting as an umpire, may be a barrister and will be appointed by the two arbitrators. The third arbitrator may also be a respected person within the insurance market. Thus a panel of three will sit to hear the case presented by both parties. The English arbitration law is currently changing as a new Arbitration Bill has recently passed through Parliament. The law on arbitration was scattered in a diffuse body of cases and the statute law was also spread across three Acts, of 1950, 1975 and 1979. This situation needed improvement. Since this chapter looks at reinsurance dispute resolution only up to 1996, it refers to the arbitration law applicable up to 1996, before the new Arbitration Bill was enacted. However it is important to mention the new bill and its coming into effect as it delivers living proof of the disenchantment with arbitration described above and below.

The Arbitration Act 1979 gives the arbitrators a certain amount of liberty with respect to procedural questions. For example, it is quite common that no full discovery will be conducted, which might, for the reasons described above, be welcomed by foreign parties. According to practitioners interviewed, there is a reluctance of arbitrators – especially with a panel of market men – to look at a large quantity of papers.

With reference to the personal qualification, the panel must have appropriate experience in the matter that is being arbitrated. An-

scope of this chapter. See: Edward Gumbel, "Auf dem Weg zu einem neuen Schiedsrecht in England", *Zeitschrift für Versicherungswesen* 21 (1994), 575–8.

60 For capacity, qualification and impartiality of the arbitrators in general, see Michael J. Mustill and Stewart C. Boyd, *The Law and Practice of Commercial Arbitration in England*, 2nd edn (London, Edinburgh: Butterworth, 1989), 247–56.

other essential requirement for an arbitrator of course is impartiality. It has become increasingly difficult to find persons to meet these requirements. The practitioners stated that this has been a kind of parallel development in volume and intensity, which has resulted in arbitrators and expert witnesses being in high demand. With respect to the number of people in the London market, reinsurance is a 'closed society' and, as the number of arbitration proceedings has increased, it has become more and more difficult to find a sufficient number of arbitrators that were not close to one party or the other. To overcome these difficulties, the Reinsurance and Insurance Arbitration Society was established in 1991 under the aegis of the Association Internationale de Droit des Assurances to promote and assist in the development of arbitration as a reliable means of dispute resolution for the insurance and reinsurance markets. Based in the London insurance and reinsurance market, the society draws its membership from organizations worldwide and aims to serve and assist the international community, not just the domestic market.

Law Applied by Arbitrators: Lex Mercatoria *in Reinsurance*

Under certain circumstances, straightforward legal approaches may lead to inequitable results. This straightforward approach concerns not only the application of law but also the arrangement of the arbitration panel and its approach to resolving the dispute.[61] A different approach which stressed market principles is called the 'equity' clause. An equity clause in the general sense is spoken of if the arbitration agreement purports expressly to dispense the arbitrator from applying the law either wholly or in part, by some provision such as the following:[62] 'The arbitrator shall be entitled to decide according to equity and good conscience and shall not be obliged to follow the strict rules of law.' Or the clause may say: 'The arbitrator shall act as amiable compositor.' In reinsurance, such an equity clause is called an 'honourable engagement'. In essence, an honourable engagement clause is a clause which attempts to allow an arbitration panel the right to determine the dispute in accordance with market principles and in the spirit of good faith.[63]

61 Butler, *Reinsurance Practice and the Law*, 25.2.

62 Mustill and Boyd, *Commercial Arbitration*, p. 74.

63 Butler, *Reinsurance Practice and the Law*, 25.3.1.

Provisions of this type raise theoretical questions of great difficulty.[64] The crucial question is: are reinsurance disputes in the London reinsurance market resolved on a *lex mercatoria* basis and can reinsurance therefore correctly be named a loophole of *lex mercatoria*, as it is by some authors,[65] with reference to an alleged ruling opinion? The up-to-date answer to this question suggests that this is not the case. A view contrary to the alleged ruling opinion requires good arguments. A reference to a prominent comrade-in-arms[66] cannot be considered sufficient. To start the chain of arguments, in the first place a definition of *lex mercatoria* in its modern context is required. But although the new discussion of *lex mercatoria* started in the 1960s,[67] and various attempts at a definition have been made in the meantime,[68] a mutual consent on the characteristics of *lex mercatoria* has not yet been found. This flaw is often the first point of criticism for its opponents. As Goode has put it in a talk entitled 'The Influence of Mercantile Practice on the Context of Commercial Law', one cannot see it or smell it, but one certainly knows that it is floating around.[69] However, in order to try a fair assessment, existing definitions basically can be said to comprise the following characteristics: *lex mercatoria* is a body of

64 Mustill and Boyd, *Commercial Arbitration*, p. 75.

65 Andreas Kappus, *"Lex mercatoria" in Europa und Wiener UN-Kaufrechtskonvention 1980* (Frankfurt/M.: Lang, 1990), 182; Fritz Reichert-Facilides, "Rechtvereinheitlichung oder Rechtsvielfalt?" in *Europarecht, Internationales Privatrecht, Rechtsvergleichung*, Official Paper 7 (Vienna: Kommission für Europarecht, 1988), 155–70, at 162, with reference inter alia to Klaus Gerathewohl, *Rückversicherung-Grundlagen und Praxis*, vol. I, p. 541.

66 Michael J. Mustill, "The New Lex Mercatoria: The First Twenty-five Years", in *Liber Amicorum for Lord Wilberforce* (Oxford: Clarendon Press, 1987), 182.

67 Clive Schmitthoff, "Das autonome Recht des Welthandels – Rechtsdogmatische und rechtspolitische Aspekte", in *RabelsZ*, 28, (1964), 47–77.

68 See: Michael J. Mustill, "The New Lex Mercatoria: The First Twenty-five Years", p. 151; Ulrich Ehricke, "Zur Einführung: Grundstrukturen und Problem der lex mercatoria", *Juristische Schulung* (1990), 967–9, at 967.

69 Roy Goode, 'The Influence of Mercantile Practice on the Context of Commercial Law' a talk given on 19 February 1996 at the Centre for Socio-Legal Studies, Oxford.

rules which have emerged out of international practice of commercial transactions; these rules are not part or the result of any kind of state enactment or the result of a court's dispensation and can claim legal observance as binding authority within the international community which runs the business concerned.

Mustill[70] answers the fundamental questions regarding the application and sources of *lex mercatoria* in the sense that it is required to be supranational and, as for its sources, he has recourse to a list compiled by Lando.[71]

To answer the question of application of *lex mercatoria* in reinsurance dispute resolution in a qualified and credible manner, it seems appropriate to go through the different possible sources subsequently. To start with public international law, it can be stated that public international regulations concerning reinsurance barely exist. Therefore this source of *lex mercatoria* can be excluded. Uniform supranational laws concerning reinsurance do not exist either, and the attempts which have been made, such as European standards and regulations for insurance and reinsurance, concern regulatory matters not dealt with in this chapter, which focuses on the legal interaction between reinsurer and cedant.

General principles of law, comprising rules such as good faith, *pacta sunt servanda*, *rebus sic stantibus*, abuse of rights and *culpa in contrahendo* are alleged sources of *lex mercatoria*. For two reasons the application of those principles cannot be qualified as *lex mercatoria* in reinsurance. First, the qualification of general legal principles as sources of *lex mercatoria* encounters the objection that general legal principles are embodied in national legal orders referring to those principles and resemble each other. The qualification of general legal principles as a source of *lex mercatoria* is therefore under dispute. And even if one does not share those concerns with regard to the qualification of general legal principles as *lex mercatoria*, one meets difficulties in affirming their application in reinsurance. As shown above, those principles are resorted to a great deal in reinsurance, not in such broad terms but within a specific scope, such as the nature of utmost good faith within the usages of reinsurance. A recourse to general principles of law

70 Michael J. Mustill, "The New Lex Mercatoria: The First Twenty-five Years", p. 172 et seq.

71 Ole Lando, "The Lex Mercatoria in International Commercial Arbitration", *International and Comparative Law Quarterly* 34 (1985), 747–68.

therefore does not help further in the solution of specific reinsurance problems.

Rules of international organization do not touch on issues relating to the private international relationships in reinsurance.

Within the scope of the definition given it is, then, obvious that *lex mercatoria* must be found – if at all – within commercial arbitration, the field where commercial disputes are supposed to be resolved with 'one's own peers'. Arbitration awards, if published, certainly could establish precedents. In reinsurance, contrary to other commercial fields such as maritime law, arbitration awards are not published and therefore cannot claim to give legal guidance. Nor are awards accessible in another way if they are not subject to an appeal. Comments on this must remain subject to the envisaged decision analysis.

Contrary to continental arbitration, in English arbitration there are two factors which limit or hinder the *lex mercatoria* from coming into existence within arbitration. We have considered above an arbitrator having a duty to decide the dispute in accordance with the law. There is also the judicial control over arbitration, the possibility of appealing against an arbitration award. And, although the scope of appeal has been narrowed down by the Arbitration Act 1979, and will be further restricted in the future through the new Arbitration Bill, the basic feature of judicial control remains.

Reliable knowledge on the spread of the honourable clause in reinsurance arbitration agreements up to now is not available because they are not published. As with other equity clauses, they appear to be the exception rather than the rule. Again, whether in those cases decisions are made according to equity is difficult to assess because they are not published. Isolated or sporadic application of market practice and equity, if not generally known and accepted as legally binding, may not qualify for claiming the existence of a *lex mercatoria*.

However, it seems fair to concede market practice in reinsurance considerable recognition in reinsurance disputes. But this recognition cannot go beyond the fact that, if an honourable engagement clause is there, arbitrators, as market men, perhaps exempt the parties from naming expert witnesses to undermine their view of a certain market practice. A further difficulty in conceding the existence of *lex mercatoria* in reinsurance, with respect to London as a dispute resolution centre, is that English law has a precise idea about when a rule becomes law and therefore binding. Market practice in the sense of a 'law merchant' has to pass a test that it is notorious, generally exercised and followed as legally binding.[72] To undermine the criteria of general exercise it is only necessary to call on an expert witness who states a practice otherwise. This demonstrates that English law is quite serious on what can be understood as established – even with a market practice that could form a single legal binding rule.

Finally, the spontaneous honouring of arbitration awards has been brought forward as an argument of *lex mercatoria*.[73] There are two objections to this, one factual and one systematic. First, experience shows that the spontaneous honouring of arbitration awards in the London reinsurance market cannot be affirmed unreservedly. For this I would like to refer to the statement of Lord Mustill, who maintains that this was so in the past, when the market was narrow, and default could be fatal. In his experience, reinsurance is nowadays the most bitterly litigious of all areas of commercial activity.[74] The interviews conducted with City practitioners support the impression that arbitration awards are not honoured with the matter of course of previous times. Furthermore, the question must be allowed how the spontaneous honouring of arbitration awards nowadays can indeed be attributed to the existence of *lex mercatoria*. A more pragmatic approach suggests that the spontaneous honouring of arbitration awards is driven by the intention of the parties involved to preserve the major advantage compared to litigation which arbitration has sustained: privacy.

Conclusion

This chapter on reinsurance disputes in the London reinsurance market presents two main conclusions. On the one hand, it reveals disputes in an area which was traditionally known as 'gentlemen's business' and was characterized by the principle of utmost good faith. On the other hand, it refutes approaches that look for results in the facilitation of cross-border legal interaction

72 Kenneth Smith and Dennis Keenan, *English Law*, 10th edn (London: Pitman Publ., 1992), 14.

73 Bernardo Cremades and Steven Plehn, "The New Lex Mercatoria and the Harmonization of the Laws of International Commercial Transactions", *Boston University International Law Journal* (1984), 317–48, at 317.

74 Michael J. Mustill (1987), "The New Lex Mercatoria: The First Twenty-five Years", p. 182.

by means of an alleged globalization of the law.[75] It has emerged that a national court may, under certain circumstances, be well suited to the requirements of cross-border legal interaction. Findings which evidence the importance of a national court for cross-border dispute resolution may not suit at a time when globalization – at least in recent socio-legal literature – is deemed to have already reached all areas of human activity and therefore seems to be reality. As regards the Commercial Court in London with respect to reinsurance disputes, a typical non-court user group can be found litigating there.

Owing to the dissatisfaction with the incalculable outcomes as well as with the increasing costs, arbitration became less popular. The special expertise of the Commercial Court, the contribution of the legal professions in London and their experience with international cases, as well as the fact that the application of foreign law is a question of evidence, have led to the Commercial Court's becoming a preferred forum for resolving reinsurance disputes. This is not to say that legal–cultural differences in using a foreign legal system – especially with respect to procedural questions – do not occur. In weighing the pros and cons, these legal–cultural differences are very minor obstacles and do not prevent the foreign parties from opting for the Commercial Court. The selective use of dispute resolution mechanisms is one remarkable feature in this respect. Whilst generally a tendency of retreat from national courts is to be observed when it comes to cases with an international element, the reinsurance community participating in the London market appears to use the legal instrument most suitable to enabling cross-border legal comparability and interaction.

References

Alzheimer, Alois. 1971. Probleme der internationalen Rückversicherung. *Versicherungswirtschaft* 12.

Brown, Anthony. 1987. *Hazard Unlimited*. London: Lloyd's of London Press Ltd.

Butler, J.S. 1993. *Reinsurance Practice and the Law*. London: Lloyd's of London Press Ltd.

Butler, J.S. and R. Merkin. 1986. *Reinsurance Law*. London: Kluwer.

75 Cf. the contributions in Gunther Teubner, ed., *Global Law without a State* (Aldershot: Dartmouth, 1997).

Cornish, Gordon. English Reinsurance Law Developments During 1994. *Zeitschrift für Versicherungswesen* 21.

Cremades, Bernardo and Steven Plehn. 1984. The New Lex Mercatoria and the Harmonization of the Laws of International Commercial Transactions. *Boston University International Law Journal* 317.

Dickson, G.C.A. and J.T. Steele. 1984. *Introduction to Insurance.* 2nd edn. London: Pitman.

Ehricke, Ulrich. 1990. Zur Einführung: Grundstrukturen und Problem der lex mercatoria. *Juristische Schulung* 967.

Gerathewohl, Klaus. 1976. *Rückversicherung – Grundlagen und Praxis*, Vol.I. Karlsruhe: Verlag Versicherungswirtschaft e.V.

Gerathewohl, Klaus. 1987. The International Reinsurance Markets Today – Developments and Perspectives. *Versicherungswirtschaft* 14.

Golding, C.E. 1987. *The Law and Practice of Reinsurance.* 5th edn. London: Witherby & Co. Ltd.

Gumbel, Edward. 1992. Neue Vertriebswege und das Beispiel des britischen Versicherungsmaklers. *Versicherungsrecht* 31.

Gumbel, Edward. 1994. Auf dem Weg zu einem neuen Schiedsrecht in England., *Zeitschrift für Versicherungswesen* 21.

Jannott, Horst K. 1982. Rückversicherung – Einige praktische Aspekte der Arbeit im Ausland. *Versicherungswirtschaft* 7/82.

Jannott, Horst K. 1987. Rückversicherung – Einige praktische Aspekte der Arbeit im Ausland. *Versicherungswirtschaft* 7/87.

Jones, Samantha J. 1992. *Compensating Victims of Mass Accidents, A Socio-Legal Analysis.* Oxford: Centre for Socio-Legal Studies and Pembroke College, University of Oxford.

Kappus, Andreas. 1990. *'Lex mercatoria' in Europa und Wiener UN-Kaufrechtskonvention 1980.* Frankfurt/M.: Lang.

Lando, Ole. 1985. The Lex Mercatoria in International Commercial Arbitration. *International and Comparative Law Quarterly* 34.

McGrew, Anthony. 1992. A Global Society? In *Modernity and Its Futures*, edited by Stuart Hall, David Held and Antony McGrew. Cambridge: Polity Press.

Mustill, Michael J. 1987. The New Lex Mercatoria: The First Twenty-five Years. In *Liber Amicorum for Lord Wilberforce.* Oxford: Clarendon Press.

Mustill, Michael J. and Stewart C. Boyd. 1989. *The Law and Practice of Commercial Arbitration in England.* 2nd edn. London, Edinburgh: Butterworth.

O'Hare, John and Robert N. Hill. 1995. *Civil Litigation.* 7th edn. London: FT Law & Tax Publishers.

Pfeiffer, Christoph. 1994. *Einführung in die Rückversicherung*. 4th edn. Wiesbaden: Gabler.

Raphael, Adam. 1994. *The Ultimate Risk: The Inside Story of the Lloyd's Catastrophe*. London: Bantam Press.

Reichert-Facilides, Fritz. 1988. Rechtvereinheitlichung oder Rechtsvielfalt? In *Europarecht, Internationales Privatrecht, Rechtsvergleichung*. Official Paper 7. Vienna: Kommission für Europarecht.

Schmidt-Prange, Dirk. 1985. Katerstimmung in der Rückversicherung und wie es dazu kam. *Zeitschrift für das Versicherungswesen* 21/85.

Schmitthoff, Clive. 1964. Das autonome Recht des Welthandels – Rechtsdogmatische und rechtspolitische Aspekte. *RabelsZ* 28.

Schulte, Andrea. 1990. *Rückversicherung in Deutschland und England: Unterschiede in Recht und Praxis*. Karlsruhe: Verlag Versicherungswirtschaft e.V.

Shelley, Toby. 1994. Maintaining the City's global role. In *The London Underwriting Centre – One year on*. London: A Lloyd's List Special Supplement, 9–10 October.

Smith, Kenneth and Dennis Keenan. 1992. *English Law*. 10th edn. London: Pitman Publishers.

Teubner, Gunther, ed. 1997. *Global Law without a State*. Aldershot: Dartmouth.

Weise, Paul-Frank. 1989. *Materielles Recht vor der internationalen Handelsschiedsgerichtsbarkeit*. Frankfurt/M.: Lang.

The Author

Christine Stammel is a German lawyer with an additional Master of Law degree (European Studies of Law, University of Bremen). She joined the Bremen research team on cross-border legal interaction in 1995 and during her studies in England was based at the Centre for Socio-Legal Studies, Wolfson College, Oxford.

Address: Waldstr.61, 46487 Wesel, Germany.

Abstract

This chapter gives an introduction to cross-border legal interaction and third cultures in the London reinsurance market. Owing to its large share of international business, the London reinsurance market represents a field which invites a study of the legal behaviour of the global players within one specific field of business. Reinsurance, so far, has not conducted legal battles in public – if there were legal battles at all. First of all, disputing parties would negotiate, dispute thus remaining in the privacy of arbitration. This could indicate a kind of third legal culture. The result of literature study and empirical research refutes statements that reinsurance still is a non-litigious area. The Commercial Court in London has taken an important role in resolving those disputes put to it by UK residents and non-UK resident parties. Fundamental changes since the end of the 1980s have taken place in the course of reinsurance business. Bad results, together with other factors, led to a reassessment of the relationship between reinsurers, cedants and the retrocessionaire. The Lloyd's crisis occurred in this decade as well. These changes have not taken place without influencing behaviour regarding the resolution of disputes within the London reinsurance market. Increased competition may have caused the turning away from arbitration towards obtaining court decisions. On the other hand, reasons inherent to the system may have caused this swing. This chapter attempts to offer an explanation of the development of dispute behaviour in the London reinsurance market during the last 10 to 15 years. The focus here is on exemplifying cross-border legal interaction and third cultures in a kind of international microcosmos. This includes a discussion of *lex mercatoria*.

4 Third Cultures versus Regulators: Cross-border Legal Relations of Banks

KLAUS FRICK

Introduction

The following study explores how banks which are active across borders deal with one another, what conflicts arise in the framework of cross-border contacts, and how these conflicts are prevented or resolved in practice.

Banking autonomy serves as an explanation for the smooth handling of international payment transactions. Practically without government assistance, but also without government control, the banks have built up a global network of institutions which effectively avoids legal and legal–cultural conflicts. Of course, this process has not escaped the attention of the legislatures. While, on the one hand, the state has a keen existential interest in a well-functioning banking system, on the other a spate of recent events – starting with the Herstatt bankruptcy caused by misguided dollar speculations, through the current discussion about the role of the banks in international money laundering, and all the way up to the spectacular collapse of the venerable Baring Bank, caused by the highly speculative transactions of a 23-year-old 'financial genius' – has roused the government supervisory authorities. Thus it is not surprising to hear increasing calls for restrictions on banking autonomy through increased government intervention; no more surprising of course than it is to see representatives of the banking industry doing everything they can to prevent their hard-won autonomy from being eroded.

This chapter is intended – using the specific example of cross-border payments transactions – to demonstrate how, on the one hand, in the process of European unification the borders for intra-European bank dealings have de facto fallen away, while on the other hand the credit institutions have, in the view of the EU Commission, still proved incapable of transferring payments as quickly and cheaply within Europe as they can within the respective member states. This is the starting point of the critique by the EU Commission, which for some time now has threatened to take legislative action if the banks do not voluntarily adopt appropriate self-regulatory measures.

An essential part of this chapter recounts the significant efforts banking industry representatives have made to keep this directive, which is waiting in draft form, from being adopted.

The banks first began the now quite strikingly evident process of internationalization at the end of the 1950s.[1] At first it was the direct investments made around the world by industrial companies and closely accompanied by their banks which stood in the foreground: the key phrases here are 'international division of labour' and 'multinationalization of conglomerates'; while since the 1980s, with the development of the international financial markets, one has witnessed an increasing globalization of the banking sector itself. This development was substantially influenced and stimulated by the development of new means of communication,[2] as well as by a progressive deregulation of the banking sector. In particular, this deregulation is the basis of the current banking autonomy, although it is not always easy to decide whether the advancing globalization is its cause or its effect.[3]

International payment transactions which, as the unquestionably most important area of cross-border banking activity, are our main focus here, have gained significance as a topic in recent years through the massive increase of cross-border economic activity. Thus the volume of world trade rose from (nominal) US$59 billion in 1950 to US$3,441 billion in 1991;[4] the leading export countries, the USA, Japan and Germany, alone had a combined share of US$1,140 billion.[5] Such exports generate a correspondingly high number of

1 Hans E. Büschgen, *Bankbetriebslehre* (Wiesbaden: Gabler Verlag, 1993), 425–6.

2 Alfred Steinherr, "Der europäische Bankensektor im integrierten Finanzmarkt", *Zeitschrift für das Bank- und Börsenwesen* (1989), 121, 124 et seq.

3 Hans E. Büschgen, "Allgemeine Entwicklungslinien", in *Europäische Bankengeschichte*, ed. Hans von Pohl (Frankfurt/M.: Fritz Knapp Verlag, 1993), 455 (466).

4 Volker Burghagen, "Auslandsgeschäft der Kreditinstitute", in *Handwörterbuch des Bank- und Finanzwesens*, 2nd edn (Stuttgart: Schäffer-Poeschel, 1995).

5 Karl-Heinz Jung, *Jahrbuch für den Außenhandel* (Stuttgart: Schäffer-Poeschel, 1992).

cross-border payments, which merely in the European area amount to around 170 million operations per year – and the trend is rising.[6] Further cross-border financial transactions result from the dramatically growing financial derivatives market. These are the forward transactions traded on the financial markets in the form of options, futures contracts or swaps: that is, all transactions where it is not the original security (stock or bond) which is traded, but rather a product 'derived' from it and which relates to the future price or interest rate of the underlying product. The Bank for International Settlements (BIS) in Basle estimates the global nominal volume of this market for the end of 1993 at US$15 billion,[7] and anticipates a further massive increase of volume in this area.

To approach the topic from the perspective of the banks, within the framework of a questionnaire survey conducted by the author in late 1994/early 1995, 45 German credit institutions were asked about their experiences in cross-border payment transactions. This questionnaire allowed the author to obtain information on the type and scope of cross-border relations between the surveyed banks and other institutions. The bases – the legal, contractual or customary-law foundations of such cooperation – were probed, as were the causes, avoidance possibilities and control strategies for certain conflict situations which can arise among banks. Further, questions were posed about the importance of a series of internationally active organizations and institutions, as well as about their publications. Also explored was how the international cooperation of the banks could be further improved. Moreover, both through this questionnaire and through a total of 14 personal interviews with bank representatives (international banking practitioners as well as banking association employees), answers were sought about whether the actors felt restricted in their activities by government intervention, whether they regarded the legal bases of their work to be adequate, or indeed whether they felt further juridification was desirable.

Already the fact that, of the 45 questionnaires sent out, 34 (a good 75 per cent) were answered and sent back indicates the banking network's own interest in this subject. However, it must also be taken into account that it was not the author himself, but rather a

6 Klaus Peter Schmid, Banken im Schmollwinkel, *Die Zeit*, 28.10.1994, 31.

7 See "Vorstände müssen Risiko aus Derivaten überwachen", *Frankfurter Allgemeine Zeitung*, 2 November 1995, 15.

member of the bank's managing board, as well as a departmental director, who sent on the questionnaires with personal cover letters to bankers they knew – presumably the response rate would have been significantly lower if the author had sent out the questionnaires himself.[8]

At the very start of the study it became clear that the conflicts, such as these can be found in the interactions between other actors, exist to only a limited degree among banks. For example, legal disputes among banks are an extremely rare exception: a fact which, in light of the enormous sums moving back and forth across the world every day, is by no means self-evident. The fundamental thesis proposed by the author is that banks occupy a special place among the various actors of cross-border legal transactions and that conflicts – which undoubtedly exist among credit institutions as well – are generally resolved by means of internal mechanisms.[9] This assessment was substantiated as early as 1966 by Kegel, in his classic study on bank transactions in German Private International Law. Kegel established that, over a period of around 40 years, no more than 24 judicial decisions had been published in Germany involving cases where lawsuits were initiated by one bank against another. He attributed this to the circumspection and experience of the banks, and assumed that banks generally shy away from trials.[10] Little has changed with respect to this assessment over the past 30 years: judicial contests between banks participating in the cross-border business are still an absolute exception. This is confirmed both by the small number of judicial procedures which deal with cross-border transactions of banks with one another, and by the views of the banks which are active across borders themselves. In the framework of the survey, all the banks questioned indicated that they overwhelmingly preferred to resolve problem cases by common agreement, and only in exceptional cases were they ready to call for judicial clarification.

8 This is a clear example of the existence of a "third culture" of the banks in their dealings with one another.

9 See Paul-Frank Weise, *Lex mercatoria: materielles Recht vor der internationalen Handelsschiedsgerichtsbarkeit* (Frankfurt/M.: Lang, 1990), 51.

10 Gerhard Kegel, "Die Bankgeschäfte im deutschen internationalen Privatrecht", in *Gedächtnisschrift Rudolf Schmidt*, ed. Erwin Seidl (Berlin: Duncker & Humblot, 1966), 215.

According to the banks which responded, even arbitration tribunals are turned to only in exceptional cases; in this respect as well, the banks, with their policy of sector-internal conflict resolution, occupy a special position among the actors in cross-border legal transactions.[11]

Against this background, the present study first examines the question of which structures and institutions are used by the banks to ensure the smoothest possible handling of the cross-border payment transactions which are the focus of attention here.

Next, the study examines the activities of the EU Commission in this area, since for some time now considerable pressure has been exerted from Brussels on the banking associations, in order to improve cross-border payment transactions with respect to their high costs, long duration and lack of transparency. Finally, the highly characteristic reactions of the banks to the activities of the EU Commission (as well as to increasing criticism among the general public) are discussed.

Fundamental Concepts of Cross-border Payment Transactions

Within the framework of international economic activities, countless payment obligations arise every day which must be fulfilled by the transfer of money between the contracting parties. Only in the past 10 years or so have the market participants, but also increasingly the politicians, begun to show an interest in the organization and functioning of cross-border payment transactions.[12] This increasing interest is rooted particularly in the enormous growth which cross-border payment transactions have displayed in this period. This growth is based on the progressive dismantling of trade barriers and the deregulation of the markets, the consequent growing international interpenetration and the intensification of cross-border exchange of goods and services.[13] Along with this, both a sharp increase in money market and foreign exchange

11 To the same effect, see also Paul-Frank Weise, *Lex mercatoria*, pp. 51–2.

12 See Bank of International Settlement, 64th Annual Report, Basle, 1994.

13 Peter Gerard, "Internationaler Zahlungsverkehr im Wandel: Konzeptionen der Deutschen Bank", *bank und markt* (1994), 20–21.

transactions and a remarkable expansion of international securities trading have occurred.

Definition of Cross-border Payment Transactions

The concept of 'cross-border payment transactions' is very broadly understood to mean any business operation which has as its object the shifting of cash or cashless monetary values beyond the borders of a defined currency area.[14] Under foreign payment transactions fall both cross-border payments by private individuals and payments by companies sent abroad, as well as payments of domestic and foreign credit institutions to one another.

International cash payment transactions are primarily of importance in connection with the travel of private individuals, and here banks are required only for converting domestic into foreign currencies. However, when, within the framework of economic interpenetration over the gradually disintegrating or at least increasingly opening borders (particularly in Europe[15]), payments must be sent abroad, at least two banks are generally involved in such monetary transfers.

Differences Compared to National Payment Transactions

Cross-border payment transactions are fundamentally different, especially with respect to the costs which arise, from domestic payment transactions. The reasons for this lie in the necessity of establishing international correspondent bank relationships for clearing the payments,[16] joining the S.W.I.F.T. organization,[17] performing currency conversions and, especially, employing qualified (linguistically competent) employees. In addition, the yield on cross-border payments – at around 1 per cent of the total payment transaction volume – is still low[18] and requires a comparatively high expendi-

14 See Emilio Albisetti, ed., *Handbuch des Geld-, Bank- and Börsenwesens der Schweiz*, 4th edn (Thur, Switzerland: Ott Verlag, 1987).

15 Generally, on the effects of the EC Single Market on the banking sector, see Steinherr, "Der europäische Bankensektor im integrierten Finanzmarkt", p. 121 (125 et seq.).

16 See on this point pp. 109–10 in this chapter.

17 See on this point pp. 104–9 in this chapter.

18 See Claudia Nicolai-Verni and Axel Michalek, "Zahlungsverkehr in Kooperation mit Partnern aus dem Ausland – der Ansatz der Commerzbank", *bank und markt* (1994), 27 (28).

ture of time and labour.[19] Finally, in the member states of the EU and the EFTA countries, to which around two-thirds of the foreign payment transactions originating from Germany are sent, different procedures have developed for handling national payment transactions, procedures which are wholly or partially incompatible with one another, so that fully-automated (and thus cost-saving) processing, as occurs at the domestic level, is still impossible at the international level.[20]

Forms of Cross-border Payment Transactions

Bank customers have various possibilities at their disposal for the cross-border transfer of relatively small amounts in the nature of personal, 'face-to-face' (that is, cash) payments. Along with an international transfer, such payments can also be made using eurocheques and credit cards, as well as cheques and bills of exchange. Eurocheques and credit cards are commonly used to pay for goods as soon as they are received. The eurocheque is a paper-bound type of payment, in which a cheque form with legally prescribed minimal elements must be filled in and signed. It is generally accepted only when presented together with the holder's eurocheque card. By contrast, credit cards are used either via terminals or via a mechanical card-reading device; the party liable to pay only has to sign. A transfer instruction is used to discharge a debt by instructing a banking institution to transfer a certain sum of money from the account (generally a current account) of the party liable to pay into the account of the payment recipient.

Eurocheque transactions

The development which the eurocheque has undergone over the past 25 years was characterized by virtually all the bank representatives interviewed as a telling example of an autonomously created, cross-border structure of international payment transactions.

On the initiative of German credit institutions, in May 1968 representatives of the banking industry from 15 European countries

19 See the customer brochures of the Bundesverband deutscher Banken (National Association of German Banks) on cross-border payment transactions, Wertpapier-Mitteilungen, 1993, 626–7.

20 Albert Wagner and Ewald Wagner, "'Low value Payments' über mehrere Korrespondenten – das Beispiel der Dresdner Bank", *bank und markt* (1994), 40.

met to discuss unifying the guidelines for cashing cheques.[21] Before this, the credit institutions of the different countries had started asking all their respective correspondent banks to cash their cheques in connection with a related guarantee card, and for this purpose had begun distributing cashing guidelines to the bank cashiers. If this development had not been recognized in time and brought under control, sooner or later countless guidelines of various banks from different countries would have piled up at the banks, with the consequence of unforeseeable risks and higher costs.

At another conference held in Paris in October 1968, the name *eurocheque* was adopted, with a certain inevitability, for the European cheque system. At the same time, agreement had to be reached on accepting a standard blank under standard cashing conditions throughout Europe. This agreement was initially reached only with regard to the cashing conditions, so that later a book with the standard cashing conditions, the 'ec-ring binder', was published in the languages of all the eurocheque countries. However, this book contained reproductions of all the different participating cards and cheques, and was therefore quite voluminous.

This was the foundation upon which the new eurocheque system started on 1 May 1969 in 15 European countries. In the following period the countries whose banks themselves issued cards were joined by so-called 'passive' countries,[22] ones whose banks did not issue cards, but did cash card-guaranteed cheques. The increasing acceptance in these countries was motivated by growing levels of tourism, especially in the Mediterranean region.

In 1972, standard cheque forms and standard cheque cards were introduced by central conventions for the cheque card procedure. There were a number of practical reasons behind this quest for unification. The practice engaged in until then of individual banks issuing their own forms constituted a barrier for the dissemination and acceptance of cheque transactions. In addition, the risk of counterfeits multiplied with the number of different forms.

In a third developmental stage, reached in 1975, it was agreed that cheques could be made out, not only in the currency of the country of origin, but also in that of the host country; the cheque guarantee was thus also extended to foreign currency cheques.

21 Ulrich Weiss, "eurocheque: 20 Jahre erfolgreicher Zusammenarbeit", *Die Bank* (1988), 370 et seq.

22 Eckart van Hooven, "25 Jahre eurocheque – ein historischer Konsens", *Die Bank* (1993), 367.

If a cardholder abroad makes out a foreign currency cheque, it is passed on within the banking system of the respective country to a central collection point. This collection point then sends the cheques or – in a document-free exchange – only their data, on to the central collecting point of the other participating country.

In the interim, the eurocheque system has become one of the largest supranational payment systems in the world: the standard forms for cheques and cards are published in 25 countries, the so-called 'active' or 'card' countries; another 15 countries accept the guaranteed cheques in payment. In 1991, over 40 million cheque cards were issued under the eurocheque system in the active countries. In the meantime, this service also goes far beyond the original framework. In Germany alone there is a network of around 20,000 money machines (there are around 80,000 of them throughout Europe) and the POS (point of sale) system, to which about 200,000 POS terminals have so far been connected in stores and filling stations, keeps expanding as well. Currently, credit cardholders can find more than 2.4 million acceptance points in Europe.[23]

The cooperation which has come about within the eurocheque framework has been described as a 'historic consensus',[24] and demonstrates the ability of the actors in the banking sector to work together successfully if a common overriding interest exists.

Cooperation of credit institutions in the credit card field

Another major point of successful cross-border cooperation of credit institutions lies in the field of credit cards.

The Credit Card System There are no special statutory regulations for the functioning of the credit card business in Europe; here is yet another broad field of activity for the creation of autonomous structures. Thus, as in many areas of banking, written, fixed practices have developed for the internationally useable credit cards of banks which are binding on all participants. These practices are roughly as follows: the credit card issuer provides the credit cardholder with a card which entitles him or her to the cash-free use of the services of a contract company upon presentation of the card. The contract company accepts the card instead of a payment and

23 Holger Berndt, "Strategie und Abwicklung des Auslandszahlungsverkehrs im Sparkassensektor", *bank und markt* (1994), 7.

24 Eckart van Hooven, "25 Jahre eurocheque – ein historischer Konsens", p. 368.

receives the settlement amount, minus a discount which basically represents compensation for the payment guarantee, from the issuer. At regular intervals, the cardholder receives an account statement listing each use of the card. Generally, the final amount is then debited directly from the cardholder's bank account.

The Eurocard International Association This association is based on the cooperation of Eurocard and MasterCard International.[25] The Eurocard International company has its headquarters in Brussels. It is owned by the national Eurocard companies of the Western European countries, which in turn are owned by credit institutions. The companies Eurocard France (F), the GZS Gesellschaft für Zahlungssysteme (D), UK Forum (GB) and MasterCard Int. (USA) each hold 15 per cent of Eurocard International. On the basis of the cooperation with MasterCard Int., NY, Eurocard credit cards are accepted by MasterCard contract partners, and vice versa.

The Eurocard business is processed over the European Data Communication System (EDCS), a data network which was installed specifically for this purpose.[26] Owing to the high growth rates in recent years, the growing internationality of business and the greater automation of the national and international clearing houses, Eurocard/Mastercard was forced to set up a worldwide communications system for authorization, clearing and settlement data. For this, Eurocard could base itself on the data transmission network set up by the EPSS S.A. (European Payment System Services, Brussels).

Europay The Europay International S.A. was founded on 1 September 1992 by the merger of Eurocheque International and Eurocard International. Through the founding of Europay, the managements of the two forerunner companies were combined to form a new board. This consists of the representatives of 10 major countries (in terms of the number of the issued cards and turnover), representatives of MasterCard International as well as two representatives from the 'small' European countries, which are combined into two regional boards. This new board is supported by five advisory committees composed of bank experts of various nationalities.

25 Hans W. Schlöter, "Von eurocheque über EUROCARD zu EUROPLUS", *Die Bank* (1987), 674 et seq.

26 Eurocard Review 1985/86, Brussels 1987, 8.

Until the founding of Europay, the two companies stood in competition with one another, had different objectives and target groups, and were based on different systems (debit card system on the one hand, credit card system on the other). To the contrary, the shareholders of Eurocheque International and of Eurocard International were virtually identical, so that the merger of the two companies into a single central organization was an altogether logical move.

The cooperation of the banks in this area lies in the support of the different credit card systems; more specifically, in the development of umbrella organizations and the formation of worldwide partnerships.[27] The task of these umbrella organizations is the development of new products and the further extension of the respective system. For Europay this means, along with the synergy effects,– the development of three new service groups: the 'pay before' (prepaid products like traveller's cheques), 'pay now' (products which immediately alter the current account, such as the eurocheque, payment at the point-of-sale via edc-Maestro or the withdrawal of cash using an ec-card at one of the many money machines located throughout Europe) and 'pay later' (products which give the customer a credit period, that is credit cards).

The company is striving to meet the requirements of a unified Europe and those of the Commission in the field of payment transactions. Thus Europay supports the demand of the Commission with respect to more transparent, cheaper and faster payment transactions[28] by now offering the possibility of making cross-border payments of up to ECU1,000 by means of a eurocheque – a possibility which is widely used despite the lack of a guarantee.[29]

edc-Maestro Since 1993 there has existed as a European Community project a cross-border electronic cash procedure called edc-Maestro.[30] This system is based on the cooperation of Eurocard International and Eurocheque International, on the one hand, with Mastercard on the other.[31] The goal of this cooperation is the

27 R. Bernhard and J. van Eldik, "Bessere Zahlungsverkehrsqualität durch Europay", *Wertpapier-Mitteilungen* (1993), 283.

28 For more details on this, see pp. 117–21 in this chapter.

29 R. Bernhard and J. van Eldik, "Bessere Zahlungsverkehrsqualität durch Europay", 284.

30 edc = electronic debit card.

31 Manfred Krüger, "electronic cash-Verfahren ab 1993 grenzüberschreitend möglich", *Sparkasse* (1992), 331.

creation of a cross-border debit card system through which national debit cards are given access to foreign POS terminals.[32] For the participants, the cooperation offers the advantage that one can draw upon the existing national systems in the areas of both electronic data processing and card issuance, thus avoiding the generation of new costs on these aspects.

The Cross-border Bank Transfer

The international bank transfer is the most important form of cross-border payment transaction. With the creation of the EU Single Market, increasingly payment transactions are no longer limited to the individual member states, but more and more frequently extend across borders. According to EU Commission data, the number of cross-border payments of amounts below the ECU2,500 limit (around DM5,000) in 1992 stood at well over 200 million. Compared with the approximately ECU26 billion worth of domestic payments in the same period, this volume is still comparatively small; the same is true for the value of cross-border payments, which for Germany currently make up only 0.03 per cent of all domestic payment transactions.

The significance of the international transfer in comparison to payments by means of a bill of exchange or cheque differs from country to country; particularly in the Anglo-American legal sphere, there are substantially more payments by means of cheque and bill of exchange than by means of transfer. Nevertheless, the following text will deal primarily with the transfer (a payment form which is especially important from the German perspective), since it is on this area that the European Union's activities and, in reaction, those of the banks as well, have focused.

The S.W.I.F.T. Network

Foreign payment transactions were initially conducted by letter, via telephone or telegraphically, but since the mid-1970s they have largely been handled via S.W.I.F.T. (Society for Worldwide Interbank Financial Telecommunication). This organization, supported by credit institutions active in international bank transactions, makes a fundamental contribution to the functioning of the international exchange of goods and services.

32 POS = point of sale.

In the interviews which the author held with practitioners from the foreign operations departments of various banks, banking associations and savings banks, reference was made again and again to the particular importance of S.W.I.F.T. for their day-to-day work. The structure, area of responsibilities and functioning of this organization will therefore be presented below to the extent that they are significant for the present discussion.

Development and organization

S.W.I.F.T. is a private-law corporation, organized as a cooperative society, which was founded in March 1973 in Belgium by 239 credit institutions from 15 countries and which commenced its activity in January 1974.[33] Today S.W.I.F.T. is owned by 2,500 banks throughout the world.[34] S.W.I.F.T. transmits financial messages between the 5,000 or so affiliated banks. The network connects 130 countries all over the world, including Eastern European and Asian countries,[35] with one another.

Access to the network is reserved to shareholders of S.W.I.F.T. s.c., as well as to their subsidiaries (banks) as submembers. However, since 1989, there also exists for a number of so-called 'participants' the possibility of using S.W.I.F.T. These participants, who numbered 78 at the end of 1991, include, besides securities brokers and dealers, various institutions, such as Euroclear and Cedel.[36]

The S.W.I.F.T. network is open throughout the year, 24 hours a day. In 1991, a total volume of 365 million messages were processed over the network, an average of 1.5 million messages per business day.

33 For details, see Wolfram W. Loh, *Das SWIFT-System, Die moderne Datenübertragung im internationalen Zahlungsverkehr* (Frankfurt/M.: Verlag W. Kohlhammer, 1983), 18.

34 See "Frankfurter SWIFT-Büro als Schlüssel für Zentraleuropa", *Frankfurter Allgemeine Zeitung*, 5 September 1995, 26.

35 Dietrich Jueterbock, "Zehn Jahre S.W.I.F.T.-Netzwerk – ein Meilenstein der Automation?", in *Die Bank* (1988), 269 (274); 'Frankfurter SWIFT-Büro als Schlüssel für Zentraleuropa', *Frankfurter Allgemeine Zeitung*, 5 September 1995, 26.

36 S.W.I.F.T., Minutes of the Annual General Meeting 1989, Brussels, 1989, 5 et seq.

Area of responsibilities and functioning of S.W.I.F.T.

The mission of S.W.I.F.T. s.c. is the planning, construction and operation of an international computer-controlled communications network for the transmission of financial messages ordered by the member banks which participate in S.W.I.F.T., as well as other allowed categories of financial institutions. Although the original area of activity was largely limited to the transmission of international transfers, today S.W.I.F.T. also transmits messages relating to international money and foreign exchange dealings, the collection and credit business, as well as other messages which are linked to cross-border banking operations. In addition, banks which maintain accounts with one another can deliver their account statements via the S.W.I.F.T. network. Beyond this, the S.W.I.F.T. group focuses on developing and marketing special network applications, as well as the related hardware and software.[37]

The message transmission time amounts (regardless of the distance to be covered) to less than five minutes, including encoding and decoding of the messages as well as confirmation of the operation by the payee bank; if it is an emergency message, it will be transmitted in less than one minute. Compared to the time (sometimes several weeks!) transfers can take by mail – the processing method which was used for around 80–85 per cent of all cross-border payment orders prior to the introduction of S.W.I.F.T.[38] – the main advantage of S.W.I.F.T. for the banks and their customers lies in this time saving.

The most important prerequisite for the functioning of S.W.I.F.T. was the standardization of the messages to be transmitted. The addresses of participating banks had to be encoded, as did the currency designations and finally the message text itself. While for the bank addresses an eight-figure, now universally accepted standard[39] and for the currencies a three-figure code[40] were developed, the encoding of messages posed a few problems. That these problems were solved – and just how well – can be judged by the fact

37 Planning for the introduction of S.W.I.F.T. II, a higher-performance network than the first system, and one which can also be used for general financial services, began as early as 1985.

38 Wolfram W. Loh, *Das SWIFT-System, Die moderne Datenübertragung im internationalen Zahlungsverkehr.*

39 S.W.I.F.T., Annual Report 1986, Brussels, 1987, 10.

40 The Alpha Code developed by the International Standard Organization could be used as such.

that the S.W.I.F.T. standards have developed into a technical language in its own right, one which in the interim has partially replaced the different national technical concepts.[41]

It is important to note that S.W.I.F.T. is not a 'supranational clearing house':[42] the messages transmitted by S.W.I.F.T. are in fact cleared over the correspondent network of the internationally active banks.[43] In banking practice, S.W.I.F.T. functions as follows: a transfer order in favour of a foreign beneficiary is sent in standardized form via the national computer centre (the regional processor called 'concentrator') to the responsible operating or switching centre.[44] (The two original switching centres have in the interim been joined by a third in the USA.) There, the order is classified into one of three categories of urgency and then transmitted via the responsible concentrator of the target country to the bank of the payee. If the payment is addressed to a bank which is not itself affiliated with S.W.I.F.T., that is to a participant, the order is brought via the S.W.I.F.T. network as close as possible to this bank and then sent on the rest of the way by mail.[45] The security of the transmission is ensured by the system already mentioned, in which the content of the transfer order as well as the payee bank are encrypted. In addition, S.W.I.F.T. messages are confirmed by the sending bank and then checked once again by the payee bank by means of an 'authenticator', a code number installed in the system. Finally, there are automatic checks which also serve to guarantee the security of correct transfer. At the bank of the payee, the S.W.I.F.T. order is then printed out (exceptionally also displayed on-screen) and then stands available to the office in charge of the specific account for crediting the amount to the beneficiary.

41 Ernst Deeg, "Wo kann S.W.I.F.T. mithelfen, Probleme zu lösen?", *Zeitschrift für das gesamte Kreditwesen*, Ausgabe Technik of 15.03.1982, p.15.

42 Jörg Etzkorn, *Rechtsfragen des international elektronischen Zahlungsverkehrs durch S.W.I.F.T* (Berlin/New York: Walter de Gruyter, 1991), 11.

43 Max Brüggemann, *Die Banktechnik des Auslandsgeschäfts*, 6th edn (Stuttgart: Schäffer-Poeschel, 1981), 23.

44 For a transfer coming from Germany, this is the switching centre in Leiden, The Netherlands.

45 See Carl-Heinrich v. Gablenz, *Die Haftung der Banken bei Einschaltung Dritter* (Munich: C.H. Beck, 1983), 44.

S.W.I.F.T.'s introduction has meant that only a very small share of cross-border payments are any longer handled by telephone, telex, letter or telegraph. Letter transmission is made using a standard blank, by which the transfer order is ensured through two signatures, which in turn are deposited at the payee bank. Transfers by telephone or telex are secured against falsification by using agreed test numbers; if the payment order is given telegraphically, codes are used in part.

The legal bases of S.W.I.F.T. s.c.

Fixed rules have also been developed for the execution of cross-border payments. Since S.W.I.F.T.'s introduction, its members have at least partially established these rules in the form of so-called 'by-laws', consisting of the Articles of Association and the General Terms and Conditions. When applying these general terms and by-laws, one must take into account that the S.W.I.F.T. s.c. is a society founded under Belgian law and is thus subject to Belgian law. This is also expressly stipulated in Clause 10 of the general terms for the relationship among the banks participating in S.W.I.F.T. Banks which only now seek a participation in S.W.I.F.T. s.c. must, in accordance with Clause 3 of the general terms, undertake to accept the general terms and thus the application of Belgian law. Clause 10, para. 2 of the general terms establishes an arbitration agreement. According to this provision, conflicts concerning the general terms between S.W.I.F.T. and its members as well as disputes of members with one another are to be resolved in accordance with the Rules of Conciliation and Arbitration set down by the Paris-based International Chamber of Commerce.[46]

Applicability of the S.W.I.F.T. rules to the relationship of the participating banks

Difficulties, comparable to the problem of whether and to what extent the General Standard Terms and Conditions apply in the relationship of the banks to one another, arise with respect to the question of the S.W.I.F.T. rules, when two banks confront one another as sender and receiver of a message transmitted by S.W.I.F.T. within the framework of a correspondent bank relationship.

The bank survey revealed that the correspondence agreements between banks do not generally include an express reference to the

46 See Publication No. 291 of the ICC of September 1980.

S.W.I.F.T. provisions. Thus only a tacit agreement on the validity of the rules comes into question. It is therefore of decisive importance that a bank which wishes to become a member of S.W.I.F.T. s.c. must first acknowledge the General Terms and Conditions and the rules contained in the so-called 'User Handbook'. One of these rules is the unconditional obligation to receive and process messages of other S.W.I.F.T. members – regardless of whether it is a correspondent bank or not – in accordance with the rules applying for S.W.I.F.T. members.[47] Thus a bank which sends or receives a message via S.W.I.F.T. knows that this will be performed on the basis of the S.W.I.F.T. rules. Therefore one can proceed on the basis of an implied inclusion of these rules in the correspondence relationship of the participating banks.

The Correspondent Bank System

If, as is generally the case for the major banks, credit institutions have subsidiaries or branch offices in the target country of the international transfer, they will use their own banking connections abroad in order to execute transfers.[48] However, this possibility can be called upon in only a comparatively small number of cases. Generally, cross-border payments of German credit institutions are processed via existing business relations with foreign correspondent banks.[49] According to the estimates of the interviewed bank practitioners, German banks work together with around 10,000 foreign institutions in the framework of such correspondent bank relations. This presupposes a credit transfer relationship between the German and the foreign bank, which is established contractually by the German institution sending a writing (in any form) to the foreign bank asking to open an account in the corresponding national currency, and simultaneously promising to establish a certain initial credit balance. This account is then effectively opened upon the written response of the foreign bank, in which this latter informs the German institution of the

47 See Karl-Ernst Brauner, *Das Erklärungsrisiko beim Einsatz von elektronischen Datenverarbeitungsanlagen* (Bonn: Margarete Wehle, 1988), 39 et seq.

48 On the example of the Deutsche Bank, see Peter Gerard, "Internationaler Zahlungsverkehr im Wandel: Konzeptionen der Deutschen Bank", pp. 20 et seq.

49 Max Brüggemann, *Die Banktechnik des Auslandsgeschäfts.*

account number and (if appropriate) the General Standard Terms and Conditions.[50]

Apart from the reciprocal account relation described above, there are correspondent relationships which take the more limited form of a simple agency agreement. Such an agency arrangement gives the participants the possibility of immediately issuing an individual payment order, which is cleared via the agreed representative capacity of a third credit institution.[51]

If the credit institution in Germany which has been given a cross-border transfer to execute does not have a credit transfer relationship with a foreign correspondent bank, there exists the further possibility of calling upon the services of the Deutsche Bundesbank. Without any promise of meeting any specific deadlines, the order is sent on to the foreign correspondent bank only after the necessary cover has been provided.

Practical Execution of a Cross-border Bank Transfer

Outgoing cross-border transfers generally occur as follows: the party who is obliged to make the payment gives his bank a transfer order within the framework of the existing credit transfer contract. The institution can then either turn directly to the correspondent bank located in the target country, to the extent that a business relationship exists with this latter bank, or it can send the order to the responsible regional bank/central giro institution, which then in turn orders a correspondent bank located abroad to execute the transfer. If the payee has an account with the correspondent bank, the latter can credit to him the amount after the equivalent amount of cover has been provided to its nostro account at the correspondent bank. If the beneficiary does not have an account at

50 On the acceptance of the General Standard Terms and Conditions through silence after sending, see Bundesgerichtshof (BGH), Decision of 18.06.1971, *Neue Juristische Wochenschrift (NJW)* 1971, 2127; and see on this the note of Helmut Kollhosser, *Juristische Rundschau*, 1972, 26; Klemens Pleyer and Dieter Ungnade, note on BGH NJW, 1971, 2126 et seq. in *Neue Juristische Wochenschrift* 1972, 681 et seq.; Dieter Ungnade, *Wertpapier-Mitteilungen*, 1973, 1133; Klemens Pleyer and Robert Battes, Geltung und Auslegung Allgemeiner Geschäftsbedingungen im Verkehr der Banken untereinander, *Der Betrieb* (1971), 1295.

51 Brüggemann, *Die Banktechnik des Auslandsgeschäfts*, 17–18.

the foreign bank that has received the order, this bank will either send it on to the bank of the beneficiary, pay out the amount in cash or deliver a cheque to the payee, a practice which is quite common in the Anglo-American legal sphere.

For transfers into some countries it is necessary to call upon several correspondent banks in different states, so that it is possible for a transfer to run through a whole chain of different credit transfer relationships. In such cases, for every cross-border credit transfer relationship existing with a foreign bank one must check which legal order applies with respect to a specific transfer and what rights and duties are derived from this for the participants. For each of the various credit transfer relationships, the result can be that a different legal order or other general conditions can apply to a bank, which can lead to different regulations with respect to the duties of the participants, the time of performance, any revocation possibilities, and so on.[52]

The Law Applying to Cross-border Transfers

The Network Contract Concept

When only two banks participate in a cross-border transfer, the issue of the applicable law is not a problem. However, quite often more than two banks are involved. This produces so-called 'transfer chains',[53] in which there are a number of contracts. For these cases it has been suggested that the applicable law should be determined in accordance with the concept of a network contract.[54] Under the network contract theory, a contractual relationship exists not only between the respective banks sending on a transfer order, but also between the principal (the party who gave the original

52 See Klemens Pleyer and Edgar Wallach, "Erfüllungszeitpunkt und Gefahrtragung bei grenzüberschreitenden Überweisungen nach deutschem und englischem Recht", *Recht der Internationalen Wirtschaft* (1988), 172 et seq.

53 Hadding, in Walther Hadding and Uwe H. Schneider, *Rechtsprobleme der Auslandsüberweisung* (Berlin: Duncker & Humblot, 1992), 15.

54 See Wernhard Möschel, "Dogmatische Strukturen des bargeldlosen Zahlungsverkehrs", *Archiv für die Civilistische Praxis*, 186 (1986), 211 et seq.

payment order) and every intermediary bank all the way down the line, up to and including the bank of the payee.

For this model to apply in practice, the network contract would first have to be recognized by the legal systems of all the countries participating in the international payment transaction. Further, all contractual relationships would have to be subject to one uniform law, since otherwise possible damage claims by the principal of a cross-border payment would have to be asserted on the basis of the respectively applicable law and the thereby resulting different claim prerequisites in each contract relationship, which would produce an intolerable degree of legal uncertainty in this area. The network contract theory has therefore quite rightly failed to gain acceptance.[55]

Instead, the following applies in cross-border payment transactions for the participating banks with respect to the applicable law under the rules of private international law: since it is not intrinsically self-evident which of the banks in the contract chain performs the 'characteristic service', it is initially an open question which national law will be applied in a case of conflict. Proceeding from the case where a German bank customer instructs his bank to make a transfer via an English correspondent bank to his English business partner, both German and English law can apply. Arguing for the application of German law is the fact that the details of the payment, in particular its amount, is established by the customer and is sent on by the German credit institution, without the English bank having any influence on these aspects. Arguing for the applicability of English law, by contrast, is the fact that the actual operation, namely the crediting of the amount to the account of the business partner, takes place in England.

In most cases, the provisions of the respective private international law relationship of the participating banks are interpreted in such a way that the characteristic service is performed by the paying correspondent bank; that is, in the above case, by the English institution.[56] Determining the characteristic service becomes more

55 See on this Ingo Koller, "Grundstrukturen des Bankhaftungsrechts unter besonderer Berücksichtigung des Zahlungsverkehrs", in *Neue Entwicklungen im Bankhaftungsrecht*, ed. Johannes Köndgen (Cologne: Kommunikationsforum, 1987), 25; Claus-Wilhelm Canaris, *Bankvertragsrecht*, 4th edn (Berlin/New York: Walter de Gruyter, 1988), para. no. 393.

56 Gerhard Kegel, "Die Bankgeschäfte im deutschen international Privatrecht", pp.215 (225); Münchener Kommentar-Martiny, Art.

difficult if a payment order passes through a series of banks in different countries. In such cases the view can be defended that each participating bank, by sending on the payment, brings it one step closer to the payee, and thus a service becomes all the more characteristic the closer it gets to the payee.[57] This view leads to the result that, for a single cross-border payment operation, as many different legal systems could apply as there are banks in different countries which participated in it.

Harmonization of European and International Banking Contract Law

The result that, under certain circumstances, several different legal systems might apply to a single cross-border payment operation has led to efforts at both the European and international levels to resolve this problem. The majority of the banks questioned also find the applicability of different legal systems to a single transfer operation unsatisfactory, and describe this problem as an essential reason for conflicts in the cross-border banking business.

Against this background, the development of a uniform law also at the international level is increasingly seen as desirable, since until now there has never existed a supranational law regulating the banking business which would prevent the problems resulting from the applicability of various legal systems.

Within the framework of cross-border banking activity, two publications of UNCITRAL[58] play an especially important role: first, the 'UNCITRAL convention on international bills of exchange and international promissory notes' of 9 December 1988, which will

28, para. no. 238; Canaris, *Bankvertragsrecht*, para. no. 2503; Oberlandesgericht Hamburg, *Versicherungsrecht (VersR)*, 1983, 350; Bundesgerichtshof (BGH), Decision of 9.3.1987, *Recht der Internationalen Wirtschaft*, 1987, 476–7; Klemens Pleyer and Edgar Wallach, "Erfüllungszeitpunkt und Gefahrtragung bei grenzüberschreitenden Überweisungen nach deutschem und englischem Recht", p. 174.

57 Thus Christoph von der Seipen, "Anwendbares Recht beim Überweisungsverkehr", in *Rechtsprobleme der Auslandsüberweisung*, ed. Walther Hadding and Uwe H. Schneider (Berlin: Duncker & Humblot, 1992), 85.

58 See, on the work of UNCITRAL, Erich Schinnerer, "Probleme 'Internationaler Überweisungen'", *Österreichische Juristische Zeitung* (1984), 205 et seq.

not be discussed here; and, second, the 'Draft of a UNCITRAL model law on international payment transactions' of 1988.[59] The organization began as early as 1982 to deal with electronic payment transactions.[60] In 1987, model rules were first presented for electronic transfer transactions; then UNCITRAL widened its work to cover all transfers – regardless of whether they were by electronic or other means. The draft version of the Model Law[61] was presented in the summer of 1991,[62] and adopted at the following Commission meeting in May 1992. It should be applicable to international transfers, whereby a transfer qualifies as 'international' when the bank of the principal and that of the beneficiary are located in different states.

The goal of the model law is to make those who participate in international payment transactions clearly aware of their duties and responsibilities. Particularly important among these is improving the quality of cross-border payment transactions with respect to both speed and costs. In addition, it should be ensured that, for the entire contract chain from the principal through the paying banks all the way to the beneficiary, equivalent (if perhaps nationally distinct) law is applied.

The Work of the Commission of the European Union in the Area of Payment Transactions within the Single Market

Cross-border payment transactions in their currently practised form have long been criticized by the Commission of the

59 Neither the bills of exchange agreement nor the model law has yet entered into effect, since until now 10 states have not ratified these conventions; however, this step is anticipated within the next few years.

60 UNCITRAL, "Electronic Funds Transfer", in *Yearbook of the United Nations Commission on International Trade Law*, 1982, vol. XIII (New York, 1982), 272.

61 Draft of 3 October 1988 (A/CN 9/WG. IV/WP 39); on the forerunners, the "Model Rules on Electronic Funds Transfers", see Erich Schinnerer, *Zeitschrift für Rechtsvergleichung*, 1985, 226; Robert C. Effros, *The Banking Law Journal*, (1988), 510.

62 See on this Uwe H. Schneider, "Das UNCITRAL-Modellgesetz über den internationalen Überweisungsverkehr", *Wertpapier-Mitteilungen* (1989), 285 et seq.

European Union. The main points of its criticism concern lack of transparency, excessive costs and unduly long durations.

Two Examples to Clarify the Present Situation

A perfect example to show how justified criticisms of the current situation of cross-border payment transactions are is offered by a case which took place at the Bonn subsidiary of a major Frankfurt bank.[63] A Zurich company complained to its own bank in late September 1994 that a transfer which had been notified from Germany in the amount of DM16,000 had still not arrived. Since the investigation undertaken by the Swiss bank had produced no answers, they advised the company to inquire via its business partner at the bank in Germany. A week later, this inquiry in Germany produced the answer that the debiting in the amount of DM16,000 had already been performed four weeks earlier: the money had been correctly sent to Switzerland. The German business partner then personally contacted the Bonn bank subsidiary to clarify what had happened to the transfer en route. To their consternation, the employees of the bank said in effect that for a 'laughable' DM16,000 it was hardly worth the effort to follow up on the delay; after all, where would a major bank be if ...

The German customer nevertheless repeated his request that the entire transfer operation be checked, since otherwise he would be constrained to contact the central bank in Frankfurt. The examination of the transfer that this produced revealed a few days later that in fact the money had been mistakenly transferred to another bank in Switzerland. Only a further 10 days later was the money finally credited to the proper account of the Swiss company.

Nor was that the end of the incident. Prompted by this example of carelessness, the customer then checked all his other recent international transfers, and thereby discovered that the Bonn bank had for some time been regularly deducting from the transfer amounts a sum of DM15, apart from the transfer costs which were being charged to the principal at the same time. Nor, as it developed, were these DM15 being credited to the respective payee bank; the bank in Germany had simply held on to them. The result of this action was that the Swiss company would have first had to send a reminder about the missing amounts in Germany. The German principal for his part would have had to inquire at his bank and

63 Following Heinz Brestel, "Aus der Praxis der Banküberweisung" in *Blick durch die Wirtschaft*, 3.11.1994, 1.

then fill in a new transfer with the improperly deducted DM15 amounts – with the risk of once again having DM15 deducted. The Swiss had already considered whether they would not have done better to simply give the money to the major German bank: 'We often do this sort of thing in transactions with offshore countries, where something always goes wrong from time to time.' Precisely why the Bonn bank chose, on its own authority, to retain in its own favour sums from transfer amounts is not known, but speculation is permitted. While valid generalizations cannot be made on the basis of this single case, it does cast a not altogether favourable light on cross-border payment transactions at a time when they are facing criticism from the public and politicians.

The fee-charging practices of German credit institutions were also at the heart of a legal dispute before the Düsseldorf Amtsgericht.[64] In this case, an Italian bank had passed on a transfer order to a German credit institution, which charged its own costs in the amount of DM50 (a rate of 0.02 per cent, but with a minimum of DM50) and deducted these on its own authority from the transfer amount of DM2,110. In so doing, the German institution argued, although no legal relation existed between it and the complainant (the principal of the transfer), it nevertheless was following an international trade practice that existed among banks, that either the order-taking bank (here: the defendant) is entitled to deduct the fee amount accruing to it from the transferred sum or the order-giving bank (here: the Italian bank of the complainant) should have expressly indicated with the payment order that the accruing charges should be invoiced to it separately.

The court ordered the defendant German institution to pay back the DM50 to the payee of the transfer on the ground that the defendant did not have any right to deduct the fee from the transfer amount. The complainant rightly referred to the EU Commission Report[65] in which, in agreement with the Banking Association, the practice of the German credit institutions was judged to be breach of contract vis-à-vis the principal of the cross-border transfer.

64 See Amtsgericht Düsseldorf, Decision of 14.12.1992, *Zeitschrift für die Internationale Praxis*, 1993, 1227; *Recht der Internationalen Wirtschaft (RIW)*, 1994, 158; on this, see the commentary of Uwe H. Schneider, *Europäisches Wirtschaftsrecht (EWiR)*, 1993, 969 and the note of Gustav Real, *Recht der Internationalen Wirtschaft* (1994), 158f.

65 Reprinted in *ZBB*, 1991, 53 et seq.

Although this decision involved only the paltry sum of DM50, its consequences are considerable. In 1992, German companies alone rendered services in a value of around DM648 billion to purchasers abroad.[66] Thus, if in just one-half of the cross-border payments operations relating to these services a corresponding fee were levied by the intermediary payee bank, at a fee rate of 0.02 per cent this would add up to fee receipts for the credit institutions of around 648 million DM. It remains to be seen whether the 'trade practice' cited by the defendant will not be incorporated into all bank contracts, since it is indisputable that the correspondent banks do participate significantly in the processing of cross-border payment transactions, and this participation has its price.[67] On the other hand, bank customers have the possibility of turning for the processing of their international transfers to one of those banks which have their own branch offices abroad and which, through so-called 'in-house solutions',[68] are capable of providing faster, and thus cost- and fee-saving execution.[69]

Measures of the EU Commission in the Area of Cross-border Payment Transactions

The responsible Italian EU Commissioner, Raniero Vanni d'Archirafi rightly believes that the Single Market can only be fully used when private individuals and companies are in a position to transfer money as quickly, reliably and cheaply from one EU country to another as they can domestically. As early as 1987, the EU Commission began working on an initiative in the area of European payment transactions. At that time the Commission was concerned with stimulating the cross-border use of the various payment card systems for withdrawals from cash machines and for payments at so-called 'points of sale'.[70] After significant progress had been achieved in this area,[71] the Commission turned to the field of cross-border transfer transactions.

66 *Statistical Yearbook for the Federal Republic of Germany*, 1992.

67 Gustav Real, "[Note on the Decision of] Amtsgericht Düsseldorf v. 14.12.1992", *Recht der Internationalen Wirtschaft* (1994), 158–9.

68 See Jürgen Terrahe, "Bedarf für ein Automated Clearing House in Deutschland?", *Wertpapier-Mitteilungen* (1993), 834.

69 Gustav Real, *Recht der Internationalen Wirtschaft* (1994), 158–9.

70 See Holger Berndt, "Strategie und Abwicklung des Auslandszahlungsverkehrs im Sparkassensektor", p. 7.

71 See on this point pp. 101–4 in this chapter.

In February 1990, the EU Commission published a 'Recommendation on the transparency of banking conditions for cross-border financial transactions'.[72] Therein it found that, owing to the interposition in general of several credit institutions, the various clearing systems, the different currencies as well as the different legal systems in the member countries, higher costs and longer durations arise for cross-border transfers than for those which take place entirely within individual member states. The first principle of this recommendation therefore suggested to the members of the European banking industry that they inform consumers via a customer brochure about the various payment instruments available for cross-border payment transactions, and the costs and durations associated with each of these instruments.

In Germany, a customer brochure elaborated by the Central Credit Committee[73] has since appeared on cross-border payment transactions. It is used in the area of the private banking industry as well as – with minor variations – by the cooperative and public credit institutions.

In September 1990, the Commission published a further discussion paper entitled 'Payment Transactions in the Single Market',[74] the so-called 'green book'. Once again, criticism was levelled at the lack of transparency, excessive costs and unduly long durations of cross-border payments. At the same time, the Commission called for better relations between the carriers of transfer transactions or other *paiement à distance* instruments. The Commission called for payments between any two states within the EU to be executed just as quickly and cheaply as within a member state.

In April 1991, the Commission created two working groups, the Payment System Users Liaison Group and the Payment System Technical Development Group. On the basis of the results of these working groups, which appeared in February 1992, the Commission presented a final report entitled 'Relief for cross-border payments: The borders fall – working programme of the Commission'.[75] In this report, the Commission highlighted the absence of a

72 Recommendation of the Commission of 14 February 1990, O.J. No. L 67/39 of 15 March 1990, reprinted in *Wertpapier-Mitteilungen*, 1990, 905 et seq.

73 Reprinted in *Wertpapier-Mitteilungen*, 1993, 627–8.

74 EC Commission, COM (90) 447.

75 Doc EN/RR/220/220931 of 28 January 1993, Resolution of the European Parliament on payment transactions in the context of

cross-border payment transaction network comparable to the domestic clearing system, and called for linking up the individual national clearing houses to a pan-European network, with the goal of achieving more efficient and transparent processing of high-volume private payment transactions.

At the same time, the leading associations of the European banking industry, assembled in the European Credit Sector Association (ECSA), were once again called upon to implement the guidelines they had worked out on cross-border payment transactions by the end of 1992. In addition, they called on the central bank governors to improve information exchange between the central banks with respect to supervision of the payment systems and the coordination of policy for reducing the risks resulting from differing payment systems within the Community, as well as to draft a list of principles concerning cooperation among the supervisory authorities with respect to common standards and guarantees.

In 1993, the Commission presented yet another report on the transparency and efficiency of cross-border payment transactions.[76] This one was based on a study performed by a consulting agency about whether and to what extent the self-regulatory measures of the banks in the area of small cross-border payments (that is, those up to ECU100) were successful.[77] The Commission characterized the results of the study, with respect to transparency, costs and speed of payments, as 'disappointing'. Within the framework of this study, 280 bank subsidiaries in the EU were surveyed, of whom 68 per cent had no written information on costs and duration of cross-border transfers, 2 per cent referred simply to general brochures, 21 per cent offered merely a price quotation, only 5 per cent provided brochures with detailed information, and a further 4 per cent mentioned the accruing costs.

With regard to the costs, the Commission found, in an examination of 1,000 transfer orders (each of ECU100) between 34 banks

economic and monetary union; European Parliament ed.: *Report of the Committee on Economic and Monetary Affairs and Industrial Policy on the System of Payments in the context of economic and monetary union.*

76 "Transparency and efficiency in cross-border payment transactions – A study of the EC Commission", *Zeitschrift für Bankrecht und Bankpraxis (ZBB)*, 1993, 275 et seq.

77 See on this *Zeitschrift für die Internationale Praxis (ZIP)-aktuell*, 1993, A 103 No. 287.

in all EU member states, that a fee averaging ECU20 per order was charged. Specifically criticized was the practice, engaged in by 43 per cent of the payee banks, of continuing to charge fees, despite express agreement to the contrary, so that the transfer amount was not credited in full to the payee.

Furthermore, this practice violates the recommendations of the leading associations of the banking industry (Spitzenverbände des Kreditgewerbes) of early 1992, which were developed as guidelines in close co-operation with the Commission in Brussels, but which naturally were not binding on the individual banks. It was also in contradiction to these recommendations that over two-thirds of the banks still provide their customers with no written information on their conditions for cross-border payment transactions, and that it is also virtually impossible to obtain written information about the duration of cross-border payments.

The transfer duration averaged 4.6 working days, with wide variations: in one case, the bank required 70 working days for the transfer, and in three cases the transfers had still not been executed 20 weeks after the orders had been given.[78]

On the basis of the studies, the EU Commission also made public criticisms of the banks. Thus the *Frankfurter Allgemeine Zeitung* in its edition of 13 August 1993 published an article under the headline, 'Banks helping themselves on cross-border payments', subtitled: 'Transfer costs of 25% / EU Commission outraged / study confirms customer anger', in which the results of the Commission's investigation were presented. Other newspapers came up with similar headlines.

If the EU Commission had until then relied on the self-regulatory measures of the banking industry, at the latest by this point, that is, in early 1993, it was forced to conclude that the efforts undertaken until then had not sufficed to attain the goals sought with respect to cross-border payment transactions. EU Commissioner Vanni d'Archirafi therefore announced an initiative of the Commission in cooperation with the European umbrella associations of the banking industry, by which observance of the guidelines was to be secured more effectively than before.

In December 1993, the Commission announced that it intended in early 1994 to perform a new study on the transparency and efficiency of cross-border transfers. Were it found that adequate progress had still not been made, the Commission threatened to issue a Directive that would have to be incorporated into national

78 *ZIP-aktuell*, 1993, A 104 No. 287.

law by 31 December 1995. This draft Directive contains – after the definition of the field of application and the required conceptual provisions in Articles 1 and 2 – provisions on transparency requirements for transfer conditions (Article 3), the information to be given after the performance or the entry of a transfer (Article 4), as well as the minimal obligations of the institutions with respect to transfers. These include the obligation to perform transfers in a timely manner (Article 5), the obligation to perform in accordance with the instructions of the payment order (Article 6), and the refund duty of the institutions vis-à-vis the principal in case of unsuccessfully concluded transfers (Article 7).

The subject of this second study was to be the question whether the written information called for could be obtained in at least two-thirds of the branch offices studied, plus the double-fee charging problem; such double-charging could only occur in a maximum of 10 per cent of the cases investigated. The results of this study are still being awaited; however, what is remarkable is the many initiatives being deployed by the European banking industry in order to prevent the threatened issuance of the Directive.

The Reaction of the Banks to the Activities of the EU Commission

After the Commission's criticisms of the practice of cross-border payment transactions made it clear that the issuance of a Directive on this subject had to be anticipated in the near future – the European Parliament had also recommended in a resolution implementing the demand for greater transparency in cross-border payment transactions via a Council Directive[79] – the leading associations of the European banking industry went into action. Besides pointing to the already-mentioned guidelines (whose implementation, however, the Commission found had failed to achieve the desired results), they unanimously expressed their doubts about both the study that had been conducted[80] and the contemplated EU Directive.[81]

79 Resolution of the European Parliament on payment transactions in the context of economic and monetary union, Bundestags-Drucksache, 12/4505.

80 See "Kreditwirtschaft fordert Hilfe von Rexrodt – Banken wehren sich gegen die EU-Richtlinie zum Zahlungsverkehr", *Frankfurter Allgemeine Zeitung*, 28 October 1994, 19.

81 Letter of the Central Credit Committee of the National Associa-

The banks first complained in unison about the definition of 'small cross-border payment' by the Commission, since in their view instead of ECU100 it should have been at least ECU1,500, which would have shown the costs to be a great deal more modest. Furthermore, the European banking industry had only begun distributing the customer information brochure in January 1993, so it was hardly objective or meaningful to investigate their effectiveness only one month later.

The criticisms levelled at the draft directive of the Commission[82] took several forms. First, it was asserted that the planned obligation on the banks (contained in Art. 6 of the draft directive) to adopt the agreement made in several payment transaction networks to impose all costs on the principal of a transfer would lead to an unjustified discrimination against the cost distribution agreements that had been reached in 94 per cent of the cases up to that time. Moreover, the paying bank had no influence over the agreement reached between the payee of the transfer and his bank with respect to handling compensation; on this, Europe-wide agreements among the banks would have to be reached, something which, however, would violate the competition law regulations in effect. Further, the contemplated so-called 'money-back guarantee', under which a standard no-fault repayment claim in the amount of the entire transfer sum against the first-paying bank would exist in the case where the transfer operation was not wholly concluded in favour of the beneficiary, stands in contradiction to German contract law. Under §§ 675, 670 BGB, the paying bank already has a valid expense reimbursement claim once it has sent on the transfer order, with corresponding crediting, to the payee's bank or to an intermediate credit institution. Moreover, there is no concept of no-fault liability in the German law of obligations, although it would be a necessary prerequisite for any such money-back guarantee.[83] (The argument was that German law of obligations has no fault-independent liability, as is presup-

tion of German Banks to the Finance Committee of the German Bundestag of 26 May 1993, reprinted in Der Bankenverband informiert, *Betriebswirtschaft und Zahlungsverkehr*, II/No. 11, 306–7.

82 See on this Holger Berndt, "Strategie und Abwicklung des Auslandszahlungsverkehrs im Sparkassensektor", p. 7, at 10–11.

83 Ibid., 11.

posed by a money-back guarantee, and thus it would constitute a breach of the German civil law system.)

In response to these objections, General-Directorate II of the European Commission, responsible for Economy and Finances as well as for Consumer Affairs, strove to arrive at a voluntary agreement among the leading associations of the European banking industry, the consumer associations and the Commission in the form of a Good Conduct Charter, which substantively – except for the money-back guarantee – would lead to regulations comparable to the draft directive, but on a voluntary basis.[84]

At the same time, the associations of the European banking industry asked the Commission not to resort to legislative measures before mid–1994, thus giving the banks time to develop suitable Europe-wide payment transaction systems.[85]

In principle, the German government too supports the idea of solving the payment transactions problem on a voluntary basis in the form of a Good Conduct Charter. In October 1994, in agreement with the Central Credit Committee, the German federal government, in its capacity as EU president, proposed to the Council that the Commission arrive at a mutually agreed regulation of cross-border payment transactions between itself and the European banking industry, and report on this subject to the Council meeting in June 1995. This agreement should enter into effect at the latest by 1 January 1996;[86] one year after entering into effect, the Commission should report to the Council on the results achieved.

Beyond this, the banks adopted a series of measures, all designed to improve cross-border payment transactions and thereby ward off legislative measures and any curtailment of banking autonomy by the EU Commission.

Measures of the Banks in Germany

In Germany, representatives of the leading associations of the German banking industry (including the Bundesverband deutscher Banken e.V. in Cologne, the Deutsche Sparkassen- und Giroverband e.V., Bonn, the Bundesverband deutscher Volksbanken

84 Ibid.

85 See "Banken gegen Richtlinie für grenzüberschreitenden Zahlungsverkehr", *ZIP-aktuell*, 1993, No. 358.

86 Holger Berndt, "Strategie und Abwicklung des Auslandszahlungsverkehrs im Sparkassensektor", 12.

und Raiffeisenbanken e.V., Bonn, the Verband öffentlicher Banken e.V., Bonn, and the Verband der Gemeinwirtschaftlichen Geschäftsbanken, Bonn) agreed in early 1993 to introduce a standard, machine-readable blank for transfers up to and including a value of DM5,000 to other EU and EFTA countries. This blank represents an important basis for rationalizing and accelerating cross-border transfer transactions.

Along with this, in response to the EU Commission's criticisms, the various banking groups in Germany have recently developed a number of systems for improved processing of cross-border payment transactions. These include, as complements to S.W.I.F.T., the Automated Clearing House (ACH), the EUFISERV-IFT project, developed by a 'payment transactions structure Europe' project group, the new international payment system of the co-operative banks, TIPANET, the pan-European payment system Unitime of the BfG Bank,[87] the new services offered by both the Commerzbank[88] and the Deutsche Verkehrs-Bank,[89] the 'Eurogiro' concept of the Postal Bank, and the cross-border POS system 'edc/Maestro'.

The above-mentioned systems and projects are typical of the efforts made by the banks to preserve their autonomy unencumbered by legislative measures, and will therefore be described below.

European Post/Giro Directors Group (Eurogiro)

The term 'Eurogiro' is the name for the cooperation of 14 European postal banks in the field of cross-border payment transactions.[90] A total of 96,000 post offices, branch offices and sub-offices are available to process the more than 40 million outgoing payments.[91] At the outset the postal banks of Belgium, Denmark, Germany, Finland, France, Great Britain, The Netherlands, Norway, Austria, Spain, Sweden and Switzerland joined forces. Later the postal banks

87 See "BfG Bank: Europaweites Zahlungssystem", *Zeitschrift für das gesamte Kreditwesen (ZfdgK)*, 1993, 1098.

88 See "Commerzbank: Zahlungsservice", *Zeitschrift für das gesamte Kreditwesen (ZfdgK)*, 1994, 327.

89 See "Geldtransfer im Zehnminutentakt", *Zeitschrift für das gesamte Kreditwesen (ZfdgK)*, 1993, 130.

90 See "Eurogiro", *Zeitschrift für das gesamte Kreditwesen (ZfdgK)*, 1993, 944.

91 See Günter Schneider, "Europäischer Zahlungsverkehr: Herausforderung und Chance für die Postbanken", *bank und markt* (1994), 36.

of Ireland and Luxembourg as well as, since July 1994, the postal bank of Japan became associate members of Eurogiro. The cooperation names as its advantages (matching the demands of the EU Commission) shorter durations, lower costs and a correspondingly greater cost transparency. In the future, a transfer should never take longer than four bank working days; the costs for document-bound orders will be limited to 0.1 or 0.15 per cent of the order amount (but with a minimum of DM10 or 15) and to a maximum of DM100 or 200.[92]

The Automated Clearing House (ACH)

Depending on their current organizational and technical level, banks have different procedures for executing a payment order to be sent abroad. One of these possibilities is the so-called 'Automated Clearing House' (ACH).[93] In this procedure, the paying credit institution sends the order (which may not exceed an upper limit of DM5,000[94]) to a clearing house in its own country or in the target country, in order thus to forward the order to the payee bank. The task of the clearing house is to bundle the incoming cross-border transfer orders and settle them between the paying bank and the payee bank. Depending on the technical form of the order, this can involve either a conventional (that is, document-bound) or an automatic (that is, digitized) order. If the paying bank wants to use an ACH, the order must be transmitted in digitized form.

The idea of the automated clearing houses comes from the countries whose central banks have not assumed the function of a common clearing house for national transfers, and which therefore had to create their own central clearing house. After all the European central banks had decided not to perform such a clearing function for cross-border payment transactions, the affected banks are faced with the necessity of acting on their own. The institutions which have their own branches in the target country of a transfer can call upon the so-called 'in-house' solution, but this only applies to a relative handful of banks, and even these do not always have branches in every other European country. In the long run, the tried

92 Ibid., 37.

93 See on this "Grünes Licht für deutsches ACH", *Zeitschrift für das gesamte Kreditwesen (ZfdgK)*, 1993, 857; Jürgen Terrahe, "Bedarf für ein Automated Clearing House in Deutschland?", 834.

94 Holger Berndt, "Strategie und Abwicklung des Auslandszahlungsverkehrs im Sparkassensektor", p. 7 (12).

and tested correspondent bank system does not offer a high enough performance capacity to handle the growing number of high-volume payment transactions.

The creation of a European ACH is therefore a task which must be accomplished as soon as possible to attain the standards called for by the Commission respecting price formation, normal durations and internationally standard message formats.[95] Currently, the ACH is being tested in Belgium, Germany, Great Britain, Italy and the Netherlands.

S-Interpay

Complementing the ACH concept, the Land Banks in Germany will in the future be offering a service called S-Interpay. This system is based on the concept of transferring to each of the individual Land Banks the responsibility for one European country, and thus tightening up the correspondent bank network.[96] Within the S-Interpay framework, every cross-border transfer order that is entered in the savings bank sector will be sent to the respectively responsible Land Bank and executed by this bank. Apart from strengthening competitiveness, the advantages which the savings bank organizations expect from S-Interpay lie in a better exploitation of existing resources. The cost and duration requirements of the EU Commission will both be fulfilled by S-Interpay. The costs will be limited to a standard amount of around DM15 per order and the transfer time will be reduced to a maximum of four days. In addition, the principal should if desired share in the costs that arise in the payee's country, in order to guarantee the crediting of the entire transfer amount to the account of the payee.

EUFISERV

EUFISERV[97] (European Savings Banks Financial Services Company) is the name given to another form of cooperation of European savings banks in the area of payment transactions. Currently, 1,698 savings banks from 16 European countries belong to the European

95 Ibid.

96 Ibid.

97 See on this Alfons Müller, "EUFISERV – Zusammenarbeit der europäischen Sparkassen auf dem Gebiet des Zahlungsverkehrs", in *Rechtsprobleme der Auslandsüberweisung*, ed. Walther Hadding and Uwe H. Schneider (Berlin: Duncker & Humblot, 1992), 203 et seq.

Savings Bank Association in Brussels.[98] Despite the differences existing between the savings banks of the various European countries with respect to their structure, legal form and business activity, the Association strives for cooperation with regard to the common European market. Already in 1990 a 'Commission 1992' set up by the European Savings Bank Association adopted a Charter,[99] in which, as the basis of future cooperation, the following key sentences were set forth.

> The common traditional characteristics of the savings banks and the existing close personal and institutional ties should be used for the European cooperation and the business capacity expanded through a pooling of resources for the benefit of the customers; a savings bank image of European dimensions should be created and a suitable procedure created in order to promote cooperation between the member institutions of the European Savings Bank Association. In addition, an open and broad-based cooperation should be implemented through which multilateral and collective activities would also be promoted, as well as the development of coordinated bilateral agreements.

In February 1990, representatives of 11 European countries founded in Brussels the company EUFISERV s.c. with the purpose of offering their customers a service which is not only as standard as possible but also as attractive as possible in terms of price and quality in the field of payment transactions.[100] When the cooperation began, the approximately 37 million savings bank customers who possess an ec-card, a credit card or a savings bank customer card received access to all the money machines of the savings banks in the EU, since the shareholders of EUFISERV – savings banks and savings bank associations – set up a system (with headquarters in Hannover) to create a European money machine network. EUFISERV S.C. concluded with the data processing company of the Lower Saxony savings bank organization (dvg Hannover) a long-term contract for using and operating the network.

Each of the member organizations is linked with dvg Hannover via a national interface, the National Interface Location. The connection within the European savings bank network now makes it possible for savings bank customers to use an on-line money

98 End of 1989.

99 See DOC D 106/89 fin-Commission 1992.

100 Alfons Müller, *Sparkasse* 1991, 413.

machine at any time, 24 hours a day. In the meantime, this network includes around 24,000 money machines, which can be operated using German, English, French or the respective national language. Travelling abroad in Europe has been made a great deal easier through this example of cross-border cooperation.

Transferts Interbancaires de Paiements Automatiés (Tipanet)

The cooperative banks, too, prefer the Good Conduct Charter for cross-border payment transactions to a Directive which they view as 'counterproductive'.[101] In the autumn of 1993, therefore, the German Volks- and Raiffeisenbanken agreed to participate in a cross-border cooperation under the name of Tipanet with the cooperative banks from Belgium, France, Great Britain, Italy, Canada, Spain and the USA.[102] In 1994, this network was expanded by the entry of the cooperative banks of Denmark, The Netherlands, Austria and Switzerland. Each day the network bundles all incoming transfers and sends them abroad in one data record via IFT (Interbank File Transfer). A significant advantage over S.W.I.F.T. lies in the use of a multinational data format, which is compatible with the various clearing systems of the partner countries and thus makes possible fully automatic processing of the data.[103]

The Code of Practice of the British Banks

The criticisms of the EU Commission have also led to reactions on the part of the banks in other European countries designed to avoid legislative measures and any accompanying curtailment of autonomy. Alongside the bilateral and multilateral agreements,[104] which result in an improvement of payment transactions not only for the German customer, but also for the respective foreign cus-

101 Bernd Rodewald, "Offen für weitere Partner: weltweiter Zahlungsverkehr im genossenschaftlichen Verbund", *bank und markt* (1994), 31.

102 See "Genossenschaftsbanken: Neues grenzüberschreitendes Zahlungssystem", *Zeitschrift für das Gesamte Kreditwesen (ZfdgK)*, 1993, 1043.

103 Bernd Rodewald, "Offen für weitere Partner: weltweiter Zahlungsverkehr im genossenschaftlichen Verbund", *bank und markt* (1994), 31, at 33.

104 See more on this below.

tomer, there are sets of rules comparable to the Good Conduct Charter of the German banks.

An example of this is the Code of Practice which was drafted in 1991 by the British Bankers' Association (BBA) in cooperation with the Building Societies Association (BSA) and the Association for Payment Clearing Services (APACS). The Code of Practice which entered into effect on 16 March 1992 is a set of rules establishing standards for the business dealings of the British banks, building societies and card issuers with their private customers.[105] The second edition of the rules, in effect since 28 March 1994 but which does not have the force of law, is regarded by the British associations as a standard and the member institutions are expected to recognise the Code of Practice as a binding set of norms.[106] The goal is to ensure the good banking practices of British banks through this set of rules, which contains a series of duties already established in the common law; of course, the banks are always free to subject themselves to even stricter measures on a voluntary basis.

The principles set down in Part B No. 5 and No. 13 of the Code of Practice are important in connection with cross-border payment transactions. According to these provisions, the customers must be given detailed explanations about the basis of the accruing fees and costs, and they must be informed about exchange rates and costs associated with foreign exchange operations. Further, customers who wish to participate in foreign payment transactions must be informed at least about the appropriate payment forms, the normal payment durations for international transfers and about the accruing fees and any costs generated by third parties.

Cross-border Cooperation of the Credit Institutions in the Field of Payment Transactions in the Form of Bilateral or Multilateral Agreements

Of course, there has always been cooperation among credit institutions at both the national and international levels.[107] This

105 Details in Klaus Vorpeil, "Code of Practice der Banken", *Recht der Internationalen Wirtschaft* (1993), 336.

106 Klaus Vorpeil, "Code of Practice der britischen Banken", *Recht der Internationalen Wirtschaft* (1994), 559.

107 See Peter Kajüter, "Internationale strategische Allianzen im europäischen Finanzsektor", *Die Bank* (1994), 196.

extends from the simple exchange of information[108] about bilateral and multilateral agreements all the way to the formation of complex structures in the field of cross-border payment transactions. The interests of the banking industry are focused – precisely because of the sharpening competition with other financial service providers – on reinforcing its competitive advantages through the most efficient cooperation possible. Recently, the number of cross-border cooperations between banks has grown significantly precisely at the European level.[109] There are various reasons for this: for one thing, private and corporate customers are increasingly demanding international services from their banks. In addition, there exists – owing to the many legal and cultural differences which remain, despite all the efforts at harmonization between the individual countries – the necessity of also being present in the respective foreign countries if one wishes to offer one's own products across borders.[110]

Since the end of the 1980s, one observes an increasing trend on the part of the internationally active banks to enter into bilateral and multilateral cooperations on a larger scale. These are characterized by a particularly careful selection of the partner and a limitation to individual business areas.[111]

In the field of cross-border payment transactions, the Inter-Bank-Online-System (IBOS) agreement was concluded in November 1991 between the Spanish Banco Santander and the Royal Bank of Scotland, through which transfers between the two institutions were made possible in only seven seconds. In the meantime, the Crédit Commercial de France and the Banco de Comercio e Industria have acquired an IBOS licence, so that more than 2,500 bank subsidiar-

108 See, for example, Henner Walkhoff, "Kreditinstitute auf dem Weg nach Europa, Ergebnisse eines Bankengesprächs in London", *Sparkasse* 1992, 180–81.

109 See Bank of England, ed., "Cross-border alliances in banking and financial services in the single market", in *Bank of England Quarterly Bulletin* August (1993), 372 (377).

110 Peter Kajüter, "Internationale strategische Allianzen im europäischen Finanzsektor", p. 196 (197).

111 Hans H. Hinterhuber and Harald P. Pechlander, "Strategische Allianzen im grenzüberschreitenden Bankensektor", *bank und markt* (1992), 22 et seq; Joachim Süchting, "Strategische Allianzen in der Kreditwirtschaft", *Zeitschrift für das gesamte Kreditwesen* (1990), 702 et seq.

ies in France, Spain, Great Britain and Portugal are now connected on-line with one another. If the participants originally only had the goal of being practically present abroad via the electronic connection of their subsidiary network without having to set up their own branch office or acquire a foreign bank, IBOS has in the interim developed into a system by means of which cross-border payments within the Single Market can be processed comparatively quickly and cheaply, something the Commission has long called for.

The German banks have also grown increasingly active. One should mention here the cooperation of the Commerzbank with the British National Westminster Bank, the French Société Générale, the Italian Credito Italiano and the Spanish cooperation partner, the Banco Central Hispanoamericano, through which high-volume payment transactions should be better processed in a single network,[112] the convention of the Westdeutsche Landesbank central giro institution with the English Standard Chartered Bank on a reciprocal customer service, the cooperation of the DG-Bank with the Caisse Centrale de Banques Populaires, Paris, the Crédit Agricole, Paris, the Rabobank Nederland, Utrecht, the Raiffeisen-Zentralbank Österreich AG, Vienna and the Banco Espito Santo, Lisbon,[113] as well as the cooperation between the Deutsche Bank with Den Danske Bank, the Union Bank of Finland and the Schweizerische Kreditanstalt, developed from the traditional correspondent bank relationships, all with the goal of ensuring that the Deutsche Bank is represented via a cooperation partner in all of the 18 EU and EFTA countries where it does not have its own subsidiaries or branch offices.

Conclusion

While in comparable areas, for example international reinsurers, one observes a development in the direction of a juridification which is fervently desired by the actors themselves,[114]

112 See on this Claudia Nicolai-Verni and Axel Michalek, "Zahlungsverkehr in Kooperation mit Partnern aus dem Ausland – der Ansatz der Commerzbank", pp. 27 et seq; "Commerzbank: Zahlungsservice", *Zeitschrift für das gesamte Kreditwesen (ZfdgK)*, 1994, 327.

113 See on this, "DG Bank: Reorganisation des Auslandsstützpunktnetzes abgeschlossen", *Zeitschrift für das gesamte Kreditwesen (ZfdgK)*, 1993, 1043.

114 See on this Christine Stammel, Chapter 3 of the present volume.

the banks active across borders have continued to strive – until now with great success – to avoid government intervention wherever possible. One guarantee that this situation will not change in the foreseeable future is the autonomous structures and mechanisms which these banks have created. These contribute not only to the most conflict-free processing possible of the various cross-border banking activities, but simultaneously to the edification of an outward image of smooth-functioning capability, thus offering few exposed flanks for legislators to attack. Even where grievances have been identified – for example by the EU Commission with respect to the transparency, speed and cost of cross-border payments – the banks have at least until now been able to block any statutory regulation through self-imposed good conduct agreements and various innovations in this sector. A further reason for the autonomous position of banks (at least in the more liberal market economies) is the increasing pressure of international competition, since no state can afford to curtail the freedoms of its own financial economy and thereby render its own credit institutions uncompetitive on the global financial markets.

However, the autonomy of the banks is not undisputed. Even if there are a series of instruments which bring considerable advantages for bank customers and which were first made possible by a broad consensus of the international banking industry (for example, in the area of eurocheque procedures and the credit card system), the banking industry has come under increasing public criticism for some time now under the slogan, 'power of the banks'.[115] It is certainly true that the credit institutions, given their central importance for the functioning of an economy and their many ties both with one another and with major corporations, do in fact possess considerable influence, and thus power. And if the concept of autonomy means not only the right to set one's own laws and live according to them, but in ethics also describes the condition of ethical maturity, in which one's own conscience determines the laws of one's action, the banks must admit the question of whether they are dealing responsibly with, or abusing, their power.

As long as, for example with respect to the money laundering issue, the actors proceed according to the motto, 'If I don't take the drug mafia's money, someone else will – so I might as well do it

115 Manfred Weber, "Phänomen 'Bankenmacht'", *Die Bank* (1995), 196; Weber "Banken sind am Unmut der Verbraucher selbst schuld", *Frankfurter Allgemeine Zeitung*, 27 October 1994, 17.

myself', laws and regulations will remain ineffective. However, if one can successfully stimulate the self-commitment of the actors prior to the enactment of legislation, as was the case for cross-border payment transactions in the form of self-created good conduct guidelines and new, high-performance and customer-friendly payment transaction systems, then actual regulation of the field by the legislators can be largely omitted as superfluous.

References

Albisetti, Emilio, ed. 1987. *Handbuch des Geld-, Bank- and Börsenwesens der Schweiz*. 4th edn. Thur, Switzerland: Ott Verlag.

Bank of England, ed. 1993. Cross-border alliances in banking and financial services in the single market. *Bank of England Quarterly Bulletin* August.

Berndt, Holger. 1994. Strategie und Abwicklung des Auslandszahlungsverkehrs im Sparkassensektor. *bank und markt*.

Bernhard, R. and J. van Eldik. 1993. Bessere Zahlungsverkehrsqualität durch Europay. *Wertpapier-Mitteilungen*.

BfG Bank: Europaweites Zahlungssystem. 1993. *Zeitschrift für das gesamte Kreditwesen*.

Brauner, Karl-Ernst. 1988. *Das Erklärungsrisiko beim Einsatz von elektronischen Datenverarbeitungsanlagen*. Bonn: Margarete Wehle.

Brestel, Heinz. 1994. Aus der Praxis der Banküberweisung. *Blick durch die Wirtschaft*, 3 November.

Brüggemann, Max. 1981. *Die Banktechnik des Auslandsgeschäfts*. 6th edn. Stuttgart: Schäffer-Poeschel.

Bundesgerichtshof (BGH). 1971. Decision of 18.06.1971. *Neue Juristische Wochenschrift*.

Burghagen, Volker. 1995. Auslandsgeschäft der Kreditinstitute. In *Handwörterbuch des Bank- und Finanzwesens*. 2nd edn. Stuttgart: Schäffer-Poeschel.

Büschgen, Hans E. 1993a. Allgemeine Entwicklungslinien. In *Europäische Bankengeschichte*, edited by Hans von Pohl. Frankfurt/M.: Fritz Knapp Verlag.

Büschgen, Hans E. 1993b. *Bankbetriebslehre*. Wiesbaden: Gabler Verlag.

Canaris, Claus-Wilhelm. 1988. *Bankvertragsrecht*. 4th edn. Berlin, New York: Walter de Gruyter.

Commerzbank: Zahlungsservice. 1994. *Zeitschrift für das gesamte Kreditwesen*.

Deeg, Ernst. 1982. Wo kann S.W.I.F.T. mithelfen, Probleme zu lösen? *Zeitschrift für das gesamte Kreditwesen*, Ausgabe Technik of 15 March.

DG Bank: Reorganization des Auslandsstützpunktnetzes abgeschlossen. 1993. *Zeitschrift für das gesamte Kreditwesen.*

EC Commission. 1993. Transparency and efficiency in cross-border payment transactions – A study of the EC Commission. *Zeitschrift für Bankrecht und Bankpraxis.*

Etzkorn, Jörg. 1991. *Rechtsfragen des international elektronischen Zahlungsverkehrs durch S.W.I.F.T.* Berlin, New York: Walter de Gruyter.

Eurogiro. 1993. *Zeitschrift für das gesamte Kreditwesen.*

Frankfurter SWIFT-Büro als Schlüssel für Zentraleuropa. 1995. *Frankfurter Allgemeine Zeitung.* 5 September.

Gablenz, Carl-Heinrich v. 1983. *Die Haftung der Banken bei Einschaltung Dritter.* Munich: C.H.Beck.

Geldtransfer im Zehnminutentakt. 1993. *Zeitschrift für das gesamte Kreditwesen.*

Genossenschaftsbanken: Neues grenzüberschreitendes Zahlungssystem. 1993. *Zeitschrift für das gesamte Kreditwesen.*

Gerard, Peter. 1994. Internationaler Zahlungsverkehr im Wandel: Konzeptionen der Deutschen Bank. *bank und markt.*

Grünes Licht für deutsches ACH. 1993. *Zeitschrift für das gesamte Kreditwesen.*

Hadding, Walther and Uwe H. Schneider. 1992. *Rechtsprobleme der Auslandsüberweisung.* Berlin: Duncker & Humblot.

Hinterhuber Hans H., and Harald P. Pechlander. 1992. Strategische Allianzen im grenzüberschreitenden Bankensektor. *bank und markt.*

Hooven, Eckart van. 1993. 25 Jahre eurocheque – ein historischer Konsens. *Die Bank.*

Jueterbock, Dietrich. 1988. Zehn Jahre S.W.I.F.T.-Netzwerk – ein Meilenstein der Automation? *Die Bank.*

Jung, Karl-Heinz. 1992. *Jahrbuch für den Außenhandel.* Stuttgart: Schäffer-Poeschel.

Kajüter, Peter. 1994. Internationale strategische Allianzen im europäischen Finanzsektor. *Die Bank.*

Kegel, Gerhard 1966. Die Bankgeschäfte im deutschen internationalen Privatrecht. In *Gedächtnisschrift Rudolf Schmidt*, edited by Erwin Seidl. Berlin: Duncker & Humblot.

Koller, Ingo. 1987. Grundstrukturen des Bankhaftungsrechts unter besonderer Berücksichtigung des Zahlungsverkehrs. In *Neue Entwicklungen im Bankhaftungsrecht*, edited by Johannes Köndgen. Cologne: Kommunikationsforum.

Krüger, Manfred. 1992. electronic cash-Verfahren ab 1993 grenzüberschreitend möglich. *Sparkasse.*

Loh, Wolfram W. 1983. *Das SWIFT-System, Die moderne Datenübertragung im internationalen Zahlungsverkehr*. Frankfurt/M.: Verlag W. Kohlhammer.

Möschel, Wernhard. 1986. Dogmatische Strukturen des bargeldlosen Zahlungsverkehrs. *Archiv für die Civilistische Praxis*, 186.

Müller, Alfons. 1992. EUFISERV – Zusammenarbeit der europäischen Sparkassen auf dem Gebiet des Zahlungsverkehrs. In *Rechtsprobleme der Auslandsüberweisung*, edited by Walther Hadding and Uwe H. Schneider. Berlin: Duncker & Humblot.

Nicolai-Verni, Claudia and Axel Michalek. 1994. Zahlungsverkehr in Kooperation mit Partnern aus dem Ausland – der Ansatz der Commerzbank. *bank und markt*.

Pleyer, Klemens and Robert Battes. 1971. Geltung und Auslegung Allgemeiner Geschäftsbedingungen im Verkehr der Banken untereinander. *Der Betrieb*.

Pleyer, Klemens and Edgar Wallach. 1988. Erfüllungszeitpunkt und Gefahrtragung bei grenzüberschreitenden Überweisungen nach deutschem und englischem Recht. *Recht der Internationalen Wirtschaft*.

Real, Gustav. 1994. [Note on the Decision of] Amtsgericht Düsseldorf v. 14.12.1992. *Recht der Internationalen Wirtschaft*.

Rodewald, Bernd. 1994. Offen für weitere Partner: weltweiter Zahlungsverkehr im genossenschaftlichen Verbund. *bank und markt*.

Schinnerer, Erich. 1984. Probleme 'Internationaler Überweisungen'. *Österreichische Juristische Zeitung*.

Schlöter, Hans W. 1987. Von eurocheque über EUROCARD zu EUROPLUS. *Die Bank*.

Schmid, Klaus Peter. 1994. Banken im Schmollwinkel. *Die Zeit*. 28 October.

Schneider, Günter. 1994. Europäischer Zahlungsverkehr: Herausforderung und Chance für die Postbanken. *bank und markt*.

Schneider, Uwe H. 1989. Das UNCITRAL-Modellgesetz über den internationalen Überweisungsverkehr. *Wertpapier-Mitteilungen*.

Seipen, Christoph von der. 1992. Anwendbares Recht beim Überweisungsverkehr. In *Rechtsprobleme der Auslandsüberweisung*, edited by Walther Hadding and Uwe H. Schneider. Berlin: Duncker & Humblot.

Steinherr, Alfred. 1989. Der europäische Bankensektor im integrierten Finanzmarkt. *Zeitschrift für das Bank- und Börsenwesen*.

Süchting, Joachim. 1990. Strategische Allianzen in der Kreditwirtschaft. *Zeitschrift für das gesamte Kreditwesen*.

Terrahe, Jürgen. 1993. Bedarf für ein Automated Clearing House in Deutschland? *Wertpapier-Mitteilungen*.

UNCITRAL. 1982. Electronic Funds Transfer. In *Yearbook of the United Nations Commission on International Trade Law*, Vol. XIII. New York.

Vorpeil, Klaus. 1993. Code of Practice der Banken. *Recht der Internationalen Wirtschaft*.

Vorpeil, Klaus. 1994. Code of Practice der britischen Banken. *Recht der Internationalen Wirtschaft*.

Vorstände müssen Risiko aus Derivaten überwachen. 1995. *Frankfurter Allgemeine Zeitung*. 2 November.

Wagner, Albert and Ewald Wagner. 1994. 'Low value Payments' über mehrere Korrespondenten – das Beispiel der Dresdner Bank. *bank und markt*.

Walkhoff, Henner. 1992. Kreditinstitute auf dem Weg nach Europa, Ergebnisse eines Bankengesprächs in London. *Sparkasse*.

Weber, Manfred. 1994. Banken sind am Unmut der Verbraucher selbst schuld. *Frankfurter Allgemeine Zeitung*. 27 October.

Weber, Manfred. 1995. Phänomen 'Bankenmacht'. *Die Bank*.

Weise, Paul-Frank. 1990. *Lex mercatoria: materielles Recht vor der internationalen Handelsschiedsgerichtsbarkeit*. Frankfurt/M.: Lang.

Weiss, Ulrich. 1988. eurocheque: 20 Jahre erfolgreicher Zusammenarbeit. *Die Bank*.

The Author

Klaus Frick is a lawyer with an additional Master degree in European Law (University of Bremen) and is currently employed by IKB Deutsche Industriebank in Düsseldorf (Germany). He has been part of the Bremen research group on 'Global Legal Interaction' since 1995 and is writing a PhD dissertation on the subject of his contribution to the present volume.

Address: IKB-Deutsch Industriebank AG, Wilhelm-Bötzkes-Str.1, 40474 Düsseldorf, Germany.

E-Mail: Klaus.Frick@ikb.de

Abstract

The banking sector serves in this paper as an example of an autonomously organized and informally regulated field of global legal interaction. In spite of regulatory attempts of nation-states and, recently, the European Commission, and also in spite of public criticism regarding costs, delays and errors in the course of money transfer from one country to another banks have been able to preserve their 'third culture'. This phenomenon is explained by highly efficient structures created and continuously developed in the course of one or two decades and by the power the sector has achieved with the globalization of the financial markets. State interference, as in the case of money laundering, has remained largely unsuccessful.

5 The Political Economy of the Chamber of Commerce of Milan: Towards a New 'Universitas Mercatorum'

VITTORIO OLGIATI

Il suffit de rappeler ... l'influence que les marchands lombards ont eue sur le développement economique de l'occident. (P. Huvelin[1])

Introduction

A Theoretical Hypothesis: Legal Certainty at Risk

The aim of this study is to take normative order seriously as a *problematic* 'need' of current cross-border socioeconomic interactions.[2] For this purpose, it deals with a historically determined territorial/functional, public/private, European infrastructure specifically concerned with global/local business activity: the Chamber of Commerce, Industry, Agriculture and Handicraft of Milan, hereinafter 'Milan Chamber'. As the analysis will show, there are a number of theoretical and practical reasons to study a service infrastructure such as the Chamber of Commerce. However, one reason

1 Pierre Huvelin, *Essai historique sur le droit des Marchés & des Foires* (Paris: A. Russeau ed., 1897).

2 Volkmar Gessner, "Praesumptio similitudinis ? – A Critique of Comparative Law", *The Proceedings of 1995 ISA-RCSL Annual Meeting, Papers Section Meetings, Supplement* 2, ed. Japan Committee for the RCSL95 (Tokio, 1995); Volkmar Gessner, (1995), "Legal Certainty in Cross-border Interactions", *The Proceedings of 1995 ISA-RCSL Annual Meeting, Papers Section Meetings, Supplement* 2, ed. Japan Committee for the RCSL95 (Tokio, 1995).

stands above any other: once again, as ever, its organizational modelling scans the evolution patterns of both capitalistic economy and political institutions in Europe.

In many discussions on socioeconomic dynamics, it is a platitude to hear that positive law ultimately prevents and/or reduces risk by guaranteeing stability, certainty and security in the course of contractual relations. In particular, the above cliché is ascribed specifically to the risks of the modern capitalistic market system, claiming that economic exchange in contemporary (westernized) society necessarily requires such a socio-technical performance. Indeed, up to the 1930s, one could effectively find a kernel of truth in such a statement. On the one hand, by virtue of the subsumption of traditional commercial rules (*lex mercatoria*) into parliamentary legislation (civil codes) which occurred in the nineteenth century – the hegemonic and monopolistic power of formal official law backed by the state was substantially unquestioned in socioeconomic matters. On the other hand, the ups and downs of both market competition and production circles were somehow predictable and/or moulded by state law policy, at least to a certain extent. Looking at this general context, it is well known, for example, that Max Weber had no hesitation in defining theoretically the relationship between law, state and economy in westernized society as a process of rationalization.

Since then, however, validity and efficacy of positive state law as a generalized medium of socioeconomic 'development' and 'control' has been eroded, increasingly challenged either by a number of legal devices related to new, informal/unofficial/semi-autonomous legal systems or by the growing incongruence between the so-called 'rational' economic calculation and broader socioinstitutional action systems. Thus, contrary to widespread stereotypes, at both the technical and the social level, not only does a formal conditional enforcement of positive state law not seem to fit any more with a strict cost–benefit management of business relations, but also economic efficiency no longer necessarily implies the use of positive law as a pivotal risk-avoiding instrument.

Proofs of the above are so clear nowadays, owing to the far-reaching impact of market economy at a worldwide level, that a substantial overturning of opinions is increasingly apparent, particularly in sociolegal scientific debate.[3]

3 Vittorio Olgiati, "Process and Policy of Legal Professionalization in Europe. The De-construction of a Normative Order", in *Pro-*

Leafing through most advanced sociolegal literature, in particular, one finds studies stating that 'Capitalism no longer demands a calculable formal legal order, requiring instead highly indeterminate discretionary government interventions, which are now functionally sufficient to underpin the self-created order of the economy'.[4] One finds also analyses suggesting that positive law might no longer be able congruently to stabilize social expectations, for the limits of its evolutionary differentiation have reached such a degree that it is likely to endanger – rather than sustain – the overall social dynamics.[5] In other words, it is argued that, far from realizing a mutual 'rationalization' at the social and institutional level, both (market) economy and (state) law have become themselves veritable risk-producing systems for the whole of society.[6]

This chapter deals precisely with this *new* – because all-embracing and globally generalized – state of affairs, not so much to thematize it in general terms, but rather to focus on some of its empirical implications: more precisely, to study how the so-called 'organized irresponsibility' of both positive state law and capitalistic economy vis-à-vis contemporary society is confronted and managed at infrastuctural level at present.

A Methodological Choice: the Policy of a Service Infrastructure

For the above purpose, a highly emblematic case will be proposed as subject matter: seemingly, a case of practical 'secondary adjustment' of local dimension; potentially, a great political project of continental (European) importance. The case, it is worth stressing immediately, is still in embryonic form: up to now, one might say that it is more an idea-in-progress than a result, a

fessional Competition and Professional Power. Lawyers, Accountants and the Social Construction of Markets, ed. Yves Dezalay and David Sugarman (London/New York: Routledge, 1995), 170–204.

4 Gunther Teubner, "And God Laughed... Indeterminacy, Self-reference and Paradox in Law", in *Critical Legal Thought: An American German Debate*, ed. Christian Joerges and David Trubek (Baden-Baden: Nomos, 1989), 410.

5 Niklas Luhmann, *La differenziazione del diritto* (Bologna: Il Mulino, 1989).

6 Ulrick Beck, *Risikogesellschaft. Auf dem Weg in eine andere Moderne* (Frankfurt-am-Main: Suhrkamp, 1986).

programme to be fulfilled than an historically tested reality. Yet, even as a mere ideal model, its substantive content is able to mobilize such a constructionist energy and symbolic appeal – for it fits basic structural trends and deep-rooted social conditions – that it has already been embodied in an official institution: paradoxically, in an ancient institution, whose origin dates back to the early rise of the market economy, the structures of which are now gaining a substantial performative renaissance.

The case in point is that of the Chamber of Commerce, Industry, Agriculture and Handicraft in Italy as defined by Law 29.12.1993 n.580; the leading model is that incorporated into the programmatic activity of the Chamber of Milan; the organizational design is that elaborated in theoretical terms by the influential review, *Impresa & Stato*, edited by the same Milan Chamber. The project that the Milan Chamber aims to fulfil is extremely ambitious: to put at the disposal of the local and foreign business community an integrated subinfrastructural service network based on that mix of skills, information and culture that characterizes the region as a unique and incomparable geoeconomic context. In other words, to provide the business community as a whole with an institutionalized – territorially settled and functionally differentiated – service system to sustain and implement the *regulation* of socioeconomic activity concerned with the area. In short, to revitalize in a postmodern fashion the mediaeval/humanistic Italian tradition of an *ordered* social organization of the *universe* of market–society relations: the (city-state) *Universitas Mercatorum*.

At the core of this programme there is, indeed, a double intuition and one strategic choice: that (1) only the aggregation of local variables could 'make the difference' in a process of valorization of economic exchanges that more and more are oriented towards a global dimension, and (2) only a truly *institutional* policy involving the whole social dynamics could cope with the challenges – and mould the risks – of current socio-economic fluctuations, so that (3) the target/need to be pursued could be based neither on mere paper law, nor on a mere 'local' legal system such as casuistic *lex mercatoria*, but on a new, general, substantial normative asset in which the entire realm of the enterprise system – the enterprise as a 'subject' – is assumed as a pivotal frame of reference.

Moving on from these premises, it has been thus defined the corresponding structure-in-context model: the Lombardy region has always played a role as a 'boundary' zone, dealing with commercial transactions and productive transformation craftmanship. Due to its geographical position the Milan Chamber was compelled to provide a special service network for the global business community. In turn, as the Milan Chamber is just one of the public/private service infrastructures in the region, and the overall normative asset of the enterprise system implies both preventive and successive checks, due to the changes occurring (and required) in the same system, the above role must be functionally oriented not towards ex post control functions, but rather towards ex ante, *observing* and *driving* functions, so as to monitor (and possibly advance) actual (and prospective) validity and efficacy of such a normative asset.

As one can see, the model, in theory, looks quite appealing and, indeed, refined. But how far can one rely in practice on the above assumptions? What sort of historically determined conditions lead to such a 'rationale'? Is it possible here and now (in the current state of affairs of the economic and institutional realms) to take the project seriously? What about the achievements of the project so far?

To try to deal with these questions the historical interplay between socioinstitutional and economic dynamics will be sketched first in order to show the limits of mere legal arrangements and the potentials of functionally differentiated infrastructures in managing at local, national and international level the imperatives of contemporary law and economy issues. This will offer the opportunity to stress the rise of neocorporatist polycentrism and discuss other new organizational models of legal and economic pluralism.

The above insights will then be contextualized by analysing the *ratio juris* of Law 580/93 on the Chamber of Commerce system in Italy: a normative framework that has been strongly influenced by the leading strategy of the Milan Chamber. Here the institutional nature of the system will be outlined with specific reference to (public–private, territorial–functional, horizontal–vertical) autonomy (that is statutory prerogatives and legislative powers), autarchy (financial and administrative self-management) and autocriny (jurisdictional and regulatory performances). The overall subinfrastructural configuration of the Italian model will be compared with other European systems. To complete the picture, the organizational mission of a special cross-border agency – the Lombard Chamber's Foreign Centre – and, more particularly, the current policy of Italian chambers abroad will be discussed also with reference to the 'diaspora' of the Italian business community in the world.

The study will then directly focus on the services provided by the Milan Chamber in relation to the variables occurring in the structure and meaning of cross-border socioeconomic interactions at present. Type and standards of the Milan Chamber's overall subinfrastructures will be described as 'cybernetic' models; that is, as steering 'methods' and steering 'bodies' set up to face the increasing fluctuations of 'glocal' dynamics (the neologism 'glocal' comes from *glo*(bal) and (lo)*cal* variables). Empirical evidence will be offered of the changing patterns of competition logic and evaluation criteria about 'internalization' and 'externalization' of regional resources.

Finally, a systematic overview of cross-border activities performed by the Milan Chamber's subinfrastructures acting as private special enterprises will be sketched. More precisely, on the basis of information gathered by personal interviews with Chamber functionnaires, the following subinfrastructures will be taken into account: (a) Cedcamera, dealing with interorganizational management; (b) Eurosportello, dealing with individual issues and/or individual actors; (c) Promos, dealing with any sort of cross-border relations promotion; (d) Formaper, dealing with specific cases of general relevance; and (e) the Arbitration Chamber and Isdaci, dealing with disputes, regulation and business ethics.

The strategic *normative* aim of the Chamber is the promotion of a new stateform by means of binding 'interest governmentality' agreements and interinstitutional collaboration networks.

The Research Fieldwork as a Symbol: Italian Metropolitan 'Glocalism'

It is a clear starting-point of this study that the idea of dealing with the Chamber of Commerce system in Italy and, more particularly, of focusing on a local case such as that of the Milan Chamber, in order to study current cross-border legal interactions in Europe, should be neither surprising nor underestimated.

At present, Italy is the fifth country in the world on the scale of economic power. Italy is also at the centre of many North–South and East–West economic and political mainstreams. It is true that its current political–institutional asset is weak and shaky, to the extent that an internal federalist secession might even occur at the constitutional level, but this is precisely a signal of the magnitude of changes that the country is facing at present. These changes are, in turn, a constitutive part of the extraordinary economic contradictions – achievements as well as failures – that characterize the same asset. In any case, the whole system is based on an equally extraordinary vitality that makes it extremely creative.[7] In fact, Italian industry is quite peculiar: the flexibility of a number of small/medium-sized enterprises counterbalances the relative inflexibility of a few big companies. In total, Italian enterprises number about five million employees, one out of 12 citizens: a density that does not seem to have an equivalent elsewhere in the world.[8]

The idea of dealing with the activity of the Milan Chamber is also based on its high emblematic value. As is well-known, Milan is the financial centre of the Italian economic system, the operational core of the political economy of the country. Milan also has the second largest commercial fairs system in Europe, after Paris. Both aspects are strictly related to the city's geographical position: as the name indicates (Milan means 'mid-land') it is located exactly at the middle of the North–South line between Paris and/or Frankfurt and Naples and the East–West line between Trieste and Marseilles. It is true that in the last decades, Milan has suffered serious problems as regards its socioeconomic development, particularly so if one looks at its direct competitors, such as – on the East–West line – Munich and Barcelona. Yet, as the recent economic boom in the Italian north-east demonstrates, Milan is a place where East–West Mediterranean and North–South continental European social currents have always met and intermingled.[9]

Indeed, it is not at all by chance that Milan and its regional territory (Lombardy) have always been characterized by cross-border socioeconomic relations. Exactly a hundred years ago, Huvelin, a famous lawyer at the Court of Paris and Lyons, in his *Essai historique sur le droit des Marchés & des Foires*, quoting authors such as Ebrenberg, Goldschmidt, Schaube and Schupfer, wrote:

> A notre époque, et dès le XI siècle, le commerce italien a acquis la préponderance dans toute l'Europe. Il suffit de rappeler les noms des grandes cités qui vivent du traffic, Venise, Gènes, Amalfi, Pise, Lucques, Sienne, Milan, Florence, et l'influence que les marchands lombards ont eue sur le développement économique de l'occident, pour nous convaincre

7 Antonio Saba, *Il modello italiano. La specializzazione flessibile e i distretti industriali* (Milano: Angeli, 1995).

8 Piero Bassetti, "Una istituzione italiana al lavoro verso la Nuova Statualita", *Impresa & Stato* 30 (1995).

9 N.N., "Tema monografico: la competitività di Milano tra le capitali economiche europee", *Impresa & Stato* 27 (1994), 9–51.

> de ce fait. Les foires italiennes sont les premières dans lesquelles se développent les grands rouages de la vie commerciale. C'est là que la première fois l'on rencontre des consuls, une jurisdiction spéciale des marchands, des usages particuliers en matière de paiements, de change, de faillites, etc.[10]

Given such historical background, the idea of focusing on the programmatic activity of the Milan Chamber appears emblematic also in another sense: it concerns not only a specific case of intertwinement between traditional skills, local culture and worldwide socioeconomic change, but also a typical case in which, as has been mentioned, cross-border interactions have always been and still are at the core of its socioeconomic and institutional *identity*.

In this respect, this study is intended, at the same time, as a sort of homage and an auspice as regards the everlasting role function of the city: a homage in relation to the anniversary of the (modern) foundation of its Chamber of Commerce, set up by means of a constitutional statute drafted by Cesare Beccaria almost exactly two hundred years ago, in 1786, and also an auspice, in relation to the need to create once again, at the close of the second millennium, a plausible (that is, based on a rationally testable discourse) and socially adequate (that is, based on fundamental needs) *constitutional* asset for overall western law–economy–society dynamics.

Milan as a Glocal Centre for Cross-border Interactions

Analysing the issues of private interest governance in Europe, Schmitter tentatively suggests that eventual outcomes will depend on competition between 'regionalization' and 'sectorialization' of EU decision making as well as the emergence of more 'direct' modes of policy implementation.[11] Taking EU 'top down' law policy devices into account, the fact that the Milan Chamber's 'proactive reaction' characterizes at present 'bottom up' socioeconomic dynamics is highly symptomatic. Of particular interest are the rate of

10 Pierre Huvelin, *Essai historique sour le droit des Marchés & des Foires* (Paris: A. Russeau ed., 1897), 279–80.

11 Philippe Schmitter, "The Future of Euro-Polity and its Impact upon Private Interest Governance within Member-States", in *Droit et Société*, 28 (1994), 659–75.

commercial interchange and the status of international business relations in the Milan metropolitan area.

As worldwide economic trends are far from being regular at present, and are likely to be quite contradictory in the future, these two aspects have been thus contextualized in order to promote a 'cognitive', rather than a 'statistical' action-oriented understanding.

> In 1992, the Milan area dealt with about 70% of all international imports and 54% of all local exports of the Lombardy region, as well as more than 25% of all imports and about 17% of all exports of Italy (Milano Produttiva, 1993). In the last few years commercial goods movement dropped.[12]

This evaluation of goods interchange has to be related to at least three other parameters: (a) the spreading of a networking economy, (b) the growing importance of service infrastructures, and (c) the cultural 'appeal' of 'country-specific' environment resources (that is, local knowledge and know-how). From this more complex evaluation framework, based not on the idea of a mere international financial/commercial competition, but on the idea of multifunctional 'glocal' interactions, a much more refined view of 'glocal' socioeconomic trends, as well as a clearer perspective of limits and potentials for enhancing the internationalization of the area has thus been obtained. In brief, it has been possible to draw a 'glocal' policy of the networking enterprise system in strategic terms. In accordance with these criteria, it seems of interest to outline some data recently gathered by various research centres.

Let us begin with data concerning the type and standard of international cooperation relations based, not on mere financial/commercial interchange only, but also on common projects, joint-ventures, high-tech transferrals, know-how intercommunications, services' cooperation and so on. Firstly, let us review the process of *externalization of local resources*. According to sample research conducted by Lombardy Unioncamere together with Lombardy Region in 1990, data show that in the Milan area only 17.5 per cent of local enterprises set up international 'agreements/relations' abroad.

A more refined telephone survey carried out on the same topic five years later by Ufficio Studi Directa – a research centre of the Milan Chamber – on a sample of the Milan area's enterprises, offers

12 Ufficio Studi CCIA di Milano, ed., "Milano Produttiva 1995", *Impresa & Stato*, Supplemento 30 (1995), 55.

a quite different picture. According to this survey, in 1995, out of 350 interviewed enterprises, 168 (48.2 per cent) set up at least one international initiative in the last three years (1992–5).[13]

From these data one could immediately argue that local enterprises are still insufficiently active in crossing their socioeconomic borders, although a change is apparent. To have a better view of such a change, it is therefore interesting to look also at the data concerning those 168 Milanese enterprises that declared they had set up one or more international initiatives. Among these enterprises, production relations (63 per cent), and trade relations (51.2 per cent), particularly through exclusive distribution, are more developed than technological (32.5 per cent) and financial (10 per cent) transferrals.

Altogether, the above data suggest that by now Lombard enterprises' international integration can be considered *intermediate*, but not really satisfying, expecially in advanced production sectors. This is mainly due to the fact that individual actions on the part of small firms are often problematic, while, in turn, 'spontaneous' activation towards internationalization is rather unlikely. Thus a promotion networking service infrastructure acting as 'subsidiary integrator' seems absolutely essential to improve the situation.

Let us turn now to the 'complementary' process: that of *attraction/interiorization of foreign resources*. According to the data gathered by 'Gruppo Class', in 1993 the number of large multinational enterprises settled in the Milan area was 496. The majority of them operate in high-tech and research sectors, in particular chemistry and pharmaceuticals (30.4 per cent). As regards their geographical origin, 70 per cent come from Western Europe, of which two-thirds are from EU countries. Major financial investors are US enterprises (25 per cent), followed by French (14.9 per cent) and German (14.3 per cent). If one compares these data with previous statistics, one immediately notices that this type of cross-border process slowed down considerably over the last few years. In any case it seems that foreign multinational enterprise do *not* intend to take on the new idea of 'internationalization' sketched above, but simply seek to exploit the 'gateway' position of the Milan area to have access to the Italian market.

These remarks are confirmed by more recent data gathered by Ufficio Studi Directa. In 1995, out of the 168 interviewed enterprises that were involved in one initiative at least, there were no

13 Ibid., 114.

enterprise fusions at all and very few joint ventures or acquisitions. In brief, there was a significant absence of what is commonly intended by the very notion of 'globalization'.[14] Undoubtedly, the above data suggest that the level of business interaction of foreign enterprises within the local economic system is rather low. If this is so, the need for the city to take advantage of infrastructural support to promote a cultural and communication framework that could stimulate a 'glocal' mutuality is immediately self-evident.

Interestingly, this task is likely to concern EU citizens basically, in fact, according to Gruppo Class data, within the overall *migration rate* in the area, the majority of foreign businessmen with positions of power in local enterprises in 1993 came from France (12.88 per cent), Germany (8.89 per cent) and England (6.44 per cent), followed by the USA (5.15 per cent) and Japan (2.11 per cent). Having said this, let us have a look now at another reference standard for current 'glocal' interactions evaluation: the demand for local infrastructural services on the part of foreign enterprises.[15]

Traditional services such as legal, fiscal and financial assistance (86.6 per cent) and management of payments and tax contributions (77.5 per cent) dominate the so-called 'outsourcing' services such as advertising and promotion (36 per cent), informatic services (39.1 per cent), projects and design (20.2 per cent) and market analysis (19.3 per cent). In other words, although the Milan area is an absolute leader in advanced tertiary services in Italy (almost one in four Italian business expert services are located in Milan), the market for these services is still relatively limited.

Chambers of Commerce as Infrastructure Providers for Cross-border Interactions

Chambers of Commerce Systems in Europe

The importance of the *ratio juris* of the Italian Chambers of Commerce system, as regards the evolutionary patterns of the European polycorporative infrastructural context, can be appreciated by considering it in a comparative perspective. According to formal–legal criteria, two different Chambers of Commerce systems, public and private, actually dominate the European scenario. By rule, 'public law' cameral systems are enforced in France, Germany,

14 Ibid., 122.

15 Ibid., 104.

Spain, Greece, Luxemburg, The Netherlands and Italy: here either economic (industry, commerce, agriculture and handicraft) entrepreneurs, personally, or enterprises, by means of their representatives, are compulsorily enrolled by law and pay a standard fee for the functioning of the Chamber. 'Private law' cameral models are enforced in Belgium, Denmark, Ireland, Portugal and England: here the same economic agents are not compulsorily enrolled and simply pay for the required services.

As the Italian law reform demonstrates, such a clear-cut unidimensional formalistic distinction does not seem to be up-to-date and in fact this is a matter of some debate at present. Taking on an extreme individualistic perspective, the 'public law' model in Spain has been declared unconstitutional recently, as the (post-francist) Spanish constitution does not allow any compulsory enrolment of an individual in a body. On the other hand, the 'private law' model in England led British Chambers' associations to set up, a few years ago, a double crediting and quality certification procedure, thus splitting the national system into two subsystems: that of Approved Chambers (relating to national standards) and that of Accredited Chambers (referring to European standards). In turn, the General Assembly of Eurochambers, the European representative organ of 29 national chambers' associations, representing altogether 1,200 local Chambers, strongly support the 'public law' model, as the public law model offers formal guarantees and uniform standards at both the social and the institutional level. As the above examples suggest, the problem of Chambers' public/private legitimation is by now a general issue that cannot be simply reduced either to a mere formal 'top down' investiture – for an empirical quality test is in any case more reliable than an official (paper law) recognition – or to a mere 'bottom up' particularistic individual (contractual) achievement, for a general public responsibility and social control is involved anyway.

From an organizational perspective, in fact, the main problem for Europe is to 'add global value' to the core system of the European economy – 16,000,000 highly diversified, territorially rooted, small enterprises – while synergizing it with local branches of multinational enterprises (about 12,000). In turn, from a political–institutional point of view, European business activity is moving towards new spaces (the so-called 'regional Euro-clusters' as well as 'world economy') irrespective of national border or official frameworks. Therefore European Chambers cannot cope with the above problem unless they orient their services towards *modular* cross-border action systems.

This orientation is precisely what the Milan Chamber is currently doing, as demonstrated by, among other initiatives, the promotion and constitution (together with Frankfurt, Paris and Madrid Chambers) of a 'Euro Centre' provided with a unique procedure for enterprises' registration. Such a procedure, in fact, exemplifies a prospective 'rationalization' (low transaction costs and univocal operational logic) in both public/private administrative and socioeconomic matters. Thus, if one considers the above mentioned 'public law' and 'private law' cameral systems according to a substantial criterion, one easily realizes how much old-styled corporatist structures and functions are still operating in many countries. Let us look at two emblematic cases: the French and Dutch models.

French Chambers of Commerce are typical 'public law' corporations. More precisely, they are territorially decentralized state organs granted relative autonomy and functional 'speciality'. They act as a sort of 'consular corps' of the state. French Chambers deal with four main work areas: information (to business community); consultancy (to state organs); management of local infrastructures (such as 121 airports, 144 harbours, 88 general warehouses, 30 congress halls, 98 transport stations) and training (French Chambers have the second largest educational network in France after the public education system). They own a unified national data bank, Telexport, and support business activity by means of 180 documentation centres, 22 technoscientific agencies (Arist), 30 libraries, 34 Euro-Info-Centres, 120 local data banks and about 2,500 publications. The whole system includes 62 local Chambers, organized in 21 regional Chambers (CRCI), represented in a national assembly (ACECI). Besides this structure, French Chambers act throughout a number of interconsular associations.

At EU level, French Chambers' organization and performance is of a high standard indeed. However, their current Napoleonic structure appears more and more questionable vis-à-vis the needs of contemporary economic dynamics. In 1995, an official report was presented to the government[16] suggesting the reinforcing of centric-oriented patterns and a 'top down' hierarchy, by merging local Chambers at department level, mainly in order to reduce costs. Needless to say, the report did not obtain the consensus of either

16 Gerdani Report. Hubert Flahault. "Le camera di commercio francesi", *Impresa & Stato* 30 (1995), 37–41.

local Chambers or the business community owing to the lack of strategic flexibility.

Dutch Chambers of Commerce also belong to the 'public law' model, but, as in the case of the new Italian system, only partially. They perform a double mission: promotion and management. Promotion concerns either local territorial/commercial infrastructural planning (in particular airports, harbours and waterways) or Dutch international trade. For this purpose, the Chambers created a number of 'Trade Clubs' of Dutch corporations operating in foreign markets of strategic importance (ex-colonies), as well as data banks such as the Eastern Europe Desk. Management concerns typical public anagraphical services such as the keeping of either enterprises' (about 75,000) and cooperatives' registers, or non-profit foundations' and voluntary associations' rolls. Also relevant is the power to confer commercial licences as well as professional licenses. Chambers' governing boards include, in addition to the Chambers' members an equal rate (20 per cent) of representatives of large firms, small firms and trade unions. At national level there exists only a private association, a sort of Chambers' Union. Although a coordinating structure has been created recently between Chambers and local state institutions, major structural and functional problems for Chambers' activity stem from the updated competence system. In The Netherlands, in fact, one could count three or four economic regions, at most, and 32 regional Chambers. Given such territorial/functional conditions, it has been hypothesized that a proper networking structuration – to reduce costs and improve quality – might offer a more advanced, plausible and socially adequate way out.

Of course, the scant observations made above do not do justice to the differences and problems occurring in other European countries, as well as the range of overall action of European Chambers at local, national and international level. There does not exist a standardized typology of cameral services, as there does not exist a uniform structuration. Interestingly, this state of affairs is not considered a negative condition at all, for it permits various degrees of autonomy as well as the chance to create partnerships. Thus this also explains why a number of vertical ('top down' and 'bottom-up') and horizontal, public/private, initiatives have been set in motion in order to develop mutual international cooperation.

As far as examples of 'top down' networks are concerned, one could mention the decision of the EU Commission to place some Euro-Info-Centres within Chambers' infrastructures; to include the

Chambers as economic advisers of BC-Net (Business Cooperation Network); and to promote the so-called 'Europartenariat', a sort of international periodical convention of small and medium-size firms aiming at strengthening economic cooperation in underdeveloped regions.

As regards 'bottom up' networks, one could mention the number of initiatives in any business matter involving public authorities, the setting up of 'contact and mutual support' cameral offices in Brussels and, above all, the creation of Eurochambers, the representative organ of 29 national Chambers' associations altogether representing 1,200 local Chambers. Indeed, Eurochambers is the largest multinational infrastructural network for business in Europe, so that an increasing number of governments (especially Eastern European and ex-USSR) are showing a great interest in its institutional organizational chart.[17]

Yet 'horizontal' networks are – and will be in the future – far more relevant. At present about 1,400 national Chambers are associated within the EU territory: 1,400 action systems, microphysically spread and articulated all over the continent, serving about 15 million enrolled small enterprises, that is, 70 per cent of overall European workplaces. In a near future, in a prospective European Union of more than 20 countries, it will be *politically* quite impossible to realize any vertically linked centre–periphery self-referential (that is, inter/intracameral) cooperation. Only territorially decentralized polycentric infrastructures, able to cross any border horizontally, could face the challenge. And this is what already gives the Chambers a leading role in prospective socioeconomic and political–institutional 'engineering'.

If one carefully considers the above horizontal (increasingly public/private) framework, one cannot but note an embryonic trend towards the spreading in Europe of cameral *olonic* systems. The olonic model, as the Greek etymology of the word 'olon', 'all', suggests, is an all-embracing organizational set, the 'moral density' of which is due to the coupling of a number of different interrelations, each one gifted with high-level self-regulatory mechanisms but also able to put in motion efficient mutual cooperation strategies, in view of common aims and shared results.

The olonic model does not have predefined functional boundaries. It is structurally flexible by definition. It is not a mere joint venture: it

17 Thomas MacPherson. "Le camere italiane ne sistema europeo", *Impresa & Stato* 25 (1994), 22–24.

is a veritable institutional organization, a group community of tasks and resources, in which each unit acts as a totality when dealing with a 'top down' system's issues and as a part in 'bottom up' internal interactions. Because of the intertwining of such patterns – the short-circuiting of units (whole–part) *double citizenship* and *mutual subsidiarity* – the olonic model realizes a high capacity of internal/external reaction, self-assertion and evolutionary adaptation. At present, the olonic model helps to describe certain sophisticated features of the so-called 'virtual corporations' such as Apple, Microsoft and Benetton. But there is hardly any doubt that it could be usefully applied particularly to industrial districts of small and medium-size enterprises, by rule, insufficiently coordinated, and to any sort of infrastructures.[18] In the evolutionary scale of organizations, in fact, it has reached the level of matching both 'top down' and 'bottom up' issues, and therefore is able to resolve the main problem of polycentrism and/or polycorporatism (horizontal and vertical *acephaly*) without reducing their own potentials for autonomy.

The trend should not be surprising: the search for new organizational models for integration at EU level is indeed under way. A significant 'great leap forward' in this area can be seen in the decline of the updated (Rome Treaty) Socioeconomic Committee and the proposal of the new (Maastricht Treaty) Committee for Regions in which the role of metropolitan areas is emphasized. This suggests that also European Chambers will become involved in the creation of a new type of socioinstitutional framework based on a specific *territorial interest governmentality*, for metropolitan areas are a typical case of 'organic' intertwining of local resources and political organization. As the president of the Milan Chamber put it:

> Our prospective task will be therefore to set up the necessary linkage between the 'space' of enterprises and the space of territorial maps, of town planning, of administrative expertise [for] besides a Europe of Regions ... there emerges the reality, not yet fully accepted and metabolized, of a 'Europe of great cities' that recalls not only experiences of the past (the role of the city-state in various ages of European history) but also that of present times, such as, for example, Hong Kong or Singapore.[19]

18 Cesare Saccani, "Sistemi olonici per aziende virtuali", *Impresa & Stato* 29 (1955).

19 Piero Bassetti, "Il cameralismo tra regionalismo ed europeismo", *Impresa & Stato* 25 (1994), 9–13.

Within such a prospective scenario (that clearly includes a new idea of 'the wealth of the nations'), one understands the importance of the proposal just made by the Milan Chamber of Commerce: the creation of a special club among European Chambers of major European cities, a polycentric network constitutionally oriented to promote joint *political* guidelines to favour the European business community as a whole at local, national, continental and world level; a polycentric network, indeed, but *not at all* acephalous for, because of its territorial/functional nature, it will act as an all-embracing Janus-headed territorial/functional gatekeeper.

Interestingly, the club's protocol, signed in 1993 by the Chambers of Amsterdam, Frankfurt, Madrid, Milan and Paris, states that political and economic changes are at a turning-point worldwide, so that leading European Chambers must express their full potential in order to enlarge their *institutional* mission from the local to the global perspective. In this respect, a direct reference to Janus, the roman God of *nomic* (normatively regulated) cross-border (city-state) interactions, is thus absolutely relevant here.

The Chambers of Commerce System in Italy

As the insights sketched above suggest, it seems that traditional pyramid-like structuration of European socioeconomic and institutional settings might give way to a sort of temple-like social architecture, in which a number of (ordered) columns realize a mutual (horizontal) coordination design and trabeations symbolize the *unitas multiplex* of the given social body.

Trends towards economic and institutional 'glocalization' however, are still strongly mediated by national infrastructures. Therefore positive organizational roles and functions of these national infrastructures at cross-border level should not be underestimated. As this is also the case with national Chambers of Commerce systems, it seems opportune to give a more detailed idea of their extraordinary operational relevance by reviewing the organization chart and missions of Unioncamere, the general representative organ of Italian Chambers of Commerce.

According to the Unioncamere 1994 Annual Report, the Italian cameral system is composed of the following (public/private) substructures: 102 Chambers; 119 decentred Chambers' seats; 23 goods stock exchanges; 43 contracting halls; 37 technology of commerce laboratories; 53 arbitration seats; 124 special enterprises; 50 Euro-Info-Centres (Eurosportelli); eight general storehouses; 985 partnerships in various business sectors; 19 regional cameral unions;

two interregional cameral unions; 18 regional centres for international trade; 15 services agencies (enterprises, associations, consortiums, research centres and so on) of general interest for the cameral system as a whole; 50 Italian Chambers' seats abroad; one Unioncamere seat in Brussels; more than 80 Chambers' libraries (with a total of 852,500 volumes plus 14,300 reviews, some of which are quite rare). Additionally, Chambers and Chambers' representatives are members of a number of banks' governing boards (for example, in Banco di Napoli alone, 30 Chambers are represented). They also run a number of specialized offices (for example, 94 offices for business training); a countless number of infrastructural partnerships in almost any business matter (commercial exibitions, credit lines, EU projects and so on); influential publications (such as the review *Impresa & Stato* and the weekly review *Sistema Italia*); special professional law lists (of gas and electric contractors and public transport drivers, for example) and rolls of special enterprises (such as those involving toxic waste) for consumers' protection. The Chambers' system's total revenue in 1993 was L.1,479,141 million.

The organization is based on the so-called 'praesidium' logic: each seat realizes 'knots' of networks in relation to the general needs of economic sectors of local industrial districts. For this purpose Unioncamere's main missions concern:

- local economic sectors,
- the cameral system,
- market regulation,
- institutional relations, and
- internationalization of business activity (basically, small and medium-size firms).

Each one of these missions is fulfilled by means of a cluster of networking systems:

- a special enterprises system,
- a partnership system,
- a regulatory system,
- a public relations system, and an
- internationalization action system.

The cameral special enterprises system is a network of (private law, 65 per cent self-financed) units whose aim is to create or implement any sort of service infrastructure in areas such as transport, marketing, training, techno-laboratoires, data banks and so on. The network's total budget in 1993 was about L.237.3 billion.

The Chambers' partnership system is a networking tool with public and/or private agents devoted to finance and to promoting basic infrastructural services, at the moment not lucrative for private investors, that nevertheless might offer a favourable 'habitat' for prospective business activities (harbours, roads, scientific research, commercial centres, environment). The total amount of money put into these joint ventures on the part of the Chambers was L.365,732.8 million in 1993.

As has already been said, the cameral regulatory system includes 23 goods stock exchanges, 43 contracting halls and 53 arbitration seats. However, new 'specialized' (sectorial) arbitration seats are increasing also, especially in housing matters. Arbitration seats enforce the so-called classic 'institutional' (predefined) arbitration rules. Interestingly, these rules match the new Italian law reform on arbitration recently enhanced in order to prevent 'attacks or interferences that might undermine the proceeding's efficacy'.[20] The same law is also specifically devoted to dealing with international arbitration and the execution in Italy of foreign arbitration decisions. The number of arbitration proceedings, with the exception of Milan, is quite low (three or four cases per year in each seat) and, contrary to common opinion, is *not* rising.

The cameral public relations system is based on the amount of information gathered by law, put at the disposal of the public or elaborated by the Chambers. The system aims at interfacing with local public institutions in particular, in order to realize an 'institutional mediation' between economy and state at territorial level.

Needless to say, the cameral internationalization business action system is considered at present a major Chambers issue. Efforts in this field are made in two main directions: (a) improving and strengthening intercameral cross-border relations, projects and so on between Italian Chambers, Italian Chambers abroad and foreign Chambers, and (b) supporting the internationalization of Italian enterprises and made-in-Italy commercialization, with particular reference to small firms. Consequently, Chambers participate, with funding and data, in various programmes set up by ad hoc cross-border infrastructures such as AssoCamerEstero and Eurochambers.

20 Unioncamere, *Rapporto 1994 sul sistema camerale* (Draft) (Rome, 1994), 1–423.

The aim is to offer a service which is both specific and systematic. For this purpose, cross-border interactions are promoted either as sectorial policies or as partnerships. Sectorial policies concern intercameral data banks, commercial fairs, legal consultancy, assistance and certification, and so on. Legal consultancy is a service on legislation matters for regional and national as well as EU institutions. Legal assistance concerns procedural inquiries about requirements concerning establishment of business and environment protection documentation. Legal certification is mainly about quality tests. In turn, partnerships with public and private, domestic or foreign agents are devoted, as mentioned above, to finance or promote basic infrastructural services, exchanges and linkages (that is, training, development cooperation, import/export and technology innovation). Main areas of intervention are eastern Europe, the ex-USSR, Latin America and the Pacific Rim.

As one can easily understand, the above networking systems, and internationalization action systems in particular, are tailored to enterprises' needs not in generic terms, but in the precise sense that they provide selective (*country-specific*) technical/functional solutions for the cases (or agents) in point. Additionally, more and more such 'country-specific' solutions are offered as prospective 'virtual' solutions; that is, as projects. Processes of cooperation and simultaneous engineering are thus becoming a real issue. Consequently, cameral cross-border infrastructures oscillating between foreign 'demands' and domestic 'offers', and vice versa, are by necessity implementing new organizational patterns and the spreading of veritable 'outsourcing' organizational systems[21] in almost any business fieldwork.

If one considers that in Italy, out of 119,022 business service infrastructures, 14,378 are located in Milan (12.1 per cent),[22] and that the Milan Chamber is a leading model (either for the Italian cameral system or for those infrastructures) as regards the promotion of the above new organizational devices, one immediately realizes how much the growth of the Italian economy at the local, national and international level owes to its advanced strategic policy.

21 Charles Sabel, "Le nuove camere di Commercio fra riforma delle istituzioni e prospettiva Europea", *Atti del Convegno* (Milan, 1994).

22 Ufficio Studi CCIA di Milano, ed., "Milano Produttiva 1995".

Milan Chambers Abroad and the 'Foreign Centre'

To complete the picture of the Italian Chambers of Commerce organizational set and, more particularly, to gain clearer perception of the proactive impact of the Milan Chamber's strategic policy on overall Italian Chambers' activities at the international level, two emblematic cameral infrastructures have to be brought to the fore: one located in Milan; the other spread all around the world.

The first was set up in 1969 by all Chambers located in the Lombardy region, and then restructured in 1976, to deal specifically with cross-border legal/business relations concerned with the region: the Centro Estero Camere di Commercio Lombarde (hereinafter, Foreign Centre). The second is the result of a spontaneous development of cameral halls, set up by Italian migrants from the last decades of nineteenth century in different continents according to different local conditions and personal attitudes. These cameral halls were legally regulated (but scarcely appreciated) by the Italian government in 1918, instrumentally controlled during the Fascist regime, informally related to Unioncamere in 1954, officially recognized as a part of Italian Chambers' organization in 1970 and finally restructured as a proper cameral networking cross-border system in 1980: the Camere Italiane Estero (hereinafter Italian Chambers Abroad).

The Foreign Centre is a private-law agency, supported by public funding but also self-financing. It serves either public or private institutions (the Lombardy Region, Lombardy Unioncamere, regional Unions, banks, enterprises and so on) as regards cross-border issues that are related to the internationalization of the regional market system, but not necessarily inherent to, or activated by, a mere market logic. Its activity basically concerns coordination programmes and organizational contacts (such as international relations, fairs, special projects and joint ventures). The work areas are information, consultancy, promotion and formation. Major functional specialization concerns the data bank on international commercial law, technical standard rules and quality certification procedures. By combining service mission and specialism, the Foreign Centre is able to organize, for example, training courses on international strategic marketing, quality planning and management and small/medium-sized enterprises' technological development; or consultancy on international legal management of trade marks and patents, credit legal operations, analysis of international treaties (for example, to exclude double taxation regimes), fiscal planning, legal arrangements on money transferrals, legal requirement for settling a business abroad, and so on.

As one can see, the Foreign Centre supports regional agents and orients regional resources towards internationalization, not according to traditional import/export interchange competition modelling, but rather – as the Milan Chamber's strategic policy suggests – according to informational collaboration to create favourable conditions to foster networks, linkages and partnership at a *normative* level. For this reason it is a typical case of an intercameral public/private joint venture aiming at 'transubstantiating' economic needs into institutional performances.

The case of the Italian Chamber Abroad is totally different and extremely intriguing. Here a veritable organizational and cultural short-circuit occurred in the last decade.[23] Up to the 1970s, one could speak of Italian Chambers Abroad as a cluster of self-created, fragmented, unconnected units, located in those cities in which historically Italian migrants settled (Montevideo, Buenos Aires, São Paulo, Istanbul, New York, Marseilles, London, Paris) or where Italian enterprises had the chance to create a stable business (Caracas, Toronto, Tunis and so on). One could also speak of long-lasting prejudices and underevaluation with regard to their socioeconomic potential, as well as of an apparent marginalization on the part of ICE, the Italian Institute for Foreign Commerce set up in 1926 by the Fascist regime. From 1980 onwards, however, a radical development took place: under the pressure of market competition, and by analysing the challenges of economic change to exploit any opportunity, it became apparent that the settlement of Italians abroad – the Italian 'diaspora' – could be conceived, not as a sign of national 'weakness', but on the contrary as one of the most powerful (cultural, demographic, political, and so on) *vital* resources of the socioeconomic dynamics of the same motherland.

This sort of Copernican cultural revolution was immediately related to the idea of defining the 'Italian diaspora' as a proper institution, as a real socioeconomic collective subject: that is, as a polycentric, multilateral, flexible, networking actor. As soon as this intuition was refined, the current economicist notion of 'Italy system' was reversed: 'Italy system' appeared as a broader social environment basically connected by means of worldwide relational/

23 Enrico Pozzi, "Verso la rete: l'esperienza storica del sistema delle camere italiane all'estero", in *Impresa e Stato*, ed. Piero Bassetti (Bologna: Il Mulino, 1995).

informational ties: communicative codes (rather than mere territorial contiguities). Finally, the intertwining of both concepts, led to the hypothesis of an operational strategic project based on a shared worldwide understanding: the development of the Italian socio-economic system at the international level as a veritable local globalizing entity.

The project has thus been enhanced de facto without any aggressive aim. Being based on shared communicative actions, it excludes neither 'top down' nor centre/periphery 'imperial globalism': it simply suggests a virtual confederative model of what might be called a 'network of glocal meta-systems'. It is also interesting to note that the convergence of economic, social and cultural issues, in which the flow of information is not less important than the transferral of material goods, now leads to a rethinking of the ethical rationale of networking business exchange (actors' identity and mutual agreements) within the Italian business community either abroad or in the motherland.

From an organizational perspective, a major outcome of the project has been, first, the financial support of the Italian goverment (rising from L.400 million in 1980 to L.7.5 billion in 1992) and then the creation in 1987 of an autonomous public/private cameral infrastructure – AssoCamerEstero, the Association of Chambers Abroad – acting as a diplomatic centre and operational 'knot' between/within the glocal dimension of the 'Italy system'. Thanks to its services, basically a real-time electronic data bank system contemporaneously operating on local, intercameral and global networks, in five years only (1987–92) AssoCamerEstero's membership rose from 14,536 to 23,000 and the self-financing budget from L.2,381 billion to L11,529 billion. Significantly, the leading role played by the Milan Chamber in the rising success of this new cameral infrastructure is absolutely uncontested.

Milan Chamber of Commerce as a Networking Infrastructure for Europe

Cross-border Interactions as a 'Constitution' Problem

What has been said so far could not be omitted. It is not a mere scholarly digression from the central topic of this study. On the contrary, it is the necessary 'cultural background' and 'cognitive frame of reference' – the so-called 'understanding net' in Habermas' term – for approaching the local experience that we are now going to discuss in detail. Nothing of a social context can be correctly understood unless the past and the present are analytically intertwined. Here and now, as at any time and everywhere, only a scientific account of the historical mainstreams enables us to cast light on the contours of the issues under scrutiny while offering a reliable analytical entry point.

Indeed, as one may have already realized, the above account leads us to a general socioeconomic and political–institutional framework in which not only traditional bureaucratic nation-state apparatuses, but also certain traits of current neocorporatist infrastructures are called into question by the emergence of more advanced models and highly problematic social needs.

Altogether, contrary to Dezalay's and Garth's suggestion, neither an alleged 'Big Bang' nor generational warfare among legal professionals endowed with special 'virtues' come to the fore as pivotal tools in 'constructing the market' of contemporary society.[24] Rather, the discussion just left open the problem of how to manage in actual practice the increasing *constitutional* insecurity (and transaction costs) of current cross-border socioeconomic interactions. Thus could cross-border interactions create conditions and criteria for a prospective 'new economic order'? Is there a case or a project somewhere that, by taking cross-border issues as a problem-solving and action-oriented frame of reference, might point out a workable 'treatment' for economic risk and legal insecurity in modern society? The strategic policy of the Chamber of Commerce of Milan is a tentative answer to these questions.

The Strategic Policy of the Chamber of Commerce of Milan

Both in theory and in practice, the programmatic activity of the Milan Chamber of Commerce is a sort of 'proactive reaction' to the socioeconomic and political–institutional trends and problems sketched above. Leafing through its official documents and reports, looking at its practice in context, one cannot but realize that, since the early 1980s, the Milan Chamber has been working to respond

24 Yves Dezalay and Bryant Garth, "Merchants of Law as Moral Entrepreneurs: Constructing International Justice from the Competition for Transnational Business Disputes", *Law and Society Review* 29, no. 1 (1995), 27–64.

to global/local changes according to a step-by step, highly refined strategy.

The starting point, of course, has been – and still is – the chaotic Italian context, which epitomizes almost *in vitro* any sort of western disordered experience. In the last decades, in particular, limits, imbalances, disfunctions and so on of economic and institutional structures in Italy have become absolutely unbearable for Italian society at large. Firstly, it became apparent that the lack of an advanced infrastructural service system capable of dealing with the needs of local and transnational businesses in modernized industrial districts was an important handicap.[25]

At the same time, the seriousness of the crisis of the nation-state also became apparent. As the president of the Chamber put it:

> The dilemma is clear: on the one hand, it is meaningless to try to revitalize this type of State-form, on the other hand, it is impossible to do without any sort of State whatever it is, being closed, as we will be, between a dangerous political anomy and the indisponiblity of trustworthy administrative reforms.[26]

Thirdly, it became evident that, in view of the challenges of worldwide market competition and the EU unification policy, the process of economic and legal interactions between citizens and businesses could no longer be treated as a matter of mere 'top down' laissez faire.

Moving on from these 'competition disadvantages', the Chamber developed a preliminary project based on two basic theoretical/practical ideas. On the one hand, it was maintained that formal–legal rules (state paper law) do not necessarily define and/or guarantee any more either functional or performative values of a given process, for the most significant criteria to measure actual value of a process is rather a test of its efficacy/efficiency standard in comparison with other processes. Consequently, *comparative quality test* criteria had to be applied to service infrastructures also, particularly in view to the rise, for the first time in Europe, of a real infrastructural market system, a 'free' commercialization of infrastructural services.

25 Antonio Saba, *Il modello italiano. La specializzazione flessibile e i distretti industriali.*

26 Piero Bassetti, "Verso l'Europa", *Impresa & Stato* 19 (1992), 12–15.

On the other hand, the social impact of asymmetric and asynchronic logic of the so-called 'semi-autonomous sociolegal orders' or 'autopoietic systems' vis-à-vis official legal and economic systems was taken into serious consideration, as well as the concurrent erosion of traditional binary codes between market and state at the structural and infrastructural level.[27] In other words, given the complex interaction of legal and economic pluralism in Italy (as elsewere), the *polycentric* and *interactional* nature of socioeconomic and political/institutional dynamics has been fully recognized.

Needless to say, once the above ideas were made clear, the project of a Chamber of Commerce acting as a *networking infrastructure* to serve the business community in any sort of 'cross-border' matter was at hand, at least in theory. The adoption of a type of reasoning and decision making based on the very notion of cross-border relations – to be understood in the broadest sense, that is with regard to any matter and in relation to any context – or, if one prefers, the overcoming and dismissal of the mere formal notions of (univocal) 'citizenship', 'belonging', 'membership' and so on, made a further contribution to refining and improving the project. In fact, the notion was not conceived as an indicator of the traditional 'vocational calling' of the city of Milan only. As a service infrastructure, the Chamber depicted *itself* as a veritable 'cross-border' action system also.

To the extent that this 'reflexive' attitude was put into action, the Chamber's 'positioning' was in turn theoretically and practically clarified: as a 'seat', as a 'seed', as a 'seal'. In synthesis, the meaning of such items is as follows:

- As a *seat*, the Chamber acts as a sort of round table system, giving access, directing and treating cross-cutting issues that in any case need a complex mediation of complex decision making. In this sense, the Chamber acts as a cross-border political agency, specializing in a method: 'administration by design'.
- As a *seed*, the Chamber acts as a sort of coupling-pin system, but in order to disseminate cross-cutting communications and issues – inputs, outputs, feedbacks – of a number of functionally differentiated and often loosely interconnected units. In this sense, it acts as a cross-border technical agency, specializing in a procedure: 'integrative networking management'.

27 Vittorio Olgiati, *Process and Policy of Legal Professionalization in Europe.*

- As a *seal*, the Chamber acts as a visible sign of a sort of *pactus foederis* – a synergic 'constitution' – between different forces, placed in different work areas and aiming at different issues, but all compelled to interact by the same insecurity and risk. In this sense, the Chamber acts as a cross-border regulatory agency, specializing in a result: 'socio-economic order'.

Trying to play the above multidimensional roles or functions, as a 'tuning' device at the crossing of a number of different systems, the Milan Chamber perceived that a further step was absolutely essential: a radical change of its formal official legal constitution, a law reform of its own updated statute. This is precisely what has been formally achieved by virtue of the enforcement of the new Law 29 December 1993 n.580.

The Normative Asset of Chambers of Commerce in Italy

The Law 580/1993 on the Chamber of Commerce system in Italy is to a very large extent a result of the policy enhanced by the Milan Chamber over the last few decades. Indeed, its normative rationale cannot be fully understood unless one compares it with the theoretical and practical guidelines described above.

Under the rule of previous corporatist law – not by chance enforced in 1934, that is under Fascist corporatism – Chambers of Commerce in Italy were conceived in legal terms as a sort of 'economic prefectures' acting at territorial level as suppletive (instrumental) public devices in matters such as certification, registration and control of economic activity. Chambers' traditional jurisdiction (Court of Arbitration) was relatively limited, owing to the dominant position of state courts. Beyond workaday performances, autonomous initiatives were also quite limited to internal particularistic concerns. In short: the Chambers suffered from scarce independence, insufficient representativeness and limited spheres of action.

Reversing such a state of affairs, the new Law 580/1993 now states that Italian Chambers of Commerce constitute a system of autonomous institutions performing functions of general interest to serve the economic system at territorial and functional level (Art.1). The new Chambers' *institutional* nature is emphasized by two pivotal tools that radically exclude any confusion with old-styled corporatist service infrastructures: structural/functional independent orientation to general aims and 'bottom up' political autonomy in both public and private fieldwork. Within this frame of reference, in turn, the Chambers' institutional autonomy emphasizes public/private cameral role/functions, *without* determining their actual performances. Autonomy, therefore, is basically assumed as a strategic orientation standard. It implies (a) independent statutory and legislative powers, (b) independent tutelage and representation of internal general interests, (c) independent financial revenue and spending management, (d) independent and alternative jurisdictional activity, and – last but not least – (e) an independent programmatic policy.

In accordance with the above self-regulation principles, Chambers' functions are *not* listed by the law: they are limited neither by disciplinary competences nor by systemic functional differentiation. Generally speaking, they concern the following main areas:

- any sort of (private) functions to support and promote business's general interest;
- subsidiary (public) functions in administrative and economic matters concerning business activity;
- delegated (public) functions concerning a variety of socioeconomic issues;
- ascribed public functions based on international conventions;
- market regulatory functions (statutory, jurisdictional and so on);
- consultative functions before public/private bodies;
- public registration functions.

As is easily realized, altogether Chambers' action can be performed at three main levels: activation/promotion, study/consultation and resolution/enforcement – exactly the three 'patterns of policy formation' that, as we have seen, characterize neocorporatist intermediary infrastructures acting as autonomous *political* agents. In order to deal with the above issues, Chambers are allowed:

- to set up and manage autonomously any structure of general economic interest at territorial and/or functional level;
- to take part in any local, national and/or international structures, projects and so on concerned with, or useful for, Chambers' general aims;
- to set up their own special economic enterprises.

All the above, however, can be fully performed in practice only with the wider support and larger participation of those who are interested, and only if a clear 'differential' quality standard is (comparatively) attainable; that is, by adopting a proper efficacy/effectiveness (not mere legalistic) criterion. Therefore, in order to realize in practice *general* interests of the economic system, the new law, for the first time in modern Italy, but rescuing an ancient tradition, allows any subgroups of the local business community to participate in proportion to the importance of their respective economic sector to the governing board (the Giunta) of the same Chambers. Thus, by virtue of such practical arrangement, Chambers' institutional autonomy as regards their own programmatic activity immediately transubstantiated into the specific form of business community's self-government.

The insertion of the business community within the Chambers' independent structure/function and autonomous policy making is likely to produce important *political* consequences as regards market regulation, also at cross-border level. This insertion realizes:

- a change in emphasis in the *servus*/service relationship,
- a substantial reassessment of public and private issues,
- a direct integration of enterprises' workforces, and
- a clear institutional input towards a networking socioeconomic regulation.

As far as the *servus*/service relationship is concerned, the Chambers take on the logic of 'serving the client' – the business community – in accordance with the most advanced organizational theorizing, that is, taking it as the pivotal *internal* component of the structure. With regard to reassessment and integration of socioeconomic variables, the Chambers' policy is strongly oriented to exploiting territorial resources as a whole: territorial localism, local knowledge of small and medium-size businesses, in particular – is considered a resource in itself and a multiplier of the added value of the area in any cross-border relation. For the purpose, a mere formal distinction between public and private institutions is simply inconceivable. And, in fact, the Chambers now act as both public and private (for example, vertical–horizontal and territorial–functional) agents.

As regards the institutional/regulatory action, the Chambers' policy aims to promote something more refined than a mere *lex mercatoria*. As is well known, *lex mercatoria* is not only a 'local' legal system, a particular legal sphere within the normative domain, concerning particular issues, techniques, actors, expertise and so on.

It is also a deterritorialized casuistic legal system. The Chambers do not underestimate it. Thus, besides the collection of merchant rules, the Chambers' role as a proper 'special jurisdiction' is stressed, dealing with business matters by means of 'specialized' decision-making systems (arbitration, conciliation and business ethics), both as alternative means to state court and state proceedings and as an autonomous/subsidiary (contextualized/institutionalized) market regulatory agency.

Altogether, these items and their relation to the above functions give evidence of the Chambers' priorities: (a) to serve the economic system as a *technostructure*, (b) to regulate and control market relations as a *jurisdictional forum* and (c) to contribute to the design of a new socioinstitutional asset by giving proofs of the possibility of a *new state form*. The logic that drives the Chambers' activities toward these priorities is based on the potentials offered by a *mixture* of the following:

- structural/functional and territorial frameworks, linked by means of a variety of praesidia – seats, networks, laboratories, consortiums and so on;
- vertical/horizontal and reticular interventions, linked by means of a number of, for example, financial, technical and normative substructures;
- operational procedures and guidelines for complex decision making and dispute resolution (contractual, participatory, authoritative, subsidiary, and so on).

Finally, by activating the entire set of the above devices, any Chamber is able to act as a *synthetic* interlocutor vis-à-vis any public or private, local, national or international authority.

As one can easily understand from the above sketchy picture, the Law 580/1993 on the Italian Chamber of Commerce system marks a real turning-point for the overall Italian infrastructure. In fact, it formally recognizes in a systematic and highly refined way a cluster of evolutionary organizational advances that were absolutely necessary for Italian socioeconomic and institutional systems in order to face the challenges of current global/local economic and legal pluralism. Significantly, however, there is hardly any doubt that the law also reflects the most advanced polycorporativist patterns of modern western society. Not surprisingly, therefore, it now constitutes a reference standard for the overall Chambers of Commerce systems in the rest of Europe also.

The Dialectics of the Milan Chamber of Commerce

The Issue

The above discussion offered a general account of the way a networking infrastructure such as the Chamber of Commerce, Industry, Agriculture and Handicraft of Milan contributes *empirically* to processes of structuration of cross-border socioeconomic interactions at the local, national and international level: by implementing a strategic 'glocal' policy by means of institutionalized, and 'glocally' generalizable, coordination mechanisms.

As we have seen, the Chamber's strategic 'glocal' policy not only condenses de facto most advanced and innovative organizational patterns of contemporary institutional theorizing, and develops de facto an all-embracing action system to manage most problematic socioeconomic needs and cross-border interactions; it also tries to suggest a workable way out of the dilemma of constitutional insecurity of the business community: to increase the value of local/territorial resources as a condition of global/functional excellence.

Yet it is one thing to draw up a refined programme and work out a well-designed organization chart, and quite another to assess empirically their actual functioning. To put it more broadly: is the current socioeconomic conjuncture, at the local, national and international level, facilitating the Chamber's efforts? How do the institutional settings react to them? What intervening variables are determining the context? And what sort of subinfrastructures are more fit to deal with them? What follows offers a selective picture of the way these questions are dealt with empirically.

Type and Standards of the Milan Chamber's Subinfrastructures

As a first general insight, one might argue that to raise the question about how and to what extent the Milan Chamber is realizing its strategic policy is an oddity, at best. No one can doubt, in fact, that the enforcement of the new Law 580/1993 marked de facto at once the accomplishment and the advancement of its original project. No one can doubt that the overall impact of the Chamber's roles and functions has been and still is de facto absolutely significant for the remodernization of the Italian socioeconomic system. Lastly, no one can doubt that the logic of its networking framework has become a reference model also at EU level, for any of its single units, as has been said, is specifically tailored to deal with the hardcore (millions of small firms) of EU business cross-border interactions.

According to the 1995 Chamber Service Guide, the Milan Chamber is a network system composed of the following units: a central seat; six subsidiary seats in the city; seven seats in the metropolitan area, of which one acts as a World Trade Centre; eight polyfunctional offices; and seven special enterprises (CED, Arbitration Chamber, Isdaci, Eurosportello, Formaper, Promos, Cisgem). First, the Chamber offers typical 'public law' (administrative) security and credential services, that is the keeping of enterprises and economic operators' rolls; handicraft and commercial business and agents' lists; professional expertise lists; special licensing registers; documents, archives and legalization forms; inspection and enforcement services. Besides these 'traditional' services, a great number of public/private (autonomous) promotion services are offered also, concerning in particular (a) market regulation, (b) assistance, (c) trade and foreign relations, (d) credit support, (e) information and the data bank, (f) research and (g) training.

On closer inspection, however, one might wonder about positive/negative conditions that the Chamber's operational substructures are facing at present. In short, what sort of 'transpositionings' or 'adjustments' related to 'glocal' issues are now on the agenda of the Milan Chamber? All cameral enterprise promotion services are not only specifically oriented but also functionally differentiated in order to serve business internationalization. Let us consider, for example, three types of fieldwork: assistance, trade and foreign relations, and information and data bank services.

Enterprise assistance services relate to any issue concerning the entire life of an enterprise activity: know-how data bank; administrative requirements; environment information, technologistic support, meeting points, scientific consultancy, budget evaluation software, fiscal vade mecum, fairs' agenda and news. Among know-how data bank devices, one can also apply, for example, to IDEM (Information Desk for Enterprise Mobility) an EU-type tested information system working through personal computers on economic and legal pros and cons concerning the setting up of an enterprise abroad. Equally, the budget evaluation software service is tailored to reclassify national budget forms in accordance with the EU budget plan as defined by EU Directives IV and VII on fiscal matters.

Needless to say, trade and foreign relations promotion services are totally devoted to cross-border cameral issues. In this fieldwork the mission is to favour the insertion of the Milan area's enterprises, small and medium-sized in particular, within cultural and operational global mainstreams. For this purpose, all service units are networking with a number of other specialized infrastructures at the national and international level (Unioncamere, Italian Chambers Abroad, Institute for Foreign Trade, Fairs, Export consortiums, Eurochambers and so on). Within this network system, EU services (such as legislative consultancy, economic information, personal contacts, cultural exchanges, technological transferrals and joint ventures) are particularly refined. Let us just mention a 'Euro Centre' service substructure such as Infodesk, a telematic network jointly created by the Milan Chamber with most important EU Chambers (Amsterdam, Frankfurt, Madrid, Paris) to promote expertise cooperation among *infrastructural* enterprises, that is the so-called 'professionalized tertiary sector'. It keeps an EU infrastructural enterprises' register and offers selective EU 'partenairiat' services, specialized consultancy, cross-border contacts and so on. Mention should also be made of 'Boritec', the International Cooperation Stock Exchange, jointly organized by the Chamber and other Italian institutions at the Milan Fair's 'International Week' annual meetings. Here thousands of cooperation and investment projects are presented and discussed in order to disseminate ideas and favour direct contacts among economic agents.

Finally, one should mention mutual cooperation agency offices set up between the Milan Chamber and various foreign public institutions (such as the State of New York and the Welsh Development Agency) and tailor-made desks or 'service antennas' (in Russia, Ukraine and Brazil). The outstanding importance of these agency offices is self-evident: they demonstrate that cameral cross-border issues can be dealt with at institutional public level also.

As far as information and data bank services for enterprise promotion are concerned, one can have a 'self-service' access to the cameral Economic Information Hall and enquiry throughout 1,200 national and international data banks on a wide range of business issues (including reports and credentials on financial and production conditions of domestic and foreign enterprises, new international market niches, work areas and clients, international promotion of patents and legal consultancy, statistical geography, partnership cooperation and selection, technological information – with data gathered from 277 scientific research centres – import–export information about legal requirements, fiscal burdens and tariffs systems; and EU economic programmes and directives).

As one can see, even considering only the above sketchy list, and ignoring a number of other relevant initiatives such as the High School for Economy and International Relations jointly created with Milan Catholic University, the type and standard of the Milan Chamber's cross-border services, already well-tested and currently running, are remarkable indeed. But is this all that the Milan Chamber can do for the business community?

If one reads carefully the Chamber's Board Programmatic Reports from 1993 to 1996, one immediately realizes that the Milan Chamber tries to answer this basic question in two ways: on the one hand, by turning the Chamber's structure and function more and more into a veritable *cybernetic* model – into a steering 'method' and a steering 'living body' able to navigate despite increasing 'glocal' socioeconomic and political–institutional fluctuations; on the other hand, by promoting a new institutional relationship between socioeconomic and sociopolitical dynamics by means of ad hoc institutional arrangements: in a nutshell, a *new state form*.[28] In fact, on a closer view, enterprises' demand for infrastructural support and promotion cannot be satisfied unless it is transubstantiated into enterprises' integration and regulation. This is what the business community mostly requires at present. The new structural/functional asset of the Chamber, therefore, is taking on a more refined 'steering compass' to respond to business needs: *market regulation through subsidiarity*.

Indeed, prospective priorities of the Chamber's policy have been recently redefined as follows: (a) *public* subsidiarity linkages at the infrastructural/technical level, (b) *interinstitutional* alliances at the territorial/functional level, and (c) *normative* aggregation at the social and business community level. As instability of socioeconomic and political–institutional settings is likely to grow in the future, the same priorities also imply a 'variable geometry' networking structuration, so that the Chamber could act as a veritable generalized integrator of the enterprise system as a whole.

Within this new framework, a major emphasis is going to be put on promotion of (a) institutional (public) services, (b) innovation and technology quality credential services, and (c) territorial communication and formation services.

28 Piero Bassetti, "La corruzione e le regole dei mercati", *Impresa & Stato* 29 (1995).

Infrastructure Provided by the Milan Chamber of Commerce

The Chamber's strategic policy is not based on special agents endowed with charismatic powers or provided with esoteric technologies. Equally, it is based, not on aggressive actions (mergers, acquisitions, colonizations and so on) against other business service infrastructures, but on a much more refined competition model: *competition by alternative means*; that is, competition by resources differentiation and diplomatic agreement (as opposed to competition by discrimination). Interestingly, such a competition by alternative means stimulating comparative levels of efficiency and efficacy without 'top down' formal–legal pressure, not only reflects and emphasizes the Chamber's empirically grounded Janus-headed public/private action: insofar as it provides alternative means, it also fosters veritable *synergic* dynamics with any infrastructure aiming, as the Chamber does, at an innovative 'rationalization' of styles of governmentality of the broader 'glocal' context.

Management and coordination

Taking these scientific insights seriously, the Milan Chamber realized the importance of their reflexive application, for service infrastructures also, particularly those networking and facing market competition. A special (private) cameral enterprise specifically tailored to management and coordination of the Chamber's internal services (Cedcamera), set up in 1972, was thus completely restructured in the mid-1980s as a 'double-propelled canalization' technostructure dealing precisely with both internal and external demands.

The technostructural core of Cedcamera is the whole Milan Chamber's information patrimony: enterprises' local, national and international data bank, official balance sheets, protest bills (about 450,000 files each year), market goods prices, roll registers and so on, plus scientific reports and statistic analysis about any relevant trend or context. In turn, the task environment of Cedcamera is the whole Milan Chamber's network information system: local, national, international cameral infrastructures, official institutions, scientific centres, private agencies and so on, and, of course, the 'glocal' business community, expertise and so on. As far as private business information is concerned, Cedcamera is able to offer data gathered from leading private agencies such as Nielsen, Dun & Bradstreet, Cemit, Sarin and Saritel. Cedcamera is also involved in cameral cooperation issues (such as Infodesk and IDEM), projects (such as Invex, an international inventory exchange system to manage information about levels of demand and offer concerning various goods in the market); and even service production. In fact, Cedcamera produces software information systems for personal computers (such as ABC enterprise budget control) and is actively working on various innovative experiments on data inspection and retrieval systems.

Cedcamera does not compete with public and/or private (solo and/or associated) service expertise, it simply sustains both business activity and these service agents by means of information the added value of which is certified either by the Chamber's institutional role or its general interests function. In this sense, Cedcamera realizes a veritable intersection policy between different social actors, whose indirect regulatory impact on 'glocal' service infrastructures goes hand in hand with its immediate technical efficacy and efficiency: so much so that it realizes a type of political service that prefigures a new cooperation relationship between production and administration.

Information and assistance

The high speed of current socioeconomic and political–institutional change, and the rise of territorial/functional 'glocalism' as a reference framework, has so far produced a significant shift: the decline of the heuristic value of statistical data (owing to their rapid obsolescence for operative action) and the rise, as a strategic function, of context-specific steering information and personalized assistance (because of their flexible application to complex scenarios). This, in short, is also the evolution pattern of the Milan Chamber's special enterprise devoted to the 'Europeanization' of the local business community: Eurosportello.

In general terms, Eurosportello acts as a medium to disseminate EU law policy information. Enterprises wishing to take full advantage of EU policy are able to obtain updated EU legal documentation, access to DG XXIII official data bases, tailored advice on EU legislation, standards, programmes, financing and so on, and BC-Net data if they wish to find a partner abroad. In actual practice, however, Eurosportello is able autonomously and directly to operationalize EU sources. Not only is it able to develop EU financing programmes on individual stock projects, to prepare reports on risk–opportunity cooperation projects and to promote cross-border personalized contacts: it has also set up its own data banks (such as 'Smirne' on Italian recognition of EU directives), publications (*Agenda Eurosportello* and *Quaderni Europei* on EU legal activity), an information system (on Videotel) and gateway desks (towards foreign countries).

As one can see, Eurosportello not only is a sort of prototype model of (prospective) EU administration; it is also a typical model of *lean enterprise*. It reacts immediately to any external variable and all its efforts are oriented to reduce loopholes, cleavages and discontinuties between 'glocal' economy and 'glocal' public administration. In this sense it is a veritable integration infrastructure.

Communication and promotion

The intensification of 'glocal' interdependences does not raise growing demands for information and assistance only, but also for communication and promotion. The current fourth industrial revolution, the infotelematic revolution, differs in fact from previous ones (mechanic–textile; electro-mechanic and chemical–nuclear) in that it is mainly based on processes of symbolic, mimetic, 'virtual' production. The social need to interact accordingly thus compels service infrastructures increasingly to consider communication and promotion (of 'social imaginary') as strategic fieldwork.

The Milan Chamber special enterprise 'Promos' fits into this scenario. It deals precisely with it as a specialized mission, by operating on two levels. On the one hand, it deals with the management of all the Milan Chamber's communicational and promotional targets, as it runs the whole organizational set of areas (halls, meeting points, offices and so on), services (such as publications, fairs and congresses), and cameral subinfrastructures that are concerned with the fieldwork. On the other hand, by coordinating reception/dissemination devices of the Milan Chamber's internal/external relations, it offers desk consultancy and assistance to public and/or private institutions, enterprises and professionals about any sort of cross-border matters (customary tools, customs rules, contracts tenders, socioeconomic reports and so on).

Up to now, Promos' clients have been local – the Milan metropolitan area (55 per cent), the Lombardy region (25 per cent), Italy (10 per cent) – but interactions at the international level are also already well established in all relevant economic areas.

Training and human resources development

Training and human resources development is another sector in which the Milan Chamber is particularly advanced. As is well known, in modern society, the post-Fordist production system – and the extension of neo-Taylorism to the white-collar service class –

requires a new type of human resources; a type of economic actors provided with a high level of education and training. This requirement is considered crucial for any enterprise not only at the level of employees, but also at the level of management and top governance, for 'glocal' competition advantages can only be achieved by means of total quality performances.

As a rule, in Italy service infrastructures concerned with this issue deal with a part of the educational process only (mainly training courses), without considering the nature and side-effects of the process as a whole. Consequently, they often waste resources and miss their aim.

Reacting to the above, in 1987 the Milan Chamber set up Formaper: a special enterprise tailored to contribute to the development of local entrepreneurialship by means of an integrated handling of information, training, research and assistance structures. Basically, Formaper's mission is to support those who wish to become entrepreneurs and those already active entrepreneurs who wish to improve their knowledge and know-how. For this purpose, it offers them data on the socioeconomic context; information about fieldwork, methods and technology; personalized projects for prospective business (between 1988 and 1995, 530 business plans were realized); analysis of subjective potentials; and organizational check-ups and strategic management advice. Formaper's teaching courses vary according either to the type of human resource (young graduates, women, boards, and so on) or to the type of target (starting up a business, how to operate abroad, cultural advancement, and so on). A particular emphasis is also put on the organization of educational courses for foreign young managers in Milanese enterprises and training programmes to improve economic collaboration between local and foreign enterprises (mainly East European, North African, Latin American and Far Eastern). Lastly, to make all these services complete, a special Formaper desk provides free of charge information and guidance on bureaucratic standards, administration and legislation procedures, market conjunctural analysis, EU, national and regional financial opportunities, and so on.

Arbitration and dispute resolution

It has been repeatedly stressed here that the Milan Chamber is strategically oriented to set up the condition to give rise to a new state form by regulating and promoting market forces. As this task implies nothing less than a general reorganization of socioeconomic relations the Chamber must establish forums where the business people may pursue their public and private interests, including their interests concerning the protection of their legal rights in private law relations.

The issue stems from the fact that, up to now, state law neatly distinguished and separately regulated public representation of business interests from the private one. In turn, representative agents of business interests in the public (political) sphere were/are used to act according to a more or less manifest 'spoils system' that in the long run, and given certain circumstances, seems to jeopardize economic performance. Additionally, these agents operate within hierarchically centralized administration structures, whose functional autonomy rests on territorial competence, but not vice versa. Lastly, neither public nor private representative agents, as such, have so far been entitled to set autonomously the means for the handling of business interests' conflicts.

As evidence shows that each one of these traditional devices turned into disfunctional tools as regards the overall socioeconomic dynamics and that the resolution of the business conflicts is increasingly required at both public and private level in order to keep under control the disruptive effects of unregulated market competition, the Chamber has emphasized its functional/institutional role as a public/private subsidiary *business authority* also.

This additional aspect of the Milan Chamber's policy, which is in line with a more general European trend towards 'commissarial' agencies, is epitomized by the renewal of an ancient attribute: the autonomous organization of infrastructures for normative regulation (arbitration, as well as self-discipline and conciliation) of conflicting business interests. Indeed, taking seriously the mediaeval Merchant Guilds' organizational principle according to which the market is an institutional device, Chambers of Commerce in Europe have always acted as public/private seats for arbitration in commercial matters. More recently, the same role gained a new momentum, due to the increasing inefficiency of ordinary (state) justice administration, the rise of new (semi-) autonomous sources of law and the diffusion of favourable sociolegal conceptions of legal pluralism in modern society. Yet what distinguishes the Milan Chamber's policy in this specific field at present is that it is not based on the above variables only, but moves forward to assess normatively the need to promote a further process, the institutionalization of the enterprises system as a proper sociopolitical system; that is, towards the official recognition of enterprises as veritable public/private institutions.

This process officially started as early as 1986, when, by reforming the pre-existing asset, a 'Chamber of National and International

Arbitration of Milan' was created as a special public/private enterprise within the Milan Chamber proper, provided with formal approval on the part of the Italian government.[29] In 1987, a new set of rules on national and international arbitration procedure was issued in order to refine the relationship between the Chamber and the parties. Standard arbitration clauses and standard arbitration agreements were also issued for the appointment of the arbitrators. In 1993, with the enforcement of the Italian Chamber's Law reform n.580, the power 'to constitute arbitration and conciliation commissions to solve disputes between enterprises and between enterprises, consumers and users' (Art. 2), was formally recognized as a constitutive part of Chambers' autonomy.

In the meanwhile, the Milan Chamber actively participated in the drafting of the Arbitration Law n. 25/1994 and the new arbitration rules of the Italian Civil Code, in force since April 1994. As a result of all the above, the Italian arbitration system maintained and even strengthened its classic character: it is an administrated or preorganized (institutional) arbitration system.

The vantage point offered by this model is twofold. An administrated arbitration system is not only a means to treat disputes that is alternative and subsidiary – not competitive or opposite – to the ordinary justice system; it is also a means to prevent a politically irresponsible treatment of business disputes on the part of private agents. In other words, it plays a Janus-headed function: on the one hand, it is a deregulating and privatizing way to prevent the ordinary justice system misfunctioning; on the other hand, it is a way to prevent a ruthless deregulation and privatization of business relations. Not by chance, the *ratio* of the new Law n. 25/1994 is to adjust the Italian model to the overall conditions of the broader 'glocal' business dynamics not only as regards general legal issues – EU Directive 5 April 1993 (on abusive clauses, point 9), international arbitration conventions, recognition and enforcement of foreign arbitration decisions in Italy and so on – but also as regards 'attacks or interferences that might undermine the proceedings's efficacy' from outside (foreign 'experts' included).[30]

29 Benito Boschetto, "Arbitrato e dintorni fra continuità e innovazione", *Impresa & Stato* 18 (1992), 14–19.

30 Feliciano Benvenuti, "L'arbitrato tra Stato e Società", *Impresa & Stato* 18 (1992), 54–9; Stefano Azzali and Rinaldo Sali, "La funzione dell'arbitrato e le Camere di Commercio", *Impresa & Stato* 25 (1994), 75–9; Guido Alpa, Ferdinando Del Re and Paolo Gaggero,

However, it is significant to note that in Italy the appeal of business dispute resolution by means of an arbitration procedure remains rather slight. In 1994, there were in Italy 53 Arbitration Chambers, of which only 17 were active, that is effectively working. Of these 17 Chambers, 14 dealt with three or four cases per year; nine dealt with one case only in 1993. Within this framework, the Milan Arbitration Chamber is simply a relative exception – or if one prefers, a singular case.

In order to have an idea of the Milanese context, consider Tables 5.1 to 5.3, concerning arbitration cases treated by the Milan Arbitration Chamber from 1987 to 1995.

As can be seen, the overall rate is of less than 30 cases per year in the last decade. The number of individuals acting as a party is increasing. And while the number of cases is increasing smoothly, the stakes are becoming smaller. It is evident that, if one wishes to explain these data, one cannot rely on a superficial look at the 'normative climate' or at economic trends at the international level. Even less can one take for granted the ability of business lawyers to act as 'moral enterpreneurs'. Rather, it is compelling to refer to *local* issues, such as the functioning of discretionary local legal systems and the lack of a proper (socially oriented) 'arbitration culture' on the part of the business community at large. According

Table 5.1: Typology of Arbitrations in the Milan Arbitration Chamber (1987–95)

	1987	1988	1989	1990	1991	1992	1993	1994	1995	Total
National	1	3	2	6	17	8	14	23	26	100
International	—	—	—	2	—	3	5	—	4	14
Ritual	1	2	—	3	3	5	6	11	13	44
Non-ritual	—	—	1	1	7	3	8	9	7	36
Undefined	—	1	1	2	7	—	—	3	6	20
By law	—	—	—	3	4	6	12	12	11	48
By equity	1	2	1	1	3	2	2	7	7	26
Undefined	—	1	1	2	10	—	—	4	8	26
Total	1	3	2	8	17	11	19	23	30	114

Source: ISDACI (1996).

Le camere di Commercio e la regolazione del mercato (Milano: CCIA, 1995).

Table 5.2: Typology of Arbitration Parties in the Milan Arbitration Chamber (1987–95)

	1987	1988	1989	1990	1991	1992	1993	1994	1995	Total
Private individuals	—	1	3	4	6	—	5	7	10	36
Corporations	2	3	1	10	26	20	23	30	44	159
Small firms	—	2	1	2	—	2	7	4	6	24
Consortiums	—	—	—	—	1	—	1	1 coop.	—	3
Public institutions	—	—	—	—	1	—	2	5	4	12

Source: ISDACI (1996).

Table 5.3: Annual Value of Arbitration Issues in the Milan Arbitration Chamber (1987–95)

	1987	1988	1989	1990	1991	1992	1993	1994	1995
Total value (in L.millions)	18,000	46	3,100	7,620	19,800	99,054	98,400	17,542	28,109

Source: ISDACI (1996).

to informal sources, in fact, it is well known in Italy that a variety of arbitration courts are daily acting privately, that is informally and unofficially, within the framework of corporativist units. Each business/product area has set up its own 'covert' arbitration court dealing with its own 'covert' arbitration rules. This type of 'black arbitration' system – the quintessence of *lex mercatoria* – is a way to excape from ordinary state justice as well as from any public and/or private dispute treatment structures (not related to such 'covert' corporatist modus operandi). To put it otherwise: it is a way to avoid *any* external (socioinstitutional) regulatory device at all.

Once this simple fact is recognized, it is apparent why the Milan Chamber strongly pursued the above mentioned law policy. This policy is now oriented towards (a) refining the 'administrated' arbitration infrastructural setting, by differentiating the same arbitration system (technical arbitration, quality arbitration, class arbitration and so on); (b) monitoring the dynamics of the arbitration fieldwork at any 'glocal' level (by collecting data on arbitration awards, legislation, market conjuncture and so on); and (c) stressing the social importance of the 'administrated' arbitration model by promoting a proper (that is, democratic) arbitration culture.

The strategic relevance of this last item has been so clearly perceived that, since 1986, a special private cameral agency (ISDACI, the International Institute for the Study of Arbitration and the Law of International Commerce) has been created, to deal precisely with the dissemination of arbitration culture throughout research, meetings and publications. Thus it is a merit of the Milan Chamber and the ISDACI to have highlighted at national and European levels the broader issue of the 'justice functions' of Chambers of Commerce as one of the major pillars for prospective socio-institutional changes in the relationship between law, economy and society.[31] Indeed, they have signalled once and for all a new infrastructural requirement: the necessity to place conflicts of business and consumer interests into an appropriate normative framework (conciliation) and to include in it, among other legal devices, up-to-date professional codes of ethics for the experts that might be involved on both sides.

Concluding Remarks

In the course of this study it has been shown how the Chamber of Commerce, Industry, Agriculture and Handicraft of Milan, as a public/private networking infrastructure, is currently constructing its strategic policy towards meeting the issues of 'glocal' socioeconomic dynamics in the Milan regional area.

In dealing with this topic, it has been observed, in particular, how the Milan Chamber takes serious note of historical experience and most advanced theoretical and operational models of western culture, to keep under normative control the risk-producing patterns of contemporary law and economy while promoting infrastructural linkages and collaboration conditions to foster the excellence of territorial/functional local resources. As these efforts move towards a prospective reassessment of economic enterprises as veritable (publicly responsible) institutions, we have also analysed the way in which the Milan Chamber performs its service mission and how it monitors needs and demands, deficits and

31 Giuseppe Tarzia, "Le funzioni di giustizia delle camere di commercio", *Impresa & Stato* 25 (1994), 97–100.

imbalances, stemming from the broader socioeconomic and institutional context. Last, but not least, we have seen how the activity of this Chamber already constitutes – owing to its highly refined articulation – a leading reference model for assessing and regulating cross-border relations in Europe.

By reflecting on the above, we can theoretically draw one simple, but substantial, lesson of general character in conclusion: whatever 'glocal' western context is concerned, the experience of the Milan Chamber of Commerce shows that the rise of a new ideal asset between *Kratos*, the irrepressible power of production forces, and *Ethos*, the normative content of societal reproduction (envisaged in the 'subsidiary regulatory authority' of the Chamber's policy) cannot be based alone on *Tecné*, the refined devices and highly sophisticated potentials of technological innovation.

As is well known, technological innovation, by its very nature, is among the most powerful variables that jeopardize normative certainty and socially based interest governmentality (rewards, status, values and so on). Thus it is apparent that what is needed to deal with the dilemmas of constitutional insecurity of present-day socioeconomic systems is a rather different tool: a new cybernetic (controlling and driving) policy based on the combination of two meaningful items: reflection ('thought' or knowledge) and art ('measure' or skills). Only such a policy, in fact, could be suitable not only to dig up from the past what can add a unique value to current country-specific resources, but also to secure a strategically oriented institutional framework for any sort of 'glocal' systems of the future. What is needed, in short, is what ancient Greeks called *Methis*, 'cunning reason': the reason able to fuse conjecture and experience, past and future, into a really context-based all-embracing project.

The values and interests that such a Janus-headed reason has to subsume and promote, however, cannot be assessed as a mere outcome of either the regulatory crisis of the state or the disorganizing and risky dynamic of current economic competition. If it is true that the claim for a 'new statuality' at 'glocal' level is related, as Ohmae puts it, to both 'the end of the nation-state' and 'the rise of regional economies',[32] it is also true that it cannot be satisfied by means of a simple juxtaposition of a variety of sources of law or a new set of rules different from state law (for example, by adding a *lex mercatoria* to other legal systems). Equally, it cannot be achieved by simply

32 Kenichi Ohmae, *La fine dello stato-nazione. L'emergere delle economie regionali* (Milan: Baldini & Castoldi, 1996).

activating current legal roles and professional expertise. Indeed, both these devices have already proved to be scarcely functional in coping with the complexity of business 'glocal' relations (particularly owing to their high degree of specialization); and it is reasonable to argue that they will become even more inadequate in the near future unless they are institutionally coupled by networking service infrastructures to the broader socionormative realm according to processes of cooperation and simultaneous engineering.

What Methis suggests, therefore, is not a mere technical intervention on technicalities. Rather, it makes a claim for an up-to-date cybernetic policy of business–society interest representation in which nothing less than a new 'glocal' constitutional framework is envisaged: that is to say, a new socioeconomic *raison d'état* based on a new conceptualization of social utility. The social need of the whole world society for a normative change of this sort is absolutely self-evident, as the infrastructures discussed in the first part of this chapter demonstrate.

The experience of the 'regulatory subsidiarity' programme of the Milan Chamber is a part of this historical mainstream. And it is not at all by chance that the normative *esprit* that characterizes it leads directly back to the great European cultural tradition of Bodin and Grotius, the founders of modern *jus gentium*.

References

Alpa, Guido, Ferdinando Del Re and Paolo Gaggero. 1995. *Le camere di Commercio e la regolazione del mercato*, Milano: CCIA.

Azzali, Stefano and Rinaldo Sali. 1994. La funzione dell'arbitrato e le Camere di Commercio. *Impresa & Stato* 25.

Bassetti, Piero. 1992. Verso l'Europa. *Impresa & Stato* 19.

Bassetti, Piero. 1994. Il cameralismo tra regionalismo ed europeismo. *Impresa & Stato* 25.

Bassetti, Piero. 1995. La corruzione e le regole dei mercati. *Impresa & Stato* 29.

Bassetti, Piero. ed. 1995. *Impresa & Stato. Una istituzione italiana al lavoro verso la Nuova Statualità.* Bologna: Il Mulino.

Beck, Ulrick. 1986. *Risikogesellschaft. Auf dem Weg in eine andere Moderne.* Frankfurt/M.: Suhrkamp.

Benvenuti, Feliciano. 1992. L'arbitrato tra Stato e Società. *Impresa & Stato* 18.

Boschetto, Benito. 1992. Arbitrato e dintorni fra continuità e innovazione. *Impresa & Stato* 18.

Dezalay, Yves and Bryant Garth. 1995. Merchants of Law as Moral Entrepreneurs. *Law and Society Review* 29.

Gerdani Report. Flahault, Hubert. 1995. Le camera di commercio francesi. *Impresa & Stato* 30.

Gessner, Volkmar. 1995. Legal Certainty in Cross-border Interactions. In *The Proceedings of 1995 ISA-RCSL Annual Meeting, Papers Section Meetings, Supplement* 2, edited by Japan Committee for the RCSL95. Tokyo.

Gessner, Volkmar. 1995. Praesumptio similitudinis? A Critique of Comparative Law. In *The Proceedings of 1995 ISA-RCSL Annual Meeting, Papers Section Meetings, Supplement* 2, edited by Japan Committee for the RCSL95. Tokyo.

Huvelin, Pierre. 1897. *Essai historique sur le droit des Marchés & des Foires*. Paris: A.Russeau, ed.

Luhmann, Niklas. 1989. *La differenziazione del diritto*. Bologna: Il Mulino.

MacPherson, Thomas. 1994. Le camere italiane sistema europeo. *Impresa & Stato* 25.

Ohmae, Kenichi. 1996. *La fine dello stato-nazione. L'emergere delle economie regionali*. Milan: Baldini & Castoldi.

Olgiati, Vittorio. 1995. Process and Policy of Legal Professionalization in Europe. The Deconstruction of a Normative Order. In *Professional Competition and Professional Power. Lawyers, Accountants and the Social Construction of Markets*, edited by Yves Dezalay and David Sugarman. London, New York: Routledge.

Pozzi, Enrico. 1995. Verso la rete: l'esperienza storica del sistema delle camere italiane all'estero. In *Impresa & Stato*, edited by Piero Bassetti. Bologna: Il Mulino.

Saba, Antonio. 1995. *Il modello italiano. La specializzazione flessibile e i distretti industriali*. Milan: Angeli.

Sabel, Charles. 1994. Le nuove camere di Commercio fra riforma delle istituzioni e prospettiva Europea. *Atti del Convegno*. Milano.

Saccani, Cesare. 1995. Sistemi olonici per aziende virtuali. *Impresa & Stato* 29.

Schmitter, Philippe. 1994. The Future of Euro-Polity and its Impact upon Private Interest Governance within Member-States. *Droit et Société* 28.

Tarzia, Giuseppe. 1994. Le funzioni di giustizia delle camere di commercio. *Impresa & Stato* 25.

Teubner, Gunther. 1989. And God Laughed ... Indeterminacy, Self-reference and Paradox in Law. In *Critical Legal Thought: An American–German Debate*, edited by Christian Joerges and David Trubek. Baden-Baden: Nomos.

Ufficio Studi CCIA di Milano, ed. 1995. Milano Produttiva 1995. *Impresa & Stato*, Supplemento 30.

Unioncamere. 1994. *Rapporto 1994 sul sistema camerale* (draft). Rome.

Wallerstein, Immanuel. 1991. *Geopolitics and Geoculture: Essays on the Changing Worlds-System.* Cambridge: Cambridge University Press.

Wilhelmsson, Thomas. 1995. Legal Integration as Disintegration of National Law. *Legal Polycentricity: Consequences of Pluralism in Law*, ed. Hanne Petersen and Henrik Zhale. Aldershot: Darmouth.

The Author

Vittorio Olgiati is a senior researcher at the Institute of Philosophy and Sociology of Law at the Milan State University and lecturer at the universities of Urbino and Macerata, Italy.

Address: Istituto de Filosofia e Sociologia del Diritto, Università degli Studi de Milano, Via Festa del Perdono 7, 20122 Milan, Italy.

Fax: 39-2-58312599

Abstract

The project that the Milan Chamber of Industry and Commerce aims to fulfil is extremely ambitious: to put at the disposal of the local and foreign business community an integrated subinfrastructural service network based on that mix of skills, information and culture that characterizes the region as a unique and incomparable geoeconomic context. In other words, to provide the business community as a whole with an institutionalized – territorially settled and functionally differentiated – service system to sustain and implement the *regulation* of socioeconomic activity concerned with the area. In short, to revitalize in a postmodern fashion the mediaeval/humanistic Italian tradition of an *ordered* social organization of the *universe* of market–society relations: the (city-state) *Universitas Mercatorum*. The chapter attempts to give an impression of this unique support structure for cross-border legal business interactions.

Part Two
Small People's Claims

6 Cross-border Maintenance Claims of Children

KIRSTIN GROTHEER

Introduction

Resolving legal conflicts in cross-border legal relations inevitably entails the difficult task of bridging legal–cultural differences. It is true that in several areas states have created internationally applicable law in the form of multilateral and bilateral treaties. Nevertheless, it is assumed that so-called 'third cultures' have developed in certain areas of cross-border legal relations. These are autonomous structures which have developed in international legal relations to bridge legal–cultural differences in the resolution of cross-border legal conflicts. In the area of the international economy, for example, a uniform trade law (*lex mercatoria*) has developed which is almost completely independent of national laws, and according to whose rules existing conflicts are settled by international arbitration courts.[1] The reasons why such autonomous legal structures develop can vary with the different legal areas. Autonomous structures can develop both in the absence of any law applicable across borders and on the basis of international treaties which, although they exist, have proved unsuccessful. By contrast, other areas of cross-border legal relations can be characterized by anomic behaviour due to the absence or unsuitability of legal regulations.

1 From the extensive literature on the *lex mercatoria* see, for example, Paul-Frank Weise, *Lex mercatoria: materielles Recht vor der internationalen Handelsschiedsgerichtsbarkeit* (Frankfurt/M.: Lang, 1990); Andreas Kappus, *"Lex mercatoria" in Europa und Wiener UN-Kaufrechtskonvention 1980* (Frankfurt/M.: Lang, 1990); Bernardo Cremades and Steven Plehn, "The New Lex Mercatoria and the Harmonization of the Laws of International Commercial Transactions", *Boston University International Law Journal* (1984), 317–48.

In the areas of the enforcement of cross-border maintenance claims, many states have concluded *multilateral* conventions designed to ensure fast and unproblematic processing between the contracting states. In addition, several *bilateral* treaties exist which are also intended to simplify the enforcement of cross-border maintenance claims.

Noteworthy in the context of enforcing maintenance claims for children is in particular the weak position of the child entitled to maintenance, or of the parent having sole custody of the child. Those entitled to maintenance are not, as is often the case in the economic sector, large, financially powerful companies which enforce their claims across borders as a matter of course,[2] but rather individual persons. Usually, a person entitled to maintenance has never before had any dealings in this area, let alone any experience in cross-border enforcement of his or her claim, so that he or she may initially be confused about the complicated, many-layered and, above all, opaque procedures required for enforcing a maintenance claim.

The very question of which international convention applies in a given case can raise substantial problems for the creditor. Thus, for the applicability of a convention, it is first decisive to which convention the country to which the debtor belongs has acceded. This depends on whether a maintenance order already exists which is to be enforced abroad, or whether a maintenance claim must be filed directly abroad.

The declaration of enforcement must be applied for in the sovereign territory of the enforcement state in which the maintenance debtor has his residence or where enforcement is to be performed.[3] For this, however, it is necessary that the creditor know the address of the debtor or the location of his assets or workplace. Moreover, the applicant must designate a person authorized to accept service in the district of the court applied to or, if so provided in the law of the state where enforcement is being sought, to establish an elective domicile. Consequently, the applicant is dependent upon legal representation in the enforcement state. Generally, this also means that the correspondence must be conducted in the national language of the country in which enforcement is being sought. It is therefore of great importance whether efficient support structures exist which

2 See Chapters 3 and 4 in the present volume, concerning the reinsurance and international banking sectors, respectively.

3 See Art. 32, para. 2 of the 1968 Brussels Convention.

are accessible to maintenance creditors to help them in enforcing their claims abroad.

This chapter will analyse whether the mechanisms existing in the field of maintenance claims enforcement are suitable for offering maintenance creditors effective support, and above all legal certainty.

The Creation of Cross-border Maintenance Claims for Children

Cross-border maintenance claims can arise for widely differing reasons. Social and family changes of individuals as well as the generally observable increase in worldwide mobility are a few of the factors in the development of such claims. Child maintenance claims can first arise as a result of family conflicts, such as when a marriage ends in divorce and the children from this marriage thenceforth live with one parent and thus have maintenance claims against the other. In addition, when a purely foreign marriage ends (for example) in Germany, it is possible that one parent will return to the respective homeland with the children. The return of a parent to the homeland is even more likely if a binational marriage is dissolved in Germany. The maintenance claims which exist after a divorce, possibly in favour of children deriving from the marriage, become cross-border claims as soon as a divorced spouse moves to another country. According to statistics from the *Statistisches Bundesamt* (Federal Statistical Office), in Germany in 1991 a total of 11,196 binational marriages in which one spouse had German nationality ended in divorce.[4] In the same year, 3,282 purely foreign and binational marriages without a German spouse were dissolved. In 1992, 11,048 binational marriages were dissolved in which one spouse had German nationality, as well as 2,593 binational and foreign marriages without German participation. In 1993, the number of divorces of binational marriages with German participation amounted to 12,426, while 2,953 binational and foreign marriages without a German spouse were dissolved. In 1994, the number of divorces of binational and foreign marriages in which one spouse had German nationality rose to 13,600, and the divorce figure for binational and foreign marriages without a German spouse

4 Including 3,392 marriages in which the husbands had German nationality and 7,804 marriages in which the wives had German nationality.

came to 4,280. In all, there were between 13,500 and 15,500 divorces annually which could lead to cross-border maintenance claims as well as – presuming there were children – to child maintenance claims. In an overwhelming majority of these cases (75–80 per cent), one of the parents was of German nationality.

The migration[5] of individual family members can also give rise to cross-border maintenance claims. Thus it is possible that the husband in a marriage entered into abroad lives and works in Germany, while his wife still resides with the children abroad (in the homeland). Such cases do not involve a divorce but rather a still-existing marriage in which the spouses nevertheless live separately in different states. In 1991 in Germany, there was a total of 142,000 married foreign men who lived apart from their wives, 97,000 of whom did so because their wives continued to reside in the homeland. Of these foreign wives, 51,000 lived with their minor children. According to the evaluation, in 1991 there were living in Germany 19,000 married men with Yugoslavian nationality and 15,000 married men with Turkish nationality, whose wives resided with the children in their homelands.[6]

Another important factor in the creation of cross-border claims is the ever-increasing mobility of the population. Thus unmarried binational cohabitation can develop from vacation acquaintances, which might lead to children as well. In addition, the ever-expanding desire to travel can mean that some children born out of wedlock are born of vacation relationships, without unmarried cohabitation ever having developed. Of course, longer-term, perhaps job-related, stays abroad can also lead to binational relationships. If such relationships end definitively, it is often the case, as with binational marriages, that the foreign partner will return to his or her homeland, so that any children will then have to pursue their claims against the parent living abroad. Thus do maintenance claims become *cross-border* claims.

Furthermore, in the past, particularly as a result of the stationing here of American armed forces, Germany saw the birth of numerous illegitimate children whose maintenance claims against the father, at a time when American troops were being progressively with-

5 Cf., on migration: Bernhard Santel, *Migration in und nach Europa* (Opladen: Leske & Budrich, 1995).

6 This result comes from a special assessment of the 1991 microcensus (Population at the Family Residence), which was conducted by the *Statistisches Bundesamt* in Wiesbaden.

drawn from Germany, have become (or could yet become) cross-border maintenance claims.

All these constellations can lead to cross-border maintenance claims; however, solid figures could not be attained about their actual scope. Not every divorce necessarily results in a cross-border maintenance procedure, since those obliged to pay maintenance may well do so voluntarily. However, it is assumed that voluntary payment of maintenance is *not* the norm. The number of married foreign men living in Germany whose wives live with their minor children in the homeland (51,000) must also be broken down further. While it is true that the figure at first appears to be very high, it must not be forgotten that this figure does not distinguish between different age groups. If one assumes that these minor children are 10 years old on average, and if we assume that a child needs to enforce a maintenance claim only once in his or her lifetime, the figure of 51,000 must also be seen as distributed over 10 years, so that annually only an average of 5,100 maintenance claims would be enforced. In addition, it is also conceivable that the participants are not aware that maintenance must also be paid (or can be enforced) across borders.

Legal Bases for Enforcing Cross-border Maintenance Claims of Children

The legal sources of maintenance claims for children, international conventions which are of primary importance for enforcing cross-border maintenance claims of children, are set forth below, with reference to German law. The discussion will first focus on the 'enforcement conventions', which enable enforcement of maintenance orders made in a contracting state within the jurisdiction of another contracting state. Secondly, a UN convention of administrative assistance, the New York Convention 1956, will be introduced. Then reference will be made to the provisions of the Rome Convention which is aimed at improving efficiency of enforcement conventions in the EU–EFTA area, but which has not yet taken effect. Lastly, the German Law on Enforcement of Maintenance Claims in Relation to Foreign States will be discussed, which is practically designed to cover the US–German cases. Bilateral treaties concerning enforcement of child maintenance claims will be dealt with later within the context of government assistance in cross-border enforcement.[7]

7 See below, "The bilateral international treaties" (p. 210).

The Enforcement Conventions

If the entitled party has already obtained a judgment in the country in which he or she resides, the question arises: what legal possibilities exist for having this judgment declared enforceable abroad? For the area of recognition and enforcement of maintenance decisions, the following are applicable: the Hague Convention on the Recognition and Enforcement of Decisions Relating to Maintenance Obligations towards Children, 15 April 1958 (1958 Hague Convention),[8] the Hague Convention on the Recognition and Enforcement of Support Act, 2 October 1973 (1973 Hague Convention),[9] as well as the two 'jurisdiction and judgment' conventions applicable in the EU–EFTA area, that is, the Convention on Jurisdiction and the Enforcement of Judgments in Civil and Commercial Matters, signed at Brussels on 27 September 1968 (1968 Brussels Convention)[10] and the Convention on Jurisdiction and the Enforcement of Judgments in Civil and Commercial Matters, signed at Lugano on 16 September 1988 (1988 Lugano Convention).[11] Furthermore, there exist a number of bilateral treaties as well.

8 *Bundesgesetzblatt* (BGBl., the federal official journal of Germany) 1961 II, 1013; this now applies for Germany only in relation to Belgium, Liechtenstein, Austria, Surinam and Hungary.

9 BGBl. 1986 II, 826; this applies for Germany in relation to Finland, France, Italy, Luxembourg, The Netherlands, Norway, Portugal, Sweden, Switzerland, Turkey, the United Kingdom, Spain, Denmark, the Czech Republic and the Slovak Republic.

10 *Official Journal of the European Communities* (O.J. EC) 1972 L 299, 32; BGBl. 1972 II, 774; in the version of the 2nd Accession Agreement of 25.10.1982 (O.J. EC 1982 L 388, 1; BGBl. 1988 II, 453) it still applies for Germany only in relation to Denmark and Belgium; in relation to Spain, France, Great Britain, Greece, Ireland, Italy, Luxembourg, The Netherlands and Portugal, it applies in the version of the 3rd Accession Agreement of 1.12.1994 (O.J. EC 1989 L 285, 1; BGBl. 1994 II, 2658).

11 O.J. EC 1988 No. L319, 9; it entered into effect on 1 January 1992 for France, The Netherlands and Switzerland. Today it also applies for Luxembourg (since 1 February 1992), Great Britain (since 1 May 1992), Portugal (since 1 July 1992), Italy (since 1 December 1992), Sweden (since 1 January 1993), Norway (since 1 June 1993), Finland (since 1 July 1993), Ireland (since 1 December 1993), Spain (since 1 November 1994), Germany (since 1 March 1995) and for Iceland (since 1 December 1995).

The New York Convention on the Recovery Abroad of Maintenance, 20 June 1956 (1956 New York Convention)[12]

Systematically considered, the 1956 New York Convention would be classified among the administrative assistance conventions, and applies for both adult and child maintenance. In the foreground of the convention is the determination to help needy persons through the creation of appropriate authorities which cooperate across national borders in enforcing their claims, to the extent that these persons are dependent on persons living abroad for their maintenance.[13]

The convention's underlying idea is to simplify the recovery procedure so that attempts to collect maintenance claims abroad do not fail because of uncertainty about the law to be applied and the enforceability of foreign maintenance decisions. However, questions about procedural costs, statutory requirements of representation by a lawyer or currency export authorizations raise considerable problems.

There is a Transmitting Agency and a Receiving Agency in each contracting state which are respectively responsible for outgoing and incoming applications for maintenance claim enforcement.

The Rome Convention on the Simplification of Procedures for the Recovery of Maintenance Payments, concluded at Rome on 6 November 1990 (1990 Rome Convention)[14]

The 1990 Rome Convention was designed to simplify the procedures for guaranteeing mutual recognition and enforcement of maintenance decisions by supplementing the provisions of the 1968 Brussels and the 1988 Lugano Convention with administrative agreements.[15] Thus it is meant to be applied in the EU only.

The 1990 Rome Convention's underlying idea of ensuring that

12 BGBl. 1959 II, 150; the convention applies for more than 50 states.

13 Preamble of the New York Convention.

14 The convention was signed by Belgium, Denmark, Great Britain, Greece, Ireland, Luxembourg, The Netherlands and Portugal, but until now has been ratified only by Italy; thus it still has not entered into effect.

15 Thus the Preamble of the Rome Convention.

those entitled to maintenance receive government assistance in enforcing their claims is indistinguishable from that of the 1956 New York Convention. Both are legal assistance conventions intended to make it easier for creditors to enforce maintenance orders abroad.

The scope of application of the 1990 Rome Convention is limited to maintenance decisions falling within the scope of application of the 1968 Brussels Convention. In order to guarantee a smooth operation in the enforcement of cross-border maintenance claims under the 1990 Rome Convention, the member states of the 1990 Rome Convention undertake to specify a central authority which must perform free of charge the tasks specified under the convention. Here one can already see a possible advantage over the 1956 New York Convention, since functioning and competence could be significantly improved by centralizing the tasks within a single agency. The 1956 New York Convention, by contrast, left it to the discretion of the contracting states whether or not to appoint one or several offices for performing the tasks.

Further, a permanent committee was set up to meet at regular intervals to discuss the operation of the convention and resolve any difficulties arising in practice. Application of this convention might indeed provide significant relief in the enforcement of cross-border maintenance claims. However, the convention has still not entered into effect, so that it has yet to achieve any practical significance.

The German Law on the Enforcement of Maintenance Claims in Relations with Foreign States – the Auslandsunterhaltsgesetz *of 1 July 1987*[16]

The *Auslandsunterhaltsgesetz* was primarily created in order to overcome the earlier existing difficulties in enforcing maintenance claims where the debtors live in the USA. The uniform law adopted in the USA by a series of states on the reciprocal enforcement of maintenance decisions between the US states, the Uniform

16 BGBl. 1986 I, 2563; reciprocity as understood in the *Auslandsunterhaltsgesetz* is guaranteed with the states of the USA (in several states, limited to child maintenance), with several states of Canada and with South Africa; see Erik Jayme and Rainer Hausmann, eds., *Internationales Privat- und Verfahrensrecht*, 7th edn (Munich: Beck, 1994), 521.

Reciprocal Enforcement of Support Act of 1950 (URESA),[17] which was created to ease enforcement of maintenance claims, in particular the execution of existing decisions, extended (in its 1968 revised version) the URESA possibilities to foreign states as well. Thus the Revised Uniform Reciprocal Enforcement of Support Act of 1968 (R)URESA[18] makes it possible to cooperate with foreign states as well, provided that in these countries the model law or an essentially similar law on reciprocity has entered into effect (§2). This prompted the *Auslandsunterhaltsgesetz*, which is similar to (R)URESA and via which one comes within the legal scope of URESA. After declaration of reciprocity, which is established by concurring declarations of the two states, there then exists to this extent a legal situation similar to that under the 1956 New York Convention, where the judicial and administrative authorities on both sides grant free assistance to those seeking the enforcement of maintenance claims.

Among other things, this is decisive for ascertaining the debtor's residence. Prior to adoption of the *Auslandsunterhaltsgesetz*, it was often impossible, owing to the absence of a general registration duty in the USA, to track down a debtor's address. In addition, the American authorities, on protection of privacy grounds, basically refused to divulge any personal data from their documents to private individuals. By guaranteeing reciprocity, the American authorities now strive to find the address within the framework of mutual administrative assistance, and they do not limit their efforts only to the requested American state.[19]

17 Uniform Reciprocal Enforcement of Support Act of 1950 (last amended 1958), reprinted in Alexander Bergmann and Murad Ferid, *Internationales Ehe- und Kindschaftsrecht*, 6th edn, vol. X (Frankfurt/M.: Verlag für Standesamtswesen, 1993).

18 Revised Uniform Reciprocal Enforcement of Support Act of 1968, reprinted in Bergmann and Ferid, *Internationales Ehe- und Kindschaftsrecht*, Vol. X, USA, No. 13.

19 Thus BT-Drucksache 10/3662; Christof Böhmer, "Das Auslandsunterhaltsgesetz vom 19.12.1986", *Praxis des Internationalen Privat- und Verfahrensrechts* (1987), 139–41, at 139; Sigmar Uhlig and Peter Berard, "Die Geltendmachung von Unterhaltsansprüchen im In- und Ausland nach dem AUG", *Neue Juristische Wochenschrift* (1987), 1521–5, at 1522.

Government Assistance in Enforcing Child Maintenance Claims at Home and Abroad

The Role of the Youth Welfare Offices in Germany

In Germany, state (*Land*) or local public offices responsible for protection of children, the youth welfare offices (*Jugendämter*), play a major role in enforcing cross-border maintenance claims for children. The youth welfare offices are of great importance above all with respect to the question of the legal representation of children born out of wedlock. According to §1705 German Civil Code (Bürgerliches Gesetzbuch – BGB), the mother has custody of the minor child born out of wedlock. Under §1706 BGB, the child has appointed an *Amtspfleger* (a guardian who will be appointed ex officio in the case where the mother of the child born out of wedlock is not of age) to safeguard certain interests. Upon the birth of a child out of wedlock, by operation of law the youth welfare offices become the *Amtspfleger*, if the child has his or her normal residence within the area of application of the Children's and Youth Assistance Law (*Kinder- und Jugendhilfegesetz* – KJHG).[20] The jurisdiction of the youth welfare office derives from §87c KJHG.

In order to ensure in all cases that the youth welfare offices are notified of cases where a legal guardianship will arise, under §57 KJHG, the registry office has a duty to inform the respective competent youth welfare office of the birth of any child out of wedlock.

The *Amtspfleger* must, inter alia, assist in the determination of paternity and the enforcement of maintenance claims, acting as the sole legal representative of the child. While this does limit the scope of parental custody, it brings advantages if maintenance claims must be enforced in the courts, since the child and thus also the parent with custody can benefit from the experience and possible specialized knowledge of the youth welfare office.[21]

However, the support of the youth welfare offices is not offered solely to children born out of wedlock: their assistance is available to legitimate children as well. Upon application of the parent having sole custody, under §1685 BGB, the youth welfare office can be appointed as a *Beistand* (legal advisor) if the respective parent is

20 See Johannes Münder, *Familien- und Jugendhilferecht*, vol. 2 (Weinheim, Basel: Beltz-Verlag, 1993), 108.

21 Cf. *Der Amtsvormund* (1990), 987, 989.

formally the only person responsible for the child's personal, financial and parental care. However, this advisory position at first has a purely internal effect. Only when, for example, responsibility for enforcing maintenance claims is transferred to the *Beistand* does the latter accede to the position of an *Amtspfleger*, who can then take binding action in legal relations with others.[22]

The youth welfare offices are obliged to support those with custody who are concerned about the enforcement of their claims. The cooperation of the youth welfare offices is also necessary when a foreign maintenance claim is to be enforced in Germany. After the foreign applications have been received by the *Generalbundesanwalt* as the competent receiving agency under the Auslandsunterhaltsgesetz, or the *Bundesverwaltungsamt* (Federal Administrative Office) under the 1956 New York Convention, the documents transmitted are first examined and prepared for the hearing of the maintenance debtor by the competent youth welfare and social welfare offices. The *Bundesverwaltungsamt* generally calls upon the administrative assistance of both cities and rural districts,[23] and thus forwards the application and the complete documents to the competent youth welfare or social welfare offices. Within the administrative assistance framework, they then contact the maintenance debtor, look into his personal and economic situation, and attempt to convince him to make voluntary payments, that is, to sign an enforceable document. If this does not work, a maintenance action or an application for a declaration of enforcement of the foreign order is filed.[24]

Both for outgoing and incoming applications, the youth welfare offices support the creditors as far as possible in enforcing their claims.

22 Cf. Johannes Münder, *Familien- und Jugendhilferecht*, vol. 1, p. 154.

23 The Länder have all adopted directives on this.

24 According to information from the *Bundesverwaltungsamt* and the youth welfare office.

How are the Conventions and the Auslandsunterhaltsgesetz *Used by Youth Welfare Offices in Germany?*

The 1956 New York Convention and outgoing applications

The 1956 New York Convention is an administrative assistance convention. For the youth welfare offices it offers the possibility of enforcing maintenance claims in the respective contracting states for the creditors, without having to conduct further correspondence with the foreign country.[25] Several youth welfare offices use this possibility to rely upon the free administrative assistance of the foreign authorities and pursue maintenance claims for whose enforcement they are responsible within the framework of existing *Amtspflegschaften* or *Beistandschaften*, with the aid of the 1956 New York Convention.

If maintenance is to be enforced via the 1956 New York Convention, the competent youth welfare office first (if the debtor's whereabouts are unknown) gathers information about the legal possibilities for finding his address and investigating his economic circumstances or about the economic situation in the participating state. The German embassies abroad and the German Institute for Guardianship (*Deutsches Institut für Vormundschaftswesen)* in Heidelberg serve as sources of information.[26]

Furthermore, before any enforcement action, it is always established whether the accruing costs which, depending on the *Bundesland,* are borne either by the *Land*'s own budget or by the parent with custody, exceed the value of the expected maintenance. In practice, the youth welfare offices try in each case to investigate the economic situation of the debtor, so as to be able to decide whether an enforcement action seems worthwhile. Because of the tough economic conditions and the very low wage levels in most of the countries which have acceded to the 1956 New York Convention, however, in most cases attempts are no longer made to enforce maintenance. The only cases where enforcement is still undertaken are those where the debtor holds property.

25 See above, on the New York Convention.

26 See further on the Deutsches Institut für Vormundschaftswesen the comprehensive discussion below.

All this would suggest that the number of maintenance claims enforced via the 1956 New York Convention must be very small. In order to verify this assumption, files were studied at the authorities which, in Germany, are entrusted with the tasks of the transmitting agency. In particular, such file analyses were expected to yield information from the German perspective about the participation of the various countries in procedures via the 1956 New York Convention and about the scope of the successful procedures. Further, the authorities were questioned about their other experiences with the 1956 New York Convention.

According to unofficial statistics from the Federal Ministry of Justice and the files studied at the transmitting agencies, in 1991 for all of Germany a total of only 53 maintenance applications were sent from Germany to foreign receiving agencies. All of the 16 *Länder* surveyed submitted answers, most of them highly detailed. The trend pinpointed by the statistics of the Federal Ministry of Justice with respect to the participation of the various states is also already evident in the results of the analysis performed.[27] The applications were sent from the German offices primarily to The Netherlands, and it is interesting that the largest share of *these* applications (10) was sent from Nordrhein-Westfalen to the Dutch receiving agency, quite evidently because of the simple geographical proximity of Nordrhein-Westfalen to The Netherlands.

In virtually all cases, a German maintenance order already existed and the goal was to get it declared enforceable abroad.[28] Interestingly, the maintenance applications were filed primarily, but not exclusively, by youth welfare offices on behalf of the creditor. Roughly 20 per cent of the analysed cases were submitted by the

27 These statistics indicate that, in 1991, the largest share of outgoing applications was sent to The Netherlands (21 applications), and that between one and five applications went to Australia, Austria, Belgium, Brazil, Denmark, Finland, France, Italy, Poland, Sweden, Switzerland, Turkey and the United Kingdom.

28 This is interesting, because in general the number of applications for execution of foreign judgments is always less than legal actions directly brought by foreign creditors. That is, generally creditors prefer to go and sue abroad instead of suing at home and enforcing the judgment abroad; see Volkmar Gessner, "International Cases in German First Instance Courts", in *Foreign Courts – Civil Litigation in Foreign Legal Cultures*, ed. Volkmar Gessner (Aldershot: Dartmouth, 1996); also Chapter 1 of the present volume.

legal representatives of the creditors and approximately 20 per cent by lawyers. The submitted orders have thus far been declared enforceable in 17 cases. Interestingly, receipt of maintenance payments was registered in 17 cases. However, maintenance payments were not registered in every case where the order was declared enforceable. This shows that the declaration of enforcement for an order does not necessarily also imply a successful outcome of the whole procedure: the receipt of maintenance payments. On the other hand, an enforceability declaration is not an absolute prerequisite for the receipt of maintenance payments either.

It was striking that the procedures under the 1956 New York Convention are characterized by very long processing times, generally running to several years. The necessary intervention of the various authorities, which in turn are obliged to process the applications, at the same time has the effect of significantly slowing down the procedure. A maintenance application must first be submitted to the competent *Amtsgericht* (local court) as receiving office, which checks the documents sent in for completeness. Then the application goes to the *Landgericht* (district court), where a preliminary examination of the application is performed to assess the application's chances of success. Only if this preliminary examination offers some hope of a successful outcome are the application and documents translated into the respective language of the country in which the claim will be enforced. Then the application is forwarded to the competent transmitting agency, that is the justice administration of the relevant *Land*, which can finally send it abroad.

Simply processing the application from acceptance at the receiving office to arrival at the transmitting agency can take, according to the assessments, between one month and one year. This period in turn depends on the completeness of the documents and their translations, but above all on the speed with which the individual authorities process the applications. The time which the Ministries of Justice of the *Länder* require as the transmitting agencies for sending out applications varies greatly. The indicated time periods range from several days to several months, this being said to depend on the completeness of the attached documents. If documents have to be objected to or additional ones demanded, the request will be sent to the applicant via the same long administrative path. And if the applicant wants to send the required documents subsequently, they are once again passed on to the transmitting agency via the same administrative path. Thus it is not surprising that this slows down the transmission process considerably.

The further development of the procedures via the 1956 New York Convention in the following years reveals the progressively declining significance of the convention. It is true that, in 1992, 56 maintenance applications were still sent abroad via this route, but in 1993 the number fell to 45, and in 1994 to as few as 38 outgoing applications. Owing to the decentralized system Germany has chosen for accepting applications, that is the delegation of these tasks to the individual justice administrations of the *Länder*, the specialized competence of the staff is possibly not as great as it would be were the application processing centralized at the federal level. Germany is the sole contracting state which has multiple transmitting agencies. Above all, the long procedural times caused by the required intervention of the various agencies means that many youth welfare offices refrain from enforcing maintenance claims under the 1956 New York Convention. Further, owing to the often poor economic conditions in the participating states, the economic effectiveness of enforcing a maintenance claim is not necessarily assured, since frequently the accruing translation costs alone exceed by far the expected maintenance payments.

The 1956 New York Convention and incoming applications

The number of maintenance applications coming in from abroad to the receiving agency, the *Bundesverwaltungsamt*, in the years 1991–4 ranged between 917 and 1,180,[29] of which around 80 per cent were successful: that is, they could be concluded with the payment of maintenance to the creditor living abroad.[30]

With respect to the payment of maintenance, in principle the debtor is obliged to pay maintenance payments directly into the account of the creditor abroad. As soon as the debtor interrupts his payments, the transmitting agencies abroad inform the *Bundesverwaltungsamt*. This office demands that the debtor resume his payments and sets a short period for him to present proof that he has done so. If such proof is not submitted, the *Bundesverwaltungsamt* levies execution.[31] However, if payment monitoring is

29 Also the number of applications coming in from abroad dropped steadily over the period from 1991 (1,180 applications) to 1994 (917 applications).

30 Information and statistics from the *Bundesverwaltungsamt*: Bad Homburg field office.

31 Information from the *Bundesverwaltungsamt*.

held to be necessary from the very outset, the payments are made into an account at the *Bundeskasse* (Federal Cash Office) in Bonn. The debtor transfers the payments to this account, from which they are sent via the *Deutsche Bundesbank* to the creditor abroad. Accordingly, the 1956 New York Convention plays an important role for the monitoring or resumption of maintenance payments, and on the whole appears to be very useful for an enforcement of foreign maintenance claims in Germany.

Although the number[32] of applications coming from abroad in 1991–4 dropped from 1,180 to 917, the total number of cases processed by the *Bundesverwaltungsamt* rose, from 3,445 to 4,152. Also on the rise were the number of new judicial procedures, the complaints and applications for enforcement orders (from 141 to 391), judicial executions (from 157 to 411) and the number of monthly payment receipts (see Table 6.1).

Table 6.1: Statistical Data of the *Bundesverwaltungsamt* on the Cases it Processed (Absolute Figures)

	1991	1992	1993	1994
Incoming applications:				
new applications	1,180	1,150	1,103	917
New court procedures				
Complaints/applications on enforcement order	141	208	363	391
Enforcements	157	173	303	411
Total number of cases processed	3,445	3,832	4,008	4,152
Total number of monthly payments received at the Federal Cash Office	691	924	971	989

The Auslandsunterhaltsgesetz

Within the framework of the applicability of the *Auslandsunterhaltsgesetz*, the German authorities can call upon the unrestricted

32 The data do not distinguish between adult and child maintenance. The following table too includes all maintenance applications submitted from abroad, independent of whether they involve child or adult maintenance.

aid of the American authorities and without charge. How important the *Auslandsunterhaltsgesetz* is for the youth welfare offices depends essentially on the interests of the youth welfare offices. If they wish to enforce the claims on their own, the *Auslandsunterhaltsgesetz* offers a support without which independent enforcement would be impossible. However, many youth welfare offices also give cases where maintenance claims are to be enforced in the USA to an organization under private law, the German Institute for Guardianship (*Deutsches Institut für Vormundschaftswesen;* hereafter German Institute) in Heidelberg,[33] so that the *Auslandsunterhaltsgesetz* is not utilized to the same extent by all youth welfare offices. In 1991, the *Generalbundesanwalt*, as central authority, was assigned to enforce the claims in 66 child maintenance cases in the United States. At the German Institute, by contrast, a total of 210 US cases were counted in which child maintenance was to be enforced. Obviously, the youth welfare offices prefer to entrust the German Institute with the enforcement of the claims. The reasons for this could be that the authorities wish to spare themselves the work entailed by the application, or that the authorities regard enforcement via the German Institute to be more likely.

The Bremen youth welfare office by itself enforces claims where the debtors live in the USA, using the *Auslandsunterhaltsgesetz*. According to information from this youth welfare office, the only cases which prove successful are those in which the address of the debtor is known. Residence searches undertaken by the American authorities generally turn up empty-handed unless the social security number of the debtor is known. In the period 1993–4, only two cases with participation of the USA were registered in which American maintenance decisions could be obtained and regular payments were also received.

The enforcement conventions

If a German order is to be declared enforceable abroad invoking one of the enforcement conventions, the youth welfare offices always turn to the German Institute in Heidelberg, which attempts to enforce the orders abroad on behalf of the respective youth welfare office for the creditor.

The necessity of bringing in a foreign lawyer to enforce the claims of the child abroad can lead to linguistic problems which, in

33 On the *Deutsches Institut für Vormundschaftswesen*, see the comprehensive discussion below.

the case of enforcement by the youth welfare offices, themselves might require the use of a translator. This in turn would raise the costs. Furthermore, most youth welfare offices simply do not have the personnel to spend time contacting various foreign lawyers and conducting the necessary (and unavoidably expensive and time-consuming) correspondence, and so on. Moreover, it is doubtful whether the youth welfare offices possess the necessary knowledge about the legal prerequisites and particular aspects concerning individual countries which must be taken into account when enforcing maintenance abroad. Here the procedure under the 1956 New York Convention for sending orders abroad for the purpose of having them declared enforceable is obviously rarely or never considered.

The enforcement conventions also contain regulations which directly affect the youth welfare offices, despite the case being turned over to the German Institute. Thus Article 1 of the 1973 Hague Convention expressly provides that it applies to recourse cases. As in most contracting states, German laws give social services agencies possibilities of recourse against the maintenance debtor.

It is true that social services are always of a supplementary nature;[34] however, if there exists – even if only temporarily – no possibility of obtaining maintenance payments from the maintenance debtor, the party seeking help who lives in Germany has a claim to subsistence aid under §30 para. 1, Social Security Code (*Sozialgesetzbuch*: SGB) and §120 Federal Public Welfare Act (*Bundessozialhilfegesetz*: BSHG).[35] The same is true for the granting of maintenance advances to foreign children living in Germany (§1 para. 1, sentence 2, Living Allowance Act (*Unterhaltsvorschußgesetz*: UVG)).[36] In practice, maintenance creditors in Germany must frequently turn to government assistance in the form of subsistence aid or maintenance advances for the simple reason that maintenance claims existing abroad cannot always be implemented immediately. This situation is taken into account by Article 1, para. 1, no. 2 of the 1973 Hague Convention. It can be applied to

34 See §2 BSHG; §1 UVG.

35 See Walter Schellhorn, *Bundessozialhilfegesetz, Commentary*, 16th edn (Neuwied: Luchterhand, 1996), Marg. Nos. 6 and 7 on §2 BSHG; Walter Schellhorn, "Das Verhältnis von Sozialhilferecht und Unterhaltsrecht – aus der Sicht der Sozialhilfe", *Familie und Recht* (1990), 22.

36 Rainer Scholz, *Unterhaltsvorschußgesetz, Commentary*, 2nd edn (Cologne: Heymanns, 1992), Marg. Nos. 3 and 4 on §1 UVG.

reimbursement claims or reimbursement orders of the above-named authorities, independent of their legal nature.[37]

Social services agencies, as public institutions as defined in Article 1, para. 1, no. 2 of the 1973 Hague Convention, are – in Germany in the case of continuing subsistence aid – the cities and the rural districts of the *Länder* and, in the case of maintenance advances, the youth welfare offices.[38] Recourse takes place through transfer of the claims by operation of law.[39] However, the substance of the claim is not changed by legal assignment, so that reimbursement claims in Germany have the same legal nature as maintenance claims.[40]

However, the question arises to what extent the youth welfare offices actually make use of this possibility. While it is true that enforcement of the recourse claims which arise from prepayment of maintenance through a maintenance advance or current subsistence aid is pursued by the social services authority itself, in practice transferred maintenance claims are generally reassigned in trust to the maintenance creditor. The public institution then enforces the claims, not on its own behalf, but on that of the child entitled to maintenance.[41] This procedure is justified by the fact that many countries do not react very positively to government demands which are enforced against a maintenance debtor as a private individual. In such cases, the interest of the countries or competent authorities, lawyers or courts in bringing about quick (or indeed any) enforcement of the maintenance claim is very limited. Proceeding on behalf of the maintenance creditor is also more advantageous with respect to utilization of legal aid abroad, since the child entitled to maintenance might be able to claim this abroad, but not the social services agency.[42]

37 Baumann, *Anerkennung und Vollstreckung ausländischer Entscheidungen und Unterhaltssachen*, 15; Verwilghen, "Rapport explicatif", *Bundestags-Drucksache* 10/258, 29: no. 88.

38 See §96 BSHG and §9 UVG.

39 See §90 BSHG, §7 UVG.

40 OLG Düsseldorf, FamRZ 1979, 543; VG Karlsruhe Der Amtsvormund 1986, col. 88; Uwe Diederichsen, in Otto Palandt (1994), *BGB-Kommentar*, 53rd edn, Munich: C.H. Beck, Introduction to §1601 BGB, Note 5c.

41 Information from the youth welfare offices.

42 Thus, for example, German Institute Expert Report of 1 October 1993, *Zentralblatt für Jugendrecht* (1993), 599.

Within the framework of the applicability of the enforcement conventions, the social services agencies are compelled to rely on institutional assistance in order to be able to enforce maintenance abroad. However, the conventions then offer a simplified form for getting orders declared enforceable abroad, so as to be able to enforce them thereafter.

The bilateral international treaties

Alongside the existing multilateral conventions there are also bilateral conventions which play a very important role in the area of cross-border maintenance claims.

Between Germany and Austria there applies the German–Austrian Social Services Convention,[43] which obliges the youth agencies of both countries to offer one another administrative assistance. Thus, if a child maintenance claim is to be enforced in Austria, the German youth welfare offices can enter into direct contact with the Austrian youth authorities. In practice they employ this method frequently, since the possibility of entering directly into contact with the competent authorities in Austria allows them to dispense with time-consuming exchanges of letters. The authorities on both sides evidently act more quickly and reliably in an administrative assistance matter – perhaps because this form makes it an official duty.[44] The German order is then declared enforceable under the 1958 Hague Convention.

Between Germany and Switzerland the German-Swiss Social Services Convention applies.[45] The youth welfare office (in Bremen, at least) handles claims to be enforced in the German-speaking cantons of Switzerland on its own. Here, too, it directly addresses the Swiss youth authorities, which then pursue enforcement of the claim. In such cases, an existing maintenance order is sent for the purpose of securing an enforcement order, which is issued there in

43 Abkommen zwischen der Bundesrepublik Deutschland und der Republik Österreich über Fürsorge und Jugendwohlfahrtspflege vom 17 January 1966, BGBl. 1969 II, 1.

44 Information from the youth welfare offices and the German Institute, according to which the German Institute is only brought in if difficulties arise with respect to the cooperation of the Austrian youth authorities.

45 Vereinbarung zwischen der Bundesrepublik Deutschland und der Schweizerischen Eidgenossenschaft über die Fürsorge für Hilfsbedürftige vom 14.7.1952, BGBl. 1953 II, 31.

accordance with the requirements of the Swiss legal system. Things are different, however, in the French-speaking cantons of Switzerland. According to information from the German Institute, since Switzerland acceded to the 1956 New York Convention the agencies there have ceased being helpful in the enforcement of maintenance claims – not only under the bilateral Convention, but in general. The cooperation of the authorities would offer – just as in the German-speaking part of Switzerland – the advantage that they could represent the maintenance creditor free of charge in a court proceeding. However, the youth agencies in the French-speaking cantons of Switzerland have refused this since the 1956 New York Convention became applicable, so that there the only possibility is to assign a lawyer to pursue enforcement of the maintenance claims or the application for an order of enforcement of the German decision. However, the accruing costs would not be covered by legal aid. Thus, in this area, the only way to save lawyer's costs is to transmit the German decision for an enforcement order in accordance with the 1956 New York Convention.

To sum up, the possibilities theoretically open to the youth welfare offices for enforcing the maintenance claims of creditors living here have been substantially improved by the existing conventions. Yet the youth agencies virtually never make use of these possibilities, instead apparently assigning most cases to the German Institute for the enforcement of claims. Only the *Auslandsunterhaltsgesetz* appears to have developed a greater significance for the youth welfare offices.

However, it is evident that the existing bilateral treaties, by providing for direct cross-border cooperation of the youth agencies, make an essential contribution to enabling the youth welfare offices to enforce maintenance claims independently.

Non-governmental Assistance within the Framework of Enforcing Cross-border Maintenance Claims for Children at Home and Abroad

German Institute for Guardianship (German Institute)

For the various reasons just discussed, not only the creditors themselves, but also the youth welfare offices, depend on institutional forms of assistance to enforce claims. The German Institute for Guardianship (*Deutsches Institut für Vormundschaftwesen*) was founded in 1906 in Frankfurt am Main with the goal of improving the legal and social situation of children born out of wedlock and their mothers by developing guardianship institutions, thus at the same time promoting child welfare generally. After earlier moves, first to Berlin and then to Hildesheim, the Institute has had its headquarters in Heidelberg since 1955.

Historical development

Since the beginning of the century, the Institute has exerted a major influence on the development of youth welfare in Germany. After the youth welfare offices were set up in 1924, they turned to the German Institute to function as a central authority. In the period 1924–6, the then director of the Institute placed greater weight on social educational aspects. Even then, however, the Institute's scope of responsibilities included dealing with maintenance issues for German children born out of wedlock whose fathers resided abroad; the same was also true for foreign children within Germany.[46] When, in 1966, the long-time director was replaced by the person who currently holds the office, the new director reinforced the legal advice offered to the affiliated youth welfare offices, believing that this was where the interest and necessity for the youth welfare offices lay. Thus, since that time, the number of personnel has increased, together with the number of cross-border maintenance claims enforced.

Current situation

The Institute has a total staff (including its bookkeeping department) of 20–25 people who work either as full-time employees or on a fee basis. The maintenance cases are processed, among others, by three lawyers. The Institute has benefited from a high degree of personnel continuity. The current director has led the Institute for around 30 years. Most of the staff are long-time employees, many of whom have been active in the Institute for 20 or more years. The work of the German Institute serves exclusively and directly public-interest purposes. The Institute is not a profit-making organization and thus does not act in its own interest.[47]

46 At that time the German Institute was handling about 5,000 paternity cases at any given moment, with an average annual replacement rate of around 1,000 cases (information provided by the German Institute).

47 Thus §3, paras. 1 and 2 of the German Institute charter.

The German Institute is financed by federal grants and through the memberships of the majority of the German youth agencies. The membership contributions from the youth welfare offices, the amount of which depends on the number of inhabitants in their respective areas, are paid by the cities or the rural districts of the *Länder*. Furthermore, a fee is charged for each case taken over, and 6 per cent of each maintenance payment which comes in through the German Institute goes to the Institute.

Among other things, the Institute gives its members legal aid in paternity and maintenance procedures abroad, including the recovery of maintenance money for children born in or out of wedlock.[48] The Institute's work focuses on supporting the youth welfare offices in cross-border cases with respect to the enforcement of maintenance claims of their wards. The majority of the youth welfare offices located throughout Germany are German Institute members, and can thus lay full claim to the assistance offered by the Institute. However, the Institute does not act exclusively for the youth welfare offices: it also handles inquiries and applications from parents with custody as legal representatives for the child entitled to maintenance, to the extent that its capacities allow this.[49]

When it takes over a case, the German Institute handles all the correspondence with foreign countries. Thanks to the large number of cases it has dealt with, very good working relations have existed for decades with many foreign authorities, lawyers and private organizations. Thanks to its extensive knowledge of other countries, the Institute is in a very good position to take the appropriate steps on maintenance enforcement abroad. Thus it is always called upon by the youth welfare offices when cross-border maintenance claims have to be enforced where a German decision already exists and must be enforced abroad.[50] Yet even in cases where a fresh action must be filed abroad, many youth welfare offices will transfer their case to the German Institute. These are usually cases where the debtor lives in the USA. Legal relations with the USA occupy a great deal of the Institute's total activities.[51]

The German Institute is frequently brought in only after the debtor has shown himself unwilling to make payments voluntarily.

48 Thus §2, para. 2c of the German Institute charter.

49 Information from the German Institute.

50 Information from the German Institute, which was confirmed by the German Institute file assessment.

51 Further on this, see below, "Legal relations with the USA".

However, if neither the competent youth welfare office nor the creditor has yet called upon him to make the maintenance payments, the German Institute always first gives the debtor a chance to shoulder his maintenance obligation voluntarily. Only if this attempt proves unsuccessful are judicial measures initiated.[52]

The German Institute also offers its support in cases where foreign creditors wish to enforce their maintenance claims in Germany. Frequently these involve applications from the former Czechoslovakia.[53] The Institute then attempts to make contact with the respective debtor, either directly or through the competent youth welfare office, in order to convince him to make the payments voluntarily. If this does not work, a maintenance action or an application to have the foreign order declared enforceable is filed.

A Study of the Files at the German Institute for Guardianship

Considerations underpinning the analysis of the data

The German Institute is the only private-law institute in Germany which, using an international enforcement convention, assists minors entitled to maintenance with enforcing their claims, handles all the related correspondence and effectively conducts the maintenance enforcement process. Since most youth agencies have become members of the German Institute, it can be assumed that the majority of all maintenance claims for children born out of marriage are enforced by the Institute. In the areas of validity of the 1956 New York Convention or the *Auslandsunterhaltsgesetz*, government offices are available as transmitting agencies, which obviates the need for the creditor to correspond with foreign offices. As the research made clear, the 1956 New York Convention is used only to a very limited extent by the youth welfare offices and private individuals. Even via the *Auslandsunterhaltsgesetz* only a small number of cases are enforced. Thus, in many cases, the Institute is called upon to handle things by the youth welfare offices despite the applicability of the 1956 New York Convention.

52 This could be derived from the evaluated data. According to the information from the Institute, this is the approach always taken.

53 On legal relations with the former Czechoslovakia, see p. 229.

The evaluated file materials

From the German Institute's records, 313 files were randomly chosen from the cases which were accepted for processing in 1991 as 'trial cases' ('T-cases')[54] and evaluated.[55] These were cases which had been accepted for processing in 1991. The only decisive criterion in the selection of the files was that the Institute was assigned to enforce the maintenance claim in 1991, not whether it involved a first inquiry which was submitted in 1991 and which immediately became a T-case or whether the T-case was based on a first inquiry from an earlier year which they only decided to enforce in 1991.

Results of the Study of German Institute Files

Distribution of the evaluated cases over the various states

Of the 313 cases, 74 per cent were, from the German perspective, *outgoing* cases: that is, the maintenance was enforced abroad, thus the creditor was located in Germany and the debtor abroad. The remaining 26 per cent of the cases were, again from the German perspective, *incoming* cases, with the debtor located in Germany and the creditor abroad; thus the maintenance was enforced in Germany.

Interestingly, outgoing applications to the USA made up 59 per cent of the assessed files. The participation of the other states never exceeded a maximum of 7 per cent. Table 6.2 gives the participation of the different states.

Of the incoming applications, 64 per cent were from the area of the former Czechoslovakia. The number of incoming applications from other countries can be seen in Table 6.3.

54 At the German Institute, "trial cases" are those in which the Institute is entrusted with the enforcement of the maintenance claim. In this respect it is irrelevant whether the enforcement actually requires going to court or whether the debtor, after being called upon to do so, voluntarily commences making payments to meet his maintenance debt. What is decisive in the classification of a case as a trial case is simply that, if the debtor does *not* pay voluntarily, judicial enforcement is anticipated.

55 In 1991, a total of 629 cases were newly accepted for processing as T-cases. Merely with respect to legal aid relations with the USA, 242 first inquiries were registered in 1991 for which maintenance was to be enforced.

Table 6.2: Distribution of the Applications going out from Germany to Various States

	More than 50%	5–7%	1–5%	Less than 1%
All African states				+
Australia			+	
Austria			+	
Belgium			+	
Croatia				+
Denmark				+
Former Czechoslovakia			+	
France		+		
Hungary				+
Italy			+	
Kazakhstan				+
Korea				+
Netherlands		+		
Norway				+
Russia				+
Scotland			+	
Sweden			+	
Switzerland			+	
United Kingdom		+		
USA	+			

Table 6.3: Distribution of the Applications coming from Abroad, Various States

	More than 60%	8–9%	4–5%	1–3%
Austria			+	
Denmark				+
Finland			+	
Former Czechoslovakia	+			
Netherlands				+
Poland			+	
Romania		+		
Slovakia				+
Switzerland				+
USA		+		

The significance of the existing legal bases for the enforcement of cross-border maintenance claims for children by the German Institute

The Enforcement Conventions and the 1956 New York Convention

In many of the cases where maintenance is to be enforced abroad, there already exists a German maintenance order and the goal is simply to get it enforced abroad. Generally, the German Institute then proceeds, invoking the 1968 Brussels Convention or the 1973 Hague Convention, to get the decision declared enforceable abroad and then to use this as a basis for pursuing enforcement. Claims against a debtor living in Denmark, Norway, Finland or The Netherlands however, are enforced via the 1956 New York Convention, although even here the German decision is transmitted for the purpose of getting it declared enforceable abroad. The reason is that, unlike the situation in many other countries, private-law institutions – such as the German Institute – which could pursue a maintenance enforcement for the creditor cheaply do not exist in these countries. True, a lawyer residing there could represent the creditor in court; however, the German Institute notes that lawyers' fees in the above-mentioned countries are very steep and not covered by legal aid. In such cases, therefore, the Institute proceeds via the 1956 New York Convention and employs the possibility opened up by the convention of using the free administrative assistance of the foreign authorities.

Which enforcement convention will serve as the basis of an application for an enforcement order naturally depends first of all on which convention the respective participating state has acceded to.The possible grounds for rejecting an application for an enforcement order are stipulated in the conventions, and thus can be anticipated. As explained earlier, the two enforcement conventions, namely the 1973 Hague Convention and the 1968 Brussels Convention, differ in only a few points. Beyond this, however, knowledge of the legal situation in the various countries, with respect to both the legal system and public policy, is absolutely necessary, since one can easily run into unexpected difficulties in connection with enforcement in the absence of a comprehensive understanding of the legal and factual situation in the country where enforcement is being sought. Minor differences between the conventions could, in connection with the legal facts, be decisive for the success or failure of an enforcement declaration application.

The application of the 1968 Brussels Convention or of the 1973 Hague Convention can depend on whether maintenance is to be enforced in favour of a child born in or out of wedlock. If a child born in marriage is involved, generally the 1968 Brussels Convention is applied, since the procedural duration through Article 34, para. 1 of the 1968 Brussels Convention is generally shorter than under the 1973 Hague Convention. Moreover, because of its broader scope of application, the former is more familiar to foreign judges and lawyers than the 1973 Hague Convention. If maintenance is to be enforced in favour of a child born out of wedlock, one must examine very carefully which convention should be applied. In some cases, the question of enforceability of maintenance claims in favour of children born out of wedlock depends on whether the maintenance is enforced under the 1973 Hague Convention or the 1968 Brussels Convention. Article 27, no. 4 of the 1968 Brussels Convention[56] can lead to rejection of the enforcement declaration of a German maintenance order if the determination of paternity on which it is based is not also adequately founded under the national criteria applied in the country where enforcement is being sought. In one Italian case, the order of enforcement for the decision was rejected under the 1968 Brussels Convention, Article 27, no. 4 of the Convention being cited. Later an attempt was made to have the decision declared enforceable under the 1973 Hague Convention, and that attempt proved successful.[57] If maintenance is to be enforced in favour of children born out of wedlock in cases where the German maintenance decision is *not* based upon an acknowledgement of paternity, it is better to proceed under the 1973 Hague Convention, since it does not contain a provision like that found in Article 27, no. 4 of the 1968 Brussels Convention.[58]

56 Art. 27, no. 4 of the 1968 Brussels Convention reads as follows: "A decision is not recognized if the Court of the state in which the decision was given, with respect to a preliminary question which involves the civil status, the legal and acting capacity as well as the legal representation of a natural person [...], contradicts a provision of the private international law of the State in which recognition is enforced, unless the decision would not have led to another result if the provisions of the private international law of the latter State had been applied."

57 Corte Superiore Palermo of 7 March 1980, *Der Amtsvormund*, 1980, 668.

58 Horst Klinkhardt, "Einige Erfahrungen mit der Geltendmachung der Unterhaltsansprüche nichtehelicher Kinder im Ausland",

However, one must note that in several countries an enforcement declaration for German maintenance orders in favour of children born out of wedlock is fundamentally impossible either under the 1968 Brussels Convention or under the 1973 Hague Convention,[59] if the maintenance decision is not supported by an acknowledgement of paternity or if the determination of paternity on which the decision rests is based exclusively on the testimony of the mother. Instead, additional witness statements and further evidence must be adduced for paternity to be unambiguously established. Otherwise, the German decision would be declared unenforceable, a violation of national public policy being invoked.[60]

The evaluation of the files confirms the information from the German Institute that, for maintenance claims to be enforced abroad in favour of children born out of wedlock, the 1973 Hague Convention is always applied if the maintenance decision is not supported by an acknowledgement of paternity. The Institute thereby avoids the risk posed by Article 27, no. 4 of the 1968 Brussels Convention. In the cases of the sampling from 1991, where maintenance was to be judicially enforced in favour of children born out of wedlock, in 12.9 per cent of the cases the 1973 Hague Convention was applied, and in 8.9 per cent of the cases the 1968 Brussels Convention.

By contrast, if foreign maintenance claims are to be enforced *in* Germany, for the application of a convention it is absolutely irrelevant whether children are born in or out of wedlock. Around 50 per cent of the incoming cases were enforced via the 1973 Hague Convention and around 50 per cent via other conventions. This is above all due to the fact that many of the incoming applications originated in the former Czechoslovakia, and these are always

Zentralblatt für Jugendrecht (1984), 161–9, at 163–4. According to the German Institute, this still applies today.

59 For example, in France and Belgium.

60 See, with respect to France, Horst Klinkhardt, "Einige Erfahrungen mit der Geltendmachung der Unterhaltsansprüche nichtehelicher Kinder im Ausland", pp. 161–9 (166 with reference to a decision of the French Court of Cassation of 19 December 1973) – according to information from the German Institute in February 1995, nothing has changed in this respect up to now; cf. German Institute Expert Report of 25 June 1992, *Zentralblatt für Jugendrecht* (1992), 489; cf. for Belgium: German Institute Expert Report of 25 February 1992, *Zentralblatt für Jugendrecht* (1992), 490.

enforced via the 1973 Hague Convention, because the Brussels Convention is not applicable there.

On account of the many cases processed by the German Institute in various countries, the employees of the Institute possess extensive knowledge about the legal requirements in the respective states, so that unanticipated problems are rarely encountered. However, the German Institute is also quite risk-averse. The study of the files revealed that, prior to submission of each application, the existing documents are examined to see whether they will satisfy the requirements of the country in which enforcement is sought. Only when all documents are complete and translated into the respective national language is the application for an enforcement order filed. Sometimes it can take a very long time to assemble the documents, since the Institute corresponds exclusively with the competent youth welfare office and this office must in turn contact the parent with custody to secure the required documents. This examination always takes place at the outset in order to keep the risk of a rejection as low as possible from the start – and evidently with some success: of the cases accepted for processing in 1991 by the German Institute, only two enforcement order applications were rejected.

If one turns to the application frequency of the enforcement conventions and the 1956 New York Convention, one finds no significant differences, at least between the 1956 New York Convention and the 1973 Hague Convention. The number of maintenance claims enforced abroad via the 1973 Hague Convention and via the 1956 New York Convention each stand at 6.4 per cent of the total number of maintenance claims to be enforced abroad. The 1968 Brussels Convention was used in 4.7 per cent of the cases. These very low figures result from the fact that, among other things, in 40.3 per cent of the cases, for various reasons, no judicial enforcement of the maintenance claim took place, and in 34.4 per cent an applicability of the 1968 Brussels Convention was excluded from the outset by the participation of the USA. A greater significance of any one convention vis-à-vis another cannot be derived from the application frequencies. However, differences could result from the success rates.

With respect to the number of cases already concluded[61] by the respective conventions, it is evident that many of the procedures implemented under the enforcement conventions were concluded.

61 Table 6.4 includes all 313 cases which were accepted for processing in 1991 and where judicial enforcement was concluded by May 1995.

The procedure was concluded in 63.6 per cent of the claims enforced under the 1968 Brussels Convention and in 87.9 per cent of the claims enforced under the 1973 Hague Convention. The study of the files confirmed, however, that procedures under the 1956 New York Convention are characterized by very long procedural periods.[62] As many as 80 per cent of the procedures via the 1956 New York Convention still are not concluded; these involve eight claims being enforced in The Netherlands and four in Australia, whose outcomes are still completely open. This confirms once again that procedures under the 1956 New York Convention are associated with very long procedural periods[63] (see Table 6.4).

Table 6.4: Procedural Status of Maintenance Cases at the German Institute under Applicable Law (N=149 Cases from 1991)

	Concluded Procedures		Unconcluded Procedures		Totals	
	Number	%	Number	%	Number	%
Brussels 1968	7	63.6	4	36.4	11	4.0
Hague 1973	29	87.9	4	12.1	33	22.1
New York 1956	3	20.0	12	80.0	15	10.1
URESA	40	62.5	24	37.5	64	43.0
Other	22	84.6	4	15.4	26	17.4
Total	101	67.8	48	32.2	149	100.0

For various reasons, however, the mere applicability of the 1968 Brussels Convention or the 1973 Hague Convention does not automatically lead to a successful outcome of the procedure. If the legal position in the country where enforcement is sought is very similar to German law, even decisions in favour of children born out of wedlock can be enforced without complications. However, determinative for whether a maintenance enforcement can be brought to a successful conclusion is the factual and economic situation in the country of enforcement. Obtaining a court decision declaring a domestic decision enforceable abroad frequently creates few

62 On the reasons for the long procedural period, see p. 204.

63 However, according to information from the German Institute – viewed on the whole – an enforcement should succeed, although it may require a good deal of patience.

difficulties, but problems *are* caused by the actual enforcement of payments owing to the predominantly low payment capability. Thus, in southern Spain, in principle maintenance is only enforced if the debtor is well-off.[64] On the other hand, the German Institute states that there are good possibilities for enforcing maintenance in Barcelona. Also in southern Italy, despite the applicability of the enforcement conventions, enforcement is attempted only in cases where the debtor possesses sufficient assets, such as hotels or land.[65]

In other countries, such as those of Asia and Africa, procedures are virtually *never* undertaken any more, owing to the low wage levels.[66] Nor is enforcement attempted in Brazil. While it is possible to have a German order declared enforceable there,[67] in practice the demands cannot be implemented, since the enforcement system simply does not function in Brazil.[68]

Thus one can see that knowledge about the economic situation and legal–cultural differences in the countries where enforcement is being sought is highly significant. The prospects for successfully collecting maintenance depend essentially on the wage levels in the individual countries, for often these also determine the real payment capability of a given maintenance debtor. In practice, therefore, maintenance claims are pursued only in countries where one can count on obtaining maintenance payments which stand in some kind of reasonable proportion to the accruing costs. Since the youth welfare offices, that is the cities, administrative districts and communities themselves, cover the fees accruing in connection with a claim enforced by the German Institute,[69] all decisions must take this economic efficiency principle into account.

64 Cf. Deutsches Institut für Vormundschaftswesen, *Zentralblatt für Jugendrecht* (1993), 497.

65 Horst Klinkhardt, "Einige Erfahrungen mit der Geltendmachung der Unterhaltsansprüche nichtehelicher Kinder im Ausland", pp. 209–42, at 209; German Institute Expert Report of 13 December 1991, *Zentralblatt für Jugendrecht* (1992), 202–3.

66 According to information from the German Institute.

67 Although Brazil has not acceded to the enforcement conventions.

68 Information from the German Institute; cf. also German Institute Expert Report of 30 April 1992, *Zentralblatt für Jugendrecht* (1992), 438.

69 In fact, in a number of German *Länder* the parent with custody is called upon to pay for costs accruing for required translations. If this parent is unwilling to bear the costs, there will be no enforcement.

The enforcement conventions are *always* used by the Institute when the maintenance debtor lives in Great Britain, France, Belgium[70] or Sweden.[71] Of the decisions submitted via the enforcement conventions, 84 per cent were declared to be enforceable in the procedures already concluded. The balance is not so positive with regard to the actually incoming maintenance *payments,* however. The number of maintenance payments received for claims enforced under the 1956 New York Convention is even lower, but it must also be taken into consideration that until now there have been only a very small number of cases concluded. Thus only two of the case files in the 1991 sampling have resulted in maintenance payments.[72] Overall, the German Institute can point to a very solid success rate: maintenance payments were registered in 64.1 per cent of the cases judicially enforced abroad (see Table 6.5).

Table 6.5: Success of the Maintenance Recovery by the German Institute in Outgoing Cases (N=78 Cases from 1991)

	Obtained Maintenance Payments		No Maintenance Payments		Totals	
	Number	%	Number	%	Number	%
Brussels 1968	3	37.5	5	62.5	8	10.3
Hague 1973	3	27.3	8	72.7	11	14.1
New York 1956	2	100.0	—	—	2	2.6
URESA	33	89.2	4	10.8	37	47.4
Other	9	45.0	11	55.0	20	25.6
Total	50	64.1	28	35.9	78	100.0

In Italy, enforcement was attempted in six cases from the evaluated file materials, three of which were brought to a successful conclusion;

70 However, Belgium did not accede to the 1973 Hague Convention, so that an enforcement there takes place via the 1958 Hague Convention.

71 In Sweden, enforcement takes place most of the time via an enforcement convention, but exceptionally also via the New York Convention.

72 In the third case concluded under the New York Convention, the complaint was withdrawn.

that is, the decisions were declared enforceable.[73] In two cases, payments were registered, both coming after the declaration of enforcement of the German order.

Study of the files revealed that attempts are no longer made to enforce maintenance in Portugal, Greece,[74] Spain and Turkey. Inquiries coming in from the youth welfare offices about the possibilities of success in these countries received the answer that any such attempt was virtually certain to fail. Thus in 1990 a total of (at least) 50 cases were registered which, on the basis of this assessment, were not accepted for processing.[75] This in turn meant that in 1991 the inquiries concerning these countries from the youth welfare offices dropped off substantially: only nine inquiries were registered.[76] The youth welfare offices evidently do take note of the expert reports published on these countries in the *Amtsvormund* (Official Guardian) and the *Zentralblatt für Jugendrecht* (Central Journal for Juvenile Law), which regularly pointed out the slim to non-existent chances of success in these states. The expert reports are expressly designed to help the youth welfare offices independently assess the success potential of a given case. In answering inquiries from the youth welfare offices, the German Institute frequently refers to an already published expert report.

Considering all the outgoing and incoming applications, one finds a dependence of the receipt of payment on the application of the conventions. Maintenance payments were obtained in 37.5 per cent of the cases enforced via the 1968 Brussels Convention, and in

73 The other three cases were not concluded.

74 Klinkhardt, “Einige Erfahrungen mit der Geltendmachung der Unterhaltsansprüche nichtehelicher Kinder im Ausland”, p. 209; German Institute Expert Report of 21 August 1989, *Zentralblatt für Jugendrecht* (1989), 549–50; German Institute Expert Report of 10 April 1991, *Zentralblatt für Jugendrecht* (1991), 414; German Institute Expert Report of 29 July 1991, *Zentralblatt für Jugendrecht* (1991), 539.

75 Distributed over the countries as follows: Turkey 23 case; Greece 10; Spain 12 and Portugal five. The number of cases is not great; according to the Statistisches Bundesamt there were, for example, 1,965,577 Turkish citizens living in Germany in 1994 and there are many divided families among them.

76 Distribution here: Turkey three; Greece two; Spain two; Portugal two.

51.7 per cent of the cases enforced via the 1973 Hague Convention. However, for the majority of the maintenance payments obtained via the 1973 Hague Convention this was not a success of the convention as such. Applications for an order of enforcement for incoming applications coming to the German Institute from abroad are generally made under the 1973 Hague Convention. Obviously, in Germany, thanks to its functioning enforcement system and also owing to the relatively strong economic situation, there are good prospects of actually obtaining the maintenance. In the final analysis, for receiving maintenance payments what is decisive is not the application of specific conventions, but rather the legal and economic situation in the country where enforcement is being sought (see Table 6.6).

Table 6.6: The Receipt of Maintenance Payments at the German Institute in Incoming and Outgoing Cases as a Function of the Application of the 1968 Brussels Convention or the 1973 Hague Convention (N=110 Cases from 1991)

	Obtained Maintenance Payments		No Maintenance Payments		Totals	
	Number	%	Number	%	Number	%
Brussels 1968	3	37.5	5	62.5	8	7.3
Hague 1973	15	51.7	14	48.3	29	26.4
Other	52	71.2	21	28.8	73	66.4
Total	70	63.6	40	36.4	110	100.0

The significance of the enforcement conventions must therefore always be considered from the perspective that maintenance claims ultimately can be enforced in only a very few of the states which have acceded to the conventions. The German Institute thus makes a preliminary selection with respect to the countries in which an enforcement of maintenance claims appears worthwhile.

Legal Relations with the USA As already mentioned, legal relations with the USA represent a great part of the German Institute's activities. Earlier, virtually no assistance was given for enforcing maintenance claims in the USA, since the laws of several US states did not allow for any claims for children born out of wedlock. A

German Institute staff member then discovered the URESA, through which legal relations could first be developed with the state of California. Thus reciprocity was declared between California and the Federal Republic of Germany (effectively represented by the German Institute); this was first manifested and formally confirmed, however, through enactment of the *Auslandsunterhaltsgesetz*.[77]

Thus, when child maintenance claims are to be enforced in the USA, the German Institute reports that it does not normally make use of the *Auslandsunterhaltsgesetz*. Instead, in such cases – after a local court examines the need for legal action to be taken – the complaints are filed directly with the central authority of the receiving state which is competent under (R)URESA. This agency then turns to a subordinate agency in the area where the debtor resides and assigns the offices of the county or district attorney to process the case (free of charge) and thus protect the interests of the creditor. Nevertheless, the address (or at least the general area where the debtor is residing) must be known for the agency to be able to take action. The debtor is then called upon by the county or district attorney to explain his position on the maintenance demand. Then either he pays voluntarily or legal action, which has already been prepared in Germany by the German Institute, is initiated. The Institute thus enters directly into the sphere of action of the (R)URESA. This procedure is made possible by the fact that the *Auslandsunterhaltsgesetz* does not restrict the long-practised approach of the Institute. It is not an exclusive regulation, so that maintenance claims can be enforced through it, but a complaint can also be filed directly with the American authorities. Thus a maintenance action is filed under the (R)URESA in 83.8 per cent of all cases where the maintenance debtor lives in the USA.

The German Institute also has access to an American agency which can help out when it is seeking an address. At the outset of any maintenance action, one always has to find out where the debtor is staying. One way to do this is via a request to the Parent Locator Service,[78] which will try to find the debtor. The advantage here is that investigations are not limited to a single state. Nevertheless, several minimum pieces of data are required for the investigation to have a chance of success. One must know at least the debtor's approximate age (or, even better, his date of birth), his place of

77 See above, p. 198.

78 The Parent Locator Service is a federal agency which provides assistance in finding addresses relating to a URESA complaint.

birth, his earlier residence and, if at all possible, his social security number.[79] Often not all of the desired data on the person are available, yet the residence of the debtor frequently *can* be identified. On the other hand, the less information provided, the longer the search will take.[80] Nevertheless, in 85.7 per cent of the US cases the current address could be found, and in 91.7 per cent of those cases the Parent Locator Service was used.

A problem arises when the debtor moves to another district after the complaint has been filed. In this case a new complaint has to be filed, since a complaint initiated in one district will not be further processed in another.[81]

As stated above, even if the German Institute enforces maintenance claims in the USA without invoking the *Auslandsunterhaltsgesetz*, it retains significance for the Institute. For processing foreign complaints in the USA under the (R)URESA, it is required that reciprocity be guaranteed with the state from which the complaint originates. Even before the *Auslandsunterhaltsgesetz* entered into effect, several US states[82] had declared that Germany was to be regarded as a country with which reciprocity did exist. But now, since the *Auslandsunterhaltsgesetz* has come into effect, reciprocity exists with further US states. One disadvantage for the German Institute did develop from this with respect to the legal relations with Texas, which only processed applications submitted via the Central Authority in Berlin. In the interim,[83] however, direct working relations between Texas and the German Institute have been established. Reciprocity still has not been declared vis-à-vis the states of Alabama, Mississippi and South Carolina, although from the German Institute at least working relations have been established with South Carolina.

Of the US cases accepted for processing in 1991 and which were enforced by means of a (R)URESA complaint, 62.5 per cent have now been concluded. The receipt of maintenance payments was registered in 89 per cent of the concluded cases. The number of maintenance payments obtained through (R)URESA complaints comprises 47 per cent of all the recorded payment receipts.

79 See Lyanne Laschitza, "Durchsetzung von Unterhaltsansprüchen in den USA", *Zentralblatt für Jugendrecht* (1994), 25–6, at 26.

80 According to information from the German Institute.

81 German Institute information.

82 For example, California, Texas, Florida, North Carolina.

83 Situation as of December 1995.

If maintenance claims are to be enforced against members of the US Army, the German Institute uses a different approach (at least some of the time). Here again, enforcement does not take place under the *Auslandsunterhaltsgesetz.* Instead, a simple letter (in English, however, and accompanied by the order and its translation) is sent to the debtor's superior officer, requesting that he 'urge' the debtor to make the maintenance payments. This approach may be effective. The debtor then arranges for a standing order under which the paymaster of the US Army withholds a regular fixed amount from his pay. The reason for the voluntary payments is probably a sense of honour which a member of the US Army – under prodding from his superior officer, if necessary – must satisfy. If this method does not successfully produce the maintenance payments, a complaint is filed in the form of a (R)URESA application and in the case of a positive decision for the maintenance creditor, the enforcement will be based on this. The Department of the Army method was chosen in 15 per cent of the maintenance claims to be enforced in the USA, but only in 25 per cent of these cases could maintenance payments be obtained.

In all, maintenance payments were registered in 76 per cent of the claims enforced in the USA.[84]

Maintenance Recovery in Incoming and Outgoing Cases Receipt of maintenance payments was registered in 37 per cent of all (incoming and outgoing) cases accepted for processing by the German Institute in 1991. Of these, payment took place voluntarily in 42 per cent of the cases, before any complaint had to be filed. The study of the files showed that in only 56 per cent of the evaluated cases did judicial enforcement take place, since (among other things) in 30 per cent of the 44 per cent of non-judicially enforced cases the debtors voluntarily assumed maintenance payments.

Table 6.7 shows how maintenance payments could be obtained for the incoming and the outgoing applications. It is striking that maintenance debtors living in Germany start making payments voluntarily much more frequently prior to the conclusion of the judicial procedure than do debtors living abroad. The debtors living in Germany are frequently foreigners from the former Czechoslovakia, Poland or Romania. The economic situation is poor in these countries, the wage levels are very low and living conditions corre-

84 These are cases in which the address could be found; in the other cases, no enforcement was made.

Table 6.7: The Type of Maintenance Recovery as a Function of Incoming or Outgoing Applications (N=107 Cases from 1991)

	Enforcement of Judgment Procedure		Voluntary Payments prior to Conclusion of Procedure		Voluntary Payments after Conclusion of Procedure		Totals	
	Number	%	Number	%	Number	%	Number	%
Incoming application	6	11.5	35	67.3	11	21.2	52	48.6
Outgoing application	12	21.8	21	38.2	22	40.0	55	51.4
Total	18	16.8	56	52.3	33	30.8	107	100.0

Note: The type of maintenance recovery could not be determined in three cases.

spondingly difficult. By German standards, the amount of the maintenance payments enforced is usually very low, frequently involving payments of DM50 a month or less. Perhaps maintenance debtors living in Germany feel a moral obligation to pay maintenance for their children living abroad (generally with the mother) because they know all too well the conditions there from personal experience. Or perhaps the debtors are simply motivated by the certitude that, should they refuse to make the payments, they are threatened with a judicial procedure and – sooner or later – compulsory enforcement. It is therefore conceivable that the debtors wish to spare themselves this social embarrassment, especially given the relatively trivial amounts they are being asked to pay. In any event, cases in which enforcement of judgment must be performed are by no means the rule in Germany, but very much the exception.

Cross-border cooperation of the German Institute with institutions of the area of former Czechoslovakia

A very important aspect within the framework of maintenance enforcement is the cooperation of the German Institute with foreign authorities and institutions, since mere applicability of a convention is still no guarantee of successful enforcement. Thus there would be little chance of successfully maintaining enforcement in the USA without the possibility of asking the Parent Locator Service to find a debtor's address. The co-operation of the German Institute with institutions located abroad can lead to quicker (and above all cheaper) enforcement of claims if these institutions are able to help not only with determining residence, but also with enforcing the claims themselves by representing creditors in a judicial procedure. In this case, the high attorney's fees are avoided, which otherwise are generally not covered by legal aid.

In the 1930s, the Central Authority for the International Legal Protection of Juveniles was established in Brünn for the area of former Czechoslovakia. This agency was patterned on the German Institute. After the Second World War, it was reformed and incorporated into the Ministry of Justice. The German Institute has cooperated with the Central Authority in Brünn for decades and the collaboration is described by the German Institute as excellent.

When, in 1993, the two successor states of the former Czechoslovakia were formed, the legal relations of the German Institute with the Czech Republic continued to run through the Central Authority in Brünn without change. In the Slovak Republic, a new organization, the Central Authority for the International Legal Protection of Children and Young People, was set up within the framework of the Ministry of the Interior in Bratislava. In the meantime, the German Institute has developed good reciprocal working relations with this agency as well. However, it is noteworthy that the area of the Slovak Republic offers significantly fewer procedures than the Czech Republic.

Both central authorities support domestic creditors in the enforcement of their maintenance claims abroad as well as foreign creditors in domestic enforcement. If a claim is to be enforced in Germany, creditors living in these two states turn with their requests to the central authority of their respective country, which in turn calls upon the German Institute, which will then take action in Germany on behalf of the foreign creditor. If enforcement of a German claim is sought in the Czech or Slovak Republic, the German Institute transmits the required documents in all cases directly to the respective central authority, which then handles the enforcement of this claim. The advantage of this cross-border cooperation lies above all in the fact that the respective institutions process the applications very quickly. If certain documents required for enforcement are still missing, they immediately inform their counterparts so that no unnecessary delays arise. Naturally, delays caused by the lack of cooperation of the *creditors* cannot be compensated by swift processing of the case by the institutions. If important documents are missing, it is usually the creditors who must procure them. Sometimes this takes a very long time, so that the whole procedure can be drawn out, and there is nothing the institutions can do about it. The legal relations with the central authority in Brünn account for the largest share of the incoming applications arriving at the German Institute from abroad, and they also run very smoothly with respect to the incoming German applications from the German Institute.[85] Of the incoming maintenance applications among the file materials studied from 1991, 65 per cent came from Brünn. However, in 69.4 per cent of the incoming cases, the debtor voluntarily paid prior to the filing of a complaint and signed an obligation document, so that only in the other cases did judicial enforcement come into question. In these remaining cases, however, 95.2 per cent of the decisions were declared enforceable, and in only one case (4.8 per cent) was an application for an enforcement order rejected. Receipt of maintenance payments was registered in 82.6 per cent of the cases. Cases sent by the German Institute to the central authority in Brünn make up 4 per cent of the sampling.

Conclusion

The study demonstrates the high degree to which the actors participating in cross-border legal relations in child maintenance cases, when pursuing their claims in another state, are dependent on support not only through international treaties, but particularly from institutions. This prompts the question whether legal globalization in this area is sufficient to offer the entitled parties the necessary support, or whether additional forms of support are required. The literature on globalization shows that, in all areas of cross-border legal relations, legal standards either do not exist or are insufficient for regulation, and thus the globalization of the law is straggling far behind the globalization of the markets. Various structures have therefore evolved in the different areas in order to close the existing gaps. One can speak here of cognitive mechanisms,[86] that is exchange relations between the participating actors which are suitable for offering such legal certainty even in cases of

85 According to information from the German Institute.

86 On the relation between cognitive elements of social order and normative rule, see Volkmar Gessner, "Kognitive Elemente sozialer Ordnung", in *Normenerosion*, ed. Monika Frommel and Volkmar Gessner (Baden-Baden: Nomos, 1996), 207 et seq.

conflict. Borrowing from Luhmann's definition of the concept of legal certainty, here too the (subjective) expectative certainty of the actors participating in the legal relations is seen as the decisive criterion for the existence of legal certainty.[87] It is important here to distinguish between structures which are classified as 'roles' and those seen as 'programmes'.[88] Explicitly referring to Luhmann's concept, Gessner likewise distinguishes between two (main) levels in the social institutions of cross-border legal relations: 'programmes' and 'roles'.[89] For the legal certainty of the actors participating in the cross-border legal relations, the institutions assigned to the 'role level' are far more important than those classified as 'programmes'. This is because the former are executive bodies which take direct action. By contrast, the 'programmes', while they may often provide important legal framework conditions, are – because they have to be implemented – unsuitable for giving the participants a (subjective) feeling of legal certainty.

In the area of the enforcement of cross-border maintenance claims, an attempt has been made to unify and globalize the law to be applied by creating enforcement conventions at the normative level. However, these conventions can only be utilized with respect to titles for which a declaration of enforcement has already been applied by a foreign court. Yet the problem of maintenance enforcement is already rooted in a much earlier phase of enforcement, that of access to these legal regulations. One must therefore ask how well-suited the support mechanisms made specially available to those entitled to maintenance really are for closing this wide gap. First, one must note that the mechanisms which currently exist in other legal areas are simply unusable for maintenance creditors. The international economic actors mentioned earlier enter into cross-border legal relations in full knowledge, understanding the risks and behaving accordingly, for example by vetting prospective business partners right at the start. And if conflicts still arise, the participants have a panoply of conflict-resolution instruments at their disposal.[90]

87 See the extensive discussion in Niklas Luhmann, *Rechtssoziologie*, (Opladen: Westdeutscher Verlag, 1983), 54, 85 et seq.

88 On distinguishing the various levels and their effects on expectative certainty in general, see Niklas Luhmann, *Rechtssoziologie* (Opladen: Westdeutscher Verlag, 1983), 85.

89 Cf. Gessner Chapter 12 of the present volume.

90 See Chapters 1, 3 and 4 in the present volume.

By contrast, children entitled to maintenance do not enter into voluntary contractual relationships forming the basis of their maintenance claims. Instead, they are involuntary actors born into the legal relationship who cannot eliminate *ab initio* the possible risk of non-performance by the person owing the maintenance. The foreign connection frequently arises only after the debtor has moved away. Insurance against the risk of non-payment by the maintenance debtor is no more available – apart from subsidiary social services – than are the other mentioned security possibilities. If maintenance debtors who live abroad do not pay, the children are forced to participate in international legal relations if they want to enforce their (in most cases paltry) claims.

In the following, we will analyse the extent to which the mechanisms existing in the field of maintenance claims enforcement are suitable for offering maintenance creditors effective support, and above all legal certainty.

Legal Certainty through Government Support Mechanisms

On the basis of welfare state considerations, in 1956, states entered into a UN Convention creating an international network through which the barriers against access to foreign courts and institutions could be surmounted, and with whose aid maintenance creditors could enforce their claims in the respective state parties to the Convention by turning to the transmitting and receiving agencies. Thus maintenance creditors are given access to foreign authorities and courts, something which is absolutely essential for enforcing maintenance claims abroad. While one must reckon with very long processing times, the Convention does offer the legal framework conditions for the cooperation of different states with differing legal systems.[91] This Convention should be seen as a first stage in globalizing the field of cross-border maintenance claims enforcement legally as well. No deregulation of the national legal orders occurs here; instead, the 1956 UN Convention and the creation of the transmitting and receiving agencies allowed the national legal norms to be embedded within 'inter-national' structures. The

91 The 1956 UN Convention guarantees an analogous course of enforcement and can thus offer certainty in this respect. Here, however, the view is represented that, in cross-border legal relations, "roles" (in this case "roles" of a governmental nature) are far more important than "programmes".

national legal norms of the foreign states are retained and rendered compatible with one another through institutionalization on a global level. This is not an institutionalization with a hierarchical structure, so there is no superior/inferior relationship between the respective participating agencies; rather, the 1956 UN Convention contains rules for a 'horizontal structure' which allows transmitting and receiving agencies to communicate with each another on a single level.

However, one must ask whether this system offers the affected maintenance creditors sufficient legal certainty to induce them to actually enforce their claims. The German transmitting agencies under the 1956 UN Convention are very rarely called upon by maintenance creditors to enforce their cross-border claims. Why? A first explanatory element is that the transmitting agencies are ill-suited for offering the entitled parties legal certainty. Under the above-mentioned definition, the transmitting agencies should clearly be assigned to the 'role level'. However, one must also take into account that these agencies are merely implementing bodies of the 1956 UN Convention, thus of a 'programme'. In this connection it should be noted that most of the government institutions which occupy a supporting position in cross-border legal relations act on the basis of international conventions. In this case, however, the transmitting agencies are in fact departments within agencies which perform a pure transmission activity. Even the local courts which, at least in Germany, are responsible for accepting the applications under the 1956 UN Convention cannot give the applicants a feeling of legal certainty. In the final analysis, this is merely an agency which sends the requests on to other agencies, at home and abroad. One never knows how motivated the specialists of the following agency will be in dealing with a request.

Often, however, maintenance creditors have absolutely no access to the mechanisms, such as the 1956 UN Convention, which create the infrastructure for cross-border maintenance enforcement in the first place and make it possible for the actors to participate in international legal relations. In cross-border child maintenance cases, alongside the age-related, very weak position of the child entitled to maintenance, there is the additional difficulty that the persons with custody frequently have their own maintenance problems to deal with. It is possible that many of those who are entitled are wholly unaware of the existing international network and its scope of application, and believe that they must themselves contact foreign lawyers, authorities and courts, for maintenance creditors can expect little support even from their own lawyers, since the latter too often do not know what to do with claims which must be enforced across borders. A truly decisive role is therefore played by advising and supporting institutions on the national level, here meaning the domestic youth agencies in particular. The caseworkers in the youth agencies are in a position to develop a relationship of confidence with some maintenance creditors, or those with custody over them. If the maintenance claims of minors are to be enforced abroad, however, a trust relationship between the entitled party and the youth welfare office is not enough to give the entitled party a feeling of legal certainty. Decisive here are the existing contacts which the youth welfare office can use to enforce the claims. For only if the caseworkers understand the sequence of the enforcement process, and in particular know the specialists responsible for handling the requests, can the maintenance creditor receive a convincing explanation of the course of an enforcement attempt and its chances of success.[92]

With respect to the procedure under the 1956 UN Convention, one cannot escape the impression that even the caseworkers of the

92 However, access to the authorities is not as simple in every state as it is in the major industrial countries. In many Third World countries, maintenance creditors do not possess the necessary possibilities of access to the authorities, and for that very reason they do not know that maintenance claims can also be enforced across borders, which support possibilities they could call upon, or how their claims might ultimately be implemented. In particular, the participation of Third World countries (which was registered in only a very few cases in the study) permits one to suppose that entitled persons living there have no idea of the legal possibilities of maintenance enforcement and also no access to the corresponding agencies. The selection process – already often described and investigated in the industrial countries (see on this Richard Miller and Austin Sarat, "Grievances, Claims and Disputes", *Law and Society Review* 15 (1980/81), 525 ff; Hubert Rottleuthner, "Probleme der Beobachtung von Arbeitsgerichtsverfahren", in *Interaktion vor Gericht*, ed. Wolfgang Hoffmann-Riem (Baden-Baden: Nomos, 1978), 109 et seq) – which ensures that the number of claims enforced in court is far smaller than the number of actually existing claims therefore plays a considerably greater role in countries where there is little legal knowledge or possibilities of access to advising institutions.

youth welfare offices do not get a sense of legal certainty from the accepting, transmitting and receiving agencies of the 1956 New York Convention. The responsibility of the different agencies at various procedural stages leads to a completely formalized, anonymous processing of the requests, which makes informal exchanges between the participating agencies impossible.

Legal Certainty through Utilization of the German Institute for Guardianship

All the above is structured differently within the framework of the collaboration of the youth agencies with the German Institute. The youth welfare offices[93] can turn with their requests on a wholly informal basis to the Institute, where they receive highly competent advice. With these consultations, however, the Institute also functions like a filter. Generally, no attempt is made to enforce a claim if the Institute gives a negative assessment of its chances of success. If maintenance debtors reside in states where attempts to enforce claims have already failed in past cases, enforcement attempts are forsworn in later, similar cases, because the youth welfare offices regard them as hopeless from the start. The filtering effect which emanates in any case from the German Institute with respect to cross-border maintenance claims of children living in Germany is further reinforced by the fact that the Institute's monthly bulletin regularly prints expert opinions which, time and again, point out the hopelessness of such efforts in certain states.

To enforce claims should the situation have improved in the interim, the German Institute regularly checks an enforcement's prospects of success by sending inquiries to the corresponding foreign authorities, thus avoiding unnecessary court procedures and undue burdens on the maintenance creditor. The Institute legitimates itself through a successful procedure in which no unnecessary costs are generated and where the interests of the child also receive consideration. In this way, over many years a trust relationship has developed between the youth welfare offices and the Institute which at the same time gives the youth welfare offices legal certainty. Were the Institute to begin pursuing maintenance claims with increasingly unpredictable outcomes, the confidence which the youth welfare offices place in the Institute would de-

93 Those persons with custody of children entitled to maintenance can also address themselves directly to the German Institute, but then they have to bear the costs incurred for maintenance enforcement.

cline because that (for them, decisive) feeling of legal certainty would disappear. For the work of the youth welfare offices, it would mean that they in turn would be unable to give the entitled parties a feeling of legal certainty.

Its many years of collaboration with local courts also give the German Institute better possibilities for monitoring the progress of the cases. In some cases, the Institute also calls upon the assistance of the 1956 UN Convention, which means that the already long chain of instances provided for by the Convention is extended by yet another link. On the other hand, however, intensive monitoring of the further procedural progress as well as a checking of payment receipts exert a positive effect on the overall success of an enforced maintenance claim. The pathways prescribed under the 1956 UN Convention and the *Auslandsunterhaltsgesetz* (AUG) always provide for forwarding to the next authority in the chain of instances of the respective legally defined sequence. This means the requesting person or the youth welfare office has only very limited possibilities for controlling the time frame. Once the request has been sent along the line of the various authorities, the applicant can often only obtain reliable information about the progress of the case by inquiring.

In cases concerning the USA, by contrast, the German Institute gets back the pre-examined request before it is sent abroad. On the basis of the experience it has acquired, the necessary time periods can be better estimated, so that after a certain length of time inquiries about the status of the case can be made. Already in this phase, the time period required for preparing the request can be checked. Frequently, however, even this is unnecessary, since the DIV (German Institute for Guardianship) is already informed about possible delays in the preliminary examination, thanks in large part to the many years of close collaboration. In particular, the collaboration between the German Institute and the US authorities (which was already practised long before the AUG entered into effect) allowed youth welfare offices to enforce maintenance across borders on behalf of their wards, thus fulfilling their responsibilities within the framework of the existing official guardianships. The collaboration of the German Institute with the youth welfare offices is characterized by a long tradition rooted in the cooperation which the Institute had already engaged in for decades with foreign agencies.

Thus, over many years a trusting collaboration has developed between the youth welfare offices and the DIV, which has led the youth welfare offices to continue turning to the Institute.[94] At this level, a parallel can be seen with the *lex mercatoria* - even though far less advanced than in international trade – insofar as the youth agencies have freed themselves, with respect to maintenance claims of minors to be enforced across borders, from the network of public law and prefer the private-law structure of the German Institute in order to surmount the fragmentation of the transmitting agencies under the 1956 UN Convention in the individual federal *Länder*. They can therefore profit without restriction from the external communication of the Institute. The Institute, which cooperates independent of international treaties, affords certainty through the long-term stability of its staff, that is the permanent presence of concrete individuals who, considered sociologically, occupy a position as personal guarantor.[95] The German Institute thus compensates for the deficits government authorities reveal in the area of the enforcement of cross-border child maintenance claims, and in Germany de facto takes over for outgoing requests the tasks of the 'central authority' as well as the transmitting and receiving agencies.

References

Bergmann, Alexander and Murad Ferid. 1993. *Internationales Ehe- und Kindschaftsrecht*. 6th edn, Vol. X. Frankfurt/M.: Verlag für Standesamtswesen.

Böhmer Christof. 1987. Das Auslandsunterhaltsgesetz vom 19.12.1986. *Praxis des Internationalen Privat- und Verfahrensrechts*.

Cremades, Bernardo and Steven Plehn. 1984. The New Lex Mercatoria and the Harmonization of the Laws of International Commercial Transactions, *Boston University International Law Journal*, pp. 317–48.

German Institute Expert Report of 21 August 1989. 1989. *Zentralblatt für Jugendrecht*.

German Institute Expert Report of 10 April 1991. 1991. *Zentralblatt für Jugendrecht*.

94 Cf. Cyril Hegnauer, "Familie und Staatsgrenzen", *Zeitschrift für Vormundschaftswesen* 38 (1983), 15, 20 et seq, who regards the German Institutute as a very competent institution and would like to see a comparable contact point for the Swiss youth agencies.

95 On concrete persons as personal guarantors, see Luhmann, *Rechtssoziologie*, p. 85.

German Institute Expert Report of 29 July 1991. 1991. *Zentralblatt für Jugendrecht.*

German Institute Expert Report of 13 December 1991. 1992. *Zentralblatt für Jugendrecht.*

German Institute Export Report of 25 February 1992. 1992. *Zentralblatt für Jugendrecht.*

German Institute Expert Report of 30 April 1992. 1992. *Zentralblatt für Jugendrecht.*

German Institute Expert Report of 25 June 1992. 1992. *Zentralblatt für Jugendrecht.*

German Institute Expert Report of 1 October 1993. 1993. *Zentralblatt für Jugendrecht.*

Gessner, Volkmar. 1996. International Cases in German First Instance Courts. In *Foreign Courts – Civil Litigation in Foreign Legal Cultures*, edited by Volkmar Gessner. Aldershot: Dartmouth.

Gessner, Volkmar. 1996. Kognitive Elemente sozialer Ordnung. In *Normenerosion*, edited by Monika Frommel and Volkmar Gessner. Baden-Baden: Nomos.

Hegnauer, Cyril. 1983. Familie und Staatsgrenzen. *Zeitschrift für Vormundschaftswesen* 38.

Jayme, Erik and Rainer Hausmann, eds. 1994. *Internationales Privat- und Verfahrensrecht.* 7th edn. Munich: Beck.

Kappus, Andreas. 1990. *'Lex mercatoria' in Europa und Wiener UN-Kaufrechtskonvention 1980.* Frankfurt/M.: Lang.

Klinkhardt, Horst. 1984. Einige Erfahrungen mit der Geltendmachung der Unterhaltsansprüche nichtehelicher Kinder im Ausland. *Zentralblatt für Jugendrecht.*

Laschitza, Lyanne. 1994. Durchsetzung von Unterhaltsansprüchen in den USA. *Zentralblatt für Jugendrecht.*

Luhmann, Niklas. 1983. *Rechtssoziologie.* Opladen: Westdeutscher Verlag.

Miller, Richard and Austin Sarat. 1980/81. Grievances, Claims and Disputes. *Law and Society Review*, 15.

Münder, Johannes. 1993. *Familien- und Jugendhilferecht*, Vols 1 and 2. Weinheim, Basle: Beltz-Verlag.

Rottleuthner, Hubert. 1978. Probleme der Beobachtung von Arbeitsgerichtsverfahren. In *Interaktion vor Gericht,* edited by Wolfgang Hoffmann-Riem. Baden-Baden: Nomos.

Santel, Bernhard. 1995. *Migration in und nach Europa.* Opladen: Leske & Budrich.

Schellhorn, Walter. 1990. Das Verhältnis von Sozialhilferecht und Unterhaltsrecht – aus der Sicht der Sozialhilfe. *Familie und Recht.*

Schellhorn, Walter. 1996. *Bundessozialhilfegesetz, Commentary*. 16th edn. Neuwied: Luchterhand.

Scholz, Rainer. 1992. *Unterhaltsvorschußgesetz, Commentary*. 2nd edn. Cologne: Heymanns.

Uhlig, Sigmar and Peter Berard. 1987. Die Geltendmachung von Unterhaltsansprüchen im In- und Ausland nach dem AUG. *Neue Juristische Wochenschrift*.

Weise, Paul-Frank. 1990. *Lex mercatoria: materielles Recht vor der internationalen Handelsschiedsgerichtsbarkeit*. Frankfurt/M.: Lang.

The Author

Kirstin Grotheer is a lawyer. In 1995, she joined the research group on 'Global Legal Interaction' at the Centre for European Law and Policy at the University of Bremen and in 1997 started an internship at the Bremen District Court.

Address: Flemingstr.15, 28357 Bremen, Germany.

Abstract

In cross-border legal relations in child maintenance cases there exist multilateral international treaties which attempt to unify and globalize the law to be applied. Furthermore, existing international treaties offer the legal framework conditions for cooperation of different states with differing legal systems. However, more important for persons entitled to maintenance are national institutions which are suited for enabling access to foreign institutions and thus to a foreign legal sphere, so that they are put in a position to actually enforce their claims abroad. Therefore support mechanisms which afford maintenance creditors subjective legal certainty are decisive. For this reason, institutions providing support in Germany, the Czech Republic and Slovakia were empirically investigated to understand how they work, and to discover to what extent these institutions are able, through cross-border collaboration, to offer maintenance creditors legal certainty in enforcing their cross-border claims.

7 Cross-border Legal Issues Arising from International Migrations: the Case of Portugal

PIERRE GUIBENTIF

Cross-border Legal Relations Involving Private Citizens: Typology and Characterization

Cross-border legal relations involving private citizens may be the result, basically, of three different types of circumstances. Individuals may get involved in legally relevant relations with individuals or entities from other countries without leaving their own country. They may develop such relations by moving from one country to another either for longer periods (which is usually qualified as migration) or for shorter periods. Concrete cross-border legal relations may arise from, or lead to, situations which are combinations of those three types of circumstances. For instance, it may sometimes be difficult to draw a sharp distinction between migration and temporary staying abroad. As recent research on Portuguese citizens living in other European countries has shown, there is a trend towards not only maintaining close relations with both host and home country, but also taking advantage of 'double socialization'. Holidays are spent in Portugal, where many families which emigrated have built a house, and journeys between the two countries facilitate different types of small trade. Nevertheless, identifying these three types may help us to define typical patterns of social situations likely to give rise to cross-border legal relations.

Regarding migrations, an important distinction is to be drawn. After somebody has left a country and settled in another one, things may evolve in two different ways. He or she may, abruptly or progressively, lose his or her social ties with the home country. This is the case for most of the nineteenth-century Portuguese emigration to Brazil, as well as, to a significant extent, for contemporary Portuguese overseas emigration. Alternatively, he or she finds a way of maintaining these ties. This is the case for most recent Portuguese emigration to other European countries. The distinction is relevant for our topic since situations of the second type are more likely to produce cross-border legal interaction than those of the first type.

Concerning the two other circumstances – temporary travelling and correspondence – it can be assumed that they will frequently be combined. They do not, as such, provide useful criteria among the possible typical social situations. On the other hand, one might single out two cases, both consisting of combinations of those two circumstances: individuals who have only occasional connections to individuals or entities from other countries (tourists, consumers purchasing goods from foreign sellers) and individuals who have built up regular personal or professional relations with partners abroad.

Three social situations have thus been identified, likely to involve individuals in cross-border legal interaction: migration with maintenance of social ties with the home country, regular contacts with foreign individuals or entities and occasional contacts. Let us now characterize the legal interactions which can arise from those three situations, considering especially the legal domains to which they may be related.

In the first situation, what may give rise to legal interactions are the social ties with the other country. Two types of social ties are likely to acquire legal relevance, actually in quite different ways: family relations and the inclusion of an individual in a larger, legally recognized community. Other relationships, such as friendship or neighbourhood (considered as having a significant role to play in the framing of the Portuguese 'welfare society'[1]), are not likely, *per se*, to acquire legal relevance, even if concrete matters based on such relations may do so.

Family relations are usually subject to detailed legal provisions in national legal systems. Admittedly, these provisions do not, most of

1 See Pedro Hespanha, *Vers une société-providence simultanément pré- et post-moderne. L'état des solidarités inter-générationnelles au Portugal* (Coimbra: Oficina do CES No. 38, 1993); João Arriscado Nunes, "'Com mal ou com bem, aos teus te atém': as solidariedades primárias e os limites da sociedade-providência", *Revista Crítica de Ciências Sociais*, no. 42 (1995), 5–25; Boaventura de Sousa Santos, "Sociedade Providência ou Autoritarismo Social?", *Revista Crítica de Ciências Sociais*, no.42 (1995), i–vii.

the time, actually govern the everyday life of the families. But they can, at any time, be invoked by individuals who want a public entity (social service or judge) to intervene in an intrafamiliar conflict. If a family relation involves individuals living in two (or more) different countries, the question will unavoidably arise as to which of the two (or more) countries' legislation will apply, or which public entity will intervene. Migrations such as Portuguese emigration to other countries in Europe have favoured such situations. Fathers have emigrated, leaving their wives and sons in Portugal. Sometimes both parents emigrate, having left the children with relatives in Portugal. Or one parent returns to Portugal, for instance after a divorce, while the other remains with the sons in the host country.

Relations of individuals to the broader communities they are part of are today shaped in terms of citizenship, that is of legal rights and duties towards the state. Some of these rights and duties may lose their relevance as a citizen leaves his or her country, others will retain it. What remains after an individual has left may be some entitlement to protection by his home country, whether in terms of consular support, or through specific welfare mechanisms that would remain applicable even if the person lived in another country. As far as duties or obligations are concerned, the main issues which have to be taken into account are taxes, military service and social security. To the extent that a person has assets remaining in his or her home country or continues to receive some income there, he or she may have to pay taxes even if living in another country. A person reaching the age of military service will have to discharge his obligations, probably by returning home to do his military service, at least as long as he has no second citizenship which would allow him to invoke a bilateral agreement governing military service obligations in cases of double nationality. Finally, even having left his or her home country, a person may remain subject to, or may opt to contribute to the social security system of his home country, in connection with benefits he will be entitled to receive from that country.

The second situation – the maintenance of regular contacts with foreign partners on the part of individuals who do not leave their home country – may acquire legal relevance as soon as significant financial or material interests are at stake. Admittedly, such interests are more likely to arise in relations between companies or associations involved in large-scale undertakings. But situations of this type involving private persons may also give rise to legal problems; for instance, relations between a company, registered in one country, and a private person, residing in another, who provides the company with paid services, whether as an employee or as a self-employed person. Such cross-border work relations raise questions of contract and possibly labour law. To the extent that payments are made, tax and social security law, of both the countries concerned, may also become relevant.

The third situation, that of persons having occasional contacts with people abroad, applies mainly to tourists, who use transport or accommodation services abroad. It could also apply to individuals purchasing goods or services from sellers registered in other countries. Such occasional relations raise, in particular, issues of product liability. Obviously, this situation can also lead individuals to suffer damages caused, intentionally or not, by third parties whom they meet in foreign countries, which may require the application of tort or penal law.

The features of these three situations allow us to justify the scope of the following analysis. First, we will focus on one of the three situations, that is, migrations. We do so, on the one hand, because this is a context where the other two situations will frequently be included: migrants are likely to have regular and occasional relations in their home country (or, after returning home, in the former host country) which are similar to those arising in the second situation; and, on the other hand, because the problems raised by the two latter situations are covered in Chapters 1 and 3 of the present volume (international contractual relations associating small or medium-sized enterprises; cross-border insurance contracts). Secondly, our analysis is limited to the fields of family and social security law, which relate to two core aspects of the situation of migrants. Furthermore, questions of social security are also an aspect of the second situation which research focusing on corporate actors does not take into account.

The features of the legal fields at stake also dictate the structure of the section entitled 'Analysis of the Selected Fields'. The domain of social security is examined first. By definition, questions of social security are inherently matters of law, and relate to almost all migrants, becoming a routine matter for the agencies in charge of those questions as well as for the persons concerned. On the other hand, legal problems in the field of the family do arise only under specific circumstances, having direct relevance only for a small part of the migrant population and triggering an official involvement which is conceived as taking place only in critical cases. That is why we deal with the questions of family law after looking at social security. A separate discussion of these two issues makes sense since they are covered by different international legal instruments and, in Portugal, are entrusted to different agencies.

This limitation of scope does, however, leave several aspects unanalysed, among which, two deserve to be mentioned. First is the handling, in practice, of cross-border tax matters,[2] a relevant question for two of the three situations. But this is actually a question which should not be analysed separately for private individuals; it is also significant for corporate actors. The second aspect is problems that could be called 'accidental cross-border relations', which could include the handling of damages caused to private persons during their stay in foreign countries, as well as the provision, in practice, of consular support to citizens abroad, whether related to such damages or not.

At the end of this introductory section, one question remains to be tackled. Up to now we have adopted – and have had to adopt – the perspective of individuals. If we want our observations to contribute to the discussion of the globalization issue,[3] we have to characterize the relationship between individual situations and the processes of globalization. This can be easily done in the case of occasional or regular contacts of individuals with individuals or entities abroad: there is no doubt that globalization is likely to favour such situations. On the other hand, migrations could be considered as belonging to a historical phase which precedes what may be considered as the processes of globalization: today it seems easier for production devices to be relocated where low-cost manpower is available, for technological as well as for legal reasons, than for people to move from one country to another in search for employment – considering in particular the current trend of economically developed countries towards severe curbing of immigration. This does not mean, however, the end of migrations, but probably considerable changes in it. That is why it is worth observing precisely what happens where legal instruments dealing with migrants' problems are implemented. It may help us to

2 About cross-border tax issues, see Alberto Xavier, *Direito Tributário Internacional* (Coimbra: Almedina, 1993). The publication of this work in Portugal is an indicator of the practical relevance of these questions.

3 On this discussion, see Chapters 9, 11 and 12 of the present volume.

evaluate these changes and thereby better to grasp the reality of globalization.

Methodological Questions

According to the objectives of the broader research on cross-border legal interaction, our aim was to make out, in the concrete case of Portugal, what infrastructures have been developed for the treatment of cross-border matters, and how the cases are handled in the framework of these infrastructures. By 'infrastructure' we mean stable, differentiated social devices, constituted by skilled staff and appropriate equipment and premises, entrusted with specific tasks related to the handling of cross-border legal matters.[4] The research started with a survey of the administrative agencies playing a central role in the field. Interviews carried out with officials of these agencies allowed us to locate some other – private or public – entities also active in the field, which were also surveyed.

The survey consisted of semi-directive interviews in which the officials were questioned on the following topics: development and organization of the service; relations with the clients of the agency and characterization of the cases submitted by these clients; relations with other agencies active in the field, on the one hand in the same country, on the other hand in other countries. In the last part of the interview, the officials were questioned directly on the legal instruments to be applied, as far as these instruments had not been spontaneously mentioned in an earlier stage. The interviews were complemented by the analysis of printed materials collected in the agencies surveyed.

Since professional skill is a crucial element of infrastructures in the sense presented above, a separate part of the survey has been dedicated to the mechanisms of training and information from which the officials may take advantage. This included interviews with persons in charge of officials' training; analysis of the relevant legal and administrative literature available in Portugal – an analysis which took into account, not only the doctrinal contents of the publications, but also the conditions under which they were drafted,

4 Even if courts obviously belong to the category thus delimited, they will be mentioned here just marginally, since they have been extensively discussed in Volkmar Gessner, ed., *Foreign Courts – Civil Litigation in Foreign Legal Cultures* (Aldershot: Dartmouth, 1996).

released and used as working tools by practitioners; and a survey of the principal relevant professional and scientific associations.

To assess the effective output[5] of the agencies under analysis, it would have been elucidating to question a sample of (potential) clients. Such a research step would have required human and material means which were not available at the time when the present work was carried out.[6] It may be assumed, however, that the lack of data coming from the clients can be at least partially compensated by the opportunity we had to confront information supplied by different public departments, or by departments belonging to different national administrations.

Portugal: a Short Characterization

Portugal presents a set of somehow contradictory features which have led social scientists to qualify the country as 'semi-peripherical'.[7] On the one hand, Portugal belongs geographically and politically to Western Europe and, thus, to what analysts of the world-system have named 'the central countries'. It has been a member state of NATO and of EFTA since the creation of these organizations. It joined the Council of Europe in 1976, two years after the collapse of the authoritarian regime implemented by Salazar, and became a member of the European Community in 1986. But, on the other hand, its economic and social indicators have for years been comparable to those of developing countries. Furthermore, the

5 About the serious difficulties the concept of effectiveness may encounter in the domains under analysis, see Pierre Guibentif, *La pratique du droit international et communautaire de la sécurité sociale – Etude de sociologie du droit à l'exemple du Portugal* (Geneva: doctoral thesis, 1995), 462 et seq.

6 Unfortunately, available sociological data on migrants in Portugal – which could partly substitute for data originally collected for the present research – are rare and have not been updated for years. See Manuela Silva *et al.*, *Retorno, emigração e desenvolvimento regional em Portugal* (Lisbon: Instituto de Estudos para o Desenvolvimento, 1984); and Maria do Ceu Esteves, ed., *Portugal, País de Imigração* (Lisbon: Instituto de Estudos para o Desenvolvimento, 1992).

7 Boaventura de Sousa Santos, "Estado e sociedade na semiperiferia do sistema mundial: o caso português", *Análise Social*, No. 87–88–89 (1985), 869–901.

country remained isolated for two decades after the Second World War because its regime, like the Franco regime in Spain, was considered as having sympathized with the regimes defeated by the Allied Forces. Finally, for historical reasons, Portugal maintains a close relationship with Portuguese-speaking African countries as well as with Brazil.

These circumstances have consequences of direct relevance for our theme. A first consequence is that Portugal has experienced strong flows of both emigration and immigration. Significant rates of emigration have been observed for centuries. The highest level was reached during the 1960s, with more then 100,000 people emigrating each year.[8] These numbers were due mainly to the shortage of employment opportunities in the Portuguese *interior* and to the huge difference between the average wages in Portugal and in other European countries. They partly had political reasons also. Immigration is a more recent phenomenon, related to the economic growth of the country since its integration into the European Community, and to the importance Portugal, as an EC country, has acquired in the view of nationals of non-European countries.[9] Thus, not only the volume of migrating population, but also the fact that the country had to face successively trends of emigration and immigration, make Portugal an interesting field for analysing how legal problems related to migrations are handled.

The specific situation of Portugal also has consequences on the level of the state apparatus. The effects of decades of authoritarianism are still noticeable in the attitudes of civil servants towards superiors or clients. They also explain how difficult it is in Portugal to obtain reliable statistical data on the activity of state agencies.[10] Furthermore, the political features of the former regime, as well as lack of financial means, have seriously hampered the development of research and education. As a result, it is still difficult in many

8 Of publications in English on Portuguese migrations, see in particular Maria Ioannis Baganha, *Portuguese Emigration to the United States 1820–1930* (New York / London: Garland Publishing, 1990).

9 For a review of recent research on immigration in Portugal, see Pierre Guibentif, "Le Portugal face à l'immigration", *Revue européenne des migrations internationales* 12, no. 1 (1996), 121–38.

10 For a recent comment on these difficulties, see António Barreto in António Barreto, ed., *A Situação Social em Portugal, 1960–1995* (Lisbon: Instituto de Ciências Sociais, 1996), 21–8.

domains to find pre-existing academic work structuring available data and supplying a fairly solid background for further research and discussion. Under these circumstances, cross-border legal issues are tackled in Portugal in a way which differs sometimes significantly from the way they are handled in other European countries, which confers a special interest on the inclusion of Portugal in this comparative research. However, these circumstances have also obviously conditioned the carrying out of the research itself in this country.

Analysis of the Selected Fields

The Handling of Cross-border Social Security Issues

The problems

Today's social security systems are organized on a territorial basis. Social security entitlements (mainly with respect to benefits) and duties (mainly obligations to contribute to the system financially) link individuals to the social security system of the country where they live. This means, in the case of migrants, that they are normally covered by the social security system of their host country. Their status, however, may become more complex. Four cases are worth a special mention. First, every time migrants travel back to their home country, there is a risk of their being affected by contingencies that oblige them to claim social benefits. How will the responsibility of providing these benefits be shared between the social security systems of home and host country? Secondly, migrants may leave children in their home country. Which of both systems will provide family allowances and other family benefits? Thirdly, on reaching the age of retirement, they will be entitled to receive a pension from the social security system they have contributed to during their working career. What happens if they have contributed to two or more national systems? And, finally, what happens if, receiving a pension from one or more countries, a migrant settles in a third country – maybe his or her home country – where he or she never paid social contributions and from which he or she receives no pension? Which social security system will provide benefits, especially health care? Which system will pay for them?

The legal solutions

In an attempt to answer these questions, a number of bilateral agreements have been negotiated between states linked by significant migratory flows, as soon as these states started to develop their welfare systems, that is since the beginning of this century.[11]

Since its creation after the First World War, the International Labour Organization (ILO) has participated in technical improvements to these instruments (named instruments of coordination) by supporting bilateral negotiations among its member states. An early concern of the ILO was the development of multilateral agreements addressing the problems faced by migrants who had worked successively in more than two countries. Efforts on this multilateral level succeeded in post-Second World War Europe. In this context there were strong practical needs for such solutions (the number of displaced persons; the rebuilding of national welfare systems now inspired by the new concept of social security agreed upon by the Allied Forces), as well as strong diplomatic reasons for tightening cooperative relations between former enemies. The ILO took advantage of this situation, first encouraging and supporting the making of an agreement on the social security of Rhine boatmen, adopted in 1950, ratified by Belgium, France, Germany, The Netherlands and Switzerland. Later, the ILO was invited by the states then negotiating the EEC treaties to cooperate in the drafting of a multilateral agreement to be applied to workers who were nationals of these states and who would circulate within them. This agreement (Convention of Brussels of 9 December 1957) was changed a few months later into Regulation No. 3 of the newly founded EEC. After a thorough revision in 1971, this agreement is still in force, now designated as Regulation No. 1408/71 of the EC, and applies to the cross-border movement of citizens of all member states of today's European Union.

In the late 1950s, the question arose as to whether the EEC social security regulation could apply to citizens of non-member states. This was denied by the EEC authorities. Thus, with a view to tightening the links between EEC member states and other Euro-

11 See Guy Perrin, "Origines du droit international de la sécurité sociale", *Revue française des affaires sociales*, no. 1 (1981), 161–205; and Guy Perrin, *Histoire du droit international de la sécurité sociale* (La sécurité sociale – son histoire à travers les textes, Tome V) (Paris: Association pour l'étude de l'histoire de la sécurité sociale, 1993).

pean countries, the Council of Europe, with the support of the ILO, drew up another instrument for multilateral coordination in Europe, the European Convention on Social Security, which was adopted in 1973.

As a result of this development, coordination between national social security systems in Europe is achieved by a complex network of bilateral and multilateral instruments. Two factors have contributed to a simplification of the picture. On the one hand, from the beginning, the role of the ILO ensured that the agreements were technically similar, and even made it possible for different instruments to have almost identical provisions regarding the same questions.[12] On the other hand, the trend towards the enlargement of the European Community – later European Union – made Regulation No. 1408/71 applicable to almost all intra-European migrations or movements of persons.

Portugal belongs to the group of European countries which joined in the effort of bilateral coordination at a later stage, after a first network of bilateral conventions between the economically more advanced European countries had been completed. To begin with, an agreement was negotiated with France. This was signed in 1957 and entered into force in 1959. In the following years and until the early 1980s, agreements were signed with all European countries with numerous Portuguese resident populations,[13] as well as with

12 This is especially the case with Regulation No. 1408/71 and the European Convention on Social Security of 1973. A description of the provisions included in these instruments cannot be undertaken in the present chapter. For a general introduction, see International Labour Office, *Social Security of Migrant Workers* (Geneva: ILO, 1974); Rolf Schuler, *Das Internationale Sozialrecht der Bundesrepublik Deutschland. Grundlagen und systematische Zusammenschau des für die Bundesrepublik Deutschland geltenden Internationalen Sozialrechts* (Baden-Baden: Nomos, 1988); Guibentif, *La pratique du droit international et communautaire de la sécurité sociale*, with further references. For the complete current EC legislation, see European Commission, *Compendium of Community Provisions on Social Security*, 4th edn (Luxembourg: Office for the Official Publications of the European Communities, 1995).

13 Spain (1962), Germany (1964), Luxemburg (1966), Netherlands (1966), Belgium (1970), Switzerland (1975), Sweden (1978), United Kingdom (1978), Norway (1980), Austria (1985). For exact references, see Guibentif, *La pratique*, annex 5.

several overseas countries. In 1986, Portugal joined the EEC, so that the bilateral agreements formerly concluded with the other member states of the EEC were replaced by Regulation No. 1408/71.[14] Later, from the time of the creation of the European Economic Area (EEA) on,[15] Regulation No. 1408/71 also became applicable in Portugal's relations with Austria, Norway, Iceland and Sweden.

International social security rules in action

The existence of these coordination agreements makes the handling of cross-border social security issues a matter of applying international or supranational rules. The question to be asked is how these rules are applied to concrete cases, considering two things in particular. First, the rules themselves, even if legally they are integrated in the national legal systems, are the result of specific drafting processes. And legal commentaries exist mainly in the context of what could be described as an international legal culture, and much more rarely in the context of national legal scholarship. Secondly, the application of the rules will often require cooperation between agencies belonging to the public administrations of different states.

14 Article 6 of Regulation No. 1408/71. The former agreements remain valid and are, under certain circumstances, applicable to movements between the two countries of persons who are not citizens of an EEC member state.

15 Strictly speaking, the law of the EEA is not identical with that of the EU. It consists of the *Acquis communautaire* at the time of the negotiation of the EEA agreement. Since then, changes to the EU regulations have been introduced to the EEA legislation from time to time, through specific EEA procedures. Thus EEA and EU legislation may differ – and have, as a matter of fact, temporarily differed. See Peter Altmaier, "Die Koordinierung der Sozialversicherungs systeme im EWR", *Sozialpolitisches Forum* (Zurich: November 1992), 3–9; Raymond Spira, "La mise en oeuvre du droit social européen: point de vue d'un magistrat", in *L'Espace social européen – Colloque de Lausanne 1992*, ed. Jean-Louis Duc (Lausanne: Institut de Recherches sur le Droit de la Responsabilité civile et des Assurances – IRAL, 1993), 217–32. In Portugal, the EEA Regulation is currently only applicable to the relations with Iceland and Norway, since Austria, Finland and Sweden joined the EU on 1 January 1995.

To answer our question, research has to be conducted on three levels. We have to consider (a) the entities in charge of applying the rules under analysis and how are they organized, (b) the means by which the knowledge of these rules and their specific application is produced and improved, and (c) on the basis of the information gathered at the two other levels, the everyday practice of international social security law itself. We will address these in turn.

The task of applying international social security rules in Portugal is today spread among several institutions. A central device is the *Departamento de Relações Internacionais de Segurança Social* (DRISS; formerly the *Departamento de Relações Internacionais e Convenções de Segurança Social* – DRICSS) at Lisbon. This public institution has responsibilities both at the level of the drafting of the instruments and at the implementation level. Officials of the DRISS, in contact with similar agencies abroad, as well as with officials of the European Commission, of the Council of Europe and of the ILO, prepare drafts for agreements to be formally negotiated by the Portuguese Ministry for Foreign Affairs with representatives of other countries. At implementation level, the DRISS takes on specific tasks related to the provisions of currently applicable instruments. One of the most important of these tasks is to decide upon requests for extension of the period a worker may be posted in Portugal.[16] Furthermore, the DRISS assists other Portuguese institutions involved in the implementation of the coordination agreements, providing legal advice and training; it assists foreign institutions in their correspondence with other Portuguese institutions; and it assists private individuals in need of information, or who have to deal with social security institutions abroad beyond the scope of the coordination instruments (for instance, requests for supplementary benefits which are not included in the conventions).

The DRISS is the continuation of an institution created in 1965, the *Caixa Central de Segurança Social dos Trabalhadores Migrantes*. As a public institution, it enjoys clear legal recognition.[17] Its tasks are strictly limited to questions of international social security coordination. Its higher officials are trained by regular contacts with the

16 This is part of a legal scheme which allows an employer to post workers abroad for a limited period, remaining subject to the social security legislation of the country where the employer is registered.

17 Recently confirmed by the approval of its new *lei orgânica*, *Decreto-Lei*, No. 320/95 of 28 October 1995.

internationally recognized specialists in matters of social security coordination.

Most of the tasks connected with the implementation of the coordination instruments are today entrusted to other social security institutions, which are mainly responsible for applying the internal Portuguese social security law. In practice, the coordination tasks are entrusted to subunits within these institutions, and these subunits sometimes have to carry out tasks related to the internal Portuguese legislation at the same time. In two larger central institutions, the *Centro Nacional de Pensões* and the *Caixa Nacional de Seguros de Doenças Profissionais*, which are in charge of matters relating to pensions, accidents at work and occupational diseases, the units responsible for international matters have a numerous staff as well as their own premises. On the other hand, the regional institutions, the *Centros Regionais de Segurança Social*, have only small informal subunits run by a few officials under rather poor conditions. These regional services are mainly responsible for sickness, unemployment and family benefit matters.

The involvement of these other institutions in the implementation of the coordination agreements is more recent than that of the DRISS. Their legal status is unclear – which, in the highly legalized Portuguese public administration system, may become a serious problem. Their staff are trained by means of occasional meetings at the DRISS and, except for the higher officials of the *Centro Nacional de Pensões* and the *Caixa Nacional de Seguros de Doenças Profissionais*, do not usually have contacts with foreign specialists.

As regards our second level of research, in Portugal general information on international coordination rules is scarce and authorized commentaries are very rare. The instruments which are most commonly invoked at the present time, the Community Regulations, are discussed in two single publications, one of them not even in Portuguese, but in English or French.[18] Thus updated information on these instruments can only be found in foreign and Community publications. This lack of information on the international coordination rules is in fact related to a widespread lack of general information on social security in Portugal. For the time

18 Sebastião Nóbrega Pizarro, *Direito de segurança social das Comunidades Europeias* (Lisbon: Caixa Central de Segurança Social dos Trabalhadores Migrantes, 1982); European Commission/DRICSS, eds., *Social Security in Europe – Equality Between Nationals and Non-Nationals* (Lisbon: DRICSS, 1995).

being, there is no journal specializing in these matters,[19] or any publication that could be regarded as an authorized handbook on social security issues in Portugal.[20] As a result, foreign publications are the main source of information on coordination rules.[21] These are not easily available to everybody, are not written in Portuguese and reflect situations and debates in which the relevant Portuguese officials and the private individuals concerned are not involved.

No wonder, therefore, that, as interviews with specialized officials reveal, the knowledge of the international rules to be applied is almost never based on such general information. According to our findings,[22] this knowledge is derived mainly from the administrative forms themselves, issued, as far as Community Regulations are concerned, by the Administrative Commission on Social Security for Migrant Workers attached to the Commission of the European Community. In their day-to-day handling of concrete cases, officials are guided mainly by the instructions included in these forms. This way of gathering information on the legislation to be applied is actually encouraged by the DRISS itself, which organizes its training sessions to a large extent as an introduction to the existing forms.

The higher officials of the DRISS, as well as officials of the *Centro Nacional de Pensões* and the *Caixa Nacional de Seguros de Doenças Profissionais*, can complete and update their knowledge by discussing these subjects with their colleagues abroad during

19 There is a *Revista Portuguesa de Segurança Social*, but it is more of an associative newsletter than a journal in the usual sense of the word.

20 There was once such a work – António da Silva Leal, *Organização da Previdência* (Lisbon: Instituto de Estudos Sociais, 1966–67) – but it has not been updated or reprinted.

21 Even on Portuguese social security, more information can be found, for the time being, in foreign publications than in Portuguese ones. See European Commission, *MISSOC – Social Protection in the Member States of the European Union* (Brussels: EC, annually updated); Gesellschaft für Versicherungswissenschaft und -gestaltung e.V., ed., *Soziale Sicherung in den Mitgliedstaaten der Europäischen Gemeinschaft* (Baden-Baden: Nomos, 1994); Danny Pieters *et al*, *Introduction into the Social Security Systems of the Member States of the European Communities*, 2nd edn (Antwerp: Maklu Uitgevers, 1995).

22 Guibentif, *La pratique*, 434 et seq.

working sessions and meetings in which they participate, in Portugal or abroad.[23] Not so the subordinate officials or those working at the *Centros Regionais de Segurança Social*, even though they have a crucial role to play in the implementation of the coordination instruments. No facilities are provided for these officials to participate in such events, even if they take place in Portugal, as was the case in October 1989 (Annual Meeting of the European Institute of Social Security) or in November 1994 (European Conference on Equality Between Nationals and Non-Nationals).

When more detailed information is needed, and especially by officials of the *Centros Regionais de Segurança Social*, they ask the DRISS, which they are allowed to do and which they actually do quite often. The relationships of cooperation and advice thus existing between the DRISS and other departments of the Portuguese social security administration create a network of contacts which we have to consider atypical in the general context of Portuguese administrative culture. Normally, a Portuguese official is allowed to communicate only with his or her superiors, that is, in the case of officials of the *Centros Regionais de Segurança Social*, with the board of the *Centro*. The 'special relationship' between officials who are in charge of the implementation of the coordination instruments, but belong to different administrative bodies, strengthens their awareness of being entrusted with a special mission, an attitude that has been, until recent years, favoured by the general concern surrounding the problems of Portuguese emigrants abroad.[24]

The structural description that has been outlined above enables us to analyse now the everyday practice of the international coordination rules – the third level of research. This analysis is to be done by dividing the area of everyday legal practice into three dimensions, according to the three bundles of social relations that it comprises, namely the relations of the officials directly in charge of the implementation of the coordination rules with (a) users, (b) officials of other countries and (c) other Portuguese officials in charge of coordination matters. We will conclude this section with some comments evaluating the practical output of the regulations under analysis.

23 The *Boletim do DRISS*, the newsletter of the DRISS, gives a periodical account of these participations.

24 Recent shifts in Portuguese migration policies, from concern for the emigrants to concern over immigration, have now modified the context in which the social security officials are doing their job. See Guibentif, *La pratique*, 114 et seq.

Relations between officials and citizens may be characterized on the basis of direct observation, as well as by examining the devices that can be considered as shaping this relationship. Data collected by these two means lead us to identify two main characteristics: relations between officials and citizens are strongly asymmetrical, run by the officials often in an authoritarian way; and questions submitted by users are handled almost publicly. Both characteristics are revealed by the spatial configuration of the premises where users are received. The subordinate position of the user is made clear from the moment of his or her first contact with the department: access to the place where cases are presented is usually restricted; the user has to ask permission to go in, which is given by a front-line official. Next, he or she has to wait for his or her turn, usually in the same room where previous users are received. This makes him or her feel like just one case among others, and seeing the difficulties previous users have in presenting their situation and defending their interests leds to a sense of helplessness.[25] The interview with the official follows, as strictly as possible, the guidelines on the printed form applicable to the case. This favours the official, who knows the form precisely, and makes it easier for him or her to avoid going into the specific detail of the case.

Up to now we have discussed general features of the relations between officials and users of public services in Portugal. The question is whether, apart from these general features, there are any specific features that could be linked to the cross-border dimension of the cases. One might expect that migrants would adopt a specific attitude as a result of their experience with the public services of other countries. Yet evidence for such an effect could not be found. This has probably to do with the fact that the emigrants who have more frequent and regular contact with the Portuguese authorities are emigrants who have settled in France, a country which has an administrative culture somewhat comparable to the Portuguese one.

There are two elements encouraging officials to adopt a more benevolent and cooperative attitude towards users of their services.

25 To this extent, the Portuguese context of social administration is comparable to the French, while it differs significantly from the German context: Franz Schultheis (undated), *Les problèmes théoriques et méthodologiques de la comparaison interculturelle. L'exemple du droit social de la famille en France et en Allemagne* (Report of a French–German research project, financed by the French CNAF and the Deutsche Forschungsgemeinschaft Bonn).

On the one hand, there is the awareness they have of the emigrant's social situation. Social problems of emigration have been an important issue in Portugal for decades and information about them has been fairly well publicized. This strengthens the motivation of officials in charge of the emigrants' social security problems. On the other hand, by dealing with cross-border cases, the Portuguese officials are able to see the way these matters are handled in other countries. This shapes criteria for the assessment of administrative behaviour which are likely to be applied to their own practice. Or, in more general terms, this distances them from their own mode of practice, and makes them more sensitive to the problems migrants may feel in their relations with public services.

The relations of Portuguese officials with officials of other countries are, and this is their main feature, highly formalized and depersonalized; contacts between agencies of different countries are, to a large extent, limited to the completion and circulation of forms. Personal relationships with colleagues from abroad are almost never mentioned in the interviews. The most frequent problems are all related to the forms themselves. The Portuguese officials complain of the fact that some agencies abroad do not complete the forms legibly; that the forms take too long to travel from one country to another; that the migrants do not ask for the relevant forms before leaving the other country, or do not receive them, which makes the treatment of the case in Portugal more difficult.

The relations between the different Portuguese administrative departments have already been described above. One point, however, should be emphasized here. At first glance, one might assume that these relations are of lesser importance for our topic, since they are relations between agencies of the same country, or even relations between departments of the same agency. Yet the fact that an agency or a department has to deal with international matters gives it special characteristics which make its relations with other agencies or departments almost like cross-border relations. In other words, if coordination agreements facilitate the relationship between agencies of different countries – and the above-mentioned formalization and depersonalization can be considered as facilitating this relationship – they are also likely to create, at the same time, inside the same country, a gap between agencies or departments which specialize in international matters and other agencies or departments.

Two factors contribute to this distance: on the one hand, the direct connection relevant departments have to the DRISS, which allows them in part to evade supervision by the board of the institutions to which they belong, and, on the other hand, the fact that these departments have to deal with rules that are almost completely unknown to officials of the other departments. This in turn makes the specialized officials act, in the view of their colleagues, as if they were 'in another world', and makes it difficult to communicate from one department to another.

The analysis sketched above enables us to formulate some short general considerations about the output of cross-border social security regulations as they are currently practised in Portugal. The main substantive goal of international coordination rules in the field of social security, reformulated according to the concepts that guide this research, is to ensure that persons involved in cross-border relations enjoy a protection similar to that of persons not involved in cross-border relations. This means, more specifically, that they should not remain unprotected between national social security systems (universality of coverage) and that, as far as they enjoy the protection of a social security system, they have the same access to the benefits under comparable conditions as other beneficiaries (equality of treatment).[26] In the case of Portugal, these goals can to a large extent be considered achieved.[27] As the number of cases and the financial amounts at stake suggest,[28] coordination has succeeded in achieving effective articulation between national welfare states. Concerning the universality of treatment, the most significant gaps are due to the situation of illegal immigrants from Cabo Verde and other African countries. The equality of treatment, broadly understood, can be considered achieved, excepting problems of geographical accessibility: part of the relevant agencies have

26 On the main principles established by the international social security law and their translation into criteria for legislative evaluations carried out in this field, see Guibentif, *La pratique*, 221 et seq, 466 et seq.

27 As was mentioned in the second section of this chapter, it is impossible, for the moment, to back this statement with a survey of the migrant populations themselves. For some information, see Silva *et al.*, *Retorno, Emigração e Desenvolvimento*, 153 et seq. and *Portugal, País de Imigração*, ed. Esteves, 48 et seq.

28 See the Annual Reports of the DRISS.

their seat in Lisbon, making it difficult for migrants residing in the inland part of Portugal to submit their problems to them. The fact that the same agencies are in charge of social security problems of both Portuguese and foreign migrants, applying technically similar rules, seems to foster the equality of treatment between these two populations, in the sense that it favours reasoning based on reciprocity: 'We have to treat immigrants the way we wanted our people to be treated when they emigrated.' There is, regarding this point, a clear difference between these agencies and agencies in charge of matters of residence.

One specific case, however, is worthy of mention, since it somehow challenges both the principle of universal coverage and the principle of equality of treatment. It is the case of Portuguese workers posted to other European countries.[29] Universality of coverage is challenged by the fact that these workers do not enjoy effective protection by the relevant regulatory administration (it is difficult for Portuguese agencies to exercise effective control over their working conditions abroad) and equality of treatment is challenged by the fact that these posted workers, covered by the Portuguese legislation, do not enjoy the same social protection as their colleague at their workplace, employed under the law of the workplace country. The way companies are using the relevant provisions of the European Regulations[30] far beyond the purposes which had guided their elaboration, and the difficulties experienced by national regulatory agencies in dealing with these cases, illustrate expressively how globalization – posted workers typically constitute a category of migrants whose emergence is likely to be associated with this phenomenon – has redistributed the room for manoeuvre of the players in the economic field.

As far as the international social security rules can be considered as effective, this is due to an important prerequisite, which is the fact that the relevant instruments have now been applicable for

29 For a recent newspaper report on these cases, see *Expresso*, 30 December 1995: "Os escravos da sala 19" (R-17–R-23). For elements of the current discussion of the problem from a German point of view (most of the Portuguese workers located abroad are posted in Germany), see *Die Zeit*, 4 August 1995, 22; 6 October 1995, 21. See also Guibentif, *La pratique*, 271 et seq, 455.

30 Articles 14–17 of the EC Regulation No. 1408/71; Decision No. 128 of 17 October 1985 of the Administrative Commission on Social Security for Migrant Workers.

about 30 years (most bilateral agreements were concluded during the 1960s, and they were, from a technical point of view, quite similar to the European Regulations applicable since 1986). This means that a long-term collective learning process could take place, involving both officials and migrants. Nevertheless, there are still problems in the everyday practice of these rules, directly related to the fact that the context of this practice is constituted by cross-border relations. These problems are mainly due to three factors.

First, after several decades of revision and enhancement, by state agencies as well as by international organizations and by the European Community, the coordination agreements have deeply transformed the conditions under which national administrations deal with cross-border issues. One of the main achievements of these agreements has been to render these issues, for those who have to deal with them, less 'cross-border', in the sense that they limit to a strict minimum the cross-border cooperation needed for handling cross-border issues. There is no doubt that this mechanism facilitates the handling of the routine cases. On the other hand, by reducing the need for effective cooperation, coordination does establish only minimal relations between the administrations of different countries and does not, *per se*, stimulate the development of an effective mutual intelligence. In these matters globalization happens, if ever, at the level of administrative mechanisms, and not at the level of social relations.

Secondly, emphasis has to be placed on the considerable differences that exist between the level of the implementation of coordination instruments and the level at which they are drafted. Certainly, the gap between the processes of their production and application is a feature shared by most legislation. Nevertheless, in several aspects the case of coordination rules seems qualitatively different. In particular, the drafting is done by people who do develop substantive cross-border relations with their colleagues abroad, whereas the officials entrusted with the implementation do not, as has just been pointed out. And the drafting process gives rise to debates and publications that aimed at an audience (in the case of the community regulations, scholars and higher officials of the more advanced European countries) to which most implementation officers cannot be presumed to belong.

Finally, the structures of administrative action play an extremely important role in the conditioning of the practical application of coordination rules. By structures of the administrative action, we mean the patterns of official–user relations, the administrative division of labour and the patterns of interdepartmental relations, and so on. This could lead us to the following general statement: if a national administration is involved in a cross-border legal relation, it will necessarily impose a broad set of national features on this relation, so that foreign elements may become almost invisible or even irrelevant. State agencies seem to be actors with a significant capacity for maintaining their definition of situations or, in other words, with little capacity for taking into account the new elements cross-border contacts may bring to the relation.[31]

The Handling of Cross-border Custody Issues

The problem

National laws give parents the right and the obligation to take care of their children, which includes first of all the right and obligation to share a common home. If parents are separated or divorced, their rights and obligations in these matters will have to differ. Usually, one parent will continue to share his or her home with the child or children, while the other parent will have an intermittent relationship with any children, based on periodic contact. The definition of each parent's status, as well as the procedures leading to this definition, may vary from one country to another.

If separated parents are living in different countries, the question will arise, in any case, as to which country's legislation is applicable. This legal question may be connected with difficult practical questions if one parent settles with the children in another country – or takes the children to another country where he or she already lives – just to escape the legislation of the first country, assuming the legislation of his or her country is more favourable and that it will be difficult for the courts of the other country to enforce their decisions abroad.

The legal solutions

The problems raised by such situations are addressed by numerous international agreements which have been drawn up mainly since the Second World War.[32] They reflect an increasing concern

31 This statement could be relevant to what has been said about the difficulties state-owned companies experience in global markets.

32 Adair Dyer, "A conferência da Haia completa cem anos de trabalho no campo do direito dos menores", *Infância e Juventude*, no. 3 (1993), 9–33.

on the part of national legislators with matters of child protection in general and of custody in particular, which lead national governments to consider ways of coordinating such legislation with foreign legislation, in the same way that other family matters have been dealt with since the end of the nineteenth century, within the framework of the Hague Conference (since 1893) or of the International Institute for the Unification of Private Law (UNIDROIT). They can also be linked to the legitimization efforts of the international organizations created after the Second World War, by means of their involvement in the development of international welfare structures aimed at implementing human rights of the second generation.

The main conventions that resulted from this evolution are the Convention on the Competence of the Authorities and on the Applicable Legislation in Matters of Child Protection (The Hague, 1961), the Convention on Civil Aspects of Child Abduction (The Hague, 1980) and the European Convention on Recognition and Enforcement of Decisions Concerning Custody of Children and of Restoration of Custody of Children (Council of Europe, 1980). Portugal has ratified the three conventions.[33] It has also negotiated bilateral conventions with France, on Judicial Cooperation in Matters of Child Protection (which entered into force in 1984)[34] and with Luxembourg, on Judicial Cooperation in Matters of Custody (ratified on February 1994).[35]

The first aim of these conventions is to guarantee that the child's case will be handled by the authorities of the country where he or she is 'habitually resident'.[36] If the involvement of authorities of other countries is requested, they have to take steps to return the child immediately, leaving the consideration of the merits of the case to the authorities of the home country. It is assumed that these authorities are best placed to consider the situation of the child. In addition, it is assumed desirable that custody matters are to be

33 For the legal acts approving the conventions, see *Diário do Governo*, 27 July 1968 (1961 Hague Convention), *Diário da República*, 21 December 1982 (European Convention) and 11 May 1983 (1980 Hague Convention).

34 *Diário da República*, 3 February 1984.

35 *Diário da República*, 5 February 1994; the signing of the convention has been briefly commented on in the diary newspaper *Diário de Notícias*, 13 June 1992.

36 Hague Convention, Art. 4.

judged under the law of the country of habitual residence as well.[37] Thereby, the application of these conventions – and this can be considered as a second aim – makes it probable that the authorities who decide on the merits of each case will do so under optimum conditions, that is by applying their home law.

International custody rules in action

As in the case of the rules governing social security, we will discuss here (a) the organizational questions, (b) the way knowledge on the applicable rules is produced and enhanced and (c) the day-to-day practice of these rules. All the relevant conventions here at stake require the contracting states to designate a 'Central Authority'. The task of this body is to channel child custody applications from one country to another, thus speeding up international procedures. The central authority receives applications from citizens residing in its country, to be channelled to the central authority of the other contracting states, which in turn have to forward these applications to the authorities in charge of custody matters, mostly family courts.

Portugal designated as central authority a department formerly called *Direcção Geral dos Serviços Tutelares de Menores*, which in July 1995 was integrated into a larger administrative body responsible for the protection and resocialization of minors, the *Instituto de Reinserção Social*. Within this institute, the application of the custody conventions has been entrusted to a small administrative unit, the *Direcção de Serviços de Estudo, Documentação e Informação Técnica* (DSEDIT). Apart from its activities in connection with the international conventions, this unit also publishes a journal which specializes in child protection questions, *Infância e Juventude*, a publication which has been in existence since 1955.

When the DSEDIT receives an application for repatriation to its place of habitual residence for a child who has been, in the words of the Hague Convention of 1980, 'wrongfully removed' to Portugal, it has to proceed in the following way: first, the application has to be made known to the public prosecutor of the place where the child is currently supposed to be found. The public prosecutor, requesting police help if necessary, tries to locate the child precisely and then to obtain his or her voluntary return. If

37 Explicitly on this point, Hague Convention of 1961, Arts 1 and 2; see also Art. 7, second paragraph of the Portuguese–French convention.

such a voluntary return is impossible, the public prosecutor files a petition in the court of his area, in order to secure the child's return. Thus the application of the international conventions in Portugal does involve not only the central authority but also local judicial authorities.

As far as the training of the relevant officials is concerned, one has to distinguish between officials of the DSEDIT and magistrates. The former have direct access to specialists working on these questions at an international level.[38] An illustration of these direct contacts is the recent publication, in the *Infância e Juventude*, of two foreign papers addressing the conventions on custody and maintenance, including a detailed assessment of the implementation of the Hague Convention on Child Abduction.[39] They have been translated by the person who is directly responsible for the application of the convention in Portugal.

In general, the training of magistrates in Portugal is a task for the *Centro de Estudos Judiciários* (CEJ), a public institute under the direct authority of the Minister of Justice, created in 1979, with the purpose of renewing the Portuguese judicial system after the country's return to democracy.[40] As such it takes on both the initial training of magistrates and their later permanent training. Within the framework of this permanent training, it organizes in particular annual sessions on 'International Agreements in the Field of Child Protection'.[41]

The CEJ has proved to be an active player in the field of international child protection. This has to do with two facts. The first is that the CEJ cooperates regularly with institutions abroad (such as the French *Ecole de la magistrature* and *Institut des hautes études*

38 Even if the attendance at international meetings is usually restricted to the head of the department.

39 Carol S. Bruch, "Casos de rapto internacional de crianças: Experiências ao abrigo da Convenção da Haia de 1980", *Infância e Juventude*, no. 3 (1993), 35–63; Adair Dyer, "A Conferência da Haia".

40 Álvaro Laborinho Lúcio, "O Poder judicial na transição", in *Portugal – O Sistema Político e Constitucional 1974–87*, ed. Mário Baptista Coelho (Lisbon: Instituto das Ciências Sociais/Universidade de Lisboa, 1989), 737–55.

41 Centro de Estudos Judiciários, *Formação Permanente – Convenções Internacionais no Domínio da Protecção de Menores (sessão de 7 de julho de 1995)* (Lisbon: CEJ, 1995).

de la magistrature[42]) and encourages its staff to get involved in international associations such as – and this is most relevant for our theme – the *International Association of Juvenile and Family Court Magistrates*.[43] In part, this may be considered a strategy for gaining autonomy and legitimacy as an institution which, since its creation, has been in a potentially uncomfortable position, caught between the magistrates' professional organizations and the government. Thus it can take advantage of a wealth of experience in the comparison of and cooperation between legal and judicial cultures. The second fact is that the CEJ has had, over the last few years, a significant role to play in the drafting of legislation which has a close bearing on the activities of the courts. This has happened notably for recent legislation on local commissions for child protection, issued in May 1991, as well as for a recent Adoption Law, issued in May 1993, which includes a chapter on international adoption. It could possibly have a role to play in the revision of the current law on guardianship and child protection, a legislation which could include a chapter on the implementation of the Hague Convention on Child Abduction.[44]

In the day-to-day practice of cross-border custody matters, a first element to be taken into account is the number of cases handled annually by the Portuguese authorities. This number is in fact quite low (an average of about 30 cases yearly[45]) compared to the number of cases handled annually by the departments in charge of international social security matters.

Secondly, it is worth considering which conventions are actually applied. Statistics issued by the DSEDIT show that the Hague Convention on Child Abduction (1980) is more often applied than the other two multilateral conventions ratified by Portugal, the Hague Convention on Child Protection (1961) and the European Conven-

42 For instance, members of the CEJ's staff participated in the meeting "Justices d'Europe" (Paris, Cour d'appel de Paris/IHEJ, November 1992) and the "European Seminar on Judicial Ethics" (London, June 1996), which means an active involvement of the CEJ in the efforts aimed at developing a European judicial culture.

43 Secretariat: Molenstraat 15, 4851 SG Ulvenhout, Netherlands.

44 The authorized handbook on this legislation has been written by scholars who currently teach at the CEJ: Rui M.L. Epifânio and António H.L. Farinha, *Organização Tutelar de Menores*, 2nd edn (Coimbra: Almedina, 1992).

45 Unpublished annual report of the DSEDIT.

tion on the Custody of Children (1980). About two thirds of the cases are lodged under application of the bilateral Portuguese–French convention. Concerning the dominance, among the multilateral conventions, of the Hague Convention on Child Abduction, one might presume that it is the result of the large number of contracting states. This is not a sufficient explanation for the differences between the European Convention and the Hague Convention. Indeed, both conventions are for the time being binding for comparable numbers of countries[46] (but, as a matter of fact, only the Hague Convention is ratified by overseas countries, such as the United States and Canada). Moreover, several countries have, like Portugal, ratified both instruments. Applications were made involving two of these countries, Luxembourg and Switzerland.

In all of these cases, the claims were made under the Hague Convention, and not the European Convention. There is a legal reason for this: the Hague Convention can be invoked by a parent even if no decision has already been taken by the authorities of the country of the child's habitual residence. He or she has only to prove the 'wrongful' removal of the child, whereas the European Convention requires a decision of the authority ruling in the concrete issue on the custody of the child. Even so, it is reasonable to state that the authorities involved probably prefer to focus their activity as far as possible on only one instrument, which is supposed to facilitate the development of routines in the relations between authorities and to favour collective learning processes.

Turning now to the concrete handling of cross-border custody cases, we will focus on the central authority. As far as the officials of the DSEDIT are concerned, the average number of cases to be handled by the department allows individual applications to be treated on an almost personal basis. They have a clear notion of the conventions' underlying principles as well as a precise knowledge of the legal provisions. In actual fact they participate as lecturers in the training sessions for magistrates organized by the CEJ. But even if they have this legal expertise,[47] they are also trying as far as

46 14 countries had ratified the European Convention by September 1995 (see *Chart of Signatures and Ratifications of European Treaties*, ed. Council of Europe, Directorate of Legal Affairs); nine had ratified the Hague Convention on Child Abduction by 1992 (Epifânio and Farinha, *Organização Tutelar de Menores*, p. 368).

47 Which is actually emphasized by the foreign consular officials interviewed.

possible to achieve voluntary solutions for the cases which are submitted to them.

The relationship with central authorities abroad is to a large extent formalized. Printed forms facilitate the collection and circulation of the necessary information.[48] Personal contacts between officials of different countries seem to be rare, limited practically to occasional meetings for assessment of the conventions, at which, however, only the head of the department usually attends. If the application of the convention does not give rise to personal contacts, it enables and indeed encourages, by contrast, permanent comparisons between the department's output and that of the central authorities of other countries. For example, officials emphasize that the number of applications sent abroad and the number of applications received are broadly 'in balance'. Differences between the departments regarding the time needed for handling applications is also an important issue.

The relationship with national magistrates is more complex, in the first place because of the division of labour between public prosecutors and the courts, which introduces an additional step into the procedures, likely to create delay and uncertainty. But the difficulties arise mainly because the procedures defined by the conventions do not correspond to the procedures defined by national laws on civil procedure. This creates hesitation whereas, as one magistrate interviewed put it, 'magistrates like certainty', a statement which confirms the accuracy of the concept of legal certainty for the approach of cross-border legal relations.[49] The parties involved consider that the origin of this problem lies in the state of the legislation. They point out that, at the time Portugal signed the conventions, no national legislation had been drawn up, so national magistrates lacked a clear framework. This led an official interviewed to make the following statement: 'Our [Portugal's] problem is we were among the first countries which signed the convention [Hague Convention on Child Abduction].'

Another problem is that of preventing judges going into the merits of the cases. It sometimes seems difficult to make clear that sending the child back to the country of his or her habitual residence does not mean that the case will not be judged, but that it will be judged by the court of the latter country.

48 See the form, "Requête en vue du retour/Request for Return", used for the communication between the departments of different countries.

49 See Chapter 12 of the present volume.

The Handling of Cross-border Maintenance Issues

The problems

There are three main issues in matters of maintenance, when cross-border family relations are in question. Which country's courts are competent to decide, considering that the private international law of different countries could designate different courts? What legislation has to govern the amount of child support obligations? How are these obligations to be enforced, considering that, if a court of the country where the child lives has decided on the claim, the debtor lives outside the direct jurisdiction of this court?

The legal solutions

The general considerations about the international conventions in matters of child protection made above with regard to custody issues apply as well to the domain of maintenance, which is covered by several conventions. Among the international institutions involved, special mention should be made of the role of the United Nations, where the New York convention on the recovery of alimonies in foreign states was passed.

Just as in custody matters, international conventions usually cover just a limited aspect of maintenance issues. They may be divided into conventions addressing the question of the legislation to be applied and those dealing with the question of enforcement of alimony decisions. The latter acquire special relevance because in many countries the court of habitual residence or domicile of the child is competent to decide, usually applying the law of the state of habitual residence of the child as well, in accordance with the main conventions on this matter. This is an exception to the general principle according to which the debtor has to be sued at his or her domicile. Since the court that decides will probably be a court of the country where the child lives, assistance has to be given to enforce the decision in another country.

The central device attempting to guarantee this assistance is the designation, in all contracting states, of agencies which will transmit the decisions from one country to another and take the necessary steps to have the decisions taken in other contracting states executed in their state. Portugal is a contracting state to the main conventions in this field, that is, the convention on the recovery of alimonies in foreign states (New York, 1956, ratified in 1964[50]), as well as of both Hague Conventions, on the applicable legislation and on the recognition of alimony decisions, in their first (The Hague, 1956, 1958; ratified 1968,[51] 1971[52]) as well as in their revised version (The Hague, both passed in 1973, both ratified in 1975[53]).[54] In the 1980s, Portugal also negotiated bilateral conventions on these matters with all Portuguese-speaking African countries except Angola. These bilateral conventions take up again most of the provisions of the New York Convention.

Even if they do not address specifically family matters, the 1968 Brussels Convention and the 1988 Lugano Convention on Jurisdiction and the Enforcement of Judgements in Civil and Commercial Matters may be invoked in maintenance cases.[55] In Portugal, however, both conventions entered recently into force (July 1992),[56] and have for the time being given rise to only a small number of cases.[57] No cases concerning matters of child maintenance have been reported to the Portuguese agency in charge of the follow up

50 *Diário do Governo*, 28 September 1964.

51 *Diário do Governo*, 22 July 1968.

52 *Diário do Governo*, 3 June 1971.

53 *Diário da República*, 2 July 1975.

54 For a report on the revision of these conventions, published in Portugal, see Luigi Battaglini, "A XII Sessão da Conferência da Haia. Um Projecto de convenção sobre reconhecimento e execução de decisões em matéria de obrigações alimentares", *Scientia Juridica* XXII (1973), 110–16.

55 Arts 1 and 57 of the Brussels Convention. On this point, see Chapter 6 of the present volume.

56 The ratification of the Lugano Convention and of the San Sebastian Convention (extending the scope of the Brussels Convention to Portugal and Spain) was approved by the Portuguese Parliament on 24 April 1991 and formalized by a Presidential Decree of 30 October 1991; see *Diário da República*, 30 October 1991. The instruments of ratification were deposited on April 1992, making the conventions enter into force on 1 July 1992 (*Diário da República*, 10 July 1992).

57 With regard to the small number of cases filed in Portuguese courts under application of the Brussels and the Lugano Conventions, see Miguel Teixeira de Sousa, "A concessão de exequatur a uma decisão estrangeira segundo a convenção de Bruxelas", *Boletim da Faculdade de Direito da Universidade de Lisboa* 35 (1994), 445–60; Dário Moura Vicente, "Da aplicação no tempo e no espaço das convenções

of the Brussels Convention's application, neither have there been cases concerning enforcement abroad of Portuguese decisions,[58] or concerning the enforcement in Portugal of foreign decisions. As a matter of fact, the Brussels and the Lugano Conventions are not mentioned in the materials edited by the CEJ for magistrates training in international family matters.[59] According to the magistrates and officials interviewed in charge of cross-border maintenance cases, they are in Portugal never invoked in matters of maintenance. Even the question of whether the department competent for the implementation of the New York and Hague Conventions would also be competent in cases involving the Brussels or Lugano Conventions has not yet given rise to any formal decision from the head of this department.

International maintenance rules in action

As in the former sections dedicated to the day-to-day handling of cross-border issues, we will examine (a) the organization, (b) the reproduction of knowledge and (c) day-to-day practice itself. The system is comparable to the one organized for custody matters. It includes an administrative body[60] which transmits the cases, and

de Bruxelas 1968 e Lugano 1988", *Boletim da Faculdade de Direito da Universidade de Lisboa* 35 (1994), 481–5. See also Erik Jayme, "Europäisches Kollisionsrecht 1995 — Der Dialog der Quellen", *Praxis des Internationalen Privat- und Verfahrensrechts* 15 (1995), 342–54, 351, mentioning only one Portuguese judicial decision invoking the Brussels Convention over the years 1993 to 1995.

58 Information supplied on July 1996 by the relevant official at the *Gabinete de Direito Europeu* of the Portuguese Ministry of Justice. This department has published an annotated edition of the conventions: *As Convenções de Bruxelas e de Lugano (Textos actualizados e jurisprudência mais significativa)*, Lisbon, 1996. This volume does not quote any decision issued by Portuguese courts.

59 Latest issue of these materials: Centro de Estudos Judiciários, *Formação Permanente – Convenções Internacionais no Domínio da Protecção de Menores — Reimpressão para a sessão de 5 de Julho de 1996*, Lisbon, July 1996.

60 The New York convention distinguishes between one entity (*autoridade expedidora*) in charge of the centralization of applications from one country and their transmission to the other country, and an entity receiving applications from abroad and channelling them to the national authorities (*instituição intermediária*). In

involves national magistrates, public prosecutors and judges in the handling of the cases. The magistrates' role is similar. On the other hand, the administrative body in charge of these matters is not the same as the one in charge of custody matters. Alimony questions are today[61] entrusted to the *Direcção Geral dos Serviços Judiciários*. This entity takes on the rather heterogeneous mission of coordinating the administrative support provided to the courts. Within this entity, the task of implementing the international conventions on alimony is assigned to a *Secção Cooperação Jurídica Internacional* (CJI), within a unit called *Gabinete de Apoio Técnico Jurídico*. This unit is responsible for the implementation of several international conventions in the field of judicial cooperation.

As far as the training of magistrates is concerned, the observations made above regarding custody issues are also applicable to the area of alimony conventions. Officials of the CJI also are involved in the training sessions for magistrates organized by the CEJ, yet their role in the assessment and redrafting of the existing conventions as well as in providing general information about these instruments seems to be less affirmative. For instance, no contacts with specialists abroad are reported. This could be due to the broad scope of activities of the CJI, or to the more technical feature of the conventions they have to implement.

As with the day-to-day practice of custody cases, applications for the enforcement of alimony decisions are not handled in massive numbers. The average number of cases filed each year lies between 70 and 80.[62] Yet, to assess the global caseload, it has to be taken into account that all files require recall correspondence to be sent to

Portugal both tasks have been attributed to one entity, a solution that seems to have been adopted by many other countries as well. For the German solution, see Chapter 6 of the present volume.

61 They have for some time been assigned to services which are part of the social security system: *Direcção-Geral da Segurança Social*, 1980–83; DRICSS, 1983–5. See Maria do Carmo Abreu, Maria Celeste Dias and Rosa Falcão, "Relacionamento e cooperação com o serviço social internacional", in *Seminário "As Migrações — Aspectos internacionais dos problemas sociais"*, ed. Departamento de Relações Internacionais e Convenções de Segurança Social (Lisbon: DRICSS, 1988), 209–22.

62 For the years 1989–95, see CJI, *Mapa estatístico respeitante a processos de cobrança de alimentos nos termos da convenção de Nova Iorque* (Lisbon, DGSJ, undated).

the national court or to the foreign intermediate institution every two months. The duration of the procedures is considered by the officials as the main problem they face in their day-to-day practice. The average duration is said to be one to two years for applications to be transmitted to Portuguese courts, and one to three years for applications to be transmitted to foreign intermediary institutions.[63] These are the longest procedures of all those for which the CJI is responsible.

In the same way as for custody, or perhaps even more clearly, one convention seems to attract the departments involved more than the other instruments. This is the New York Convention. Officials explicitly complain of overlap between the conventions. Apart from this problem, the conventions do not seem to cause major problems of interpretation. Their provisions are, according to officials interviewed, more procedural than substantive, especially compared to conventions on custody matters.

Contacts with applicants are seldom personalized. What matters is the documents needed to complete the file. The applicants have to follow precisely a standard formulation included in an appendix to the Portuguese edition of the New York Convention.[64] Debtors are described as anticipating the non-intervention of Portuguese courts on decisions taken abroad. Efforts are made to obtain voluntary payments, but seem to have little success. Usually, debtors do not answer until they receive the notification of the court of their domicile. The enforcement of the decision is said to be frequently hampered by the illegal situation of Portuguese workers, in Portugal as well as abroad, which makes it difficult to cooperate with the employer.

The relationship with institutions abroad does not seem to raise problems.[65] There are no personal contacts. The level of

63 See CJI, *Cooperação judiciária internacional* (Lisbon, DGSJ, undated), short report handed out to magistrates during the training course organized by the CEJ in 1994.

64 See Epifânio and Farinha, *Organização Tutelar de Menores*, 442 et seq.; CEJ, *Formação Permanente – Convenções Internacionais no Domínio da Protecção de Menores (sessão de 7 de julho de 1995)*.

65 This statement of the Portuguese officials is to some extent challenged by certain data collected in Germany. See Chapter 6 of the present volume. It has to be noted, however, that these data concern mainly the late 1980s. Significant changes could have taken place in the meantime, related to the implementation of Portugal's integration into the European Community.

information about these institutions is low: for instance, Portuguese officials admit to not knowing how their foreign correspondents organize what is practically the most important work for the implementation of the conventions, namely the translation of applications as well as of accompanying documents. Nor do they report substantive pictures of the agencies of the various different countries. As in the case of the custody convention, the only identifiable element is a slight degree of competition between the institutions of different countries, mainly relating to the number of cases transmitted and especially to the duration of the procedures. But it is also shown in matters such as, for example, problems encountered with the employers of the debtors who do not collaborate with the authorities. The first comment on this point is: 'Our colleagues abroad have the same problem!'

No special difficulties are reported regarding cooperation with the national courts. The level of information of public prosecutors and judges is considered to be improving, which allows the courts to play an important role in providing the public with information on the potentialities of international conventions on alimony. The intervention of the public prosecutor, with the cooperation of the police, in order to locate debtors, to estimate their incomes and to prepare enforcement measures, is described as being efficient.

Comparative Considerations

The analysis of three quite heterogeneous fields does not allow us to draw general conclusions, but the comparison of these fields provides valuable suggestions for the scholarship of international law in action.

Common Features

First of all, it is to be emphasized that in all three domains here under discussion, there is a significant role for national administrations, aimed at facilitating the handling of cross-border legal issues with which individuals may be confronted. Assistance for citizens facing problems in other countries seems to be taken for granted as one of the tasks of modern welfare states. This finding confirms the hypothesis of the relevant role of the state in cross-border issues, which has been defended in the introduction to this volume.

The significance of this role is enhanced, from the viewpoint of administrative officials, by the fact they do not see any private body (particularly associations which run activities at the international level) likely to help individuals effectively.[66] Although the importance of non-governmental agencies is generally recognized in humanitarian matters, this seems not to be the case in the more trivial field of day-to-day cross-border social relations.

The impact of national policies for fostering individual cross-border individual relations is, however, limited by a notable *effet pervers*. In two of the three fields here under analysis (social security and custody), specialized agencies handling cross-border matters experience more difficulties with agencies of their own countries than with similar agencies abroad. Contact with international matters leads them to develop a specific administrative culture which may prove difficult to reconcile with the administrative culture of agencies that do not have any international involvement.

Our findings suggest an ambivalent assessment of the relationship between agencies in charge of cross-border questions in different countries. On the one hand, the high level of formalization of contacts between institutions, and the lack of direct personal cooperation, do sharply restrict the type of international cooperation that could lead to an effective international administrative and legal culture.[67] The high level of formalization in the handling of international conventions, as shown by the relevance of printed forms, has an impact not only on the practical treatment of cases, but also on the reasoning of officials, a phenomenon which is also likely to reduce the relevance of everything that could be considered

66 It is worth noting here that the officials interviewed do not mention the International Social Service (ISS) as a player in their domain of activity. As a matter of fact, the representation of the ISS has just recently been reorganized, and the new *Associação Portuguesa para o Serviço Social International* (APPASSI, created in 1992) will take some years to establish effective links of co-operation with all relevant public departments. See the leaflets isued by the APPASSI: *O serviço social internacional* (Lisbon, May 1995); *O que é a Associação Portuguesa para o Serviço Social Internacional? O que se pretende através dela?* (Lisbon, undated). For the activities of the ISS prior to the creation of the APPASSI, see Abreu, Dias, Falcão, "Relacionamento".

67 However, it could be assumed that geographical and linguistic factors are likely to compensate partly for these institutional factors. See the cooperation between German and Swiss agencies mentioned in Chapter 6 of the present volume.

as pertaining to legal culture, at least as far as international law is concerned. Thus, using the concepts suggested by Volkmar Gessner,[68] one could argue that the fostering of 'programmes' reduces the probability for the practice to give substance to 'roles'.

On the other hand, it is precisely this formalization which enables officials to compare the output of their own department with that of other countries. This comparison is likely to give them new criteria for assessing their activity and their relationship to users, and thus to modify, in the long run, the national administrative culture of their agencies. In more general terms, even where no 'third culture' seems to have a significant development, collective learning processes take place, on the part of both citizens and relevant officials. In the case of Portugal, these processes are strongly favoured by the country's joining the European Community.

Nevertheless, there are emerging 'third cultures', even if such developments are limited to certain sectors, for instance in magistrates' training departments, or among higher officials in charge of the drafting of social security coordination instruments. The problem is that these 'third cultures' have a very weak impact on the daily handling of problems arising in the context of cross-border relations.

As far as national law is concerned, it is noticeable that all the instruments here under analysis share the same purpose: to ensure that, as far as possible, administrative bodies and magistrates deal with their own national law. This could be considered as reducing the relevance of the cross-border legal culture issue.

There is a phenomenon worth mentioning, even if it has no apparent connection with the problems raised by the day-to-day handling of cross-border legal issues under application of international agreements. It has to do with the drafting of the instruments, but is also likely to condition the development of international doctrine on these matters: and that is the competition, noticeable in the three fields, between international agencies (ILO v. European Union in the field of social security; Council of Europe v. Hague Conference in the others).[69]

68 See Chapter 12 of the present volume.

69 For comparable findings, see Wolfgang Zaschke and Kurt Tudyka, "Internationale Verrechtlichung der Sozialpolitik", in *Internationale Verrechtlichung – Jahresschrift für Rechtspolitologie* 7, ed. Klaus-Dieter Wolf (Pfaffenweiler: Centaurus-Verlagsgesellschaft, 1993), 169–205.

Significant Differences

Looking at these fields from the viewpoint of legal culture, the most interesting difference is the one between the custody field and the other two fields. It is only in the custody field that we find more debates which address the legal issues themselves, as well as a body of legal scholarship developed as a direct result of the day-to-day handling of cases. In the field of international and European social security, there are some publications, but the officials in charge with the day-to-day handling of the individual cases do not mention them as tools for their activities.[70]

Several explanations for this difference may be offered. One lies in the nature of the provisions of the custody conventions. These conventions contain several discretionary provisions which require a general principle to be developed as an aid to guiding decisions. Another explanation could be found in the cultural features of the administrative department in question. Being responsible for the editorial content and the publication of a journal, it had to develop scientific contacts in Portugal and abroad, which fostered the legal discussion of the conventions.

Final Remarks: on the Limits of Our Findings

Anticipating the comparison between our findings and those gathered in other countries, it makes sense to single out those aspects which are specific to Portugal and which may influence what has been observed throughout our research.

Probably the most important fact to mention here is Portugal's position as a country of emigration, whereas most countries in Europe are countries with large immigrant communities. In all matters under analysis, the image of the emigrant, less favoured than others in Europe, is a significant motivating factor for officials who have been interviewed. This image can also condition their attitudes in another way: they may feel a special need to defend their output, against the prejudice they assume to exist, on the basis of which they might be too tolerant with their nationals (for instance emigrants coming back with their children without the consent of the other parent).

Another specific feature is the paucity of the legal culture. With a relatively small number of legal scholars, it is hard to find enough specialists, in matters such as the conventions discussed here, to

70 For some references, see note 18.

sustain active debate likely to lead to a new doctrine corresponding to Portugal's practical problems.[71] This should be taken into consideration in assessing the relevance of findings about the importance of printed forms in the reasoning of the officials who have been interviewed.

Finally, some features of the Portuguese administration should also be taken into account, in particular the sharp lines of demarcation between different administrative departments. These features certainly have an influence on our findings concerning the gap between agencies in charge of international matters and other public departments. They can probably be related to what has been called the 'semi-peripheral' nature of the Portuguese state, briefly discussed in the third Section of this chapter. The state apparatus includes the same set of departments and is supposed to take on the same functions as 'central states', but economic shortages and the heritage of decades of authoritarian regime make civil servants strongly dependent upon their hierarchy. And considering the weak capacity of citizens to defend their rights, there is little chance for the demands of the clients to become an effective counterweight to the narrow 'top down' orientation of administrative rationality, and a factor favouring interdepartmental cooperation.

References

Abreu, Maria do Carmo, Maria Celeste Dias and Rosa Falcão. 1988. Relacionamento e cooperação com o serviço social internacional. In *Seminário 'As Migrações – Aspectos internacionais dos problemas sociais'*, edited by Departamento de Relações Internacionais e Convenções de Segurança Social. Lisbon: DRICSS.

Altmaier, Peter. 1992. Die Koordinierung der Sozialversicherungs systeme im EWR. *Sozialpolitisches Forum*. Zurich: November.

Baganha, Maria Ioannis. 1990. *Portuguese Emigration to the United States 1820–1930*. New York, London: Garland Publishing.

Barreto, António, ed. 1996. *A Situação Social em Portugal, 1960–1995*. Lisbon: Instituto de Ciências Sociais.

Battaglini, Luigi. 1973. A XII Sessão da Conferência da Haia. Um Projecto de convenção sobre reconhecimento e execução de decisões em matéria de obrigações alimentares. *Scientia Juridica* XXII.

71 For some additional elements on this point, see Pierre Guibentif, "Rechtskultur und Rechtsproduktion. Das Beispiel Portugal", *Zeitschrift für Rechtssoziologie* 10 (1989), 148–69.

Bruch, Carol S. 1993. Casos de rapto internacional de criânças: Experiências ao abrigo da Convenção da Haia de 1980. *Infância e Juventude* 3.

Centro de Estudos Judiciários. 1995. *Formação Permanente – Convenções Internacionais no Domínio da Protecção de Menores (sessão de 7 de julho de 1995)*. Lisbon: CEJ.

Dyer, Adair. 1993. A conferência da Haia completa cem anos de trabalho no campo do direito dos menores, *Infância e Juventude* 3.

Epifánio, Rui M.L. and António H.L. Farinha. 1992. *Organização Tutelar de Menores*. 2nd edn. Coimbra: Almedina.

Esteves, Maria do Ceu, ed. 1992. *Portugal, País de Imigração*. Lisbon: Instituto de Estudos para o Desenvolvimento.

European Commission. 1995. *Compendium of Community Provisions on Social Security*. 4th edn. Luxembourg: Office for the Official Publications of the European Communities.

European Commission. Annually updated. *MISSOC – Social Protection in the Member States of the European Union*. Brussels: EC.

European Commission/DRICSS, eds. 1995. *Social Security in Europe – Equality Between Nationals and Non-Nationals*. Lisbon: DRICSS.

Gesellschaft für Versicherungswissenschaft und -gestaltung e.V., ed. 1994. *Soziale Sicherung in den Mitgliedstaaten der Europäischen Gemeinschaft*. Baden-Baden: Nomos.

Gessner, Volkmar. ed. 1996. *Foreign Courts – Civil Litigation in Foreign Legal Cultures*. Aldershot: Dartmouth.

Guibentif, Pierre. 1989. Rechtskultur und Rechtsproduktion. Das Beispiel Portugal. *Zeitschrift für Rechtssoziologie* 10.

Guibentif, Pierre. 1995. *La pratique du droit international et communautaire de la sécurité sociale – Etude de sociologie du droit à l'exemple du Portugal*. Geneva, doctoral thesis.

Guibentif, Pierre. 1996. Le Portugal face à l'immigration. *Revue européenne des migrations internationales* 12, no. 1.

Hespanha, Pedro. 1993. *Vers une société-providence simultanément pré- et post-moderne. L'état des solidarités inter-générationnelles au Portugal*. Coimbra: Oficina do CES, No. 38.

International Labour Office. 1974. *Social Security of Migrant Workers*. Geneva: ILO.

Jayme, Erik. 1995. Europäisches Kollisionsrecht 1995 – Der Dialog der Quellen. *Praxis des Internationalen Privat- und Verfahrensrechts* 15.

Leal, António da Silva. 1966–7. *Organização da Previdência*. Lisbon: Instituto de Estudos Sociais.

Lúcio, Álvaro Laborinho. 1989. O Poder judicial na transição. In *Portugal – O Sistema Político e Constitucional 1974–87*, edited by Mário Baptista Coelho. Lisbon: Instituto das Ciências Sociais/Universidade de Lisboa.

Nunes, João Arriscado. 1995. 'Com mal ou com bem, aos teus te atém': as solidariedades primárias e os limites da sociedade-providência. *Revista Crítica de Ciências Sociais*. 42.

Os escravos da sala 19. 1995. *Expresso*. 30 December 1995.

Perrin, Guy. 1981. Origines du droit international de la sécurité sociale. *Revue française des affaires sociales*. 1.

Perrin, Guy. 1993. *Histoire du droit international de la sécurité sociale* (*La sécurité sociale – son histoire à travers les textes, Tome V*). Paris: Association pour l'étude de l'histoire de la sécurité sociale.

Pieters, Danny, in collaboration with Gabriel Amitsis, Eberhardt Eichenhofer, Claude Ewen, Bent Greve, Francis Kessler, Ilidio das Neves, Maria B.C. Pacheco Turnes, John Schell, Adrian Sinfield, Josée van Rooij, Gijsbert Vonk, Gerry Whyte and Nick Wikeley. 1995. *Introduction into the Social Security Systems of the Member States of the European Communities*. 2nd edn. Antwerp: Maklu Uitgevers.

Pizarro, Sebastião Nóbrega. 1982. *Direito de segurança social das Comunidades Europeias*. Lisbon: Caixa Central de Segurança Social dos Trabalhadores Migrantes.

Santos, Boaventura de Sousa. 1985. Estado e sociedade na semiperiferia do sistema mundial: o caso português. *Análise Social*. 87–88–89.

Santos, Boaventura de Sousa. 1995. Sociedade Providência ou Autoritarismo Social?. *Revista Crítica de Ciências Sociais* 42.

Schuler, Rolf. 1988. *Das Internationale Sozialrecht der Bundesrepublik Deutschland. Grundlagen und systematische Zusammenschau des für die Bundesrepublik Deutschland geltenden Internationalen Sozialrechts*. Baden-Baden: Nomos.

Schultheis, Franz. Undated. *Les problèmes théoriques et méthodologiques de la comparaison interculturelle. L'exemple du droit social de la famille en France et en Allemagne*. Report of a French–German research project, financed by the French CNAF and the Deutsche Forschungsgemeinschaft, Bonn.

Silva, Manuela, in collaboration with Rogério Roque Amaro, Guy Clausse, Custódio Conim, Madalena Matos, Manuel Pisco and Luis M. Seruya. 1984. *Retorno, emigração e desenvolvimento regional em Portugal*. Lisbon: Instituto de Estudos para o Desenvolvimento.

Sousa, Miguel Teixeira de. 1994. A concessão de exequatur a uma decisão estrangeira segundo a convenção de Bruxelas. *Boletim da Faculdade de Direito da Universidade de Lisboa* 35.

Spira, Raymond. 1993. La mise en œuvre du droit social européen: point de vue d'un magistrat. In *L'Espace social européen – Colloque de Lausanne 1992*, edited by Jean-Louis Duc. Lausanne: Institut de Recherches sur le Droit de la Responsabilité Civile et des Assurances.

Vicente, Dário Moura. 1994. Da aplicação no tempo e no espaço das convenções de Bruxelas 1968 e Lugano 1988. *Boletim da Faculdade de Direito da Universidade de Lisboa* 35.

Xavier, Alberto. 1993. *Direito Tributário Internacional.* Coimbra: Almedina.

Zaschke, Wolfgang and Kurt Tudyka. 1993. Internationale Verrechtlichung der Sozialpolitik. In *Internationale Verrechtlichung – Jahresschrift für Rechtspolitologie* 7, edited by Klaus-Dieter Wolf. Pfaffenweiler: Centaurus-Verlagsgesellschaft.

The Author

Pierre Guibentif is a lawyer and sociologist teaching at the Instituto Superior de Ciencias do Trabalho e da Empresa (I.S.C.T.E.) and the Universidade Autónoma, both in Lisbon.

Address: I.S.C.T.E., Avenida das Forcas Armadas, P-1600 Lisbon, Portugal.

Fax: 351 1 796 47 10

E-mail: Pierre.Guibentif@iscte.pt

Abstract

The aims of the research carried out in Portugal are, on the one hand, to analyse the cross-border legal problems of individuals (to be compared with the case of corporate actors) and, on the other hand, to highlight the treatment of cross-border legal problems in the context of what could be named a semi-peripheral legal culture. The research surveys several public departments as well as private associations dealing with matters of international social security and family law. The data which have been collected lead to the following considerations: the practice of the international law currently applicable in these domains (bilateral and international agreements) is conditioned mainly by personal relations between officials, strengthened by regular contacts between public agencies of the involved countries as well as between these agencies and international organizations, and by the concrete procedures organized on national level for the implementation of the agreements. These findings confirm, to some extent, the hypothesis of the prevailing relevance of 'roles' in the handling of cross-border issues, and of 'programmes' in the handling of domestic issues. The resolution of the problems faced by individuals is hampered especially by the weak knowledge individuals as well as most of the subordinate national officials have about the rules to be applied, and by the gap that exists between the public departments specializing in international matters and other national agencies, as well as between an élite among the officials – those who are involved in international networks of specialists, thus belonging to a kind of specific 'third culture' – and the other officials.

8 Obtaining Information on Foreign Legal Systems

ANDREAS PETZOLD

Introduction

Cross-border legal interaction takes place in a world of sovereign states and autonomous legal systems which only to a marginal degree have harmonized or unified their law, mostly in order to facilitate economic exchanges. If a citizen of one country has a legal claim against a citizen of another country, major information problems have to be resolved: which law applies, which procedures are available, which institutions and legal professions have to be approached, what costs will occur, how civil servants or judges will behave, and what delays have to be expected? No single citizen, no small or large enterprise, no mega-law firm has this information available for all countries of the world. They all need institutional support, in particular those actors who only occasionally are confronted by a situation in which the legal system of another country becomes relevant.

The study we have undertaken observes the role of German embassies, consulates and German Chambers of Industry and Commerce Abroad in supporting those global actors who lack experience in international matters and have few resources to get the information necessary for successful resolution of their cases. It is a modest study but it may make a small contribution to the discussion on the role of the nation-state in supplying support structures for cross-border transactions,[1] to the discussions on legal certainty in situations of insufficient legal information[2] and to recent claims for institutional modernization in order to enable the welfare state to cope with the 'debordering of the OECD system'.[3]

1 See the Introduction to the present volume.

2 See Chapter 12 of the present volume.

3 See Chapter 11 of the present volume.

Consulates

Consular Posts in a Global Net of Information Sources

Consular posts, as part of diplomatic representations, are spread globally and gather, among a great variety of other tasks, legal information on the respective receiving state. Germany currently has 224 posts established in 101 countries,[4,5] providing a network of public and – at least in theory – accessible information centres. As public service institutions, their tasks and their accessibility are determined by law.

Legal regulation of consular services

Among other tasks, consulates provide a service outpost for use by nationals abroad and for those at home regarding their legal interest in the receiving state. In their range of activities, consulates are bound to the limits of the respective consulate district, international law and the laws of the receiving state in general, and the legal and administrative provisions of the sending state in particular.

Tasks and limits of the German consular service

The Vienna Consular Convention (VC)[6] is the basis for the *Gesetz über Konsularbeamten, ihre Aufgaben und ihre Befugnisse* (Law on Consulate Servants, Their Tasks and Authorities),[7] in short Konsulargesetz (KG), providing a catalogue almost identical to the tasks named in the VC and expressly stating the same limitations to consulate activities.[8]

While legal representation of nationals of the sending state before tribunals and other authorities has a broad and detailed definition,[9] the question as to the degree to which a consular post is obliged to support a national in need of advice is left relatively open. The obligation to protect and assist in such matters is derived

4 Klaus Hoffmann, *Konsularrecht – Kommentar zum Konsulargesetz und Kommentar zum Gesetz über den Auswärtigen Dienst* (Starnberg: Schulz, ed. Jan. 01, 1996, no. 800).

5 Excluding Honorary and Honorary General Consulates.

6 2 September 1969, Bundesgesetzblatt Part II, 1586.

7 11 September 1974, Bundesgesetzblatt Part I, 2317.

8 §4 KG.

9 §5 III KG.

from the General Protection Clause of para. 1 KG and its origins in Articles 5a and 5e of VC.[10]

Under German law, the parties eligible to request these services are individuals[11] and corporations,[12] regardless of their place of residence. Receiving states may regulate such services through statutes which in general apply to consulate posts.[13]

Extent of legal advice given by consulate posts

Provided these legal conditions are met, the depth and thoroughness of legal advice given depends on the policies of the German Department of Foreign Affairs, the Auswärtige Amt (AA). How far these undergo changes may be concluded from a joint notification issued by the German Federal Secretary of Justice with the Department of Foreign Affairs in 1958 concerning the question of consulate legal assistance. It states that any activities of consular posts shall be restricted to inquiries otherwise unavailable and not easily to be found in legal literature. Expressly, the foreign service was not to be seen and used as a source for obtaining legal information.[14] More recently, this issue is only mentioned as an area of vast competence[15] with certain self-restrictions to avoid raising any doubts about the independence of the receiving states' judiciary,[16] limiting the foreign service to truly diplomatic considerations. Any inquiry shall be denied upon indications that the official reply may be used as evidence in a legal dispute.[17]

As mentioned above, the consular officer is obliged to avoid any possible conflict with the receiving state's regulations on legal counselling, whereas he is free to gather lawfully obtainable information on social, cultural and legal developments of this state, and to provide interested parties with this information.[18] This has a certain potential for conflict, since a sending state's national may go so far as to interfere with the receiving state's domestic affairs.[19]

10 Hoffmann, "Konsularrecht", no. 800, 2.6.4.3, fn 4.
11 Ibid., 2.6.1.1.
12 Ibid., 2.6.1.5.
13 Ibid., 2.6.4.1, 23.
14 *Anwaltsblatt*, 8 (1958), 170.
15 Hoffmann, "Konsularrecht", no. 800, 2.6.4.1, p. 22.
16 Ibid., p. 23.
17 Ibid., p. 24.
18 VC, Art. 5c.
19 Hoffmann, "Konsularrecht", no. 800, 2.6.4.3, 28(1); VC Art. 55 I.

The information provided has to be assessed according not only to its 'bilateral effect', but also to correctness and reliability. As with all public services, the party legitimately inquiring has a right to accurate replies. Thus consulate posts generally are advised to expressly deny responsibility for the correctness of the information given.[20]

Empirical Approach

Assumptions

Public service institutions generally tend to follow their own ideals and goals in the services they provide. Besides political influences, traditions guide and limit changes and the quest for improvement.[21] With the Department of Foreign Affairs highly dependent on its own past, one may assume that this large institution will find it rather difficult to adapt its services to the needs of the society it is supposed to serve by providing reliable information for private persons and corporations in an effective manner. On the other hand, diplomatic representations of all countries are under strong pressure from export-oriented business sectors to support the business relations between sending states and receiving states. Germany, being one of the main exporters in international trade, might have organized its representations accordingly.

Research Method

In order to assess the actual quality of legal advice rendered, consulate posts of the AA were asked by written request for legal advice in the following matter:

> A small German law office inquires regarding a client's outstanding accounts against a debtor of nationality and residence in the respective country. In question are the procedures of recognition and enforcement of a German executory title under the respective jurisdiction and recommendable ways for out-of-court settlements.

This fictional case was designed to represent the average daily case of an average lawyer's practice. The value in dispute, DM8,000, was

20 Ibid., 2.6.4.1, p. 23.

21 Alexander Drenker, *Diplomaten ohne Nimbus! – Beobachtungen und Meinungen eines deutschen Presseattachés* (Zurich/Freiburg: Atlantis, 1970).

kept rather low. The intention was to create a small legal conflict without sufficient assets to generate great interest among other legal parties potentially involved. Also the image of the inquiring party (created through letterhead, content and style) was not that of a large and possibly influential law firm, but of the modest office of a single practising lawyer from a rural area with little to no experience and connection to law and business agencies dealing on an international level.

The replies to this letter were evaluated not according to correctness of the answers – the verification of the information would have required a project of a different dimension – but according to their presentation and their practical value to those seeking the information. We evaluated the replies for their style and technical quality, for the length of time that lapsed between inquiry and reply, for the apparent recentness of sources used, and for the degree of specialization of the department responsible for the reply. Further evidence can be drawn from educated assumptions on the frequency, and thus the apparent routine, in answering such requests.

The practical value of a reply largely depends upon the degree of regard taken to the initial request. A primary indication is given by the successful individualization of the reply, and the attempt to relate the answers specifically to the actual case. A list of knowledgeable lawyers to contact is potentially very useful and locally easy to obtain, although the usefulness of the lists we received with the replies varies a great deal. Also we made a general classification as to whether the consulate regarded the reply as final information or offered further support, and of how much practical value this was to the inquirer.

Further, it was of interest whether the reply referred to existing bilateral treaties concerning the recognition and enforcement of judgments (title enforcement treaties) and whether – and, if so, in what way – the consulate refers to a possibly existing German Chamber of Industry and Commerce. In reference to the economic insignificance of the case in question, a merely statistical view on the average conclusion given by the consulates seems to be of further value, for example whether they tended to suggest dropping or (legally) pursuing the case.

Most important for our purposes was the ability and willingness of the replying person to provide information about the legal–cultural environment which may foster or hinder the enforcement of the German judgment.

Data Evaluation

A total of 196 inquiries were airmailed to German embassies and General consulates at the addresses published annually by the AA.[22] The evaluation was based on the 151 responses that were received.

In order to provide a comparative overview, the replies received were classified geographically, taking into consideration the socio-economic levels of different areas of the world. Statistical evidence is more valuable if replies received from Europe, North America, the Far East and Oceania can be compared with each other. German representations in less-developed regions such as South America, Africa and the Middle East are compared separately.[23]

22 Vertretungen der Bundesrepublik Deutschland im Ausland, supplement to the Bundesanzeiger.

23 European replies were received from Austria, Belgium, Bulgaria, Cyprus, Denmark, Finland, France, Great Britain, Greece, Hungary, Iceland, Italy, Luxembourg, Malta, Netherlands, Norway, Portugal, Romania, Russia, Spain, Sweden, Switzerland and Turkey. Replies for North America came from Canada, Mexico and the United States. Replies from South America came from Argentina, Brazil, Chile, Colombia, Costa Rica, Cuba, Dominican Republic, Ecuador, El Salvador, Guatemala, Haiti, Honduras, Jamaica, Nicaragua, Panama, Paraguay, Peru, Trinidad, Uruguay and Venezuela. Replies from Oceania came from Australia and New Zealand. Replies from Africa were received from Algeria, Angola, Botswana, Burkina, Burundi, Cameroon, Egypt, Ethiopia, Gabon, Ghana, Ivory Coast, Kenya, Lesotho, Libya, Madagascar, Malawi, Mali, Morocco, Mozambique, Namibia, Nigeria, Senegal, Sudan, Tanzania, Tunisia, Uganda, Zambia and Zimbabwe. Replies from the Middle East came from Bahrain, Bangladesh, India, Iran, Iraq, Israel, Jordan, Kuwait, Lebanon, Nepal, Oman, Pakistan, Qatar, Saudi Arabia, Sri Lanka, Syria and Yemen. Replies from the Far East were received from Brunei, Burma, China, Hong Kong, Indonesia, Japan, Laos, Malaysia, Mongolia, Philippines, Singapore, South Korea and Thailand.

Research Results

Duration of the Reply

The number of days that passed between the time the inquiry was mailed and the time the reply was received determines the duration passed. Mail delivery did not cause major delays. This can be derived from the fact that, in all regions, we found the figures widely spread. For example, replies from Europe took from two to 36 days, in one instance even 95 days. Replies from South America took from eight to 97 days. On average, the periods for each region ranged between 20 days (Europe) and 34 days (Africa). In total, the average duration for reply was 28 days. The fact that there is no clear relation between the duration and the remoteness of the location of the answering consulate suggests that the inquiries spent the larger part of this time awaiting processing on the desk of the person in charge.

Technical Quality of the Reply

It was of great interest whether (and to what extent) the responding office made use of word processing instruments, and whether these were used for editing texts formulated in advance. The traditional picture of the individually written letter, dictated to a typist, has generally changed into one of a letter assembled from a computer file, possibly by the clerk herself or himself. We rated whether the office in charge did use modern word-processing units and whether they actually made use of the possibility to tailor the information to the specific inquiry.

Replies with an orderly appearance and proper spelling were rated as 'appropriate' and 'specific', provided the above terms were met; whereas responses with a poor appearance and issued in a negligent manner were rated as 'poor'. The statistical evaluation shows that a mere 5 per cent of the respondents were using modern equipment to rationalize and improve their work, 20 per cent of the replies had an appearance suggesting the early stages of information services. The vast majority, however, met the criteria traditionally expected from official communications issued by government services: that is, not making use of the potential of word-processing equipment.

There is no apparent indication that offices in certain regions of the world are generally better equipped than those in other parts. In fact, diplomatic representations closest to the centre of computerization, such as those in the Far East, seem to have the lowest technical standard, with a third of the replies indicating a lack of an appropriate use of modern office equipment.

Relevance to the Current Situation

This criterion examines the recentness of the information supplied with the reply. In most replies, the content of the advice itself or an indication of the last update provides clear evidence on when the information had been gathered. Ratings were given as 'current' for information apparently not older than one year at the date of issuance, as 'recent' for those replies based on information dating back not more than three years, and as 'outdated' for replies clearly indicating a last revision more than three years before. Some replies, however, did not allow any conclusion and were rated as 'recent'.

According to this rating system, about half of all replies were current. A third discredited themselves by being based on outdated information, and the remaining 15 per cent had recently been updated. Examining the distribution of these results, it becomes apparent that a high degree of rationalization in answering the inquiries (for example, in Europe, North America and Oceania) leads to information that is formulated in advance and thus is frequently outdated. Part of the effort saved through rationalization, then, should be reinvested by regularly revising the information. Areas from which replies were usually issued on a more individualized basis (such as South America) show better results under this criterion.

Another observation aims at the effects of administrative supervision between the embassy in a certain country and its respective general consulates. Although the replies might differ in appearance and slightly in content, the level of thoroughness and care put into this part of the service tends to be similar, whether in the case of a high rating (such as Turkey) or of poor results (such as France).

Distribution of Competent Departments

Depending on the administrative structure of the representation, the replies were issued by four different kinds of departments: a legal department within the representation, the general embassy staff, the general consulate staff or, in some cases, even by the consul herself or himself.

With regard to the embassies, the ratio between legal departments and general staff in answering the inquiries is almost constant in most of the examined regions. Except for those in Europe, legal departments are available in about two-thirds of all embassies. The fact that only 30 per cent of the replies from European embassies were answered by such specialized departments stands without apparent explanation. Inquiries directed at consulates were almost evenly answered by general staff, special legal staff and by the heads of the representations themselves.

Frequency of Legal Contacts

The frequency of the representation's legal contacts could be related to the quality of the reply. It can be assumed that a reply referring the inquirer for further information to the legal office with which the consulate usually deals is based on broader practical experiences than a reply merely stating the theoretical legal situation of the case in question. The evaluation of the frequency of legal contacts was rated 'apparently frequent', 'less frequent' or 'hardly any contacts'. Indications are provided by the degree of familiarity in giving advice about further practical procedures or a practical evaluation of the case.

Overall, 7 per cent of the representations apparently had little to no routine in dealing with legal matters of this kind. A further minority of 32 per cent shows some routine in supplying legal advice, and the majority of 60 per cent seem to do this routinely and to be well prepared to supply information on legal procedures in their receiving state.

Broken down to the geographical areas in question, it becomes apparent that representations in less-developed areas also display less routine in answering these inquiries. Of the respondents, only 8 per cent in South America, 14 per cent in Africa, 20 per cent in the Middle East and 7 per cent in the Far East seem prepared for inquiries of this type. In more thoroughly developed Europe and North America, all representations seem to be prepared. The apparent routine in these matters is connected to the industrial importance of the respective region, rather than whether the representation is a consulate or an embassy.

Quality of the Advice

Formal individualization

Under this criterion, we question the depth of consideration given to the reply. The degree of individually focused care in processing inquiries may reflect on the general quality of the reply in the eyes of the inquirer. The responses varied from anonymous brochures attached to a compliment slip, to individually addressed but standardized letters, to replies individualized even in content to be truly considerate to the inquirer.

The overall result, rating 40 per cent under 'general consideration' and the same portion under 'individualized replies', does not reflect the same geographical distribution of results by region. It differs in that diplomatic representations in North America and Europe show the least consideration, with two-thirds of the responses not reflecting the individual case at all, and a mere 10 per cent providing individually directed advice. The remaining areas of the world show the opposite result. Here two-thirds of the replies consider the case in question individually, with only the offices in South America weakening this trend to a small degree.

Lawyers list

It can be extremely helpful for someone needing to solve a legal problem in a foreign country to be referred to a legal office with local practice. Neglecting the question at this point whether it is economical to increase the number of parties professionally involved in the dispute, and thus the costs, we evaluate how much such lists – if at all – are of practical use.

Most of the replies included a list of lawyers to contact. Only 20 per cent of the replies from North America were lacking this information. Other regions rated 25 to 34 per cent, with the exception of Europe, where 40 per cent of the representations did not supply this kind of information.

Granted that a list is been supplied, this does not ensure its practical use. This aspect can be rated according to the provision of additional information, such as the required language of correspondence of the respective office, their fields of major activities or any other detail of potential importance. Following this approach, within Europe an additional 6 per cent of the lists received proved to be useless since they lacked detailed information. The other regions showed slightly higher ratings, except for North America and the Middle East, where all of the lists received appeared to be well prepared and updated.

Offers of further support

The initial response received and examined here may not be the only information or support the inquirer receives from her or his diplomatic representation. The consulate may offer help for any further inquiries or even support in further proceedings with law-related institutions. As part of their activities in the receiving state, consulates may even go as far as supporting the interests of their compatriot inquirer by interceding locally with the supposed debtor.[24] We examined whether the replies contained any such offers and whether these were of any practical value or were merely polite, diplomatic phrases.

Overall, only 27 per cent of the representations offered further support. Out of these, another 30 per cent would not have been helpful to the inquirer, thus reducing the share of supportive offices to less than one-fifth of the replies received. Replies from North America and Oceania were the most helpful, with half of the replies promising valuable support. Offices in the Far East rated 30 per cent here, with the lowest figures for offices in Africa (10 per cent) and South America (4 per cent). Of the European representations, 17 per cent were rated helpful.

Legal–cultural information

The practical value of legal steps such as the initiation of an enforcement procedure depends on the legal–cultural environment. Courts or court clerks may be more or less accessible, they may cause delays or they may expect bribes. The simple information on the inquirer's legal position hides the cultural context which determines the actual value of this position. In the assumed situation of the German creditor, the replies stating that he only needs to obtain a recognition of his title in the Supreme Court of the receiving state differ drastically from those which told him that the law as practised in that country may allow the local debtor easily to delay this act for decades.

We considered it necessary for any of the replies to contain at least some information on the legal–cultural context in the respective country. We split up this criterion to show which of the replies gave general legal–cultural information and which referred more specifically to the practice in the respective administration of justice. It seemed desirable to get a brief evaluation of the effects these circumstances have on the presented case.

Almost 60 per cent of the replies received from the European representations gave a quite considerate insight into the legal–cultural effects on the case in question. On the other hand, it is worthwhile to point out that more than one in eight offices did not make any legal–cultural reference at all and the same number remained rather

24 Hoffmann, "Konsularrecht", no. 800, §1, 1.1, 2.6.4.3 a.

general in their remarks. This differs substantially from the North American offices, where, mostly by referring to the higher legal costs, all replies made at least indirect reference to the case.

In South America, only three offices described the actual effects of 'dragging legal procedures', while one reply did not make any reference to practical aspects at all; 80 per cent of the inquiries were answered with only some legal-cultural information, and without specific indications regarding the pursuit of such civil matters. From the legal practitioner's point of view, this makes it the region with the least informative replies.

Among the offices in Oceania, the general consulates in Australia appeared to have considered this aspect thoroughly, as both sent introductory descriptions on the probable procedures to be expected. Other replies were equally informative, although less detailed.

Of the replies from African offices, 80 per cent did consider the differences in the legal–cultural systems. Because of the absolutely unique characteristics among the African legal cultures, one would expect the African replies to meet the level of an appropriate introduction to the legal–cultural situation, yet less than a third of them did. The same goes for legal cultures in the Middle East, except that more than a third of the representations here did not make any legal–cultural considerations at all. Replies from the Far East, however, met these standards, with half of the letters being very considerate and another 20 per cent at least considering the differences from the western legal culture.

Reference to treaties on the recognition and enforcement of foreign civil judgments

In Europe, the enforcement of a foreign judgment is regulated by the Brussels, San Sebastian and Lugano Conventions.[25] In addition,

25 European Convention on Jurisdiction and Enforcement of Judgements in Civil and Commercial Matters (European Civil Jurisdiction Convention), former Brussels Convention of 27 September 1968, binding in relation to Belgium, France, Italy, Luxembourg and The Netherlands (since 29 July 1972), to Denmark, Great Britain and Ireland (since 9 October 1978), to Greece (since 25 October 1982) and Spain and Portugal (since 26 May 1989). The Lugano Convention serves as the parallel convention between member states of the EU and EFTA since its ratification through Germany, applicable with Finland, France, Italy, Luxembourg, The Netherlands, Austria, Portugal, Norway, Switzerland and Sweden.

Germany has concluded a number of bilateral conventions aimed at facilitating international civil lawsuits.[26,27] Because many practising lawyers in Germany and elsewhere are not familiar with these important conventions, one could expect the embassies and consulates to point to their relevance in the case put to them. Out of thirty representations in the twenty-one contracting European states, twenty-five replies contained such an indication. No mention was found, for example, in the replies from Portugal and Spain. Being the youngest contracting states, their representations seem to lack practical experience. Besides the European conventions, bilateral conventions were mentioned by the representations in Israel and Tunisia. Many other offices could and should have mentioned such treaties in their replies to an obviously inexperienced German lawyer.

Reference to Chambers of Industry and Commerce

Whether legal departments of consulates can be of substantial help as far as the overall situation in a legal dispute is concerned needs to be assessed. As shown above, they may provide an initial representation of the legal position and may go as far as to initiate mediating contacts with the respective debtor. Their diplomatic status prevents them, however, from getting directly involved with legal authorities of the receiving state and thus supporting their compatriot's pursuit directly. As private, binational organizations, chambers usually have fewer restrictions imposed on them, and are accordingly eligible to become directly involved with authorities in the country where they are located.[28]

Focusing on the interest of the party inquiring information from his consulate, the kind and quality of contact between the consulate and the corresponding chamber of foreign trade become important. The replies received were examined as to whether they refer to the services of a locally existing chamber at all and how detailed these references are with reference to the presented case.

26 Towards Israel: Abkommen mit Israel über die gegenseitige Anerkennung und Vollstreckung gerichtlicher Entscheidungen in Zivil- und Handelssachen vom 20.7.77.

27 Toward Tunisia: Deutsch–Tunesischer Vertrag über die Anerkennung und Vollstreckung gerichtlicher Entscheidungen in Zivil- und Handelssachen vom 19.7.66.

28 See the section on 'International Chambers of Industry and Commerce', below.

Of those consular posts which responded, a total of 85 were located in the purview of one of the German Chambers of Commerce Abroad.[29] Only a few more than a third of these bothered to mention the existence of this institution in the receiving state. Out of these, a majority of two-thirds provided a mere outline of the services the particular chamber would be able to provide. Only 23 per cent of the replies which made references indicated these services more specifically, for example by sending a brochure or stating details of the Chamber's chances of collecting outstanding assets. One in eight replies did not provide any primary information at all.

There were, however, wide disparities to be observed in the various regions examined: 42 per cent of the offices in Europe gave a reference, topped only by the 55 per cent in North America. It seems that here the communication with the various chambers works best,[30] and their role is more widely acknowledged, as all of the replies provided general-to-specific information on the chamber's activities. The conclusion drawn from data on Oceania, Africa and the Middle East provide a different picture. Although chambers are mentioned slightly less than the average, those offices which did mention the existence of a local German chamber provided more or less detailed information right away. Here, not a single reference without further details was found. This shows that, wherever primary contacts between these institutions are established, these channels seem to work well. This particular finding can be contrasted with the situation in the Far East, where one letter did provide excellent information, yet out of seven possible cross-references, this was the only one. In this region, containing the fastest developing economies in the world, our findings may indicate that German authorities evidence very little participation in the activities of national businesses.[31] This finding is even more valid for representations in South America, where only two out of 13 possible references were received, both pointing out nothing more

29 As published by DIHT, Deutsche Außenhandelskammern im Ausland, Cologne, 1992.

30 Still almost every other office failed to mention the Chamber's existence.

31 Contrary to the aims set as per Michael Schaefer, *Berufsbild: "Diplomat" – Auswahl und Ausbildung der Anwärter des höheren Auswärtigen Dienstes der Bundesrepublik* (Baden-Baden: Nomos, 1995), 23.

than the mere existence of a German Chamber of Industry and Commerce or Trade in the receiving state.

Concluding advice

Finally, we evaluated the kind of concluding advice that was given with the reply. Every response was evaluated with regard to the way it encouraged the inquirer's subsequent action. We chose to divide the responses according to whether they suggested legally pursuing the case, using a debt-collection agency, or dropping any further legal action. We also categorized respondents who showed indifference to this aspect of the inquiry.

Following the first option of further legal pursuit produces further legal costs such as those for lawyers acting as agents or for required translation services.[32] For the inquiring lawyer, this is difficult to implement – especially considering the value in dispute and the responsibility for the client's interests. The option of assigning the claim to a debt collection agency implies a margin of estimate costs narrower than that of a legal pursuit; yet there usually are substantial minimum fees involved, with equally significant contingency fees. The option of dropping any further action considers that no further expenses will evolve on the account of this claim and that the actual financial loss will consist of the claim's actual net value minus depreciation due to uncollectable accounts.

28 per cent of the replies did not suggest a particular course of action. Overall, 38 per cent of the offices suggested legally pursuing the case, while 24 per cent recommended calling upon a collection agency. A dismissal of further pursuits could be interpreted from only 10 per cent of the replies received.

Replies from Europe and the Far East were very similar insofar as the great majority opted for either legal pursuit or choosing a collection agency. Replies from Africa and the Middle East show a high similarity in suggesting further legal action while remaining indifferent on the issue otherwise – a conclusion predominant in the replies from North America and Oceania. South America is the sole

32 Hanno von Freyhold and Enzo L. Vial, "Report on the Cost of Judicial Proceedings in the European Union", in *Cost of Judicial Barriers for Consumers in the Single Market – A Report for the European Commission (Directorate General XXIV)*, ed. Hanno von Freyhold, Volkmar Gessner, Enzo L. Vial and Helmut Wagner (Bremen: Zentrum für Europäische Rechtspolitik an der Universität Bremen (ZERP), October/November 1995).

region that mainly suggest dropping the case,[33] with a smaller fraction suggesting pursuing it legally.

Discussion

Here we discuss whether the above findings meet the quality standards to be expected from a public institution.

Technical Criteria

In formal terms, the requirements include a timely response that is issued in a competent and appropriate manner and is based on current sources. To the inquirer, the practical value of the reply depends upon the regard shown to his request. Impersonal responses which provide unfeasible information and are hesitant in their further commitment create suspicion as to the trustworthiness of the information received. Replies taking into account the cultural subjectivity of the inquirer display a profound understanding of the tasks of foreign services. Their responses may be cross-checked with certain information that is absolutely essential. With access to this information, the responsibility for the appropriate implementation grows. This requires the options to be weighed by the economical scope of the case. These criteria are oriented according to the situation of our fictional law office when entrusted with the case in question. They are generally valid, yet even more so for information provided by public service institutions.[34]

The inquiries were processed by the respective consular post on average after three to five weeks. Adding another one to two weeks for mail delivery, the inquiring lawyer had received his answer in an average of between four and six weeks. In reality, this means having to put any further efforts in this case on hold. If one receives a considerate and informative reply, this seems to be a reasonable period of time. Considering the usual terms under which public officers work, it also seems like a period one should expect. A large proportion of the replies, however, were not individualized in rela-

33 Except for the three replies pointed out above under "Legal–cultural information", which gave this advice in a detailed analysis of the presented case, most other South American replies expressed this suggestion in an unprofessional and sometimes blunt manner.

34 On the obligation to inform and to caution, especially for consulate personnel, see Gottfried Hecker, *Handbuch der konsularischen Praxis* (Munich: Beck, 1982), 48, A 79.

tion to the case in question and contained merely formalized information sheets. The average duration for replies with little to no individualized content generally does not differ from the overall average duration. Considering the short time it takes to evaluate an inquiry and put a standardized reply together, this is another indication that for the longest part of the duration before reply, the inquiries were awaiting processing in the departments of the individual posts.

Furthermore, almost 20 per cent of the replies took more than 45 days before they were processed.[35] A reply received after this length of time appears to be of little value to the inquiring party, as the case had to be carried on in the meantime. Some particularly long periods were excused by the fact that the appropriate respondent had been absent or otherwise not available for some time; however, a service that commonly prides itself on comprising generalists[36] should find it easier to compensate short-term shortages of capacities in certain positions.

Also some replies advise the inquirer to send any further correspondence through the AA's courier service, probably as an insurance against unsafe and uncertain structures of the postal service in the respective region. This service provides that all mail and other deliveries destined for diplomatic representations and their personnel will be delivered as diplomatic cargo and thereby will not be held up by foreign customs and postal regulations. However, since this is commonly unknown to the inquirer, all initial correspondence gets unnecessarily delayed – if delivered at all. Therefore this advice should be included in the above-mentioned compilation of addresses of the diplomatic representations. Since this list is issued on a regular basis, it can be easily revised.

Regarding the impression of the competence of the responding department, the data do not allow any clear conclusions. There is no indication that the degree of consideration given in a reply relates to the degree of specialization of the issuing department. The most distinguished answers were drawn up by a mixture of the type

35 For example, two of the replies from the USA took 46 and 65 days; others from Denmark took 65 days; from Poland 95 days; from Venezuela 97 days; from Ghana 71 days; from Bangladesh 108 days; from Saudi Arabia 66 days; and from Singapore 46 days.

36 Hoffmann "Konsularrecht", 40.3. A II; Karl Th. Paschke, *Reform der Attaché-Ausbildung* (Baden-Baden: Nomos, 1975), 13; Schaefer, "Berufsbild Diplomat", p. 23.

of departments.[37] Possibly the aforementioned system of training the diplomatic staff as generalists, serving equally well in many positions, explains this observation.

The written quality of the replies varies in a similar way. As shown above, there is no indication that offices in cosmopolitan cities are better equipped and their staff better trained than those in provincial areas. About half of the offices examined were using word-processing computers for their correspondence, yet hardly any of them actually make use of the editing possibilities or use them to personalize their responses. This leads to the incongruity of a list of lawyers typed on an ancient typewriter many years ago, reproduced by an equally ancient photocopier, as an enclosure to a laser-printed brochure.[38] Worth mentioning is the number of typewritten replies that were mailed after being corrected by hand. There seems to be a general shortage of skilled typists – a circumstance which deprives some answers of their official nature.[39]

The authority of an official response is also influenced by the recentness of the information. Just as with the general processing of requests and the actual drawing up of replies, the maintenance of commonly used enclosures is primarily a question of office management. As shown above, about 30 per cent of all replies had enclosures that were obviously outdated. A list of some 35 law offices with the last revision dating back four years or more almost certainly con-

37 Competence had to be denied certain representatives of either group as well: a consul, who adds in handwriting to a typewritten reply, "P.S.: Your title cannot be executed here", or the judicial department of a large embassy writing, after 28 days, "The Embassy regrets to inform you that it cannot be of any help in this matter".

38 The most favourable reply we received came from the embassy in Abidjan, Ivory Coast as an excellent example of efficient use of modern office equipment. Prefabricated texts of the Federal Office for Information on Foreign Trade (Bundesstelle für Außenhandelsinformationen), Cologne, were edited by word-processing according to information required to evaluate the presented case.

39 Within one week we received two replies from a South American embassy, with neither making reference to the other. In numerous places, the letter was corrected in the blue ink of the undersigned. In their replies the authors – obviously – came to very different evaluations of the case.

tains some outdated information.[40] The same goes for general information sheets on title enforcement treaties that had not been adapted according to ratification processes in the sending state.

As also shown above, the routine in dealing with these kinds of requests does not assure a valuable and applicable reply to the inquirer. An examination of those who apparently routinely receive such inquiries and those who gave considerate regard to giving a legal–cultural perspective of the case shows that most of the offices familiar with the request did consider this legal–cultural perspective. Conversely, a substantial proportion of the considerate replies were given by consulates with less routine in these matters. The only valid conclusion in this regard is that frequency is an indication, but by no means a guarantee, of thoughtful replies – and that the decisive factor lies in the behaviour of the individual clerk.[41] Primarily focusing on the interest of the inquiring party, a regular routine in answering these requests may serve as counterproductive. A mere routine reference to a law office may not be a reasonable kind of support at all,[42] and prefabricated information sheets leave little possibility to comment on small, yet crucial, details of the case.[43]

Content-related Criteria

This last aspect is supported by the evaluation of the criterion 'Formal Individualization'.[44] We found an obvious relation between the degree of industrialization, and thus international trade, of societies in a certain region and a tendency to issue fewer individualized replies. The less industrialized the region of the receiving

40 Hecker, "Handbuch der konsularischen Praxis", §2, IV, 3, A 99, considers it unacceptable to recommend a lawyer who is not in practice any more.

41 Other valuable evidence can be drawn from the coincidence mentioned under note 39, as one of the replies was considerate and informative and the other quite formal with little information on the possibilities of further procedures.

42 See "Lawyers List", above.

43 Out of the minority of the replies which did mention the existence of a local international chamber of commerce (see "Reference to Chambers of Industry and Commerce" above), less than a third referred to the chamber's particular services. Out of all replies received, only two mentioned locally active, commercial collection agencies.

44 See "Formal individualization", above.

state, the more individualized the replies tended to be. The degree of consideration and the range of details answered satisfactorily stand in no apparent relation to either one of these trends.

Besides more-or-less general information sheets, another enclosure widely used was the lists of recommended law offices. With geographical distance and cultural differences, the difficulties in making contact with law-related institutions increase. Therefore these lists help a great deal in overcoming this initial barrier, although the reasonability of being able to contact a lawyer in a southern province of India from Germany seems debatable. Having this possibility within Europe, though, certainly makes sense and seems mandatory for an informative reply. Only a few replies showed regard to any economic considerations. The primary question of the inquiring law office regards the costs probably involved in collecting the claim in question. The value in dispute needs to stand in proportion to the efforts necessary. Most likely, merely the costs of international telecommunication may make this case unfeasible. It may not be the task of a consular post to decide this economic question on behalf of the inquirer, but who else other than this institution can provide a reliable basis for his calculation? By simply providing addresses for further legal pursuit without providing an idea of the length of time and third-party support required, the inquirer is badly positioned. As mentioned above, this situation worsens with cultural differences, when the importance of the consulate's role increases accordingly. Therefore, in providing a solid and informative response, these lists can be seen only as the last piece in a range of extensive information on the judicial system within its legal–cultural context. Hardly any of the answering offices used them in this context.

As for the specific criticism of these lists, the criteria for selecting certain offices were not always transparent. Mostly classified and presented as 'trustworthy offices in the consulate's district',[45] these lists contained anywhere from one or two, to 10 or, in some cases, 40 or more, recommendations.[46] Except for a distinction as to the

45 As recommended by Hecker, "Konsularrecht in der Praxis", §2 IV, 3 A 100; criteria on "trustworthiness", ibid., A 104.

46 In one reply from Canada, apparently only the offices corresponding in German were considered to be trustworthy. A reply from France emphasized using the salutation "maître" when corresponding with lawyers (with the next sentence giving the international telephone access code for France). One reply from Brazil cited its list of law offices from the International Lawyers Guide issued in Germany.

language of correspondence and preferred field of practice found in most lists, the inquirer is given no criteria for a final choice.[47] A few offices had asked their 'attorney of choice' for a brief evaluation of the case leading to a power-of-attorney form sent right along with the reply. Neither of these suggested dropping the pursuit in view of the small value in dispute. Even in this dialogue the inquirer is left alone with his estimate on the further development and of the future legal costs of this case.

Impersonal, formal replies, that for these reasons prove to be insufficient and of no practical value, are a greater threat to the informing institution's credibility than a reply confessing uncertainties and lack of information but issued on a personal basis.

To overcome the obstacles presented by different and foreign legal institutions, an introduction to the legal culture of the respective country is just as helpful and necessary as providing the addresses and so on of their representatives. We did show above that the degree to which this introduction is provided varies a lot. The inquiring law office is inexperienced in international disputes and its conception of foreign legal cultures is at least indifferent, more than likely characterized by common prejudices. Ignoring these, the fact that probably all the receiving states of the consular posts that did reply have codified procedural laws does not imply that these laws are being implemented according to the idea of the modern constitutional state.[48] The complete ignorance of certain, possibly incomprehensible, particularities of the foreign legal culture causes suspicion on behalf of the inquirer.[49] Knowing the discrepancies between the way

47 On a few lists, the name of a particular office bore a mark next to it – usually in the same ink the undersigned used – for no apparent reason.

48 A few replies from North and South America provided the simple but valuable hint of pursuing whether one is obliged to register an execution against an individual in a country. The inquirer may consider the ways of successfully bringing the action against the debtor himself.

49 The reply from a Central African state, war-torn at the time, is very likely to be misconceived in this manner. At great length, the consular officer describes the court procedures and required formalities. No reference is made to the actual suspension of the judicature and the fact that he personally is more likely to be evacuated at some point in the near future. Instead, he recommends filing for recognition of the claim at the Supreme Court.

legal procedures are set up in theory and work in practice from its own experience, the inquiring office is most likely to be helped with brief information on the effect that some of the differences in legal culture will have on the pursuit in question.[50] Obviously, a diplomatic representation needs to fulfil the difficult role of informing the compatriots about the actual conditions in the receiving state, yet restraining from criticizing, or interfering with, the inner affairs of their hosts.[51] The degree to which this criterion is being implemented in the service can be concluded from three replies received from a state in the Middle East. The clerk at the embassy suggested dropping the case, whereas one consulate pointed out that the debtor will probably and successfully strive to delay the case over many years, and a second consulate transferred the inquiry to its attorney of choice for further consideration. Only either direct, specific advice or practical background information can help the inquirer form a reasonable basis for his own conclusion, yet, among the replies received, these thoughtful answers are by far in the minority.

While it is debatable, and a question of policy, how far offices of the AA should include cultural references in their replies in addition to strictly legal information,[52] certain content-related criteria are mandatory for replies when the information is available. In the question of further support to be offered,[53] the consulates are bound

50 The consulate officer in a South American state describes the difficult procedures by putting the usual periods of appeal of only three to five days in relation to the faulty infrastructure of the country. Absolutely important is a reference to the possible differences in the laws of legal costs, which may change the economical approach of the pursuit completely.

51 The range of the resulting "diplomatic solutions" went from "We do not know of a single case of a successful enforcement" to a careful hint, such as "Under certain circumstances this procedure may be expedited through presents". We found almost blunt remarks such as "Lawsuits are guided through corrupt dealings" and polite, yet clear evidence such as "There may be a problem for you resulting from the custom in this country to obtain judgements preferably in favour of the local party".

52 Hoffmann accepts the subjective element in advising the "explicit task of the Consulate Officer to recommend legal means according to regional customs and their effectiveness", ("Konsularrecht", §1, 1.1, 2.6.4.3, 29).

53 See "Offers of further support", above.

by regulations to provide support beyond an initial informative reply.[54] Within the restrictions of their diplomatic status,[55] an attempt to mediate between the inquirer and the debtor can be a promising way to begin resolving the dispute. The office may proceed by issuing letters demanding payment or may even invite[56] the debtor to the representation's premises for a talk about the subject.[57] Considering that these means are considered mandatory in the regulations of the AA, the result of merely 27 per cent of the offices offering some kind of support seems surprising. Yet an inquirer claiming this kind of support would probably not achieve a positive outcome, as enforced efforts – which depend upon the conception of the respective officer – are rarely successful.[58]

Another mandatory criterion is the reference to existing title enforcement treaties.[59] Most of the offices referred to the Brussels Convention, but few did so if a bilateral treaty was in force. Representations in Spain and Portugal, recent members of the Brussels

54 Hecker, "Konsularrecht in der Praxis", §2 IV, 1, A 90 referring to AA internal regulation RES 52/15; Hoffmann, "Konsularrecht", §1,1.1, 2.6.4.3, fn 4, referring to extensive interpretation of the General Assistance and Protection Clause of §1 KG and Articles 5a and 5e VC, respectively.

55 See "Tasks and limits of the German consular service", above.

56 "Summoning" the debtor would express a degree of authority the representation cannot execute over citizens of the receiving state. The consulate is urged to carefully avoid this conception.

57 The Auslandskostenverordnung, Bundesgesetzblatt (BGBl.) I 1980, 21 on the basis of the Auslandskostengesetz, BGBl. I 1978, 301 provides the regulation scheduling the costs for these measures, with detailed provisions regarding charges for the initial and for each successive letter (Fig. 210, 211), as well as for personal talks with the debtor (Fig. 212).

58 A unique reply from Gothenburg to the inquirer offered to communicate to the debtor that the consulate would advise the creditor on the appropriate legal means against the debtor. Unique in a different way was the approach of three representations (one in Eastern Europe, one in East Africa and one in Central Asia) that suggested making an entry in the appropriate immigration or visa file of the alleged debtor to compel payment upon the next application for permit of entry.

59 See "Reference to treaties on the recognition and enforcement of foreign civil judgments", above.

Convention (respectively San Sebastian Convention), failed to mention this legal aspect.[60] This illustrates the correlation of the introduction of laws and the awareness of their existence and applicability. A lack of mention of the relevant treaty in two other replies leads back to the aforementioned observation of insufficient office management, as those answers were lacking other qualities, too.[61]

A further piece of information that is available to all of the representations is the local presence of German Chambers of Commerce Abroad. They were founded as bilateral associations with the Deutsche Industrie- und Handelstag,[62] together with an equivalent organization in the receiving state. Their general purpose is to promote business relations between the two countries. In particular, they can be of support in preparing individual enterprises to conduct business in the partner country and in settling particular business deals – up to the point where remaining outstanding amounts are in question. This makes them the ideal source of information for the case in question here. Provided the inquiring law office is one without international experience and does not know about their existence, the diplomatic representations in the receiving state should be the ones to know. Their obligation to refer to these organizations when approached with any business-related inquiry is widely accepted.[63] The chambers should be well known in the international community and, as they are service-oriented organizations, it should be easy for the consulates to obtain information to be passed on to inquirers. Yet, as shown above,[64] only about a third of all representations in the vicinity of German Chambers of Commerce Abroad passed on such a reference. A discussion as to whether it is the consulates that have to provide a more thorough picture of the institutions based in their districts, or whether it should be the chamber's job to create a greater awareness of its existence not only

60 This is an example of the problems arising out of the use of information sheets, as it requires quite some effort to keep them updated.

61 Throughout the replies from this country we detected processing periods above average, poor appearance of the letters, outdated enclosures and information sheets and a lack of the aforementioned references to existing Chambers of Commerce Abroad.

62 DIHT (Federation of German Chambers of Industry and Commerce).

63 Hoffmann, "Konsularrecht", §1, 1.1, 2.6.4.1, 23.

64 See above, "Reference to Chambers of Industry and Commerce".

in the community abroad but also in its country of origin, seems fruitless. As public authorities, it is the consulates' duty to provide all obtainable and obviously applicable information. On the other hand, it lies in the nature of the chambers' institution as (usually) self-funded organizations to make themselves known. The examples shown above support the assumption that the clarity of the services provided depends on well-functioning links between these institutions in the receiving state.[65]

The inquiry specifically asked for possible ways of securing an 'out-of-court recovery' of the claim. Similar to the evaluation of the information sheets, only the smallest part of the more individualized replies made such a reference.[66] This low response may be explained by the fact that, as diplomatic representations, they are held to avoid the mentioning of the existence of truly independent organizations who collect assets from alleged debtors in whatever way they assess to be effective.[67]

Overview

The overall picture of the quality of legal advice given by consulates developing from the foregoing evaluation is one of a few

65 As mentioned under "Reference to Chambers of Industry and Commerce", either references were shallow and without any detailed evidence or the inquiry was passed on to the chamber right away (where in two cases the inquiry must have been lost, delaying the final reply by up to 109 days in two other incidents). In relation to the effort they would require, more detailed references to the chamber"s services (such as description of services) were rare.

66 For the significance and relevance of "out-of-court recovery" see Chapters 1 and 6 of the present volume.

67 The same office that referred to giving presents in order to speed up legal procedures (note 51) admitted the existence of freelance debt-collectors but refrained from recommending them. An office in Northern Africa assumed that such "out-of-court pursuits" rely on "out-of-the-law activities" and therefore were not recommendable. An officer posted to a Central African state misread "außergerichtlich" (out of court) as "außergewöhnlich" (unusual) and politely excused himself for not being able to provide further information. One of the four offices which referred to this particular detail at all asked for clarification about the term "out-of-court recovery".

thoughtful, creative responses and a few dreadfully ignorant and useless replies. The great majority provide some of the information that is required and obtainable, but remain below the potential the existing sources allow.

A major cause of the overall insufficient service seems to lie at the conceptual level of the individual officers in charge. The nature of the consulate service as a part of public administration, instead of a service-oriented branch, and the corresponding conception of the individual clerk and his task, appear for example in generally long processing periods. The fact that certain inquiries need to be answered within a certain period of time in order to be of any value, is not considered in this system. On the average, there is no difference in replies from strongly formalized working offices which routinely deal with similar inquiries, from those of smaller representations that proceed on a more individualized basis. Mediating efforts on a personal basis would be helpful in this particular kind of case. The consulate law provides the regulations to do so, yet hardly any of its branches ever make use of these provisions.

Regarding office management, all offices in one particular country seem to apply surprisingly low standards to their services,[68] or meet low standards with regard to the recentness and appearance of the information supplied. Binding structures and the smart and appropriate implementation of modern office equipment would help to create a more credible picture, with a reduction of administrative effort at the same time. It would also allow the possibility of focusing more individually on the inquiries received. Again, these ideas require an approach on the individual level, but they need to be articulated on a more general level first.

Another important tension for an institution that sees its role in traditional administration but that is asked to perform a service-oriented task is its tendency to view this task of legal advice in abstract terms. In one respect, we detected a common lack of cost awareness. With regard to further pursuits, many recommendations were clearly uneconomical and therefore useless for the client. The question for substantive or adjective law is, particularly in the case in question here, ruled by the question of the feasibility of the required procedures. Except for the replies from North America, the question of the applicable costs was not mentioned in any answers. Another aspect rarely pointed out was whether it was possible in some states to transfer assets out of the country. The

68 As pointed out in note 61.

hindrance may be caused by the national currency regulations or by the mere fact that the particular currency is unconvertible.[69] A greater cost awareness would also lead to more frequent recommendations to undertake mediating attempts on behalf of the creditor. In the case of using the service of debt-collection agencies, the cost is more obvious, and the inquirer can calculate his risks better. Further, in view of the lengthy periods which communications between the inquirer and the consulate require, the replying offices would be more helpful if they provided more complete information at one time about any of the alternatives suggested.

A similar call for improvement refers to higher cultural awareness. The better the answering officer explains the conditions that the inquirer will be confronted with, the more realistic an overall assessment of the planned pursuit can be. To underline the importance and the possible effects of this aspect, the aforementioned reply issued in a war-torn African country[70] can be contrasted to the majority of the replies received from South America. These were not only unique in the way that a great part of them rated low under formal criteria. Another aspect they had in common was that almost all of them, in view of the insuperable legal–cultural obstacles, closed with the frank and undiplomatic advice to drop any further pursuits and write off the claim.

International Chambers of Industry and Commerce

Chambers of Industry and Commerce as a Source of Information

Consulate posts and chambers of industry and commerce abroad form a network of worldwide representations. In contrast to a particular country's public service system of diplomatic representations, the system of international chambers is not centrally organized. The German-based chambers of industry and commerce abroad examined here are usually founded as an association of the German DIHT's[71] organization, *Außenhandelskammern*,[72] and,

69 As pointed out in replies from Algeria, Cuba, Ethiopia, Greece and Tunisia.

70 See note 49.

71 See note 62.

72 AHK – Chambers of Commerce Abroad.

depending on whether enterprises under foreign ownership are permitted, a local interest community in the respective country. Their major purpose is to promote and support industrial and trading relations between the two countries.[73] Under this objective, they offer legal and financial services to any inquiring party.[74] Usually run as private limited companies, they are profit-oriented institutions.[75] Therefore they are free to quote charges for the services rendered.[76]

Empirical Approach

Assumptions

As private organizations, it may be assumed that the chambers have a better understanding of the kind of information required by the inquiring party in the case in question. In contrast to public service institutions, they can be expected not to be bound to traditional structures and procedures, but to be well adapted to the actual requirements of internationally involved industrial circles.

73 In geographically large countries, various chambers are established to serve certain regions only, for example, in Brazil, where the Câmara de Comércio e Indústria Brasil–Alemanha provides offices in Rio de Janeiro and São Paulo and branches of the latter in Curitiba and Salvador. In the USA, there is the German American Chamber of Commerce, Inc., in New York and Atlanta; the GACC of the Midwest in Chicago and Houston; and the GACC of the Western USA, Inc., in Los Angeles and San Francisco.

74 Under the jurisdiction of the respective receiving state, they underlie the same regulations and limitations as consulates (see "Consular Posts in a Global Net of Information Sources", above).

75 Most of the replying chambers signed as Pty. Ltd., Inc. or a respective equivalent. It is not intended here to examine how these legal denominations express any of the chamber's economic intentions. It appears noteworthy, however, that throughout Germany the chambers of commerce and industry are non-profit organizations.

76 Here, their policies vary. Some replies included complimentary, detailed information on the case in question; others provided information about their services and the respective charges only. These can be substantial. The office in Mexico City offered to send a brochure for DM85, plus postage; and initial counselling was quoted by the London office for DM350. Most of the chambers approached offer reduced fees or free services for members of the organization.

A global view of the services of the chambers of industry and commerce cannot be as comprehensive as the evaluation of the consulate replies. Their existence stands in direct relation to present and potential economic relations, whereas diplomatic representations are maintained primarily under political objectives. Yet, wherever consulates and chambers are coexistent, substantial evidence may be drawn from a comparison between the quality of the economic and political representation in the respective region of the world and in the extent to which these systems suit legal demands.

Research method

The same fictional case as stated earlier[77] was airmailed to 51 German Chambers of Commerce Abroad.[78] The 47 replies[79] were evaluated under the same criteria as those received from consulates, with adaptations and additions where required by the different nature of the service.[80]

Research Results

Evaluation of Criteria on Formality[81]

Statistical results

The average reply took 16 days to process and mail to the inquirer. Subtracting an appropriate period for airmail delivery, this leaves about a working week for handling the inquiry and issuing the

77 See "Research Method", in the second section of this chapter.

78 See note 29 and corresponding text.

79 Replies were received from North America from Toronto, Edmonton, Montreal, Los Angeles, Chicago, New York; from Europe from Madrid, London, Dublin, Brussels, Lisbon, Athens, Salonika, Milan, Paris, Luxembourg, Vienna, Oslo, Stockholm, Helsinki; from South America from Mexico City, Guatemala, Caracas, São Paulo, Rio de Janeiro, Curitiba, Salvador, Porto Alegre, Lima, Buenos Aires, Quito, Santiago, Bogota, La Paz; from Oceania from Melbourne and Sydney; from Africa from Tunis and Johannesburg; from the Middle East from Teheran and Riyadh; and from the Far East from Bombay, Madras, Tokyo, Kuala Lumpur, Bangkok, Seoul and Jakarta.

80 For cost implications, see note 108 and corresponding text.

81 Following the same order as in the evaluation of consulates above.

response. For replies without detailed individual consideration, this period seems more than sufficient, yet it is shorter than the general expectations of moderately efficient offices.[82]

Only one of the replies received had an inappropriate appearance through having been issued in an outdated manner. One out of every five replies had made full use of word-processing capabilities, leaving 80 per cent of the replies as orderly, yet not notably efficiently produced. The one reply rated as poor in appearance was also the only reply that obviously had been based on outdated information. Of the others, 38, that is 85 per cent of the total, were rated as being based on recent sources, and the remaining 13 per cent appeared to comprise current information.

The distribution of competent departments shows a relatively high degree of specialization, as eight out of 10 replies had been processed by staff members who signed as being in charge of legal affairs or something similar. Only two out of 10 replies were issued by the general staff of the representation. As numerous replies referred to the services, not only of legal offices, but also of local collection agencies,[83] the assumption on the apparent frequency of legal contacts[84] was altered to that on the frequency of third-party involvement. Three-quarters of these seemed to be quite accustomed to referring to independent services and, except for a single, apparently completely independent office, all other representations had at least some similar experiences they were willing to communicate.

Discussion

The data show that the internal organization of the examined representation offices is quite professional, with speed- and quality-oriented handling.[85] Except for the reply from Brussels, which was unprofessionally issued, comprising outdated information and

82 With disproportionately long handling periods of 44 to 47 days, three offices in Mexico City, Tehran and Kuala Lumpur contributed heavily to the average of 16.3 days. Neglecting these three results only, the figure drops to 13.5.

83 In contrast to this, only two of all consulate replies referred to services rendered by others than law offices.

84 As surveyed above, under "Frequency of Legal Contacts".

85 The office in São Paulo, Brazil, was the only office in the whole survey that, for speedier communication, proposed in the future to communicate by fax.

poorly written, the general average standard is high. Another generalization is that 80 per cent of all representations provide special legal departments. Thus the system of these Chambers of Commerce Abroad gives a competent impression in dealing with even further specialized, locally established institutions which have the potential to provide further support for the inquirer.

Summing up, there is a need in particular locations for improvements in their handling performance, yet the apparently smooth cooperation with local institutions shows that the structure implemented by the vast majority of the offices is functioning and able to serve the inquirer well.

Evaluation of Content-related Criteria[86]

Statistical results

With regard to formal individualization, we received no replies that were completely standardized without any regard to the individual inquirer. In fact, more than half of the replies expressed some consideration of the particular case and another quarter referred to the case directly and thoroughly. Only the remaining quarter of the offices did not refer to the particulars of the case in question.

Further procedures were proposed by 36 offices and generally implied either legal pursuits or debt-collection procedures: 17 proposed commercial debt collection,[87] seven opted for legal pursuits[88] and 12 suggested a combined approach.[89] We could further differentiate as to the detail in which these suggestions were laid out in the reply received: 25 per cent provided a general idea of the

86 Following the same order as in the evaluation of consulates above.

87 Considerate in a different way was the response from Greece, which argued against employing any collection agencies, as this would increase the debtor's risk of insolvency.

88 Differentiating a reply from France stating that a successful legal liquidation of the claim without the services of a local law office is only possible in theory. The reply from Ireland described the procedures of recognition and enforcement of the title as time consuming and most probably fruitless.

89 These were to be combined upon advice from various South American representations, where lawyers apparently play a fundamental role when dealing with collection agencies. Both approaches were to be tried separately in the case of South Africa, where the legal procedures were considered to be possible only in theory.

proposed procedures; 60 per cent implied an estimate on the period of time required and costs involved; 15 per cent were very exact in describing all the details involved.

Of these 36 replies offering further services, 20 offices named expressly a third party they would entrust with the further procedures. Of these, 18 seemed to rely on familiar connections with these institutions and only two replies made recommendations that did not appear to be trustworth. Eight replies provided detailed information on the particular law office or debt-collection agency, thus enabling the inquirer to estimate the possible effectiveness of the proposed procedure. The remaining 16 offices preferred to proceed independently, depending on self-reliant means[90] or withholding details of further procedures at this stage of the inquiry.

The evaluation of explanatory legal–cultural evidence in the replies was split into whether a merely general perspective was given, whether the explanation was given from a primarily economical point of view, and whether the inquirer received truly considerate information referring directly to the case in question. Some 17 per cent of all replies did not contain any legal–cultural reference at all; 30 per cent supplied a general perspective of the legal prospect in the case in question, and an equivalent number of replies provided an evaluation from a primarily economical point of view. The remainder, still one in five answers, gave a thorough and specific evaluation of the legal–cultural implications in the specific society. Of all 35 responses that in this regard contained advice to the inquirer, only four were incomprehensible or otherwise not practical.

Of the replies, 12 came from representations in countries bound to agreements with Germany for reciprocal enforcement of judgments. Of these, five did not mention the existence of the relevant treaty in their response.[91] Worth mentioning is the fact that none of the chambers advised entrusting the respective German consulate

90 The reply from South Korea was unique, emphasizing the effectiveness of continuous and amicable intervention of the chamber on behalf of the inquirer.

91 Besides not mentioning existing treaties, there also was a case of pointing out a treaty that actually is non-existent: The reply from Mexico City offered to supply further information on it – against prepayment of the aforementioned fee (see note 76). Despite knowing a German executory title existed, the respondent from Brussels advised that the procedures in Belgium legally require representation by a Belgian lawyer, which is false.

with contacting the debtor.[92] While we found numerous consulates referring the inquirer to the respective, locally established German chamber, none of the chambers' replies referred to services or information obtainable from the respective consulate.[93] In this regard, further data could therefore not be surveyed.

Among the replies examined here, a total of 35 did supply some kind of concluding advice to the inquirer. Four of these offered expressly indifferent conclusions.[94] Referring to the economically insignificant amount of the claim, they favoured simply dropping the case and advised the client to write the claim off, avoiding further legal steps that implied further costs. A third of the replies advised entrusting a local law office with further pursuit of the matter and the majority (20 replies) favoured pursuing the claim through means of debt-collection services, whether from their own branch or from independent agencies.

Discussion

The fact that all replies had been issued individually and that three-quarters gave varying degrees of consideration to the case in question, can be seen as further support for the evidence stated above that the organizing structure of the particular offices is more or less well functioning.

The results also show that chambers, asked for advice in a primarily legal question, tend to consider pragmatic ways of pursuing legal claims. When examined for further procedures proposed, 29 out of 36 replies proposed means of debt collection.[95] Solely judicial means were only proposed by seven.[96] This particular finding

92 For the potential of this procedure, see note 58.

93 See above, "Reference to Chambers of Industry and Commerce".

94 The reply from Venezuela stated that the amount of the claim in question is commonly regarded as "not interesting". It closed by recommending an "independent" debt-collection agency, leading to the assumption that this kind of organization draws its interest from a relatively high margin rather than from the total amount of the claim.

95 The response from Portugal was unique, suggesting obtaining "reliable" information on the liquidity of the debtor.

96 What can be seen as typical of replies from South America is stated most clearly in the reply received from Chile. The advice given here was to avoid any court or other legal settlement under all circumstances.

may be derived from the fact that some chambers offer their own debt-collection services or may be economically interested in bringing in agencies with which they are in some way connected. Yet proceeding strictly judicially tends to be a tedious undertaking whereas, by the nature of profit-sharing agreements, entrusted collection agencies promise more time-effective results. Our finding that three-quarters of these replies described the proposed procedure from a cost-oriented point of view supports this.

Of the offices which were willing to be of further support, almost two-thirds regularly assign third parties to pursue the objectives of the inquirer abroad. Given that these agencies provide reliable services, the inquirer benefits from the fact that they are usually locally established and familiar with relevant particularities in the respective society. It can be assumed that this intimate way of being able to provide services, not from outside, but from within a foreign society, explains the result shown above, according to which eight out of 10 replies provided at least general legal–cultural insights into the respective foreign structures. The fact that in foreign societies even the economy works differently has generally been included in the replies.[97] Half of them described the cost effects of the pursuit and one out of five supplied even more extensive information.

In summarizing the findings on the applicability of the replies received, it needs to be emphasized that a substantial part focuses on a cost-oriented approach when it comes to considering differing options of further procedures. Chambers of Commerce Abroad also find it easy to overcome difficulties in dealing in foreign structures by employing domestic institutions. Yet a lack of neutrality of the information supplied becomes obvious when information sheets are 'sponsored' by a debt-collection agency, recommended on a different sheet,[98] and in these instances the option of pursuing further through legal action does not receive any recognition at all.

97 The deepest insight was probably supplied by the office in Indonesia, describing debt collection agencies as "quite successful, yet varying with the approach of the executing authorities".

98 Such sponsorship was found in the reply from Norway. It differed regarding the direct way of advertisement or recommendation, where advertising material of independent agencies was enclosed with the chamber's reply. In the reply from Los Angeles, the chamber virtually advertised the services of a particular commercial debt-collection agency without supplying any further information on the same.

A differentiation of the results according to regions shows similar results under each criterion and does not allow any conclusions regarding variances in the particular socioeconomic or legal–cultural development. Each particular region has underperformers and (fewer) overperformers, according to a particular criterion[99] or even a range of criteria.[100] It may be assumed that reasons for this can be found, not so much at the organizational level, as within the complex of human resources.

Conclusion

When comparing the services of consulates with those of Chambers of Commerce Abroad with regard to their capability for supplying legal information on the respective receiving state and possibly providing legal assistance, one tends to follow the classical conception of public service institutions versus profit-oriented service agencies. On the one hand, the support given by the public service tends to be inexpensive, the information supplied is agreed to be correct by all standards[101] and its authority may be of help when needed to persuade individuals. On the other hand, the advantages of Chambers of Commerce Abroad over the consulate service as sources of information and support abroad may be found in the latter's disadvantages: chambers respond more quickly and are more flexible, and when collecting information for their reply they give more consideration to the inquirer's motives and find it easier to obtain and provide insights and information from within the business environment in the respective foreign country.

To assess each of the two systems' capacity to be of help and potential support, we need to reflect on the criteria set by the original case in question. In the original inquiry, the small law office will probably find it equally easy to contact either one of the institutions in the receiving state, as their addresses are commonly available. With regard to the consulate service, it is probably comparatively unknown that providing advice and support in such

99 See note 82 and the corresponding text.

100 See "Discussion" (p. 315) and note 91.

101 For the question of liability for information supplied in the consulate service, see Hecker, "Handbuch der konsularischen Praxis", §2 II, A 75.

matters is part of its duties mandated by law.[102] The self-supporting structure of German Chambers of Commerce Abroad, on the other hand, is probably equally unknown. Both systems therefore do indeed have potential to increase both their publicity and their effectiveness through higher demand for their services.

For a small office in a rather rural area to achieve a helpful and sound consultation, the inquirer requires primary information on the particular legal culture in which the client hopes eventually to execute his title. The major difference in this regard lies in the different approach the institutions obviously take, which may be explained by a different self-esteem: as a branch of the international economy and being financially independent themselves, the chambers naturally take a more cost-oriented approach to their counselling; whereas the consulate service, being run by bureaucrats from within their structures, just as naturally tends to focus on the foreign legal structure as it is set up abroad. Considering the great discrepancies between the law and the possibilities of its realization,[103] the information supplied by the chambers generally tends to be of higher quality, as they suit the aforesaid situation better.

Executory treaties are supposed to make the enforcement of executory titles easier.[104] Exact and comprehensive information on the state of the treaty and the procedures implied are essential for the inquirer in the aforesaid situation. Neither the replies received from the consulates[105] nor those from the chambers were clear on the existence of the relevant treaty; nor were they truthful on the procedures implied.[106]

Besides the legal situation of his client's interests, the inquiring lawyer has to evaluate possible means of out-of-court settlements, whose importance increases with the length of time required for court procedures in the receiving state. Hardly any of the consulate

102 See "Tasks and limits of the German consular service" at the beginning of this chapter.

103 See notes 88, 89, 95.

104 At least in theory: see note 103.

105 See "Reference to treaties on the recognition and enforcement of foreign civil judgments" (p. 294).

106 No mention was found in the replies from Madrid, London, Dublin, Brussels and Lisbon. Interestingly enough, the existence of the relevant treaty was also unknown in Portugal and Spain, the youngest contracting states; also see notes 88, 96.

replies made informative references to this area. This comes as a surprise, since for them the possibilities for mediating communications with the foreign debtor are provided by law. This tool found just as little consideration among the chambers' replies.[107] The most popular advice provided here was to entrust a debt-collection agency with the claim. As mentioned above, this procedure does contain the potential advantage of providing fast and clear evidence on the possibilities of financially settling the case, yet the disadvantages for the creditor seem to be considerable as well. Without any evaluation of the potential outcome, the creditor has to bear a sometimes substantial basic fee and, provided the collector is successful, is liable to pay a contingency fee on top.[108] In contrast to legal costs in most countries, payment of these charges by the debtor cannot be pursued. We also detected a certain risk for the creditor hidden in the way some of the collection agencies were recommended by the chambers. To reduce these costs, a lawyer's client frequently doing business in a particular region of the world may be advised to become a member of the respective international chamber. He or she would then be eligible for favourable rates.[109]

All this information is needed as quickly as possible, not only for economic reasons, with interests mounting on the outstanding amount, but also for the relationship between the counselling lawyer and his or her client: the law office cannot be expected to wait for weeks and sometimes months for an initial answer to continue

107 See note 90.

108 For example, for the value in dispute the German Irish Chamber charges a basic fee of DM200, plus a contingency fee of 10 per cent at a 50 per cent member discount; the New York office of the German American Chamber of Commerce, Inc., charges a DM1,000 basic fee, no contingency fee, with a 20 per cent member discount; the Camara de Industria y Comercio Argentino–Alemana, Buenos Aires, charges a basic fee of DM150 and a 9 per cent contingency fee, with 50 per cent off for members; the German–Korean Chamber in Seoul charges a DM450 basic fee and a DM1,000 contingency fee with a 50 per cent reduction for members; and the agency recommended by the Los Angeles office (see note 100) charges a contingency fee of 20 per cent. For the costs of debt collection through trade chambers, see Holger Müller and Götz-Sebastian Hök, eds, *Deutsche Vollstreckungstitel im Ausland* (Neuwied: Luchterhand, 1988).

109 See note 76.

to counsel in the case. In this regard, the chambers proved to be organized more efficiently. The chambers' replies do not allow a valid comparison as to the different quality of legal information supplied by representations of these two institutions in the same region.[110]

To expect all consulates to become more service-oriented is probably just as illusionary as to expect the Chambers of Commerce Abroad to place their own economic interests behind the need for truly considerate and helpful counselling. Yet there may be a realistic approach in aiming at better communication between the two institutions wherever they are coexistent. Wherever this is not possible, for the consulate service comprising the sole representation and thus the only source for its nationals to obtain legal information, the understanding of its function ought to become more service-oriented.

References

Drenker, Alexander. 1970. *Diplomaten ohne Nimbus! – Beobachtungen und Meinungen eines deutschen Presseattachés*. Zurich, Freiburg: Atlantis.

Freyhold, Hanno von and Enzo L. Vial. 1995. Report on the Cost of Judicial Proceedings in the European Union. In *Cost of Judicial Barriers for Consumers in the Single Market – A Report for the European Commission (Directorate General XXIV)*, edited by Hanno von Freyhold, Volkmar Gessner, Enzo L. Vial and Helmut Wagner. Bremen: Zentrum für Europäische Rechtspolitik an der Universität Bremen. October/November.

Hecker, Gottfried. 1982. *Handbuch der konsularischen Praxis*. Munich: Beck.

Hoffmann, Klaus. 1996. *Konsularrecht – Kommentar zum Konsulargesetz und Kommentar zum Gesetz über den Auswärtigen Dienst*. Starnberg: Schulz.

Müller, Holger and Götz-Sebastian Hök, eds. 1988. *Deutsche Vollstreckungstitel im Ausland*. Neuwied: Luchterhand.

Paschke, Karl Th. 1975. *Reform der Attaché-Ausbildung*. Baden Baden: Nomos.

Schaefer, Michael. 1995. *Berufsbild: 'Diplomat' – Auswahl und Ausbildung der Anwärter des höheren Auswärtigen Dienstes der Bundesrepublik*. Baden-Baden: Nomos.

110 As we had anticipated in "Assumptions", above.

The Author

Andreas S. Petzold has qualifications in law and business management. Having spent some time on practical work in the United States, he currently works in international trade in Bremen, Germany.

Address: Raiffeisenstr. 20, 28857 Syke, Germany.

E-mail: apetzold@uni-bremen.de

Abstract

This chapter is the result of an empirical study conducted among German consulates and Chambers of Industry and Commerce, which were asked to provide legal information in a cross-border civil claim. The answers received were evaluated as to their usefulness from the inquirer's service-oriented point of view.

With numerous representations spread all over the world, both the Foreign Service and German Chambers of Industry and Commerce Abroad provide a network of local sources of information for those seeking legal advice in matters involving the legislation and legal practice of the respective state. It was expected that their replies would provide sufficient indication of how to proceed in the dispute in question, but among the consulate representations we found only a few that provided practical information, that seem to have understood the need to explain the legal cultural environment of their host country and that fulfilled the service-oriented nature of their task. The Chambers of Industry and Commerce Abroad showed a more professional orientation. The study supports a view that, unlike globally acting, large companies with sufficient assets to conduct studies of cross-border legal problems on their own, players on a smaller scale find that the gap between the globalization of business opportunities and legal structures of the nation-states is too wide to cross when having to rely only on support structures available to the general public.

Part Three
Law and the New World Order

9 Global Legal Interaction and Present-day Patterns of Globalization

ANTHONY G. McGREW

Introduction

The end of the Cold War brought to a close the bipolar geopolitical order and the superpower rivalry which dominated international politics for almost half a century. But historic as it is, this shift in the geopolitical order may have distracted our attention from a more profound restructuring of the modern global order: the dramatic (even traumatic) reorganization of international political space propelled by processes of globalization which is said to be unfolding before us.[1] Globalization appears to be eroding the Westphalian norms[2] upon which the modern inter-state system is constructed, namely a political order naturally organized into territorial, bounded, sovereign political communities or 'political spaces'. The intensification of patterns of global and regional interconnectedness dissolves the boundedness of modern nation-states as political, legal, economic and other social activities transcend territorial borders. In this sense globalization is subverting the dominant pattern of modern political organization which assumes that notions of political space and political community are rooted in, and defined by, the bounded, territorial nation-state. Rather than a world order constituted by 190 sovereign political spaces, each anchored within the impermeable boundaries of the nation-state, globalization is creating a much more complex architecture of political power and political space.

1 John Ruggie, "Territoriality and Beyond", *International Organization* 41(1) (1993), 139–74.

2 Used here in the sense of an ideal type of international political order rather than a historical description of the Westphalian settlement which (arguably) is identified with the emergence of the practice of modern sovereign statehood. See Steven Krasner, "Compromising Westphalia", *International Security* 20(3) (1995), 115–51.

The academic controversies which surround globalization are legion. Even within established traditions of social and political enquiry there is often little common ground between what on the surface appear to be similar ideological approaches to the study of globalization. But despite this diversity of approaches and interpretations there is an observable clustering of accounts around shared intellectual 'fault-lines'. In particular, a key 'fault-line' concerns the issue of historical continuity and change: theoretical approaches differ markedly as to whether the present-day phase of globalization is believed to articulate a radically new epoch in world history, a process of transformation or restructuring of the global political economy, or a historically contingent phenomenon that is by no means unprecedented. Three distinctive 'positions' in the debate about globalization can be identified: the globalists, the sceptics and the transformationalists. Each delivers a distinctive response to the questions: what is new about globalization; and what are its political consequences?

It would appear that globalization delivers a serious challenge both to conventional conceptions of politics and municipal law which assume a strict separation of the domestic and the international spheres, 'inside and outside' the state, respectively, and to the modern conception of state sovereignty. This chapter seeks to locate the discussion of cross-border legal interaction in the context of this wider discourse concerning globalization and sovereign statehood.[3]

Globalization: a 'Shrinking World'

Today goods, capital, people, knowledge, images and communications, as well as crime, culture, pollutants, drugs, fashions and beliefs, readily flow across territorial boundaries. Transnational networks, social movements and relationships are extensive in virtually all areas of human activity. The existence of global and regional systems of trade, finance and production binds together the prosperity and fate of households, communities and nations

3 This chapter is based partly upon research conducted for the Globalization and Advanced Industrial State project (funded by the UK Economic Social and Research Council), based at the Open University, UK, under the joint direction of Professor David Held and myself. It reflects some of our earlier collaborative work. I am also indebted to my colleagues on the project, Dr David Goldblatt and Dr Jonathan Perraton.

across the globe. Territorial boundaries are therefore arguably increasingly insignificant insofar as social activity and relations no longer stop – if they ever did – at the water's edge. But is all such activity evidence of globalization?

Modelski defines globalization as 'the process by which a number of historical world societies were brought together into one global system'.[4] This suggests a process embodying both a spatial and a historical reach. Accordingly, we can begin to conceive of globalization as a process which generates flows and connections, not simply across nation-states and national territorial boundaries, but between global regions, continents and civilizations. This invites a definition of globalization as: 'an historical process which engenders a significant shift in the spatial reach of networks and systems of social relations to transcontinental or interregional patterns of human organization, activity and the exercise of power'. This definition provides for a crisper conceptual differentiation between processes occurring at different spatial scales, namely, globalization, regionalization and internationalization. If globalization is understood as transregional interconnectedness, then regionalization can be conceived as the intensification of patterns of interconnectedness between geographically contiguous states which define the contours of a regional subsystem. Flows of trade and finance between the three major regions in the world economy would count as globalization, and flows within them as regionalization.[5] Within Europe it is possible to identify a regional political and economic space which reflects an institutionalized regional system and in Asia–Pacific APEC (Asia–Pacific Economic Cooperation) defines the boundaries of an evolving regional economic complex. Of course, this is not to argue that globalization and regionalization are contradictory tendencies; on the contrary, there are very strong reasons to assume they are mutually reinforcing processes. Finally, internationalization can be characterized in terms of clusters of networks, flows and interactions between two or more nation-states. In keeping with these conceptual clarifications, clearer distinctions between

4 George Modelski, *Principles of World Politics* (New York: Free Press, 1972).

5 For a good discussion of regionalization and regionalism, see Barry Buzan, *People, States and Fear*, 2nd edn (Brighton: Harvester Press, 1991) and Louis J. Cantori and Steven L. Spiegel, *The International Relations of Regions : A Comparative Approach* (Englewood Cliffs, California: Prentice-Hall, 1970).

incidences of global legal interaction, and other forms of transnational legal interaction, can be made.

Alongside the changing scale of human social organization and the exercise of power, globalization also reflects a historical dynamic. Over the 'longue durée', the global condition has evolved from limited interaction between largely discrete world civilizations to a single states system which constitutes, for humanity, the key organizing principle of modern political life. Globalization therefore has to be understood as a historical process. From the age of discovery in the early modern period, through the European world empires of the late nineteenth century, to the modern era of transnational capitalism, globalization has acquired quite distinctive forms shaped by prevailing material, ideological and social formations. It is by no means only, or even largely, a modern or late twentieth-century condition. Over the course of world history it is possible to distinguish analytically between distinct historical forms of globalization, from that of the pre-modern age, the early modern era of the voyages of discovery, through the 'long nineteenth century', to the present era of late modernity. This is not to suggest an evolutionary or teleological account of world history; on the contrary the very concept of historical forms of globalization embraces a view of historical change which stresses discontinuity and contingency. Comparing and contrasting the dominant features of different historical forms of globalization offers the prospect of substantive response to the question posed by many sceptics of the globalization thesis: what's new? For it offers the possibility of a systematic and rigorous understanding of what is distinctive about its present-day articulation. However, such an undertaking is beyond the scope of this chapter and is dealt with elsewhere.[6] Instead, it may be of greater value here to explicate the analytical framework which informs such historical comparison before exploring the dominant features and patterns of modern globalization.

The Historical Form of Present-day Globalization

As indicated above, globalization embodies a set of processes which generate a multiplicity of linkages and interconnections which transcend the regions and societies which make up the modern world

6 David Goldblatt, David Held, Anthony McGrew and Jonathan Perraton, *Global Flows, Global Transformations* (Cambridge: Polity Press, forthcoming).

system: the concept therefore has a spatial connotation. Social, political and economic activities are becoming 'stretched' across the globe, so that events, decisions and activities in one part of the world can come to have immediate significance for individuals and communities in distant parts of the globe. But globalization also implies an intensification, or increasing density, in the flows and patterns of interaction or interconnectedness between the states and societies which constitute the modern world community. Alongside the 'stretching' goes a 'deepening' such that even though 'everyone has a local life, phenomenal worlds for the most part are truly global'.[7] Moreover, the extensity and density of global (and regional) networks and flows is mediated by the existence of physical, normative and symbolic infrastructures, such as systems of air transport, the global trade regime, English as the language of science and business respectively. These infrastructures are in turn a product of prevailing technological conditions and capacities, so that the scope and scale of global interactions in any epoch is significantly influenced by such (technological) interaction capacity.[8] Furthermore, infrastructures contribute over time to the regularization of networks, flows and interactions and by degrees to their developing institutionalization.

Globalization has a differential reach and impact reflecting structural asymmetries in the geometry of global power relations. States, communities, groups and households are differentially enmeshed in global networks and flows so that control over, as well as impact of, globalization varies enormously between, as well as within, societies. Patterns of hierarchy and stratification mediate access to sites of power whilst the consequences of globalization are unevenly experienced. The fact that today the majority of world trade is between OECD (the western) nations, as it was in earlier epochs, illustrates the long-standing historical patterns of hierarchy and stratification in the global trading order. Processes of globalization also imply a level of 'systemness', in that patterns of regularized interaction create a totality of relations, with its own dynamic, in which agents – be they states, institutions, comities or individuals – are embedded.[9] Finally, the dominant modes and instruments of

7 Anthony Giddens, *Modernity and Self-Identity* (Cambridge: Polity Press, 1991).

8 Barry Buzan, Charles Jones and Richard Little, *The Logic of Anarchy* (New York: Columbia University Press, 1993).

9 Anthony Giddens, *A Contemporary Critique of Historical Materialism V1* (London: MacMillan, 1981).

globalization differ across time, from military conquest, in earlier periods, to modern forms of spontaneous association and organization, as with transnational social movements such as Greenpeace.

To summarize: historical forms of globalization differ along several analytical dimensions: the extensity or scope, that is, 'stretching' of networks and connections across time and territorial space; the density of interactions, that is, 'deepening'; interaction capacities, infrastructures and the institutionalization of networks and interactions; their 'power geometry' in terms of the 'geography' of uneven impact/control; and the dominant modes of globalization. Historical comparisons must also be sensitive to the distinctive patterns of globalization evident in different domains of social and human activity. Thus the history and geography of economic globalization depart in significant ways from the history and geography of military globalization. It is these identities and differences between patterns of globalization in each of the key institutional domains of social power (the economic, political, military, cultural, legal, and so on) which are vital to a proper understanding of the nature of modern globalization. Following the work of Mann and Giddens this account is predicated upon a multicausal analysis of globalization which seeks to understand how it is articulated in each of the key institutional domains of social power.[10] Here the focus will be upon the economic, political and legal domains.

The Economic Domain

The spatial reach of present-day systems of production, distribution and exchange has significant implications for the competence and effectiveness of national economic policies.[11] Few would disagree that the globalization of economic forces has transformed the parameters within which national economic management is pursued. Although distinctive national styles of economic management exist, Gourevitch observes a general policy convergence

10 Michael Mann, *The Sources of Social Power*, vol. 1 (Cambridge: Cambridge University Press, 1986); Anthony Giddens, *The Consequences of Modernity* (Cambridge: Polity Press, 1990).

11 Jeffrey Frieden, "Invested interests : the politics of national economic policies in a world of global finance", *International Organization* 45(4) (1991), 425–53; M.C. Webb, "International economic structures, government interests and international coordination of macroeconomic adjustment policies", *International Organization* 45(4) (1991), 309–43.

amongst the advanced capitalist states, specifically in respect of broad macroeconomic measures.[12] Thus, in the 1980s, the demise of the Keynesian strategy of 'managed capitalism' – within the advanced capitalist countries – was traced, in part, to an intensification of 'interdependence' which undercut the effectiveness of the fiscal and interventionist policies necessary to sustain it.[13] In a highly competitive but interconnected global economy, national economic strategies, together with the domestic political coalitions which underpin them, have become increasingly sensitive to world economic conditions. Foreign exchange trading in the world's financial centres averaged about $650 billion a day in 1989, equivalent to nearly $500 million a minute, or approaching 40 times the value of daily world trade.[14] By 1992, turnover exceeded $1 trillion, which was in excess of the entire annual GDP of France and the UK combined. Alongside the creation and expansion of global 24-hour foreign exchange trading in the postwar period, there has also been a massive increase in international bank lending, bond trading, securitization and financial derivatives.[15] International trade, too, has grown dramatically since 1945 and by the 1980s was considerably higher as a percentage of GDP for most countries than in the late nineteenth century.

Two aspects of international economic processes are central to these developments: the internationalization of production and the globalization of national financial markets, organized in part by a relatively small number of powerful transnational corporations. Multinationals account for between 25 per cent and 33 per cent of world output, around 70 per cent of world trade and 80 per cent of world investment. Most transnational companies organize production, marketing and distribution on a regional or global basis. Global 'sourcing' of production is commonplace in all sectors. Even though all transnational corporations have a national base, their activities are predominantly geared to maximizing their

12 Peter Gourevitch, *Politics in Hard Times* (New York: Cornell University Press, 1986), 33.

13 Peter Gourevitch, *Politics in Hard Times*; Robert Cox, *Power, Production and World Order* (New York: St. Martins Press, 1987).

14 Jeffrey Frieden, "Invested interests: the politics of national economic policies in a world of global finance", pp. 425–453, at 428.

15 Jeffrey Frankel, ed., *The Globalization of Equity Markets* (Chicago, University of Chicago Press, 1994).

international competitive position and profitability, so that individual national subsidiaries operate in the context of an overall corporate strategy. Investment and production decisions therefore may not always reflect local or national conditions. Thus the operation of multinationals has accelerated the trends towards a new international division of labour and the process of global economic restructuring. With the internationalization of production has come the globalization of banking and of legal and financial services. Information technology has transformed the finance sector, so that a single global financial market now exists with almost round-the-clock trading.

Advances in transport and communication technology are rapidly eroding the boundaries between hitherto separate national markets – boundaries which were a necessary requirement for national economic management.[16] Markets, and thus societies, are becoming more vulnerable to one another. The stock market crash of October 1987 and the devaluation of sterling in September 1992 illustrate the way in which violent movements in international financial markets impinge directly upon the monetary and fiscal policies of individual national governments and, thereby, individual households and citizens. The existence of transnational networks of production, investment and exchange ensure that few national markets or sectors of national economies can insulate themselves entirely from international conditions or external competitive pressures. However, the erosion of national economic autonomy is not, of course, uniformly experienced across countries or economic sectors: some countries and some markets can insulate themselves from transnational economic forces by, among other things, attempting to restore the boundaries or 'separateness' of markets and/or to extend national laws to regulate internationally mobile factors and/or adopt cooperative policies with other states for the coordination of economic and industrial policies.[17] In addition, the

16 Geoffrey Garrett and Peter Lange, "Political responses to interdependence: what's 'left' for the left?", *International Organization* 45(4) (1991), 539–65.

17 Robert Gilpin, *The Political Economy of International Relations* (Princeton: Princeton University Press, 1987); M.C. Webb, "International economic structures, government interests and international coordination of macroeconomic adjustment policies"; Tariq Banuri and Juliet Schor, eds., *Financial Openness and National Autonomy* (Oxford: Oxford University Press, 1992).

growing regionalization of the world economy is fuelled in part by the opportunities it affords for states to combat the more damaging consequences of global competitive forces. Economic activity appears increasingly to be clustered around several poles (amongst them the EU, North America, Asia and the Pacific rim) although it is not necessarily at odds with a more globalized and integrated world economy.[18] Economic and financial globalization generate profound questions concerning the possibilities for the pursuit of national economic autonomy.

The Political Domain

In the postwar era, states have become increasingly enmeshed in institutions of geogovernance. Governments now participate in an expanding array of international regimes and organizations which have been established to manage specific global issue areas, such as trade, the oceans, space, telecommunications and so on. The growth in the number of these new forms of multilateral association reflects the rapid expansion of transnational activities, the growing interpenetration of foreign and domestic policy and the corresponding desire by most states for some form of international governance and regulation to deal with collective policy problems.[19]

New forms of multilateral and multinational politics have evolved and with them distinctive styles of collective decision making involving governments, intergovernmental organizations and a whole variety of transnational pressure groups and organizations.[20] For example, the deliberations of the Earth Summit in Rio de Janeiro in June 1992 were attended by delegates from over 120 governments and scores of transnational and national environmental pressure groups and other transnational organizations. A world of flows and connections promotes associations, loyalties and allegiances which transcend national boundaries and thus creates the potential for

18 Kym Anderson and Robin Blackhurst, eds., *Regional Integration and the Global Trading System* (Brighton: Harvester, 1993).

19 In 1909 there were 37 International Governmental Organizations (IGO) and 176 International Nongovernmental Organizations (INGO). In 1989, there were nearly 300 IGOs and 4,624 INGOs (see Anthony McGrew, "A Global Society?" in *Modernity and Its Futures*, ed. Stuart Hall, David Held and Tony McGrew (Cambridge: Polity Press, 1992), 8–12).

20 Phillip Cerny, *The Changing Architecture of the State* (London: Sage, 1990).

new kinds of transnational 'imagined communities'. This is especially visible in respect of new social movements, such as the women's and environmental movements, but also in respect of many diaspora ethnic and cultural communities which retain a sense of hyphenated identities. Onto the global mosaic of national communities, globalization is overlaying new kinds and forms of political community which transcend territorial boundaries. Such developments present a challenge to the conventional constructions of the 'political' and to established notions of citizenship, as well as political community. As Walker notes, new social movements are testament to a 'new politics' which considers the state as 'only one of a number of political spaces in which to act and in which questions about freedom, obligation, community, and so on, must be posed'.[21]

These developments suggest, on the one hand, the emergence of a 'protoglobal civil society', whilst bodies like the G7, on the other hand, bringing together the world's advanced capitalist states, operate as a kind of 'global directorate' or global proto-state institution. Yet as Zürn observes, the limited effectiveness of mechanisms of international governance has significant consequences for national governments: 'since the rise of international governance is slower than the process of globalization, the loss of effectiveness of national politics is not adequately replaced by effective international institutions. This causes a substantial deficit in the capacity to govern in all issue-areas'.[22] In addition, international mechanisms of governance lack the legitimacy for independent action, which further compounds this deficit in 'the capacity to govern'.

The Legal Domain

In parallel, the development of international law has subjected individuals, governments and non-governmental organizations to new systems of legal regulation. Over the postwar period there has been a phenomenal expansion in the number, form, scope and functional jurisdiction of international legal agreements, from multilateral treaties to protocols and conventions. This expansion has been particularly marked in the commercial, technological, cultural

21 Rob Walker, "International Relations and the Concept of the Political", in *International Relations Theory Today*, ed. Ken Booth and Steve Smith (Cambridge: Polity Press, 1995), 105.

22 Michael Zürn, "The Challenge of Globalization and Individualization", in *Whose World Order?*, ed. Hans-Henrik Holm and G. Sorensen (Boulder Colorado: Westview Press, 1995).

and administrative domains. Accompanying the growth of this global legal infrastructure is an extraordinary array of transnational legal interaction, from the extraterritorial application of municipal law to international arbitration and the internationalization of legal standards and codes. The Brussels Convention, which codifies rules for cross-border legal interaction, is indicative of the emerging infrastructures of legal globalization.[23]

International law now recognizes rights and duties which transcend the claims of nation-states and which, while they may not be backed by institutions with coercive powers of enforcement, have nonetheless far-reaching consequences. While it is the case that national legal sovereignty has most often been the victor when put to the test, the 'contest' between national sovereignty and international law is increasingly evident across many sectors of legal practice, from commercial law to family law. In the European Union, the passing of the Single European Act, which replaces unanimity with 'qualified majority voting' within the Council of Ministers for a significant number of issue areas, openly compromises the doctrine of national legal sovereignty.

In recent decades, the subject, scope and source of international law have all expanded while opinion has shifted against the traditional doctrine that international law is and should be exclusively law between states. The growing complexity and density of commercial legal interaction has generated significant discussion about the emergence of 'transnational law' (such as *lex mercatoria*) and 'delocalized' commercial arbitration.[24] As Schmitthoff observed 'we are beginning to rediscover the international character of commercial law ... the general trend of commercial law everywhere is to move away from the restrictions of national law to a universal, international conception of the law of international trade'.[25] Public international law has also evolved in such a way that the international legal understanding of sovereign statehood itself is changing subtly to reflect the principles of democratic legitimacy. In this sense, international public law is 'increasingly concerned with

23 But see its limited effect in other contributions to this volume.

24 See Chapter 10 of the present volume.

25 Clive M. Schmitthoff, "International business law: A New Law Merchant" in *Clive M. Schmitthoff's Select Essays on International Trade*, ed. Chia-Jui Cheng (London, Martinus Nijhoff Publishers, 1988), 27.

issues which impinge on what were once considered matters of domestic policy'.[26]

To conceive of national legal systems as completely autonomous organisms is thus to ignore the complex interactions between external and internal factors in the continuing evolution of legal practice. More radically, the very idea of a single site of legal sovereignty embodied in the state is destabilized by patterns of global legal interaction which erode the boundaries between domestic and international law, foreign and domestic legal systems and practices, and internal and external juridical authorities. As Dezalay concludes, in the legal domain, globalization 'throws new light onto the old question of autonomy or, if one prefers, the singularity, of national juridical cultures'.[27] In so doing, it invites serious questions about the traditional primacy accorded to the principle of national legal sovereignty.

The historical form of contemporary globalization exhibits many distinctive attributes. In particular, it embodies the complex articulation of globalization across all the key domains of social power – the economic, the cultural, the political, the legal and the military – combined with a chronic intensification of patterns of global interconnectedness and heightened consciousness of the 'global condition'. Moreover, a highly developed worldwide infrastructure of communication and transport delivers a historically unprecedented potential for intensive, as well as regularized, global (and regional) interaction and organization, but within the context of a highly regulated and institutionalized global order. Present-day patterns of globalization define the contours of a global system which exhibits a high level of 'systemness' such that events, decisions and actions in one part of the world can very rapidly acquire worldwide ramifications, whilst institutionalized networks of global and regional interconnectedness lock together (in highly complex ways) the fate of peoples and communities in remote corners of the globe. But it would be foolish to read these developments as prefiguring the emergence of a world community.[28] For globalization is a highly

26 James Crawford, *Democracy in International Law* (Cambridge: Cambridge University Press, 1994), 14.

27 Yves Dezalay, "The Big Bang and the Law: the internationalization and restructuration of the legal field" in *Global Culture*, ed. Mike Featherstone (London: Sage, 1990), 281.

28 Chris Brown, "International theory and international society: the viability of a middle way?", *Review of International Studies* 21 (1995).

uneven process and is associated with the reproduction of global hierarchies of privilege, control and exclusion. It fragments as it integrates, so that some regions, states, communities and households are tightly enmeshed in global or regional networks, while others are marginalized. It thereby contributes to processes of national and international social and political fragmentation and stratification, processes which are far from conducive to the emergence of global solidarity. Accordingly, globalization should be conceived as a dialectical process, since it stimulates 'mutually opposing tendencies' of global integration versus fragmentation, universalism versus particularism, and cultural homogenization versus differentiation.[29]

Globalization and its Disjunctures[30]

Modern processes of globalization and regionalization call into question traditional assumptions about sovereign statehood, but the idea that globalization emasculates or immobilizes the state, contributing to its inevitable decline, is more myth than substance.[31] There is no direct linear correlation between the intensification of globalization and the apparent erosion of state power. On the contrary, it is equally associated with the expanding jurisdiction of state authority through the creation of international agencies and regimes.[32] Recent studies demonstrate that the consequences of globalization for any state are mediated by its location in the hierarchy of power, domestic institutional structures and the mobilization

29 Anthony Giddens, *The Consequences of Modernity* (Cambridge: Polity Press, 1990), 64; Anthony McGrew, "A Global Society?": p. 74.

30 The concept of disjunctures is borrowed from the work of my colleague, David Held (see David Held, "Democracy, the Nation-state and the global system", in *Political Theory Today*, ed. David Held (Cambridge: Polity Press, 1991); David Held and Anthony McGrew, "Globalization and the Liberal Democratic State", *Government and Opposition* (1993); and David Held, *Democracy and Global Order* (Cambridge: Polity Press, 1995).

31 Joseph A. Cammilleri and Jim Falk, *The End of Sovereignty? The Politics of a Shrinking and Fragmenting World* (Aldershot: Edward Elgar, 1992); James N. Rosenau, *Turbulence in World Politics* (Brighton: Harvester Wheatsheaf, 1990).

32 James Rosenau, *Turbulence in World Politics*.

of countervailing political and economic strategies.[33] Governments and politicians, contrary to much globalization hype, are not immobilized by global and regional forces; the state continues to matter. Rather, in the modern era, the state and state power arguably are being restructured. As Keohane argues, globalization does not prefigure the demise of sovereign statehood, but it is strongly associated with the emergence of a new 'regime of sovereignty' which is gradually supplanting the 'Westphalian sovereignty regime'.[34]

This restructuring is captured in the growing external disjunctures between the 'de jure' claim of states to 'effective supremacy over what occurs within their territories' and the political practices of states confronted by overlapping global, regional, multilateral and transnational networks and power structures.[35] As the preceding 'mapping' of contemporary patterns of globalization demonstrates, these disjunctures are evident, to varying degrees, in all the key domains of state power from the political and the economic to the legal. Furthermore, these disjunctures also catalogue the limits to the modern state's claim to 'de facto' sovereignty, or what might be better labelled 'autonomy', under conditions of globalization and regionalization. Importantly, in assessing the impact of 'external' disjunctures, it is essential to recognize that sovereignty, particularly in its legal sense, is only eroded when it is displaced by forms of 'higher' and/or independent legal or juridical authority which curtail the rightful basis of decision making within a national polity. For sovereignty is understood here to mean the locus of political authority within a community which has the undisputed right to determine the framework of rules, regulations and policies within a given territory and to govern accordingly.[36] Moreover, sovereignty

33 Andrew Hurrell and Nyare Woods, "Globalization and Inequality", *Millenium* 24(3) (1995), 447–70; Paul Hirst and Grahame Thompson, *Globalization in Question* (Cambridge: Polity Press, 1996).

34 Robert Keohane, "Hobbes Dilemma and Institutional Change in World Politics: Sovereignty in International Society" in *Whose World Order?*, ed. Hans-Henrik Holm and G. Sorensen (Boulder Colorado: Westview Press 1995), 165–86.

35 David Held and Anthony McGrew, "Globalization and the Liberal Democratic State".

36 David Held, *Models of Democracy*, (Cambridge, Polity Press, 1989).

must be distinguished from state 'autonomy', understood as the capacity of state managers and agencies to articulate and pursue their policy preferences without resort to formal or informal international cooperation or collaboration.

The very idea of the sovereign state as 'a national community of fate', an autonomous organism which governs itself and directs its own future, sits uneasily alongside the globalization of economic production and exchange, the internationalization of security, the growing significance of international regimes, legal interaction and global institutions, the internationalization of domestic policy and the domestication of international policy. For globalization involves a growing separation or distancing of sites of political decision making from the communities, local or national, which are the subjects (intended or unintended) of such decisions. This has profound consequences for the modern doctrine of sovereign statehood which asserts the primacy of the state's authority within its own territorial boundaries and presumes a capacity to secure the welfare and security of its citizens.[37] Yet this 'idea is challenged fundamentally by the nature and pattern of global interconnections ... National communities by no means exclusively "programme" the actions, decisions and policies of their governments and the latter by no means simply determine what is right or appropriate for their own citizens alone'.[38] Furthermore, under conditions of globalization, the realization of domestic programmes is intimately connected with external initiatives, and vice versa. Autarky, as a political project, no longer appears feasible. National policy agendas are converging as the parameters within which decision making occurs are, in some domains, decisively shaped by the enmeshment of states (and their societies) in global and regional systems. To argue that these developments foreshadow the end of the nation-state is nevertheless to misread the modern conjuncture. What is occurring is best conceived as a reconstitution of sovereign statehood – the Westphalian sovereignty regime – decisively engineered by processes of globalization and regionalization. The significant disjunctures between the ideology and practice of sovereign statehood, exposed in the preceding discussion, suggest that global and regional

37 Robert. H. Jackson, *Quasi-states: Sovereignty, International Relations and the Third World* (Cambridge: Cambridge University Press, 1990).

38 David Held, "Democracy, the Nation-state and the Global System", p. 202.

patterns of enmeshment are displacing 'notions of sovereignty as an illimitable, indivisible and exclusive form of public power ... Sovereignty itself has to be conceived today as already divided among a number of agencies – national, regional and international – and limited by the very nature of this plurality'.[39] This post-Westphalian 'sovereignty regime' is characterized by a notion of sovereign statehood in which, as Keohane observes, 'Sovereignty is less a territorially defined barrier than a bargaining resource for a politics characterised by complex transnational networks'.[40]

Associated with this reconstitution of sovereignty is a reordering of international political and, thereby legal, space. The existence of global and regional networks of activity, international regimes, global and regional institutions of governance, transnational social movements, global and transnational legal interactions, and other kinds of transnational association can be interpreted as the emergence of new kinds of 'political (and legal) space' which escape the boundedness of the territorial state.[41] Whereas traditional approaches to international relations presume that territorial boundaries define the 'spatial containment'[42] of politics and juridical systems within the nation-state, globalization defines a politics of 'spatial inclusion'. For globalization dissolves the boundaries between local, national, regional and global spheres of political action reconstituting them as overlapping 'political spaces'. Under the conditions of modern globalization, politics – understood as who gets what, where and when – is no longer synonymous with the bounded territorial space of the nation-state. Nor is the language of 'levels of politics' – the local, national, global – entirely appropriate when these spheres of political action are by definition mutually constituted. Similarly, in the legal domain, domestic law and practice is no longer insulated from 'external' forces. The application of foreign law in domestic courts may well still be an unusual occurrence in most

39 David Held, "Democracy, the Nation-state and the Global System", p. 222; Paul Hirst and Grahame Thompson, *Globalization in Question*.

40 Robert Keohane, "Hobbes Dilemma and Institutional Change in World Politics: Sovereignty in International Society", pp. 165–86.

41 Anthony McGrew, "World Order and Political Space" in *A Global World?*, ed. James Anderson, Christopher Brook and Alan Cochrane (Oxford: Oxford University Press, 1995).

42 Rob Walker, "International Relations and the Concept of the Political".

states, but the practice itself has serious implications for the idea of national legal space. Accordingly, it may be more appropriate today to think in terms of overlapping (local, national, global) 'political (and legal) spaces'. Globalization therefore implies a spatial reorganization of social life in which political and legal space is no longer solely coterminous with national territorial space.

Concluding Reflections

The structural implications of modern globalization for the modern state are arguably profound.[43] The 'globalists' read into the present conjuncture the emergence of a 'global society',[44] while the 'sceptics' argue that globalization is more 'globaloney' than substance.[45] The 'transformationalist' account delivered here is therefore open to both theoretical and empirical disputation. But that debate is dealt with more fully elsewhere.[46]

This chapter commenced with a limited ambition: to offer an analytical framework, albeit a partial one, which locates processes of global legal interaction within a more general enquiry into the form of modern globalization and its implications for sovereign statehood. It has located the practice of cross-border legal interaction in a broader understanding of contemporary globalization. In terms of this enquiry, since sovereignty, autonomy and cultural particularities are so strongly expressed and institutionalized in the legal domain, evidence concerning the practices and dynamics of global legal interaction therefore holds out the promise of fundamental insights into both the transformative impact of, and, significantly, the limits to, the present phase of globalization. For, arguably, one of its most distinctive characteristics is its legal and juridical aspects.

43 Anthony McGrew, *The Transformation of Democracy? Globalization and Territorial Democracy* (Cambridge: Polity Press, 1997).

44 Martin Albrow, *The Global Age* (Cambridge: Polity Press, 1997).

45 Steven Krasner, "Economic Interdependence and Independent Statehood", in *States in a Changing World*, ed. Robert H. Jackson and Alan James (Oxford: Oxford Univeristy Press, 1993), 301–22; Winifried Ruigrok and R. v. Tulder, *The Logic of International Restructuring* (London: Routledge, 1995).

46 Anthony McGrew, *The Transformation of Democracy? Globalization and Territorial Democracy*; David Goldblatt *et al.*, *Global Flows, Global Transformations.*

References

Albrow, Martin. 1997. *The Global Age*. Cambridge: Polity Press.

Anderson, Kym and Robin Blackhurst, eds. 1993. *Regional Integration and the Global Trading System*. Brighton: Harvester Press.

Banuri, Tariq and Juliet Schor, eds. 1992. *Financial Openness and National Autonomy*. Oxford: Oxford University Press.

Brown, Chris. 1995. International theory and international society : the viability of a middle way? *Review of International Studies* 21.

Buzan, Barry. 1991. *People, States and Fear*. 2nd edn. Brighton: Harvester Press.

Buzan, Barry, Charles Jones and Richard Little. 1993. *The Logic of Anarchy*. New York: Columbia University Press.

Cammilleri, Joseph A. and Jim Falk. 1992. *The End of Sovereignty? The Politics of a Shrinking and Fragmenting World*. Aldershot: Edward Elgar.

Cantori, Louis J. and Steven L. Spiegel. 1970. *The International Relations of Regions: A Comparative Approach*. Englewood Cliffs, California: Prentice-Hall.

Cerny, Phillip. 1990. *The Changing Architecture of the State*. London: Sage.

Cox, Robert. 1987. *Power, Production and World Order*. New York: St Martin's Press.

Crawford, James. 1994. *Democracy in International Law*. Cambridge: Cambridge University Press.

Dezalay, Yves. 1990. The Big Bang and the Law: the internationalization and restructuration of the legal field. In *Global Culture*, edited by Mike Featherstone. London: Sage.

Frankel, Jeffrey, ed. 1994. *The Globalization of Equity Markets*. Chicago, University of Chicago Press.

Frieden, Jeffrey. 1991. Invested interests: the politics of national economic policies in a world of global finance. *International Organization* 45, (4).

Garrett, Geoffrey and Peter Lange. 1991. Political responses to interdependence: what's 'left' for the left? *International Organization* 45, (4).

Giddens, Anthony. 1981. *A Contemporary Critique of Historical Materialism VI*. London: MacMillan.

Giddens, Anthony. 1990. *The Consequences of Modernity*. Cambridge: Polity Press.

Giddens, Anthony. 1991. *Modernity and Self-Identity*. Cambridge: Polity Press.

Gilpin, Robert. 1987. *The Political Economy of International Relations*. Princeton: Princeton University Press.

Goldblatt, David, David Held, Anthony McGrew and Jonathan Perraton. Forthcoming. *Global Flows, Global Transformations*. Cambridge: Polity Press.

Gourevitch, Peter. 1986. *Politics in Hard Times*. New York: Cornell University Press.

Held, David. 1989. *Models of Democracy*. 1st edn. Cambridge: Polity Press.

Held, David. 1991. Democracy, the Nation-state and the global system. In *Political Theory Today*, edited by David Held. Cambridge: Polity Press.

Held, David. 1995. *Democracy and Global Order*. Cambridge: Polity Press.

Held, David and Anthony McGrew. 1993. Globalization and the Liberal Democratic State. *Government and Opposition* 28, (2).

Hirst, Paul and Grahame Thompson. 1996. *Globalization in Question*. Cambridge: Polity Press.

Hurrell, Andrew and Nyare Woods. 1995. Globalization and Inequality. *Millenium* 24, (3).

Jackson, Robert H. 1990. *Quasi-states: Sovereignty, International Relations and the Third World*. Cambridge: Cambridge University Press.

Keohane, Robert. 1995. Hobbes's Dilemma and Institutional Change in World Politics: Sovereignty in International Society. In *Whose World Order?*, edited by Hans-Henrik Holm and G. Sorensen. Boulder, Colorado: Westview Press.

Krasner, Steven. 1993. Economic Interdependence and Independent Statehood. In *States in a Changing World*, edited by Robert H. Jackson and Alan James. Oxford: Oxford University Press.

Krasner, Steven. 1995. Compromising Westphalia. *International Security* 20, (3).

Mann, Michael. 1986. *The Sources of Social Power*, Vol. 1. Cambridge: Cambridge University Press.

McGrew, Anthony. 1992. A Global Society? In *Modernity and Its Futures*, edited by Stuart Hall, David Held and Anthony McGrew. Cambridge: Polity Press.

McGrew, Anthony. 1995. World Order and Political Space. In *A Global World?*, edited by James Anderson, Christopher Brook and Alan Cochrane. Oxford: Oxford University Press.

McGrew, Anthony. 1997. *The Transformation of Democracy? Globalization and Territorial Democracy*. Cambridge: Polity Press.

Modelski, George. 1972. *Principles of World Politics*. New York: Free Press.

Rosenau, James N. 1990. *Turbulence in World Politics*. Brighton: Harvester Wheatsheaf.

Ruggie, John. 1993. Territoriality and Beyond. *International Organization* 47, (1).

Ruigrok, Winifried and R. v. Tulder. 1995. *The Logic of International Restructuring*. London: Routledge.

Schmitthoff, Clive M. 1988. International Business Law: A New Law Merchant. In *Clive M. Schmitthoff's Select Essays on International Trade*, edited by Chia-Jui Cheng. London, Martinus Nijhoff Publishers.

Walker, Rob. 1995. International Relations and the Concept of the Political. In *International Relations Theory Today*, edited by Ken Booth and Steve Smith. Cambridge: Polity Press.

Webb, M.C. 1991. International economic structures, government interests and international coordination of macroeconomic adjustment policies. *International Organization* 45, (4).

Zürn, Michael. 1995. The Challenge of Globalization and Individualization: A View from Europe. In *Whose World Order?*, edited by Hans-Henrik Holm and G. Sorensen. Boulder, Colorado: Westview Press.

The Author

Anthony McGrew is a political scientist and is Senior Lecturer in Government, Faculty of Social Sciences, The Open University, Milton Keynes, MK14 7QS, UK.

Telephone: 44(0) 1908 654441
Fax: 44(0) 1908 654488
E-mail: A.McGrew@open.ac.uk.

Abstract

Theoretical accounts of globalization differ markedly as to whether the modern phase of globalization is believed to articulate a radically new epoch in world history, a process of transformation or restructuring of the global political economy, or a historically contingent phenomenon that is by no means unprecedented. Three distinctive 'positions' in the debate about globalization can therefore be identified: the globalists; the sceptics and the transformationalists.

This chapter seeks to locate the discussion of cross-border legal interaction in the context of this wider discourse concerning globalization and sovereign statehood. In doing so it takes up the issue discussed in the introduction to this volume and delivers an account of the dominant features of present-day globalization and some critical reflections upon its implications for the modern state. The chapter commences by refining the concept of globalization and then examining the dominant patterns of modern globalization, including global legal interaction. It concludes with a critical assessment of the consequences for sovereign statehood of the developing contradictions between traditional notions of legal and political sovereignty and the dynamics of current global and regional connectedness. In this respect it argues that globalization is transforming traditional notions of sovereign statehood.

10 Reflexive Legitimacy in International Arbitration

REZA BANAKAR

Introduction

'When corporate executives in China or the former Soviet Union find themselves in conflict with their business counterparts in other countries, the fax receiver at the Stockholm Chamber of Commerce rings continuously.'[1] Arbitration in international commercial transactions has been used for more than two centuries to settle transnational disputes among businessmen. However, during the last few decades the market for arbitration as a special legal service has undergone rapid expansion.[2] This expansion has been brought on by the current globalization process, and it clearly contributes to the continuance and further development of globalization. The recent developments at the Chamber of Commerce in Stockholm (CCS) is a case in point. Established in 1917, the CCS arbitrated until recently mainly in domestic commercial disputes. But during the past few years, the caseload of international commercial disputes at CCS has been multiplied many times. Today, hundreds of international arbitration cases are processed each year in Stockholm. In China, there are some 100,000 commercial contracts with an arbitration clause which designates the CCS as the arbitrator.[3] Stockholm is, however, far from being alone in experiencing a substantial intensification of cross-border global legal interaction.

1 Quoted from an article on the Stockholm Chamber of Commerce: Stockholm världsmästare på skiljedom, in *Jusektidningen* 1994, 11.

2 In the following pages, "arbitration" refers to international commercial arbitration.

3 An interesting question in this regard is whether and how the legal culture and legal practice at the Chamber of Commerce in Stockholm affects the development of the markets in the former Soviet Union and China. This question will be the subject of a separate investigation.

The globalization of law, enhanced markets and advances in communication and transport technologies have raised our awareness of the emergence of a new legal infrastructure that is characterized by its potential to transcend both cultural and national boundaries. Furthermore, the function of law is not *only* related to, or to be understood by, the needs of business actors. As pointed out by Dezalay and Garth, 'the particulars of legal practices ... become quite important in the shaping of markets generally ...'.[4] Law is, therefore, shaped and reshaped by the economic, political and cultural forces creating the global village, while it operates to regulate and shape globalized transnational and transcultural relations. Law is simply an integral part of the globalization process.

The scale of the globalization of law is further illustrated by the rapidly increasing number of arbitration centres providing 'international justice' during the last few decades. According to the 1992's *Guide to International Arbitration and Arbitrators*, there are 120 arbitration centres in the world. Dezalay and Garth[5] point out, however, that the above-mentioned guide does not cover all such centres. They name at least 20 new centres that spread across the world from such faraway places as Sydney, Singapore, Bahrain, the Ukraine, Egypt, Tunisia, Bermuda and the USA. The results of this transnational, globalized practice of spreading justice has brought forth the need for a new examination of our traditional concepts of law.

There are also signs that arbitration may be acquiring some kind of autonomous legal status in relation to national legal systems.[6]

4 Yves Dezalay and Bryant Garth, "Merchants of Law as Moral Entrepreneurs", *Law & Society Review* 29 (1995), 27–64, at 30.

5 Yves Dezalay and Bryant Garth, "Merchants of Law as Moral Entrepreneurs".

6 Many disputes arising out of international commercial transactions are referred to arbitration rather than to litigation in court. To resolve these disputes, *lex mercatoria* or law merchant is frequently used. *Lex mercatoria* encompasses rules which have been accepted by the businessmen engaged in the practice of international commercial trade and partly, therefore, it has been defined by some scholars as "the autonomous law of international trade". See, for example, Aleksandar Goldstajn, "Reflections on the Structure of the Modern Law of International Trade" in *International Contracts and Conflicts of Laws – A Collection of Essays*, ed. Peter Sarcevic (London: Graham & Trotman/Martinus Nijhoff, 1990), 18.

This assumed trend towards a higher degree of legal autonomy is, of course, viewed with great scepticism by those legal scholars who maintain that the concept of law is as a function of centralized national law.[7] Notwithstanding the scepticism of monolithic positive law, it is generally agreed that arbitration, as an organized activity for normative regulation of international business transactions, does overcome differences in national legal cultures. If left to the usual legal mechanisms for conflict resolution at national levels, such differences can cause insurmountable legal obstacles to cross-border legal interaction. In questions of international commercial dispute, arbitration has features which enable it to transcend the limitations imposed by many national legal systems in the resolution of such disputes, and such features ought to be sufficient to bestow this procedure with special legal and cultural characteristics not shared by municipal law.[8] At the same time, arbitration illustrates signs of 'legal reflexivity', in the sense that it appears to establish norms of procedure, organization, membership and competence that alter the process of decision making from being a mere function of the market, or of the courts of law or other legal agencies, to being a process sensitive to the needs of the disputing parties.[9] These reflexive features of arbitration, as will be illustrated, are necessary for its emergence as an autonomous legal subculture while creating the framework within which it can legitimize itself.

The primary purpose of this study is to investigate the process of arbitration and its development as a legal and cultural entity. The recent changes within the field of arbitration are, however, intimately related to the intensification of global exchanges and the growth of 'world society'. It follows that any sociological study of

7 It is only under the reign of modernity that legal pluralism is conceived as legal aberration. Cf. Hanne Petersen and Henrik Zahle, *Legal Polycentricity – Consequences of Pluralism in Law* (Aldershot: Dartmouth, 1995). Certain elements of the arbitration process clearly belong to and were developed in the pre-modern era. The very notion of *lex mercatoria* belongs, for instance, to the Middle Ages.

8 Below, the terms "municipal", "local" and "domestic" law will be used as synonyms. They all refer to the national or internal law of a state, as opposed to international law.

9 Cf. Gunther Teubner, "Substantive and Reflexive Elements in Modern Law", *Law & Society Review* 17 (1983), 239–85.

arbitration must be conducted in the light of the current globalization process. Furthermore, the notion of legitimacy is used as a device for analysing the development of arbitration and its effects on the construction of global relations.[10] This study is, therefore, inspired by the underlying assumption that the basic principle of legitimacy governing public life of a society is a function of the *internal* and *external* legal cultures in that society.[11] When the general attitude towards law and legal processes changes, the legal system has either already been subjected to changes or will be altered accordingly.

The main questions which are initially posed to guide us through the abstract world of global relations as they pertain to law and commerce are the following. How does the international business community utilize the existing legal infrastructures to regulate its transnational activities and to resolve disputes which might arise from these activities? How do the needs of international commerce affect the development of law as an element of the 'changing global order'? How is the intercultural make-up of cross-border exchanges structured, and how does it affect the development of legal infrastructures which are used by international commercial exchanges? Finally, how is this law, in relation to national cultural systems, constructed and from which sources does it obtain its legal and political legitimacy? These are a few of the questions which will be scrutinized in this chapter from a general sociological perspective on law.

This chapter is organized in four parts. The first relates the development of arbitration as a market to the rule of law and

10 Legitimacy constitutes one of the essential units of every legal system determining the way the law is validated. Lawrence M. Friedman offers the following definition of the concept of legitimacy: "Legitimacy is an attitude of respect or approval for law and legal processes; the sense that law as a whole, or some parts, structures or processes, is or are valid." Cf. Lawrence M. Friedman, *Law and Society: An Introduction* (Englewood Cliffs: Prentice-Hall, 1977), 77.

11 External legal culture refers to the legal culture of the population at large, while internal legal culture refers to the legal culture of lawyers, judges and other functionaries of the legal system. Cf. Lawrence M. Friedman, "Legal Culture and the Welfare State", in *The Dilemmas of Law in the Welfare State*, ed. Gunther Teubner (Berlin: Walter de Gruyter, 1986).

legitimacy; the second investigates the existing interrelationships between law and economics, both at national and international levels. The third part focuses on the role played by lawyers in the production of the supranational legal infrastructures used by international businesses. Finally, in the fourth part, a number of questions are formulated to inspire further study. The question whether the present dominant paradigm applied in law, social sciences and sociolegal studies is sufficient for investigating supranational legal structures is posed.

Legitimacy and the Rule of Law in International Relations

Law, Legitimacy and Culture

Legitimacy is a concept used to indicate the strength of the feelings and attitudes that the governed have towards the law, its processes, institutions and the results that it produces. Legitimacy is about the people's faith in law, a factor which can vary considerably from culture to culture.[12] The notion of legitimacy is hardly a new topic in jurisprudence or in social philosophy. Aristotle, in his work on ethics, touched, for instance, upon legitimacy through his definition of the concept of justice as 'the sovereign virtue'. He argued that justice, which corresponds to the lawful and fair, embraced everything from equal distribution to legitimacy and the social institutions related to its enforcement. Much later, Weber drew attention to the significance of legal–rational legitimacy by sharply distinguishing it from other actions motivated by 'self interest', 'individual weakness and helplessness', 'loyalty' and 'tradition'.[13]

12 Cf. Lawrence M. Friedman, *Law and Society: An Introduction*; Günter Bierbrauer, "Toward an Understanding of Legal Culture: Variations in Individualism between Kurds, Lebanese, and Germans", *Law & Society Review* 28 (1994), 243–64; James L. Gibson and Gregory A. Calderia, "The Legal Cultures of Europe", *Law and Society Review* 30 (1996), 55–85.

13 Rational legal legitimacy laid the foundation for all bureaucratic systems by fostering the idea of impersonal legal norms "based on formal fixed rules of the game which are supposed to be detached from human feelings". Cf. Adam Podgórecki, *A Sociological Theory of Law* (Milano: Dott. A. Giuffrè Editore, 1991), 76.

Other theorists, such as Habermas, have focused on the relation between legitimacy and political stability.[14]

Looking back through the sociolegal literature, it seems that the rule of law, legitimacy and legality are generally treated as three closely interwoven concepts, which together lay the cornerstone of legal and social order in a modern nation-state. Modern legal thought, not to mention the social scientific theories that have followed the breakthrough of modernity, has specifically employed 'legitimacy' as the category that embraces all issues pertaining to most of the fundamental political and legal problems, such as the question of authority, obedience, order and disorder in society. It is generally assumed that, within the modern democratic legal systems which rely heavily on voluntary compliance, the citizens are more likely to obey a legal order when they believe in its legitimacy. If we accept that attitudes are translated into behaviour, then attitudes towards legitimacy 'may be the very glue that binds a society together'.[15]

Some of the theories emphasizing the necessity of legitimacy in legal practice assume, on the one hand, the existence of a causal relationship between culturally grounded values and mores of the citizens of a nation-state and, on the other, the formation of judicial order and legal practice of that state.[16] Expressed differently, legitimacy captures the problematic relation between consent and authority in a democratic society. According to Philip Selznick,[17] 'Some rule ... and others obey, because they share certain beliefs called principles of legitimacy'. These principles are clues to what Selznick calls 'the ethos of a culture or epoch'.[18]

14 Jürgen Habermas, *Legitimation Crisis* (London: Heinemann, 1976).

15 Friedman, *Law and Society: An Introduction,* p. 144.

16 Max Weber, who in a systematic way introduced and developed the concept of legitimacy in sociolegal studies, does not, however, share this view. He argues that the modern western legal system, working in accordance with its own internal logical formal rules of procedure, does not require extralegal values in order to justify itself morally, politically or in any other way. Cf. Max Weber, *Economy and Society*, 3 vols., edited by Guenther Roth and Claus Wittich (New York: Bedminister Press, 1968). Weber's views will be discussed in detail in the next part.

17 Philip Selznick, *The Moral Commonwealth* (Berkeley: University of California Press, 1992).

18 Ibid., 268. Selznick also relates law to justice, legitimacy and the notion of *community*. He writes: "Beyond the specifics of positive

However, the legal rules that regulate the behaviour of international commercial actors are no longer subject to the principles of legitimacy as it was conceived by municipal law and in terms of culturally determined attitudes towards the law and its processes. As previously pointed out, the growth of arbitration is mainly due to the increased frequency of cross-border transactions and worldwide financing, the economic integration of markets in Europe and other parts of the world, and the intensification of competition among an increasing number of 'players'.[19] This intensification of transnational – and therefore transcultural – activities clearly calls the assumption regarding the causal relation between culture and legitimacy into question.

Legitimacy: a Traditional Discourse

Legitimacy and legality, treated as sociolegal problems, necessarily involve the (Anglo-American) conception of *rule of law* implying an autonomous body of norms and procedures to which everyone is subjected.[20] The rule of law has great affinity with notions of *Rechtssicherheit* (legal certainty) and *Rechtsstaat* in German, and *rättssäkerhet* and *rättsstat* in Swedish. The common denominator in these concepts consists of their emphasis on the role played by the *state* in the creation and application of laws. Furthermore, it is assumed that a special relationship exists between the state and its citizens, which is defined self-referentially, that is, in terms of legality and valid law, themselves defined in terms of the judicial order and the state. The rule of law underlines even the significance of *justice* in the construction of the legal order and in the practice of law, while assuming, as expressed by Weber, that all

law are the *premises* of the legal order, to which appeal can be made in the name of justice and community. The premises create legitimate authority; they are the source of civic obligation. The duty of officials and citizens to obey the law is grounded on the implicit constitution, which in turn presumes community membership. At bottom, fidelity to law is fidelity to community" (ibid., 445).

19 S. Tamer Cavusgil, "Globalization of Markets and Its Impact on Domestic Institutions", *Indiana Journal of Global Legal Studies* 1, no.1 (1993), 83–100.

20 Shirley Castelnuovo, "Public Interest Law: Crisis of Legitimacy or Quest for Legal Order Autonomy", *Research in Law and Society* 2 (1979), 231–49, at 232.

legal actions, constructions and their social consequences ('legal authority') are based on 'rational grounds'.[21]

The rule of law is, therefore supposed to embody the following three main principles: (1) it expresses the absolute predominance of valid law, safeguarding citizens against arbitrary exercise of power by authorities; (2) it requires the equal subjection of all – including officials – to the valid law administered by the courts of the country; (3) it guarantees that citizens' personal rights and freedoms are formulated and protected by the rule of law rather than by abstract constitutional declarations.[22] The legal system responsible for the reproduction of such concepts of law often, but not always, embraces a *systematic* understanding of law. The law is, therefore, described for example, in the spirit of Hans Kelsen, as a continuous chain of legal norms related to and dependent upon each other in a logical manner.[23] The notion of law as a legal system must, furthermore, be free from internal contradictions, which means that it cannot have more than one centre. Thus the myth that 'the legal system emanates from the state' is created.[24] This understanding of law is further developed with the help of notions of coercion, justice and rights. The law, on the one hand, protects the citizens while, on the other, it controls aspects of their behaviour through the application of sanctions. This definition conceals an assumption regarding the relationship between law and culture. Firstly, law is regarded as a reflection of cultural values and norms. Secondly, the judicial system as a whole is supposed to be constructed in accordance with one, and only one, system of cultural norms.

This ideologically based (normative) assumption regarding the monolithical construction of a legal system does not, of course, necessarily have to have a de facto existence, a fact obvious even to

21 Max Weber, *Economy and Society*.

22 This mainly preliminary clarification is closely based on A.V. Dicey's definition of the rule of law in Albert Venn Dicey, *Introduction to the Study of the Law of the Constitution* (London: Macmillan, 1968), 188.

23 Needless to say, there are many other ways of defining the legal system. The reason for my emphasizing this definition is that it often lays the ground for the legal education in faculties of law in Sweden.

24 Anna Christensen, "Polycentricity and Normative Patterns", in *Legal Polycentricity – Consequences of Pluralism in Law*, ed. A. Pettersen and H. Zahle (Aldershot: Dartmouth, 1995), 234.

many of its advocates. A number of theorists, philosophers and sociologists of law alike have tried to argue against and demonstrate the fallacy in this supposition.[25] The strength of such ideologies lies not so much in their empirical descriptive values but in their normative nature, that is in the fact that they do not have to correspond to some already existing state of things.[26]

When we approach global levels, the underlying principles of the rule of law seem to lose their validity and applicability. Such notions as the state and coercion, the possibility of an existing singular cultural value system, and the idea of a legal system with similar functional characteristics to those of municipal law become both intangible and impracticable. The fact that a global legal phenomenon such as arbitration is by nature transnational, that is it exists at a level above the nation-state, transcending national cultures as currently defined by geopolitical boundaries, does not necessarily mean that global law has no need for legitimacy, but only that it must obtain it – and when necessary, *create* it – from other sources than those anchored in the rule of law.

Legitimacy: a Theoretical Excursus on Substantive, Formal and Reflexive Rationality in Law

The concept of legitimacy is often associated with Max Weber's sociological discourses on law, political domination, rationality and authority. Weber[27] conceptualized law as a morally and politically neutral system of abstract rules, and approached legitimacy

25 See John Griffiths, "What is Legal Pluralism?", *Journal of Legal Pluralism and Unofficial Law* 24 (1986), 1–55; Jørgen Dalberg-Larsen, *Rettens enhed – en illusion? Om retlig pluralisme i teorien og praksis* (Copenhagen: Akademisk Forlag, 1993); Boaventura de S. Santos, *Toward a New Common Sense – Law, Science and Politics in the Paradigmatic Transition* (New York, London: Routledge, 1995).

26 All modern legal systems are, however, today forced to function in a multicultural social environment. This means that issues related to the problems confronted by a judicial system dominated by a belief in a monocultural nature of the construction of legal rules, while trying to function in a multicultural society, need to be addressed. Cf. Reza Banakar, *Conflict Management in a Multicultural Society* (Lund: Institute for Sociology of Law, 1995).

27 Max Weber, *Economy and Society*.

from the angle of power, domination and authority.[28] Therefore Weber's perspective on this issue emphasizes how law as a rationally constructed system of legal rules is used to produce political legitimacy. In this context, law becomes an instrument for securing political domination in a modern state. To achieve this, the *formal* – and not the substantive – properties of the law are developed and utilized. This means that, according to Weber, the rational authority of law (based on rational legal domination) does not have to assume the existence of a causal relation between the sociocultural values of the citizens and the legal rules and judicial practices of the state in order to secure its legitimacy. Under the rational legal authority of a bureaucratic state apparatus, any legal norm can be created or changed without endangering the legitimacy of the state by a procedurally correct enactment. In other words, government actions will be regarded as legitimate as long as they are in accordance with the formal procedures and legitimate rules of the existing legal system.[29] (The unconditional acceptance of this line of reasoning, which relies on the ideology of positive law, leads to certain problems pertaining to the ethical consequences of legal rational action. For example, it means that the authority of Nazis in Ger-

28 According to Weber, *domination* is the "probability that certain specific commands (or all commands) will be obeyed by a given group of persons" (ibid., 212). Domination can, however, be legitimate or illegitimate. In modern western democratic societies, it is legitimate domination which is of importance. This type of domination is what Weber calls *authority.* Weber (ibid., 215–16) distinguishes between three ideal types of domination on the bases of which authority is made legitimate:

1. *rational* grounds resting on a belief in the legality of enacted rules and the right of those elevated to authority under such rules to issue commands (legal authority);
2. *traditional* grounds resting on an established belief in the sanctity of immemorial traditions and the legitimacy of those exercising authority under them (traditional authority);
3. *charismatic* grounds resting on devotion to the exceptional sanctity, heroism or exemplary character of an individual person, and of the normative patterns or order revealed or ordained by him (charismatic authority).

29 Cf. Roger Cotterrell, *Law's Community: Legal Theory in Sociological Perspective* (Oxford: Clarendon Press, 1995), 134–6.

many is to be viewed as legitimate.) In Weber's legal–positivist view, the legitimacy of government actions is, therefore, not tied to specific sociocultural values. It is the logical structure of the positive law which provides it with the legitimacy it needs. To use Professor Cotterrell's words,[30] it means that 'law frees itself from the sources that could challenge its legitimacy'. The thesis introduced in the previous sections, that the legal rules applied by a democratic state must necessarily reflect certain specific social values shared by the majority of the citizens, who are to submit themselves to the authority of the state rules, seems therefore to be incompatible with Weber's view on legitimacy.

Now let us change our angle of approach from domination and authority to the ideal types of social action developed by Weber. This change of perspective entails the examination of the concept of legitimacy with the aid of ideal types of *purposive rationality*, *value rationality*, *affectual action* and *traditional action*. In a modern democratic state based on authority, that is, on rational legitimate domination, submission to the rules of the state is an act motivated above all by purposive rationality. However, it can be argued that acts motivated by purposive rationality are rooted in the society's sociocultural value system. An actor who chooses to act in a rational purposive manner pursues self-interested goals by *rationally* selecting among various means for achieving those goals. This process presupposes at least one sociocultural value emphasizing the desirability of the actor's self-interested goals, which can well be the result of a system of values that promotes self-interests and endows it with some intrinsic worth. Hence there can exist a relationship between legitimacy and socio-cultural value systems, even according to Weber's social theory.

This interpretation of Weber has not gone uncontested. Weber is rather categorical in containing that law as a framework of rational, purposive action requires no social values for securing its legitimacy. Professor Cotterrell[31] maintains, for instance, that, 'although attempts have been made to argue that, in fact, Weber's concept of legal domination implies the acceptance of certain values as he formulates it, the argument seems hard to sustain'. This does not mean, however, that 'contemporary Western law can or will

30 Roger Cotterrell, *The Sociology of Law: An Introduction*, 2nd edn (London: Butterworths, 1992), 156.

31 Roger Cotterrell, *Law's Community: Legal Theory in Sociological Perspective*, p. 141.

retain the role that Weber sees as essential to this role' of providing a commonsense frame for *purposive rational action*.[32] Furthermore, adds Cotterrell, 'changes in the nature of the Western state may necessitate a different kind of legitimation from that provided by law alone'.[33]

The ambiguities existing in Weber's approach to the relationship between rational legitimacy and authority is, however, of great importance to the following pages in relation to a sociological understanding of arbitration. These ambiguities are caused by the intrinsic character of positive law which, by developing its formal properties, tries to free itself from the need for moral justification. This is, in turn, reflected in the tension between the formal and substantive properties of modern law. The modern rational drive towards an increase in the procedural formality of law does not allow itself to be integrated with the growing demands for substantive justice.[34] In this chapter it will be argued that legitimacy *ought to be* a function of popular consent, and that the legal rules underpinning the legal domination of the modern state *ought to* reflect a general system of values in society. We can call this a 'general' definition of legitimacy underlining the sociopolitical consequences of legal actions. However, we will also try to illustrate that, as Weber pointed out, legitimacy can be obtained even when the system of rationally made legal rules does not, and perhaps as is in the case of many cross-border legal interactions, *cannot* reflect the values of the people directly involved. This sociologically limited type of legitimacy, which can be obtained by following the correct legal procedures and does not require taking into account the sociopolitical consequences of legal actions, will be called 'particular' legitimacy. In this sense we will be using two concepts of legitimacy: the first one (the 'general' or sociologically comprehensive definition) emphasizing the necessity of consent as a *normative* prerequisite of rational legal domination, the second one (the 'particular' or sociologically narrow definition) highlighting the actual functions of the law in a *descriptive* manner. In the modern society both of these categories of legitimacy can be observed. To distinguish them from each other helps us also to illustrate the existing *tension* between these two methods of obtaining legitimacy.

32 Ibid., 156.

33 Ibid., 157.

34 Cf. Reinhard Bendix, *Max Weber: An Intellectual Portrait*, 2nd edn (London: University Paperback, Methuen & Co. Ltd, 1962), 437.

The *normative* version of legitimacy used in this study lies closer to that of Jürgen Habermas than to Weber. Habermas[35] argues that legitimation is one of the functions of the sociocultural sphere in a modern society; therefore legal domination is not enough to secure the legitimacy of modern western states. Legitimacy means, according to Habermas,[36] that 'there are good arguments for a political order's claim to be recognised as right and just ... *Legitimacy means a political order's worthiness to be recognised*' (original emphasis). Legitimacy must be examined and understood at the level both of system analysis and of social interaction in order to take into account both systems' imperatives and the subjective reactions of the individual citizens. Habermas limits the application of his concept of legitimacy to the claims made by the state or on its behalf, arguing that it is only political orders which can have and lose legitimacy.[37] This means, therefore, that 'multinational corporations or the world market are not capable of legitimation'.[38]

The strength of Habermas' examination lies in his recognition that modern states are ultimately dependent on the sociocultural sphere of society for legitimacy. Its shortcoming, in the context of the study of arbitration, lies in restricting its domain of analysis to the functions of the state. This inadequacy of Habermas' treatment of legitimation becomes especially apparent when recent growth of global relations is highlighted, and the changed role of the state and the 'fading' boundaries of national cultures are taken into account.

Some of Habermas' main ideas are developed in opposition to Niklas Luhmann's *system theoretical* assumptions. According to Luhmann, the increased complexity of modern society necessitates the differentiation of subsystems such as law, economics, politics and science. These subsystems are normatively closed; that is, they function self-referentially, in accordance with their own internal logic, reproducing their constituent elements by referring to themselves. They are, however, cognitively open in a sense that they selectively absorb information from their environment. This theory is also known as *autopoiesis*.

The notion of social subsystems as self-referential and therefore *autopoietic* is originally borrowed from the work on the nature of

35 Habermas, *Legitimation Crisis*.

36 Jürgen Habermas, *Communication and the Evolution of Society* (London: Heinemann, 1979), 178.

37 Ibid., 179.

38 Habermas, *Communication and the Evolution of Society*.

living systems by biologists Hamberto Maturana and Francisco Varela,[39] which they described in general terms as machines. Maturana and Varela postulated that living systems like cells maintain their autonomy and unity through their very own operations. Applying this idea to the legal system, Luhmann concludes that legal procedures are self-referential in the sense that the legal system never refers to norms or rules of procedure outside its own system when it is functioning.

If the legal system is normatively closed, as Luhmann insists, it follows that it enjoys total autonomy in relation to other subsystems, which also means that it must be self-sufficient in regard to its need of legitimacy. The legal system must therefore be *self-legitimizing*, for as Richard Lempert and Ann Arbor,[40] who also start their discussion from an autopoietic premise regarding the legal system argue, 'to depend upon political, social or ethical forces for authority is to be vulnerable to the encroachment of such forces on decision making'. Furthermore, echoing Max Weber's description of *rational legal authority*, Lempert and Arbor sustain, that the 'legal system is self-legitimating when its rules and rulings are accepted because they are legal'.[41]

The theory of autopoiesis also implies that none of the existing subsystems in society are capable of steering the self-regulation of the other subsystems. Subsystems are normatively closed, which means that they do not allow external interference in their internal normative operations. It can therefore be concluded that no single subsystem can, by way of controlling the normative operations of other subsystems, control the whole of the society. Following Luhmann, Gunther Teubner argues against the possibility of steering society from a single control centre and points out that the only alternative is to rely on the self-regulation of subsystems, or to regulate legally processes of self-regulations.[42] The aim of this regulation of regulations is to promote forms of *reflexivity* that produce

39 Hamberto Maturana and Francisco Varela, *Autopoiesis and Cognition* (Dordrecht: D. Reidel, 1980).

40 Richard Lempert and Ann Arbor, "The Autonomy of Law: Two Visions Compared" in *Autopoietic Law: A New Approach to Law and Society,* ed. Gunther Teubner (Berlin: Walter de Gruyter, 1987), 157.

41 Lempert and Arbor, "The Autonomy of Law: Two Visions Compared".

42 Teubner, "Substantive and Reflexive Elements in Modern Law".

self-limitations in order to counter both negative side-effects and internal contradictions in steering.

Teubner distinguishes between formal, substantive and reflexive rationality in law. Reflexive law does not, according to Teubner, 'merely adapt to, or support, natural social orders. Quite contrary, it searches for regulated autonomy'.[43] Reflexive law does not require the enforcement of particular substantive rules and does not set particular goals to be achieved in a regulated area. Instead of 'authoritatively' determining the social function of other subsystems, or trying to regulate their input and output performances, reflexive law tries to establish norms of procedure, organization, membership and competence that can '*further the development of reflexive structures within other social subsystems*'.[44] This, in turn, affects the mode of decision making within subsystems, changes the status of participants of the system, and makes the overall processes of decision sensitive to side-effects and externalities. All these arrangements have a common goal: they try to achieve new effects through an alteration of procedures, that is, through procedural rather than formal or substantive law.[45] Collective bargaining and codetermination are examples of reflexivity in existing labour law named by Teubner.[46] As we shall see, even legal regulation of arbitration, which is but the regulation of commercial transactions – that is, regulation of a self-regulated area of the market – illustrates signs of reflexivity. It will also be argued that rational reflexive law does have its own brand of legitimacy, which we can call *reflexive legitimacy*. The question remains whether the reflexive legitimacy is in fact enough to legitimate the process of such cross-border interactions as in arbitration. By not focusing on the necessity of the consent of those directly affected by the law, reflexive rationality comes closer to Weber's discourse on rational legal domination than to Habermas' understanding of legitimacy.

Legitimacy of Contracts: a Paradox or a Fallacy?

From the perspective of western law, we live in an individualistic contractual society. This standpoint is to some extent confirmed by the significant contribution made by contractual relations in the organization of social life. Entering a contract through

43 Ibid., 254.
44 Ibid., 275.
45 Ibid., 257, 267, 275.
46 Teubner, "Substantive and Reflexive Elements in Modern Law".

an exchange of communications with an offer and an acceptance between legal equals is, for instance, one of the most mundane and frequently recurrent daily events in commercial relations. It is so commonplace that the freedom to enter a contract – not involving illegalities – is seldom questioned or regarded as an issue in need of further inquiry. For some reason, it just does not seem plausible to question, for example, the *legitimacy* of a voluntary bargain between free individuals on a matter not prohibited by law and this is not only because to question the legitimacy of a contract appears to entail posing a paradox. On the one hand, a contract constitutes a legal act and as such is in need of a legal process which can publicly uphold and legitimize it. On the other hand, a contract is a *private* agreement between two or more individuals, not necessarily concerning the public sphere. The difficulties in examining the legitimacy of a contract can just as well be caused by an analytical fallacy: legitimacy is, as it was defined above, a function of legal processes and institutions and therefore is a legal derivative, while entering a contract is a social action with economic and legal connotations. A contract can be valid and enforceable, or null and void, but not legitimate or illegitimate. It is only the legal structures upholding a contract which can be analysed in terms of legitimacy.

The problem presented above is, however, slightly more complicated and cannot be dismissed by simply labelling it as an analytical fallacy. We have departed from what we called earlier a 'particular' definition of legitimacy. In this sense our definition is rather narrow in scope, leaving out, for instance, the political dimensions of the concept of legitimacy. If we now widen our conception of legitimacy so that it even comprises political consequences of various legal actions, we shall see that questioning the legitimacy of a contract is a relevant question worth further reflection. Imagine two large companies – Volvo and Renault, for example – entering a contract aimed at coproducing a motor car. This transnational contract cannot be regarded *only* as the action of two legal subjects because it will affect a portion of the French and Swedish economies and the lives of thousands of people in those countries. In such a situation, not only is the legal means used to bring about the contract in need of legitimacy, but so is the very action of entering the contract in the first place.

The paradox raised here is, however, enhanced by the fact that the very notion of contract is a *Gesellschaft* factor, underlining the right of an individual to freely enter into a contract. Legitimacy used in its 'general' sense is, on the other hand, one of the prerequisites of a law constructed in the spirit of *Gemeinschaft*, emphasizing the consent of the governed. To put it differently, the paradoxical situation we experience here might be due to the fact that we seem to be questioning an ideologically grounded issue; that is, the freedom of contract, the individual's right of free choice or the very value of individual rights and freedoms, the basis on which the western legal system is founded. The paradox might also be, to use Gunther Teubner's expression, the result of an evolutionary trend away from *control* towards *autonomy* and *sensitivity* to the environment.[47] The focus of attention here is on the consequences of self-organizing tendencies inherent in modern law as a social system: those so-called *reflexive* qualities of the law which, only by structuring action systems and without imposing any particular normative substantive standard, govern the quality of the outcome of legal processes. We can find the political counterpart of this legal development from *Gemeinschaft* to *Gesellschaft,* or from *control* to *autonomy*, in the gradual transformation of policies based on *solidarity* to policies designed to strengthen social organization through *subsidies* in all western European countries.

To explore the legitimacy of the law which promotes a special kind of contract is what this chapter intends to accomplish. To enter into a contract is to perform an action with legal connotations, which requires *legitimacy.* However, it is not the everyday contracts which constitute the object of this investigation, but the international business agreements. It is not even the act of entering into a contract which is being investigated, but the consequences of the arbitration clauses attached to such contracts to resolve any possible disputes which might arise in the course of commercial transactions. It is, therefore, not the contract itself but the legal means through which it is internationally upheld that is addressed on the following pages. Furthermore, in order to illustrate the existing tension between the two 'general' and 'particular' definitions of legitimacy, both these approaches will be applied in this study. Sociopolitical issues are, however, considered only insofar as they are caused by the process of arbitration. As previously argued, 'legitimacy *ought to* be a function of popular consent ... and reflect a general system of values in society'.[48]

47 Ibid., 64.
48 See the previous section: *Theoretical Excursus.*

Before providing an example of the mechanisms used by arbitration to obtain and create this legitimacy, we should perhaps take a closer look at the complex relationship between law and economic factors in general, and the actual laws regulating international commercial transactions in particular.

Law and Commerce

Doing without Law

Countless social and legal scientists are intrigued by the dynamic interrelationship between law and society in general, and law and economics in particular. Some agree that at least part of the key to understanding certain types of legal institutions, created in various societies during various social evolutionary periods, is found in the economic organization of these societies.[49] The interdependence and interrelatedness of law and economics, manifested in legislation and realized through the actions of commercial actors, have especially attracted the attention of many researchers with an interest in law and society. As a special theme within sociolegal studies, the investigation of problems posed by the relationship between law and economics has often resulted in developing a perspective on the divergent modes of non-legal regulation. Although these modes of regulation are *extralegal*, they nonetheless actively contribute to the production and reproduction of the normative structure of society. Such non-legal normative mechanisms, together with the legal system, laid the foundation used for cooperation between individuals and groups, thus helping to integrate the highly differentiated structure of modern societies.

49 Sir Henry Maine, *Ancient Law* (London: John Murray, 1885); Karl Renner, *The Institution of Private Law and Their Social Functions* (London-Boston: Routledge and Kegan Paul, 1949); Emil Durkheim, *The Division of Labour in Society* (1968) (Glencoe, Ill.: Free Press, 1933); Max Weber's *Law in Economy and Society*, and James Willard Hurst, *Law and Social Process in United State's History*, The Thomas M. Cooley lectures (Ann Arbor, 1960) are only a few among many attempts to investigate law and economics. For an overview of classical studies pertaining to law and economics, see Katherine S. Newman, *Law and Economic Organization: A Comparative Study of Preindustrial Societies* (Cambridge: Cambridge University Press, 1983).

Formal and informal agreements play an important part in this process of social integration. In order to plan and give continuity to social life so that different forms of cooperation can survive the passage of time and various unforeseen social changes and 'disturbances', agreements must be made and honoured by social actors.[50] The main function of these agreements is to minimize the possibility of socially unacceptable behaviour by actors who have agreed to perform a particular function. Furthermore, agreements are made to guarantee the fulfilment of actors' expectations of each other's conducts in relation to the subject of the agreement. The formalization of these agreements through, for instance, agreeing to the terms of a written legal contract is sometimes necessary to support and guarantee the continuity of behaviour.[51]

The best known sociolegal examination of the role played by such agreements in regulating business relations is conducted by Stewart Macaulay.[52] In his study of business practices in Wisconsin, Macaulay raises questions regarding the good of contract law, its function and the way it is used by business people. He finds that businessmen frequently ignore the important legal aspects of their contracts and agreements. When they have succeeded in reaching an agreement during their informal social encounters, they usually try to keep their word as if they were bound by a formal contract. Even disputes arising from the breach of contract are frequently settled without reference to the contract, or legal sanctions.[53]

50 Cf. Per Stjernquist, *Samhällsordningens dubbla grundvalar* (Lund: Institute for the Sociology of Law, 1995).

51 Cf. Volkmar Gessner, "The Globalization of Legal Certainty", paper prepared for the Oñati workshop on *The Infrastructure of Cross-Border Legal Interaction* (final version is Chapter 12 of the present volume).

52 Stewart Macaulay, "Non-Contractual Relations in Business: A Preliminary Study", *American Sociological Review* 28 (1963), 55–67.

53 This is, at least in part, due to the fact that litigation can intensify rather than resolve disputes. As Aubert pointed out, "when a conflict of interest passes from the stage of negotiation to that of litigation, one of the parties must be prepared to suffer a total loss", which can result in a fierce struggle between the disputing parties. See Vilhelm Aubert, "Law as a Way of Resolving Conflicts: The Case of a Small Industrialized Society", in *Law in Culture and Society*, ed. Laura Nader (Chicago: Aldine Publishing Company, 1969), 286.

Business people actively seek to avoid legal formality and the use of law and lawyers in their affairs because in their opinion it is bad for business. In most situations a contract is not needed and could have negative consequences, mainly because its functions are often served by other mechanisms. It also means that the business community could avoid most of its problems without resorting to detailed planning or legal sanctions. Besides, it has been observed that there were many effective non-legal sanctions which made the use of law unnecessary.

In the Shadow of Law

Businessmen are not obliged by law to keep informal agreements which are reached during their occasional social encounters, such as those made during lunch breaks.[54] They do, however, try to keep their word to one another in order to maintain a system of mutual trust necessary for their business relationships. A business relationship founded on the basis of mutual trust depends heavily on customs, usages, traditions and informal sanctions within the business community. In other words, such a relationship is founded on 'living law', hence the disinclination to use legal formalities. In that sense, the business community comes very close to becoming one among many subcultures existing in a modern society. Customs and usages of the business community can, under special circumstances, introduce new subcultural behavioural patterns. The City, that is, the part of London governed by commercial circles and high finance, is a case in point. The City is defined as a mechanism 'where the economic rationale of profit as a standard of conduct serves to generate a sub-cultural code of ethics for practices manifested as sanctioning devices [in order] to prohibit malpractice and deviancy from the accepted code'.[55] The City has, in other words, its own internal non-legal mechanism for regulating commercial conduct.

A closer examination of the behaviour of international bankers can further demonstrate the significance of customs in regulating commercial transactions. Frank R. Ryder argues, for instance, that

54 The informal agreements referred to here are those which lack any concrete basis on grounds of which it could be shown that they were ever reached.

55 Christopher Stanley, "Serious Money: Legitimation of Deviancy in the Financial Markets", *International Journal of the Sociology of Law* 20 (1992), 43–60, at 43–44.

it is the practices and the routines developed by the banking community, for regulating their daily transactions without asking 'why' or 'what' in regard to their undertakings, which enable them to operate in a satisfactory fashion.[56] Although it is the practice of the banking community which generally determines how the dealings are carried out, the banks, nevertheless, try to conduct their business in accordance with the law of international trade. This must not, however, be misunderstood, because they use the law, not so much to protect the banks against fraud and malpractice, but against the possible risk of insolvency. Within the banking community, the risk of fraud is minimized not so much through the application of laws but by emphasizing the importance of mutual trust and taking into consideration the customer's reputation in business. Therefore, to an outsider, the banking system might seem to be built, at least in part, on shaky ground. Nonetheless, it works because the internal normative structures of the community – what Stanley called 'a sub-cultural code of ethics for practices'[57] – is strong enough to guarantee the exclusion of business actors who, as the result of malpractice, lose their reputation from future dealings. Furthermore, as is pointed out by Ryder, 'both explicitly and implicitly, the custom of the trade, the usage and, in more modern times, the practices, is allowed to bend the law'.[58] According to Gessner, these giant actors of the global market 'are inclined to put their legal claims into the background and work on the basis of mutual trust or economic dependence'.[59] Thus such global actors as international banks try not to use law to regulate the substantive make-up of their contractual relations, but only to safeguard themselves against the risk of liquidation.[60]

56 Frank R. Ryder, *Legal Problems of International Banking* (London: Sweet & Maxwell, 1987).

57 Stanley, "Serious Money: Legitimation of Deviancy in the Financial Markets".

58 Ryder, *Legal Problems of International Banking*. See p. 1.

59 Volkmar Gessner, "Global Approach in the Sociology of Law: Problems and Challenges", *Journal of Law and Society* 22, 1 (1995), 86.

60 It is perhaps of interest to point out that one of the contract types which are flourishing is "the bank contract". Many bank contracts belong to the innominate contract types in the sense that they deviate from the standard contract types. These innominate contracts are considerably more flexible than the statutory types; they "can easily be adjusted to new experiences and needs and make

In a more general discussion pertaining to international contracts, Aleksandar Goldstajn puts forward a rather similar thesis.[61] According to Goldstajn, 'thanks to the generally recognized principle of the freedom of contract, autonomous business practices not only differ from municipal laws but also ignore or even negate them'.[62] As far as sales laws are concerned, merchants hardly care about law. Businessmen are interested in their business transactions in view of which the law constitutes a background structure.[63] To sum up, within both national and international relations, businessmen, when possible, seem to refrain from using legal measures to ensure the desired outcome of their transactions.

However, it is a mistake to assume that to abstain from using the law constitutes a purely non-legal action. As stressed by Niklas Luhmann, 'the legal system includes all acts or failures to act which are selected by reference to its mode of operation'.[64] It means that even when an actor, in this case a businessman representing a commercial interest, decides consciously *not* to write a legal contract or *not* to litigate, he might still be using the legal system as a point of reference and therefore acting in relation to the law. To abstain from litigation, or to choose other alternative and informal modes of dispute resolution, can therefore be a legally affected action. It is acting in the shadow of law. What is often demonstrated in the daily activities of the courts of law or other legal agencies and in private litigation or prosecution is the dysfunctions of the law.[65] This means that the majority of actions influenced by *successful* legal regulations are never reflected in, or registered by, various legal institutions.

maximal individualization possible" (Goldstajn, "Reflections on the Structure of the Modern Law of International Trade", p. 20). This is also one of the results of the fact that the bankers' application of the law is dictated by their practical needs, commercial usages and customs.

61 Goldstajn, "Reflections on the Structure of the Modern Law of International Trade".

62 Ibid., 18.

63 Ibid., 18–19.

64 Niklas Luhmann, "The Self-Reproduction of Law and its Limits", in *The Dilemma of Law in the Welfare States*, ed. Gunther Teubner (Berlin: Walter de Gruyter, 1986), 112.

65 H.L.A. Hart, *The Concept of Law* (Oxford: Oxford University Press, Original edition 1961, Reprint 1988), 39.

The interaction between legal and non-legal structures or action systems similar to what Macaulay described concerning business relations at national level can be observed even at the international level. The difference is that, at the level of international relations, the national unity of law is broken, while at the same time agreements – even legal contracts – might appear socially less secure. A common culture, mutual trust and perhaps a close face-to-face relationship strengthens both formal and informal contractual agreements between businessmen at national levels. Such socio-cultural mechanisms seem, however, not to be able to cement the international commercial relations where the buyer and the seller live in different parts of the world. There are, nevertheless, both legal infrastructures, such as international commercial arbitration, and mechanisms with social psychological characteristics similar to what we described as 'living law' (such as the custom of merchants) which nonetheless contribute to the regulation of these relations.

International Commercial Arbitration

Arbitration as an alternative to litigation

International commercial arbitration is a special legal procedure for settling commercial disputes without getting involved in the time-consuming and rigid formalities of a public judicial process. Thus arbitration provides an alternative to formal litigation. It does not, however, replace all sociolegal functions of litigation in international commerce, but rather coexists with court procedures.[66] It is even suggested that arbitration illustrates the significance of norms of the 'living law', which in this case would refer to those mainly informal customary rules used to regulate and integrate the activities of the international business community, as it is distinguished from the lawyer's law or the state's law.[67] These customary rules, arbitrary and hypothetical as they may sound to an outsider, constitute the very essence of the international business community, a fact that has, especially during modern times, contributed to the revitalization of the old European *law merchant* and heavily enhanced the expansion of arbitration as a system of conflict resolution sensitive to the business community's identity, needs and functions within the larger community.

66 Cf. Martin Domke, *The Law and Practice of Commercial Arbitration* (Illinois: Callaghan & Company, 1968).

67 C.f. Cotterrell, *The Sociology of Law: An Introduction*, pp. 32–6.

Arbitration and litigation show a great many similarities regarding the question of facts pertaining to the conflict at hand. Furthermore, they have the same main objective: to resolve disputes and normalize relations. The proceedings of the two processes are also somewhat similar. They can, nevertheless, differ on certain important points owing to the *framework* within which these issues are examined. As Cotterrell expresses it, 'the rules of law which provide such a framework in litigation are at most a minor part of the arbitration process'.[68]

Because of the 'technical' nature of international commercial disputes, as well as the needs of disputing parties for privacy and a speedy resolution of their conflict, litigants frequently choose an arbitrator rather than municipal courts. What makes domestic courts less attractive than arbitration is their often lengthy legal procedures – which is a function of the above-mentioned highly formal 'framework in litigation' – and the fact that they are often open to the public, with a minimum amount of privacy.[69] Thus such international commercial disputes are instead submitted to arbitration in order to be determined privately and swiftly through one or more independent third parties, the *arbitrators*. Arbitration is expected not only to be quicker but also to be less expensive than litigation, a fact that is often questioned and even regarded as 'illusory'.[70] It has also been stressed that litigation, when brought before national courts, can threaten the organization, hegemony and solidarity of the international business community, jeopardizing the autonomy of their customary rules and practices. The autonomy of arbitration is of course not absolute, although it does, through its relatively subtle and swift procedures, minimize the disintegrating effects that many commercial disputes can have on

68 Ibid., 3.

69 One of the advantages which arbitration is supposed to have over litigation is that it is not public. This means that the stigmatic effects of the legal process and its possible effects on businesses of the disputing parties is minimized. Cf. Vilhelm Aubert, *Inledning till rättssociologi* (Stockholm: Almquist & Wiksell, 1980).

70 John N. Adams and Roger Brownsword, *Understanding Law* (London: Fontana Press, 1992), 173; D.M. Day and Bernardette Griffin, *The Law of International Trade*, 2nd edn (London/Dublin/Edinburgh: Butterworths, 1993), 184; Britt-Mari Blegvad, Per Olof Bolding and Ole Lando, *Arbitration as a Means of Resolving Conflicts* (Copenhagen: New Social Science Monographs E6, 1973).

the unity of the rules of the international business community. In short, from a sociological point of view, arbitration can, owing to some of its special characteristics (which will be analysed more closely below) provide a more successful method of maintaining and reproducing the business community's internal *normative* construction. This is achieved, at least in part, by promoting and developing the reflexive rationality of law inherent in arbitration. As mentioned above, the 'rigid' procedural framework of litigation, characteristic of 'conventional' positive law, constitutes only a minor part of the process of arbitration with its touch of 'anti-formality'. This is mainly due to the fact that, in arbitration, law is used as 'a system for coordination of actions within and between semi-autonomous social sub-systems'.[71] In this context, we can describe arbitration as a global subsystem, which is trying to coordinate the self-regulatory activities of another global subsystem, that is the international commercial community.

Characteristics of arbitration as compared to litigation

According to Swedish law, which is similar to other municipal rules regulating arbitrators, a person or a temporary tribunal is chosen by the parties in accordance with the terms of the arbitration agreement, or by default through a court. Arbitrators are often familiar with the business customs and trade practices in the area of dispute. They are bound to follow certain elements of judicial process but they may in general adopt whatever procedure they choose.[72] Furthermore, they are not bound by the exclusionary rules of the law of evidence;[73] they must, however, conform to the rules of

71 Teubner, "Substantive and Reflexive Elements in Modern Law".

72 Blegvad and others maintain that "Swedish advocates are more constrained by the Swedish Rules of Procedure than for instance their Danish colleagues are by the corresponding Danish Law. This is perhaps due to the fact that there has existed since 1929 a special law in Sweden on arbitration" (Blegvad *et al*, *Arbitration as a Means of Resolving Conflicts,* see p. 119). This is even reflected in the explicative way the Stockholm Chamber of Commerce points out that the arbitrators decide the case on the basis of substantive law and not *ex aequo et bono* – as a result of fair dealing and good conscience, that is on the basis of equity – or according to some similar "equitable" principle.

73 Exclusionary rules in the law of evidence prohibit the proof of facts in particular ways.

natural justice and maintain the principles of justice. Arbitrators' decisions are usually not open to review by the courts and can be final, although cases may be referred to a court on appeal.

A tribunal normally consists of three arbitrators. Each party chooses one and the two selected in turn select a third, who then acts as the chairperson of the tribunal. The three arbitrators enjoy equal standing and each has only one vote. Their decisions need not be unanimous but they must be by majority rule. Various agencies of the state and certain private organizations may assist in carrying on arbitration proceedings to a successful conclusion.[74]

It is, however, possible to conduct an arbitration without the use of institutional rules (such as those laid down by, for instance, the Stockholm Chamber of Commerce). This means that the parties themselves make provisions for the mode of appointment. In such cases they are said to opt for an 'ad hoc' arbitration,

> i.e. one in which the arbitrator decides on procedures, subject only to the general legal rules and to the limits set for him by the parties. If, on the other hand, they opt for an institutional arbitrator, i.e., one appointed by a named body, then the method of his appointment and the procedures he adopts will be governed by the rules laid down by the relevant institution. An institution in this context may be a trade association or an International Court of Arbitration.[75]

Arbitration, therefore, is not a conceptually constructed formal legal process with substantive goals. It is rather based on what Teubner calls procedure orientation;[76] that is, it is a rationally oriented and institutionally structured procedure for making decisions, which is one of the main characteristics of *reflexive* law. In fact arbitration can be regarded as a legal activity based on the reflexive rationality of the law.

Arbitration and legal cultures

As an *international* legal process, arbitration illustrates certain features that clearly distinguish it from legal issues related directly to domestic law. These features are specifically unique because they

74 The Stockholm Chamber of Commerce, *Arbitration in Sweden*, 2nd revised edn (Stockholm, 1984), 1–5.

75 D.M. Day and Bernardette Griffin, *The Law of International Trade*, 184–5.

76 Teubner, "Substantive and Reflexive Elements in Modern Law".

shape and under-pin complicated economic relations at a supranational level, which in turn influence the social relations at national local level. These features are as follows. First, arbitration possesses a seemingly mundane contractual character, that is, it is based on voluntary agreement of the parties. The agreement to refer to an arbitrator is also contractual. As a result, some scholars have argued that even the arbitration award, when it is finally made, has a contractual effect, which means that it can be acted upon as a contract. Secondly, despite the fact that arbitration must generally observe procedures of due process in the same way as a court hearing, it is, nevertheless, surrounded by an atmosphere of *relative* informality and it is this relative informality which is supposed to speed up the process. Thirdly, arbitration possesses an intercultural dimension, in the sense that the arbitrator can usually speak the language of both parties and is familiar with their laws and procedures. Fourthly, it seems that arbitration is to some extent independent of national municipal courts (but not necessarily independent of national law, an issue which will be discussed in the next section); that is, it leaves the parties free to determine the outcome of issues. Such freedom includes the right of the parties to authorize a third party or an institution to make such a determination. This is also related to the fact that arbitration does not impose a set of substantive norms on the outcome of processes. Fifthly, arbitration is a transnational global phenomenon; that is, as a legal process it has the potential to transcend geographical and national boundaries traditionally used to determine jurisdiction of every legal culture. Finally, arbitration is a lucrative business and is actively promoted by most countries across the world, a fact that is closely linked to its global nature. It can, therefore, even be regarded as a global subsystem.

Thus, owing to the salient globalized legal character of arbitration, two closely interwoven issues of sociological interest can be raised. The first bears upon the relation between arbitration as a legal process and local cultures. The question posed is *whether*, and if so *how*, arbitration is culturally rooted. The second issue touches on the internal cultural construction of arbitration as a field of legal practice or a global subsystem. The question addressed here is *whether*, and if so *how*, arbitration separates itself from national legal customs that are grounded in local cultures.

Lex Mercatoria

A new law merchant

The merchant law of the Middle Ages, known as *lex mercatoria*, was originally created and developed in continental Europe as a customary body of laws by the international merchant community. The aim of these laws was to regulate the community's commercial transactions.[77] Thus *lex mercatoria* emanated directly from commercial relations and the *world economies'* needs for normative regulations and a mechanism for dispute resolution. Compared to the systems of world economies and international commerce, which have existed throughout history, law merchant is, therefore, a relatively new phenomenon.[78]

Lex mercatoria, however, was not a law in the formal sense of the word as it existed in modern states and it usually did not have any impact on the workings of national courts. In a much wider sense, it was a law consisting mainly of general rules of customs and usages which were often handed down from one generation of

77 According to De Ly, "the term *lex mercatoria* was used in an English collection around 1290 called the *Fleta,* where customs written down as and in *Consuetudo vel lex mercatoria,* written by Malynes in 1622". Filip De Ly, *International Business Law and Lex Mercatoria* (Amsterdam: North-Holland, 1992), 72.

78 Wallerstein maintains that there has existed two main types of world systems: *world empire*, which was politically and military unified, such as the Roman or Persian empires, and *world economies*, which existed throughout history, without being dependent on the unifying force of military or political factors (cf. Immanuel Wallerstein, *The Modern World System: Capitalist Agriculture and the Origins of the European World Economy in the Sixteenth Century* (New York: Academic Press, 1974). World economies, therefore, were not dependent on political and military domination for their survival, but were "held together by loose networks of economic production and exchange and contained numerous sovereign or semi-sovereign states which competed fiercely" (Stephen K. Sanderson and Thomas D. Hall, "World System Approaches to World Historical Change" in *Civilizations and World Systems*, ed. Stephen K. Sanderson (Walnut Creek: Altamira Press, 1995), 96. Thus, following Wallerstein"s thesis, we can conclude that economics is a far more effective means of domination and unification than politics or military force.

merchants to the next, and implicitly accepted by them in their daily economic activities.[79] (Codes did exist in the case of *law of the seas*, but not even these codes possessed any authoritative legitimacy, since they had grown spontaneously out of mercantile customs.) The constituent rules of this law often possessed an inherent vagueness which does not, and cannot have counterparts in modern law. The old *lex mercatoria* was in all respects an example of 'living law',[80] but it was a very special kind of living law. Not only was it 'intrinsically different from the local law applied to other strata of the population', but it was also 'cosmopolitan'.[81] Schmitthoff isolates four factors which gave the old *lex mercatoria* the cosmopolitan properties that contributed to its internationalization during the Middle Ages.[82] These factors are (1) the unifying character of the law of the fairs; (2) the universality of the customs of the seas; (3) the special courts dealing with disputes; and (4) the activities of the notary public.

The mediaeval *lex mercatoria* was gradually incorporated into the various European municipal systems of law.[83] Its incorporation

79 Clive M. Schmitthoff, *Commercial Law in a Changing Economic Climate,* 2nd edn (London: Sweet & Maxwell, 1981), 2.

80 Advocates of legal positivism maintain that it is only the official law, emanating directly or indirectly from the state, which is to be regarded as law. Furthermore, law is backed by formal sanctions and the force of the state. Eugen Ehrlich criticized this positivistic definition of law from a sociological standpoint and argued that many areas of life are regulated by such norms not derived from, or backed by, the state in any way. Within these areas people follow "rules" despite the absence of official sanctions. Ehrlich called such rules the "living law" and meant that they oblige without the official force and formal threat of sanctions. Cf. Eugen Ehrlich, *The Fundamental Principles of Sociology of Law*, originally published in 1936, translated by W.L. Moll (New York: Arno Press, 1975). For a critical appraisal of Ehrlich's views on law see Cotterrell, 2nd edn. *The Sociology of Law: An Introduction*, pp. 25–31.

81 Schmitthoff, *Commercial Law in a Changing Economic Climate.* See p. 18.

82 Clive M. Schmitthoff, 'International Business Law: A New Law Merchant', *Current Law and Social Problems* (University of Western Ontario, 1961), 129–53.

83 In eighteenth-century England, for example, "law merchant" was integrated into common law and the special commercial courts

took place for different reasons, in different degrees and in diverse manners, but it did, according to Schmitthoff,[84] coincide with the consolidation of the ideas of national sovereignty of the European countries. It could be, to use Weber's discourse on authority, that by incorporating *lex mercatoria* into their national laws the new sovereign states tried to control the activities of one of the most influential sectors of their societies – the community of merchants – and integrate them and their commercial operations in the political life of the state, thereby consolidating the state's own political legitimacy. Another closely related reason for implementing this incorporation can be found in the enhanced significance of commerce and foreign trade for the livelihood of the European nations. Thus the old *lex mercatoria*, which was originally a customary law based on the practices and usages of merchants, obtained 'universal' acceptance through the newly appropriated authority of sovereign states. Despite this incorporation into national laws, *lex mercatoria* maintained its original customary character.

Lex mercatoria became the object of renewed scholarly interest, of jurisprudential examination and systematic reconstructions and modifications from the end of the 1920s. This new interest, which was intensified during the 1950s and 1960s, was due mainly to international commercial law's attempts to free itself from restrictions exerted by national laws and move towards a more universal, international conception of the law of international trade. In brief, the international commercial conditions required 'an autonomous international trade law, founded on uniform rules and accepted in all countries'.[85] As regards the existing differences between the mediaeval and the modern *lex mercatoria,* Schmitthoff writes:

> The new *lex mercatoria* is very different from the medieval one. It differs in particular, in two aspects. First its international character has to be reconciled with the concept of national sovereignty on which the world order is still founded and which is the *fons et origo* of all laws. Secondly, while the growth of the medieval *lex mercatoria* was haphazard and unplanned, developing from usage to custom and then to law,

were replaced by the Royal Courts, using a jury consisting of merchants. See Michael Bogdan, *Comparative Law* (Stockholm: Norstedts Juridik, 1994), 108.

84 Schmitthoff, "International Business Law: A New Law Merchant".

85 Schmitthoff, *Commercial Law in a Changing Economic Climate.* See pp. 20–21.

> the modern *lex mercatoria* is the deliberate creation of formulating agencies and is expressed in international conventions or model laws or in documents published by such bodies as the International Chamber of Commerce.[86]

The manner in which merchants actually conduct their business has had considerable influence on the way the municipal laws on trade are shaped. Some scholars seem to agree on the importance of international customs, which lay the foundations for trade usages, in the construction of law merchant. This means that the unwritten customs and usages by merchants are adopted into municipal law by influencing – if not determining – both the content and interpretation of contract terms. The Swedish law on trade (köplagen) from 1905, for example, was constructed in respect to *lex mercatoria.*

Four scholars in particular have contributed considerably to the development of the modern *lex mercatoria*: Edouard Lambert (theory of *droit corporatif international,* 1934), Clive Schmitthoff (theory of the *new law merchants*),[87] Berthold Goldman (theory of *lex mercatoria,* 1984) and Phillipe Kahn (theory of the *société internationale des commerçants*, 1961), who introduced new ideas about the source of international business law. Partly as a result of Professor Berthold Goldman's work, *lex mercatoria* achieved a new status during the 1960s in France. He is even regarded as the father of the new *lex mercatoria.*[88]

In short, the emergence of a new *lex mercatoria* is the result of the growth of international trade. Furthermore, there are hardly any doubts about the fact that *lex mercatoria* has exerted considerable influence on recent developments in arbitration and arbitral case law.[89] The legal status of *lex mercatoria*, both as a set of self-regulatory rules of law developed by the body of international business community and in its dignity as an autonomous legal system is, however, a source of heated controversy among legal

86 Schmitthoff, *Commercial Law in a Changing Economic Climate*, p. 21.

87 See Chia-Jui Cheng, ed., *Schmitthoff's Selected Essays on International Trade Law* (Dordrecht: Martinus Nijhoff, 1988).

88 Ugo Draetta, Ralph B. Lake and Ved P. Nanda, *Breach and Adaptation of International Contracts: An Introduction to Lex Mercatoria* (New Hampshire: Butterworth Legal Publishers, 1992), 2.

89 De Ly, *International Business Law and Lex Mercatoria.*

scholars. Is *lex mercatoria* a *legal construction* founded on 'delocalized' norms or is it simply a special function of municipal national legal systems? Draetta and others describe this dispute in the following way:

> There are a number of customary principles and detailed rules which are generally applied to international business contracts. This body of principle and rules, the *lex mercatoria* or the new merchant law, has been identified by certain scholars, particularly in continental Europe, as an emerging legal system distinguished and autonomous from national legal systems. Other academic commentators have strongly opposed the proposition that the *lex mercatoria* is a system of law capable of being enforced by its own terms. The opponents maintain that 'delocalization' is impossible: contracts must be governed by a specific national law, either selected by the parties or determined by applicable conflict of laws provision.[90]

Schmitthoff maintains that, in order to understand this new law, we have to put aside our predilection for orderliness and take *lex mercatoria* for what it was in the Middle Ages and for what it will be again: unsystematic, complex and multiform, but of bewildering vigour, realism and originality.[91]

Not all international commercial contracts refer to the rules of *lex mercatoria* and not all arbitral awards apply such rules. However, those which do are no longer based exclusively on national municipal law. They are, instead, dependent upon the notion of *lex mercatoria* as a legal system, an assumption which is undoubtedly highly problematic to many lawyers. According to Goldman, *lex mercatoria* is a legal system with the potential for creating an *autonomous* arbitral conflict system. Its construction as an autonomous legal system is, however, incomplete.[92] Goldstajn reasons in a similar fashion when he sustains that '*lex mercatoria* can be defined

90 Draetta *et al.*, *Breach and Adaptation of International Contracts: An Introduction to Lex Mercatoria*. See p. xiii.

91 Clive M. Schmitthoff, *The Unification of Law of International Trade*, 1964, reprinted in *Schmitthoff's Selected Essays on International Trade Law*, ed. Chia-Jui Cheng (Dordrecht: Martinus Nijhoff, 1988), 170–87.

92 De Ly, *International Business Law and Lex Mercatoria*. See pp. 213–14.

as the autonomous law of international trade'.[93] Goldstajn develops his thesis in the following way:

> Although international trade has two sources – international legislation and international trade usages – it is nevertheless a single body of rules which constitutes a system that functions independently of municipal law. Although one of its sources – international legislation – may be part of municipal legislation, this does not affect the fact that the *lex mercatoria* is autonomous.[94]

Goldman's theory on lex mercatoria

Goldman distinguished in his analysis of *lex mercatoria* between substantive transnational rules, customs and usages, contracts, general principles of law and international commercial arbitration. With regard to transnational substantive rules, he qualifies them as French rules 'tailored to international situations and [which] may be followed by other jurisdictions'.[95] Customs and usages are considered to constitute formal sources of law, which are not dependent on acceptance by the parties. But the real sources of *lex mercatoria* are to be found in the general principles of law in international contracts and arbitral awards, which are effectively used in international trade to fill any gaps which other sources may have left. Goldman stresses, furthermore, the need to develop *autonomous* conflict rules for international commercial arbitration.[96] These will contribute to the resolution of problems caused by the application of the rules of conflict of the state of arbitration and those of the state whose law was applicable to the merits of the dispute.[97]

According to De Ly, Goldman uses a formal conception of law-creating sources, which are binding on themselves and are not binding by virtue of national law: 'As non-national sources, they create a non-national autonomous legal system.'[98]

93 Goldstajn, "Reflections on the Structure of the Modern Law of International Trade". See p. 18.

94 Goldstajn, "Reflections on the Structure of the Modern Law of International Trade".

95 De Ly, *International Business Law and Lex Mercatoria*. See p. 211.

96 Ibid., 212–13.

97 Ibid., 213.

98 Ibid., 214.

Arbitration as a global subsystem

The development of *lex mercatoria* is related to the growth of arbitration as a legal field. Both arbitration and *lex mercatoria* illustrate signs of a polycentric legal construction which is especially relevant to the discussion at hand. Arbitration's polycentricity, that is the fact that it uses diverse legal sources such as formal law, customs and usages of merchants, and so on, cannot, however, exist without its *reflexive* property. It should be postulated at this juncture that arbitration is not simply a legal phenomenon or merely a function of the municipal law, but is a subsystem at the level of world society. Arbitration has an inherent tendency towards achieving greater autonomy, which can be illustrated with the help of Niklas Luhmann's conceptual apparatus, described in a previous section. Arbitration reconstitutes itself, as a global subsystem, by reproducing its own institutional legal structures (such as Chambers of Commerce) and normative characteristics (a definition of what is to be regulated, which sources are legally valid, what is to be regarded as a dispute and how to go about resolving these disputes). Its (cognitive) relation to its environment is governed by its attempt to *coordinate* the operations of other subsystems.[99] It is this external function of arbitration which requires that it adjust itself to its environment that takes into account other subsystems' operations and, as a result, functions in an openly legal–polycentric manner. The fact that it is polycentric and uses diverse sources for its reproduction apparently conflicts with its intention to achieve legal autonomy, for it means that it is not only referring to its own constituent elements to reproduce itself. This paradox will disappear when we take into account that arbitration's relation to these sources, which are features of other operational subsystems such as an economy, are mainly cognitive. It uses them in a reflexive manner as sources of information concerning its attempts to observe and coordinate other subsystems, and not as a normative guidance for regulating its own internal operations. In other words, arbitration does make use of normative external sources, but it then uses them to regulate the international commercial relations. This mode

99 Let me stress this fact that arbitration – owing to its reflexive rationality – has a *cognitive* and not a *normative* relation to its environment. It does not endeavour to control the internal (normative) functions of other subsystems like the economy. It only tries to *coordinate* their functions while allowing them to freely choose and develop their own normative features.

of regulation is determined by arbitration's (internal) normative mechanism.

It is also important to note that arbitration, in contrast to the mechanisms of dispute resolution governing transactions at national levels, influences the way international commercial exchanges are conducted without determining the way contracts are formed or agreements are reached, or what these contracts are about. The municipal trade laws, as Schmitthoff points out, are 'increasingly governed by rules which are derived from the principle of social responsibility, a principle which demands the protection of the economically weaker, in particular the consumer, the employee and the small investor'.[100] Such tendencies are drastically decreased within the law of international trade which, for example, lacks the protective provisions of the Unfair Contract Terms Act of 1977. There are of course a number of protective substantive rules influencing the law of international trade, but these rules are few and relatively weak, a fact which is hardly surprising since they are against the interests of international commerce.[101] Arbitration is the mechanism of conflict resolution within the law of international trade and, not surprisingly, reflects a clear lack of interest in substantive aspects of contracts.

100 Schmitthoff, *Commercial Law in a Changing Economic Climate.* See p. 18.

101 As it regards the lack of substantive elements in *lex mercatoria*, the following qualification must be made. It is true that those parties which at the national level are qualified as "weaker parties" (employees, consumers and so on) are not fully protected by the rules of *lex mercatoria*. But *lex mercatoria* has developed certain mechanisms to protect the interest of, for instance, Third World parties against the dominating interests of the multinational enterprises, in order to prevent corruption and to protect the environment. There are also normative orders such as INCOTERMS consisting of substantive elements which aim to strike a balance between the interests and influence of commercial actors. Finally, the work of UN organizations often leads to rules which are not binding, but are nevertheless taken into account by the international community and possibly even by various arbitrators. However, the fact remains that, by comparison, the above-mentioned substantive rules are considerably weaker and fewer in number than the protective elements of municipal laws.

At this stage, we can establish that the application of the notion of legitimacy to arbitration, if by legitimacy we refer to some substantive qualities of legal decisions existing beyond those determined by the customs and usages of merchants (like some abstract notion of global morality or justice), is highly problematic. Scholars have pointed out that international commercial law is, to a large extent, founded 'on the autonomy of the will of the contracting parties'.[102] Arbitration, which should be understood in the context of international commercial law, is in turn dependent on the autonomy of the parties in two stages: arbitration authorizes the parties to settle not only the law that will govern the arbitration but also the law that will be applied to the substance of the dispute.[103] The emphasis is clearly on the procedural features of arbitration offering the contractual parties the settlement of their disputes in view of their trade usages and their needs. It also means that arbitration, as the result of its inherent reflexive qualities, obeys the logic of procedural legitimation. If arbitration is reflexively constructed, as it is assumed here, then it does not – in contrast to 'responsive law' – concern itself with the substantive aspect of legal outcomes. Arbitration lacks all forms of participation and patterns of communication particular to open-ended legal constructions.[104]

The Role of Lawyers

So far we have examined theoretical constructions used for creating and maintaining a supranational legal infrastructure for the regulation of cross-border commercial interaction. We now look at the way this meta-national legal reality is seen by some of its actors.

Lawyers and Legal Rationality

Lawyers are said to understand 'the secrets of power', which puts them in an almost unique position to influence the outcome of large or small power struggles. The key role assigned to lawyers in regulating the intricate game of power is partly due to the fact that law in reality does not always reflect or function in accordance to

102 Clive M. Schmitthoff, ed., *The Sources of the Law of International Trade* (London: Stevens and Sons, 1964), 6.

103 Schmitthoff, *The Unification of Law of International Trade*. See p. 155.

104 Cf. Bo Carlsson, "Communicative Rationality and Open-ended Law in Sweden", *Journal of Law and Society* 22 (1995), 475–505.

its conceptual rationality. To put it differently, if the law was such a formal rational construction, as it often claims to be, no rational actor with the ability to read a law book should – at least in theory – need the assistance of a lawyer for any legal representation. However, besides the conceptual rationality of law, which is far from flawless, there is even its working rationality. Thus experience has taught the rational clients of the legal system that they are, in most cases, in need of 'insiders', that is people with legal know-how and experience, who can tell them about the ways of the 'living law' and help them to utilize the working rationality of law as efficiently as possible to resolve practical problems swiftly.[105] Even lawyers at times need legal representation; this because no one lawyer alone can master the conceptual and the working rationality of all various areas of law. In this sense, lawyers play a central role in producing the social order and maintaining the status quo in society.[106]

This role of lawyers, as 'insiders' with insight into the practices of law, is to a great extent a function of the modern society. The most salient feature of modernity, as was observed by Weber, is its almost impulsive drive towards an ever-increasing degree of *formal* and *substantive* rationality aimed at attaining increased technical efficiency in controlling both the material and the human environments. The formal rationality more or less shapes all social systems as economy, politics, education, culture and law, which in turn determine in part the formation of diverse institutions in modern society. Friedman maintains that a 'modern economic order cannot exist without the 'functional prerequisite' of a modern legal order.[107] The

105 The need for "insiders" can also be explained as a result of the legal system's dynamic character and the fact that many of its constituent elements are constantly being reproduced in various forms diverging from the way they were originally formulated in official documents. As is pointed out by Cotterrell (*The Sociology of Law: An Introduction*, 2nd edn, see p. 2) "legal doctrine ... is continually being shaped in the practice of courts and other agencies of interpretation by reference to assumed social processes of law". It is only an "insider" who has the advantage of following and observing the sociolegal reshaping of legal doctrines in practice and fully comprehending its practical legal consequences.

106 Cf. Lawrence M. Friedman. Lawyers in Cross-Cultural Perspective. In *Lawyers in Society*, vol. 3, ed. Richard L. Abel and Philip S.C. Lewis. (Berkeley: University of California Press, 1989), 1-26 (17).

107 Ibid., 16.

economy needs transactional certainty. Business must be able to plan. The legal system must sustain and support property rights and the sanctity of contract. It has to be sensitive to commercial needs.' Law, however, does not succeed in fulfilling all the necessary functional prerequisites in a formal rational manner. Thus law has many defects, some of which are due to the very construction of the legal order and others the results of application of law on areas of life not suitable for formal legal steering. These flaws can be used and misused mainly by the 'clients' in order to promote their particular interests. To use these deficiencies they need practical knowledge of how the law actually works; that is they need lawyers.

What was said above in regard to the role of 'insiders' was based on the state of affairs at the national level. There are, however, reasons to extend this line of reasoning to the global level. The role of 'insiders', if not in fact enhanced, is not weakened at the global level. Freyhold maintains, for example, that the relative legal openness and flexibility that New York demonstrates in handling cross-border interactions and thus even towards foreign legal cultures is brought about, not so much by the legal system itself, but by 'the lawyers' specific working conditions as well as by their professional values'.[108] Furthermore, it is postulated that a so-called 'third culture' expressing autonomous legal structures has developed at the global level, especially in relation to arbitration. This 'third culture', 'international lawyers', which is supposed to be independent of national legal cultures, is in many ways a function of international legal *practice* with its special sociocultural and economic prerequisites. According to Freyhold, 'legal rules specifically governing cross-border interactions are rather scarce', which may mean that lawyers themselves are required to create autonomous law for processing their legal undertakings.[109] (To connect Freyhold's observation to our previous discussion regarding the reflexive character of arbitration as a global subsystem, we can say that lawyers, by trying to create an 'autonomous law', which is even related to their role of 'insider', are reproducing the cognitive and normative structures particular to arbitration.) Thus the role of *practice*, and therefore the need for 'insiders', is even more striking

108 Hanno von Freyhold, "The International Practice of New York Lawyers", paper prepared for the Oñati workshop on *The Infrastructure of Cross-Border Legal Interaction*, 1996. See p. 2.

109 Hanno von Freyhold "The International Practice of New York Lawyers".

at the global level than at the national level. Notwithstanding this fact, the lawyers' general attitude towards international relations is far from unambiguous. As we shall see in the next section, becoming a part of this 'third culture' does not necessarily constitute an attractive prospect for all lawyers.

Anomy in Cross-border Legal Interactions

Many lawyers with long experience in municipal legal practice do not willingly engage themselves in cross-border legal disputes. They often take the easy way out by declaring themselves 'not competent enough' in such legal matters. This can simply be because they do lack the necessary expertise in the area; it can also be because their training in law and their experiences in legal practice compel them to equate law with official law, which clearly emphasizes predictability and uniformity of legal decisions and singularity, and the formality of law as a system of legal order. These ideals seem either to evaporate in the global heat of international relations or to lose their sharp legal edge when they are applied to cross-border legal disputes. The typical 'nightmare' situation, now to give an example from *public* international law, which some lawyers mention, consists of child abduction cases involving countries that have not ratified the relevant international treaties. These child custody disputes very often have to be resolved, not through the symbolic or even the sheer rational force of official law and by application of legal rules, but rather by 'international co-operation based on mutual trust'.[110] To some lawyers such a 'procedure' is nothing more than the legal construction of a world of 'make-believe', that is pretending to conduct legal matters by actually using international relations pivoting on such non-legal factors as economic and/or diplomatic pressure or mutual respect and cooperation. Similar strategies based on extralegal factors, such as mutual trust and the business reputation of the parties involved, are even used within private international law to regulate transactions.

Thus what discourages many lawyers from getting involved in what Freyhold compares to a 'jungle' of cross-border legal interactions[111] is a general feeling of uncertainty, which is usually due

110 Michael Bogdan, "Trans-Border Abduction of Children" in *Scandinavian Studies in Law*, vol. 36 (Stockholm: Juristförlaget, 1992), 62.

111 Freyhold, "The International Practice of New York Lawyers". See p. 7.

to a lack of sufficient legal regulation in many international legal transactions. Many lawyers find it difficult to cope with the apparent arbitrariness of many legal decisions taken at this level. This lack of enthusiasm is even reflected in the legal scholars' cautious approach especially to public international law and in their seemingly never-ending discussions about whether such a thing as international law *really* exists and whether the rules of international law are *really* legal rules.[112] (This in spite of the fact that most legal scholars hold that international law is a constituent element of the international sphere. It performs functions typical of a legal system or, to put it differently, it has the same function at the international level as the national law has at the national level.) Needless to say, there are good reasons for conducting a critical appraisal of the ontological basis of international law. When, for instance, the US diplomatic staff were taken hostage in Tehran, there was no way of enforcing international law, nor was there any method for legally determining whether or not Iran had violated that law in the first place.[113]

It is perhaps not all that surprising when Hans Kelsen takes what appears to be an extreme view and compares (public) international law with 'primitive law'.[114] He maintains that international law without national legal order would be 'an inapplicable fragment of legal order'.[115] On the surface, this wariness is brought about by the disturbing absence of coercive powers in the international sphere, which for many lawyers uphold the municipal law of states and, in the absence of a legislative, judicial and executive power, give the whole legal process uniformity and legitimacy.

Lawyers working with private international legal relations, on the other hand, regard this 'uncertainty' as a challenge and a problem resolved by formalization, rationalization and routinization of international legal activities. They are familiar with anomic situations which can be caused by insufficient 'normative guidance of

112 Cf. Torsten Gihl, "The Legal Character and Sources of International Law", in *Scandinavian Studies in Law*, vol. 1, ed. Folke Schmidt (Stockholm: Almqvist & Wiksell, 1975).

113 Robert L. Kidder, *Connecting Law and Society* (New Jersey: Prentice-Hall, 1983), 18.

114 Hans Kelsen, *General Theory of Law and State* (London: Geoffrey Cumberlege, 1946).

115 Ibid., 348.

either legal or cultural nature'[116] and they use their knowledge of law and their practical legal know-how to cope with them. When it comes to resolving large international disputes, usually well established and respected judges and lawyers, with many years of experience at the municipal level, are employed to deal with intricate legal and cultural obstacles involved in bringing about a speedy resolution more or less acceptable to all parties. These anomic features are caused by the underlying cultural or rather transcultural and plural character of cross-border legal contacts. The fact that there are devices built into the very structure of formal law to permit the centralized legal system to incorporate informal law – for instance the 'custom of merchants' or the internal rules of indigenous people – in its system of rules does not necessarily diminish the anomy which might prevail over certain cross-border interactions. It has even been postulated that a latent cultural conflict exists in cross-border legal interactions.[117]

International commercial arbitration, which constitutes the kind of cross-border interaction central to the topic of this study, has, over the past 20 years, undergone considerable formalization, institutionalization and even what we might call 'Americanization'. Partly owing to this formalization process, but also as a result of increased intersubjectivity and harmonization of expectations in some areas of international relations, not to mention the intensification of transcultural contacts, anomic situations seem to have been brought under greater control than before. They are, however, still part and parcel of cross-border legal interactions.

Let us now go back to our original question regarding the role of legitimacy in arbitration. The study conducted by Dezalay and Garth sheds some light on the way arbitration obtains and creates the legitimacy it needs to function as valid law at a global level. In this process, the lawyers play a major role.[118]

116 Volkmar Gessner and Angelika Schade, "Conflicts of Culture in Cross-border Legal Relations: The Conception of Research Topics in the Sociology of Law", in *Global Culture*, ed. Mike Featherstone (London: Sage, 1994), 254.

117 Gessner and Schade, "Conflicts of Culture in Cross-border Legal Relations".

118 Dezalay and Garth, "Merchants of Law as Moral Entrepreneurs".

Legitimacy through Charisma and 'Juridicalization'

Dezalay and Garth introduce a number of factors that either directly or indirectly contribute to the discourse on the legitimacy of international commercial arbitration. The first two factors they name are 'grand old men and technocrats'. The relatively few grand old men (and it seems that they are all *men*!) are usually renowned professors, judges and other highly respected practitioners, who have 'risen to the top of their national legal professions and gained financial independence before being asked to serve as arbitrators'.[119] The general story is that these 'grand notables' regard arbitration, not as a career, but rather as a duty. International commercial arbitration, as a new field of legal activity, received the initially required legitimacy needed for its survival as a legal field from the personal legitimacy of 'grand old men'. Dezalay and Garth describe this legitimacy in terms of 'the grand notables' aura or charisma, without analysing its sociocultural significance at a global level.[120] What is defined here as 'charisma' is but a form of traditional rationality, to use Weber's typology, which is firmly anchored in the legal culture at the national level. What these highly respected senior practitioners of law have done can thus be defined as the transformation of national cultural values into international security. Through the charisma, eminence and respect attributed to them, qualities which are primary functions of their social status at local levels, they have succeeded in guaranteeing the continuity of certain behavioural patterns at a global level. It also reminds us of Kelsen's view that international legal order, without municipal law would be but 'an inapplicable fragment of legal order'.[121]

Now that international arbitration has achieved an established legal status, these 'grand old men' come under increasing criticism and are defined as 'dinosaurs' by the new generation of practitioners who were drawn to arbitration, not because they believed in such mottos as 'arbitration is a duty', but rather because of the rapid expansion of arbitration as a business during the 1980s. The new generation of arbitrators legitimize their field of activity, not through traditional rationality and charisma, but through their professionalism. They show that they are technically better equipped in procedure and substance, and contrast their qualities to the 'ama-

119 Ibid., 36.

120 Ibid., 36–7.

121 Kelsen, *General Theory of Law and State*. See p. 348.

teurism' or 'idealism' of their predecessors.[122] Technocrats rely on legal education and guidance on institutions like the International Chamber of Commerce (ICC) rather than 'grand old men', while striving for increased juridicalization, routinization and rationalization of arbitration. By doing this they are increasing the autonomy of their field from the national level and municipal law. At the same time, it seems that the 'rigid' procedures of litigation are replacing the flexible rules of international commercial arbitration. In short, they pay perhaps too high a price for establishing the autonomy of their field and reducing the anomic situations occurring in cross-border interaction. The juridicalization of international commercial arbitration makes it 'slower and more costly but also more uncertain, than recourse to courts'.[123]

Another group that, despite their internal rivalry, complement each other and together vitalize, form and legitimize the field of arbitration consists of academics and practitioners. Academics try to demonstrate their theoretical mastery of arbitration, while practitioners emphasize the significance of 'solid case law and thorough analysis of the facts'.[124] Finally, the rapid expansion of the market for arbitration, followed by multiplication and diversity of places and institutions of arbitration, promotes intense competition among merchants of law.[125] ICC facilitated this competition by transforming the field in the 1980s. International commercial arbitration is, as a result of competition, the dominance of technocrats and ICC's guidance, now 'institutionalised as a generally accepted private legal process applicable to transnational business disputes'.[126] This competition among key actors serves, according to Dezalay and Garth, to construct legal legitimacy and at the same time promotes law in the service of merchants.[127]

Change of Paradigm?

A brief review of our discussions in the previous sections regarding the process of arbitration and expansion of *lex mercatoria*,

122 Dezalay and Garth, "Merchants of Law as Moral Entrepreneurs". See p. 38.
123 Ibid., 58.
124 Ibid., 42.
125 Ibid., 45.
126 Ibid., 59.
127 Ibid., 29.

not to mention the role played by lawyers and their knowledge of the *working* rationality of law, would illustrate that the traditional discussions regarding legitimacy in its 'general' sociopolitical sense and the rule of law are not applicable at the global level. At this level, the authority of law and legal decisions can be legitimized neither by the authority of the state nor by the general consent of a national community. There is simply no globalized state and no transnational community of the governed ordinary people which can reflect the general cultural system of values or national characteristics of any particular group. The only consent that arbitration searches for and tries to obtain in order to legitimize its operations is the consent of those merchants directly involved in the dispute concerning how their conflict ought to be processed. This despite the fact that there are always people at national level who are affected by such decisions at transnational levels. The consent of these people at national level is not required in arbitration. The community of merchants, which at best constitutes a dubious sociocultural entity lacking sentiments of solidarity, is the closest we can find to the idea of a transnational community. The 'community of merchants' is integrated, not through psychologically, socially or culturally determined needs, but through rational economic action. As a community, it is therefore one dimensional. Arbitration is undoubtedly a highly polycentric and pluralistic legal phenomenon. The fact that the traditional concepts of authority, legitimacy, community and the rule of law cannot, without further alterations, be applied to arbitration does not, however, necessarily mean that arbitration cannot or need not be sociopolitically legitimized.

Dezalay and Garth's interesting study can help us further in this discussion and assist us in formulating new questions based on the problem of legitimacy as discussed earlier. It is plausible that the 'grand old men', by using their position and status at the national level, initially brought legitimacy to the field of arbitration, but the field is no longer solely or mainly dependent on the charisma of its elders. Along with the general expansion of the field and intensification of competition among the merchants of arbitration, we can observe a drive towards achieving greater autonomy in the field through, among other things, juridification of arbitration. The significance of 'charisma' is therefore dramatically reduced – and with it the dependence of the field on municipal legal cultures – and replaced by the routinization, rationalization, formalization, Americanization and, finally, juridicalization of the field. Our first question is whether this development means the creation of a 'third culture', that is, a 'global legal culture'. Irrespective of the way our answer to this first question may be based and formulated, we can put forward a second question which helps us explore the relation between the apparently semi-autonomous cultural field of arbitration and the values and norms at the national municipal level. To express it differently, we can ask to what extent the field of arbitration uses values and norms of national legal cultures, and to what extent it produces its very own values. The focus of attention will therefore be on the qualities related to *normative* closeness and openness of the field as a social subsystem. It is even interesting to examine the possible interaction between different values: those of the field itself and those of the national legal cultures.

With the help of the reviewed literature and a fairly large number of empirical studies done on legal cultures, a tentative answer to the above questions can be provided. A global legal culture is developing with its own specific norms and values. This global phenomenon is not, however, completely independent of national legal cultures and cannot be comprehended without taking into account the values and norms which create and maintain the foundations of national legal orders. This is partly because, as we have seen in the case of arbitration, global legal activities in general do not replace but coexist with national legal mechanisms. Furthermore, the role of lawyers, who have received their initial training and professional identity within the framework of municipal law, cannot be neglected. These lawyers, even when they specialize in private or public international law and *internalize* values of the global legal culture, still maintain many of their original legal values which have been produced within national legal cultures. These values affect their understanding of law even at the global level. Their working conditions and the immediate legal tasks at hand can force on them new perspectives on legal problems, but it cannot and need not force them to abandon their original legal values. It is therefore possible that the developing global legal culture is in fact a *process* reflecting the interaction between the legal cultural values at the municipal level and the operating imperatives of global subsystems such as international trade, which are mainly responsible for producing the working conditions of the lawyers. The reproduction of this relational process constituting the global legal culture is facilitated through the application of the reflexive rationality of law.

The above questions, through the examination of legal cultures involved in the field, touch rather indirectly upon the issue of legitimacy. To approach legitimacy in a more explicit manner, we can give our attention to the mechanism of social integration of the field as a system. Is the field dependent on some sort of popular consent at national level? Do all those who are affected by the activities of the field share the basic values of the culture of its practitioners? Or perhaps neither the clients nor other parties involved need to see their own moral reflection in constituent norms or activities of the field. As Luhmann points out, the basic consensus about highest-order goals and norms is no longer likely, and the unity of different social systems must be guaranteed by other means to integration than a common ethical belief.[128] Thus 'members of the same society – in our case the international community – do not have to morally agree about "the good", they merely must accept a much more abstract series of dichotomies or disjunctions'.[129] This means that all the social environment of a system needs, in order to guarantee the legitimacy of a social system, is to accept its binary schemes. Thus the final question is whether international commercial arbitration, as a metanational legal system, can guarantee its legitimacy, not by anchoring its values in certain national cultures, but by obtaining acceptance for the way it actually functions.

What causes the difficulties in applying the concept of legitimacy to arbitration in a satisfactory manner is in fact a sign of the paradigmatic inadequacies of this concept at the global level. Legitimacy is a product of municipal legal thinking and practice emphasizing the necessity of the consent of the governed. When discussing legitimacy at the global level, we must first identify our target group. Are we talking about legitimacy of legal procedures from the perspective of the contractual parties or from the point of view of the people affected at the national level by legal regulation of international commercial activities? Arbitration can, through the application of its reflexive rationality, obtain 'particular' legitimacy, that is legitimacy in its sociologically narrow sense of the concept. It cannot however, provide legitimacy in its 'general' sociopolitical sense. Although this may not be significant as it regards the process of arbitration and the settling of international commercial disputes, it will nevertheless exert an influence on the shaping of the basic elements of arbitration as a global legal culture. Global legal struc-

128 Niklas Luhmann, *The Differentiation of Society* (New York: Columbia University Press, 1982).

129 From translator's introduction to Luhmann's *The Differentiation of Society*.

tures developed in this manner will consist of reflexive legal relations lacking sociopolitical legitimacy.

Final Comments

To summarize the main discussions in this chapter, we can conclude that arbitration is a *highly* polycentric legal process. The significance that various sources have at the municipal level in making legal decisions is clearly accentuated and developed as a legal practice. Its polycentric character goes hand-in-hand with its reflexive qualities. Certain aspects of arbitration indicate the emergence of a *reflexive* global legal structure. Reflexivity and polycentricity inherent in arbitration facilitate the *internal* social integration of the international business community and the community's *external* global integration in the world society. This is done by way of enhancing the regulated autonomy of the customs and usages of merchants. Arbitration helps the international business community to strengthen its own self-regulation. It is reflected in the fact that arbitration is neither a rule-oriented nor a purpose-oriented process. It emphasizes instead procedural rationality. Finally, a thesis may be put forward which accommodates both our discussions about legitimacy and reflexivity. Arbitration has developed methods of legitimizing itself as a legal process. Since its function as a regulator of international commerce is reflexive, its legitimacy is also obtained in a reflexive manner. Dezalay and Garth's account of the latest development in arbitration, underlining a trend towards increased legalization and professionalization, supports the thesis regarding what we may call *reflexive legitimacy*.

To study arbitration, one therefore needs a conceptual apparatus which is produced by and is suitable to the legal 'reality' of transnational relations. The necessity of comparison with the municipal conditions will, however, remain. Law will always be understood by what it is at the local level, and the global law – even in its most autonomous condition – will always be a function of national law. In contrast to municipal law, which is totally engulfed and constantly influenced by cultural, political, economic and psychological developments, global law, as it pertains to arbitration, lives a rather one-dimensional economic life. This does not mean that the cultural factors are not present, but rather that the dominance of economic relations seems to be an undisputed fact: other social and cultural factors seem to be constantly overshadowed by the sheer force of the economic factors. Hence the necessity for the construction of a new paradigm for the study of global relations which can help us to clarify our target groups, and more effectively highlight the one-dimensionality of the global relations.

References

Adams, John N. and Roger Brownsword. 1992. *Understanding Law*. London: Fontana Press.

Aubert, Vilhelm. 1969. Law as a Way of Resolving Conflicts: The Case of a Small Industrialized Society. In *Law in Culture and Society*, edited by Laura Nader. Chicago: Aldine Publishing Company.

Aubert, Vilhelm. 1980. *Inledning till rättssociologi*. Stockholm: Almquist & Wiksell.

Banakar, Reza. 1995. *Conflict Management in a Multicultural Society*. Lund: Institute for Sociology of Law.

Bendix, Reinhard. 1962. *Max Weber: An Intellectual Portrait*. 2nd edn. London: University Paperback, Methuen.

Bierbrauer, Günter. 1994. Toward an Understanding of Legal Culture: Variations in Individualism between Kurds, Lebanese and Germans. *Law and Society Review* 28.

Blegvad, Britt-Mari, Per Olof Bolding and Ole Lando. 1973. *Arbitration as a Means of Resolving Conflicts*. Copenhagen: New Social Science Monographs.

Bogdan, Michael. 1992. Trans-Border Abduction of Children. In *Scandinavian Studies in Law*, Vol. 36. Stockholm: Juristförlaget.

Bogdan, Michael. 1994. *Comparative Law*. Stockholm: Norstedts Juridik.

Carlsson, Bo. 1995. Communicative Rationality and Open-ended Law in Sweden. *Journal of Law and Society* 22.

Castelnuovo, Shirley. 1979. Public Interest Law: Crisis of Legitimacy or Quest for Legal Order Autonomy. *Research in Law and Society* 2.

Cavusgil, S. Tamer. 1993. Globalization of Markets and Its Impact on Domestic Institutions. *Indiana Journal of Global Legal Studies* 1, no.1.

Cheng, Chia-Jui, ed. 1988. *Schmitthoffs Selected Essays on International Trade Law*. Dordrecht: Martinus Nijhoff.

Christensen, Anna. 1995. Polycentricity and Normative Patterns. In *Legal Polycentricity – Consequences of Pluralism in Law*, edited by A. Pettersen and H. Zahle. Aldershot: Dartmouth.

Cotterrell, Roger. 1992. *The Sociology of Law: An Introduction*. 2nd edn. London: Butterworths.

Cotterrell, Roger. 1995. *Laws Community: Legal Theory in Sociological Perspective*. Oxford: Clarendon Press.

Dalberg-Larsen, Jørgen. 1993. *Rettens enhed – en illusion? Om retlig pluralisme i teorien og praksis*. Copenhagen: Akademisk Forlag.

Day, D.M. and Bernardette Griffin. 1993. *The Law of International Trade*. 2nd edn. London, Dublin, Edinburgh: Butterworths.

De Ly, Filip. 1992. *International Business Law and Lex Mercatoria*. Amsterdam: North-Holland.

Dezalay, Yves and Bryant Garth. 1995. Merchants of Law as Moral Entrepreneurs. *Law & Society Review* 29.

Dicey, Albert Venn. 1968. *Introduction to the Study of the Law of the Constitution*. London: Macmillan.

Domke, Martin. 1968. *The Law and Practice of Commercial Arbitration*. Mandelein, Illinois: Callaghan & Company.

Draetta, Ugo, Ralph B. Lake and Ved P. Nanda. 1992. *Breach and Adaptation of International Contracts: An Introduction to Lex Mercatoria*. Salem, New Hampshire: Butterworth Legal Publishers.

Durkheim, Emil. 1933. *The Division of Labour in Society*. Glencoe, Illinois: Free Press.

Ehrlich, Eugen. *The Fundamental Principles of Sociology of Law*. New York: Arno Press. Originally published in 1936, translated by W.L. Moll.

Freyhold, Hanno von. 1996. The International Practice of New York Lawyers. Paper prepared for the Oñati workshop on 'The Infrastructure of Cross-Border Legal Interaction'.

Friedman, Lawrence M. 1977. *Law and Society: An Introduction*. Englewood Cliffs, NJ: Prentice-Hall.

Friedman, Lawrence M. 1986. Legal Culture and the Welfare State. In *The Dilemmas of Law in the Welfare State*, edited by Gunther Teubner. Berlin: Walter de Gruyter.

Friedman, Lawrence M. 1989. Lawyers in Cross-Cultural Perspective. In *Lawyers in Society*, Vol. 3, ed. Richard L. Abel and Philip S.C. Lewis. Berkeley: University of California Press.

Gessner, Volkmar. 1995. Global Approach in the Sociology of Law: Problems and Challenges. *Journal of Law and Society* 22, no. 1.

Gessner, Volkmar. 1996. The Globalization of Legal Certainty. Paper prepared for the Oñati workshop on 'The Infrastructure of Cross-Border Legal Interaction'.

Gessner, Volkmar and Angelika Schade. 1994. Conflicts of Culture in Cross-border Legal Relations: The Conception of a Research Topic in the Sociology of Law. In *Global Culture*, edited by Mike Featherstone. London: Sage.

Gibson, James L. and Gregory A. Calderia. 1996. The Legal Cultures of Europe. *Law & Society Review* 30.

Gihl, Torsten. 1975. The Legal Character and Sources of International Law. In *Scandinavian Studies in Law*, Vol. 1, edited by Folke Schmidt. Stockholm: Almqvist & Wiksell.

Goldstajn, Aleksandar. 1990. Reflections on the Structure of the Modern Law of International Trade. In *International Contracts and Conflicts of Laws – A Collection of Essays*, edited by Peter Sarcevic. London: Graham & Trotman/Martinus Nijhoff.

Griffiths, John. 1986. What is Legal Pluralism? *Journal of Legal Pluralism and Unofficial Law* 24.

Habermas, Jürgen. 1976. *Legitimation Crisis*. London: Heinemann.

Habermas, Jürgen. 1979. *Communication and the Evolution of Society*. London: Heinemann.

Hart, H.L.A. 1988. *The Concept of Law*. Oxford: Oxford University Press. Original edition 1961.

Hurst, James Willard. 1960. *Law and Social Process in United States History*, The Thomas M. Cooley lectures. Ann Arbor: University of Michigan Law School.

Kelsen, Hans. 1946. *General Theory of Law and State*. London: Geoffrey Cumberlege.

Kidder, Robert L. 1983. *Connecting Law and Society*. Englewood Cliffs, NJ: Prentice-Hall.

Lempert, Richard and Ann Arbor. 1987. The Autonomy of Law: Two Visions Compared. In *Autopoietic Law: A New Approach to Law and Society*, edited by Gunther Teubner. Berlin: Walter de Gruyter.

Luhmann, Niklas. 1982. *The Differentiation of Society*. New York: Columbia University Press.

Luhmann, Niklas. 1986. The Self-Reproduction of Law and its Limits. In *The Dilemma of Law in the Welfare States*, edited by Gunther Teubner. Berlin: Walter de Gruyter.

Macaulay, Stewart. 1963. Non-Contractual Relations in Business: A Preliminary Study. *American Sociological Review* 28.

Maine, Sir Henry. 1885. *Ancient Law*. London: John Murray.

Maturana, Hamberto and Francisco Varela. 1980. *Autopoiesis and Cognition*. Dordrecht: D. Reidel.

Newman, Katherine S. 1983. *Law and Economic Organization: A Comparative Study of Preindustrial Societies*. Cambridge: Cambridge University Press.

Petersen, Hanne and Henrik Zahle. 1995. *Legal Polycentricity – Consequences of Pluralism in Law*. Aldershot: Dartmouth.

Podgórecki, Adam. 1991. *A Sociological Theory of Law*. Milano: Dott. A. Giuffrè Editore.

Renner, Karl. 1949. *The Institutions of Private Law and Their Social Functions*. London, Boston: Routledge & Kegan Paul.

Ryder, Frank R. 1987. *Legal Problems of International Banking*. London: Sweet & Maxwell.

Sanderson, Stephen K. and Thomas D Hall. 1995. World System Approaches to World Historical Change. In *Civilizations and World Systems*, edited by Stephen K. Sanderson. Walnut Creek: Altamira Press.

Santos, Boaventura de S. 1995. *Toward a New Common Sense – Law, Science and Politics in the Paradigmatic Transition*. New York, London: Routledge.

Schmitthoff, Clive M. 1961. International Business Law: A New Law Merchant. *Current Law and Social Problems* 2.

Schmitthoff, Clive M. ed. 1964. *The Sources of the Law of International Trade*. London: Stevens and Sons.

Schmitthoff, Clive M. 1981. *Commercial Law in a Changing Economic* Climate. 2nd edn. London: Sweet & Maxwell.

Schmitthoff, Clive M. 1988. The Unification of Law of International Trade. Reprinted in *Schmitthoff's Selected Essays on International Trade Law*, edited by Chia-Jui Cheng. Dordrecht: Martinus Nijhoff. Originally published in 1964.

Selznick, Philip. 1992. *The Moral Commonwealth*. Berkeley: University of California Press.

Stanley, Christopher. 1992. Serious Money: Legitimation of Deviancy in the Financial Markets. *International Journal of the Sociology of Law* 20.

Stjernquist, Per. 1995. *Samhällsordningens dubbla grundvalar*. Lund: Institute for the Sociology of Law.

Stockholm Chamber of Commerce. 1984. *Arbitration in Sweden*. 2nd revised edn. Stockholm.

Stockholm världsmästare på skiljedom. 1994. *Jusektidningen* 11.

Teubner, Gunther. 1983. Substantive and Reflexive Elements in Modern Law. *Law and Society Review* 17.

Wallerstein, Immanuel. 1974. *The Modern World System: Capitalist Agriculture and the Origins of the European World Economy in the Sixteenth Century*. New York: Academic Press.

Weber, Max. 1968. *Economy and Society*, 3 vols., edited by Guenther Roth and Claus Wittich. New York: Bedminister Press.

The Author

Reza Banakar is a sociologist of law. Until 1997, he worked as Senior Lecturer and Research Fellow at the Institute for the Sociology of Law at

Lund University (Sweden). Currently, he is holding the Paul Dodyk Fellowship at the Centre for Socio-Legal Studies, Wolfson College, Oxford.

Address: Centre for Socio-Legal Studies, Wolfson College, Linton Road, Oxford OX2 6DU, UK.

E-mail: reza.banakar@socio-legal-studies.oxford.ac.uk

Abstract

The primary purpose of this chapter is to investigate the process of arbitration and its development as a legal and cultural entity. Furthermore, the notion of legitimacy is used as a device for analysing the development of arbitration and its effects on the construction of global relations.

Subsequently, the following questions are posed. How does the international business community utilize the existing legal infrastructures to regulate its transnational activities and to resolve disputes which might arise from these activities? How do the needs of international commerce affect the development of law as an element of the 'changing global order'? How is the intercultural make-up of cross-border exchanges structured, and how does it affect the development of legal infrastructures which are used by international commercial exchanges? Finally, how is this law, in relation to national cultural systems, constructed and from which sources does it obtain its legal and political legitimacy?

Part Four
Conclusions

11 Binding Territoriality and Functionality? Globalization Meets the Law

JÜRGEN NEYER

Introduction

One of the main topics in international relations theory in the last decade has been changes in the structure of the OECD system.[1] The number of contributions arguing for a decline in the importance of the principle of territoriality,[2] the demise of the state,[3] the end of sovereignty,[4] or even a general trend of debordering[5] of social

Thanks to Ali Cem Budak and Volkmar Gessner for critical remarks and discussion of earlier versions of this chapter. The usual disclaimer applies.

1 The term "structure of the OECD system" denotes the sum of interactions and institutions in and between the member countries of the OECD. The focus of this chapter is explicitly restricted to those countries, owing to the fact that the empirical studies in this volume do not undertake research in countries other than those belonging to the OECD.

2 John Ruggie, "Territoriality and Beyond: Problematizing Modernity in International Relations", *International Organization* 41(1) (1993), 139–74.

3 Cf. the contributions in Michael Mann, ed., *The Rise and Decline of the Nation State* (Oxford: Basil Blackwell, 1990); and Wolfgang Hein, "Die neue Weltordnung und das Ende des Nationalstaates", *Nord-Süd aktuell* 1 (1990), 50–9.

4 Cf. Joseph A. Cammilleri and Jim Falk, *The End of Sovereignty? The Politics of a Shrinking and Fragmenting World* (Aldershot: Edward Elgar, 1992).

5 Cf. Lothar Brock and Mathias Albert, "Entgrenzung der Staatenwelt. Zur Analyse weltgesellschaftlicher Entwicklungstendenzen", *Zeitschrift für Internationale Beziehungen* 2, no. 2 (1995).

processes is immense. James Rosenau, for example, has pictured international relations as 'postinternational politics',[6] Mark Zacher has traced the 'decaying pillars of the Westphalian Temple'[7] and Ronnie Lipschutz has speculated about the rise of a 'global civil society'.[8] In international political economy, a number of contributions have similarly highlighted the argument that the concept of an international economy composed of nation-states is challenged by the emergence of a global market for goods, capital and services,[9] the rise of the region state[10] and a transnationalization of social processes.[11]

In trying to cope with all these big issues, however, theorizing became increasingly unaware that there probably is some kind of connection between the level of global structures and the local level of the individual. Furthermore, theorizing about global changes suffers heavily from its often inadequate empirical foundations – and, especially in the social sciences, from its neglect of legal infrastructures. It is at these three points that the present volume provides helpful assistance. In bringing together an analysis of global changes and detailed empirical studies of the legal difficulties individual and business actors face when embarking on cross-border affairs, this volume adds some meat to the bones of often highly abstract theorizing. What can a political scientist contribute to this endeavour? Social scientists are used to thinking in terms of interaction, deriving hypotheses about the behaviour of individual actors under the circumstances identified, and testing these hypotheses by means of empirical data. That is exactly what this chapter sets out to do.

6 James N. Rosenau, *Turbulence in World Politics* (Brighton: Harvester Wheatsheaf, 1990).

7 Mark W. Zacher, "The Decaying Pillars of the Westphalian Temple: Implications for International Order and Governance", in *Governance Without Government: Order and Change in World Politics*, ed. James N. Rosenau and Ernst-Otto Czempiel (Cambridge: Cambridge University Press, 1992), 58–101.

8 Ronnie D. Lipschutz, "Reconstructing World Politics: The Emergence of a Global Civil Society", *Millenium* 21, no. 3 (1992), 389–420.

9 John H. Dunning, *Multinational Enterprises and the Global Economy* (Workingham: Addison-Wesley, 1993).

10 Cf. Kenichi Ohmae, "The Rise of the Region State", *Foreign Affairs* 72, no. 2 (1993), 78–87.

11 Cf. Jürgen Neyer, *Spiel ohne Grenzen. Weltwirtschaftliche Strukturveränderungen und das Ende des sozial kompetenten Staates* (Marburg: Tectum Verlag, 1996).

In building upon international relations theory and international political economy, this chapter argues that economic globalization implies a growing gap between the functional logic of economic actors, which act according to opportunities provided by the market, and the territorial logic of politics, which remains closely related to the states' systems. Or, to put it in different terms, the end of embedded liberalism has at its centrepiece a shift in bargaining power between transnational private interests and national public power. It will be argued, however, that this gap leads, not only to regulatory deficits of the welfare state and a corresponding change in the function of modern statehood, but also to a regulatory response by transnational actors and a new mixture of parallel transnational private and national public legal regulations. Investigating the problematics of establishing cross-border legal certainty in a debordering OECD system therefore means that we are witnessing a variety of challenges to the nation-state which point to the growing inadequacy of a purely territorial understanding of its functions in coping with non-territorial interactions.

The present chapter will, as a first step, briefly introduce the reader to the already existing literature in international relations theory and international political economy. It aims at inquiring into the categories of different disciplines for facilitating a conceptual framework for an interdisciplinary understanding of the impact of increasing cross-border interaction[12] on the relationship between territorial and interest specific representation. Secondly, the chapter will examine how far we can observe in the legal realm a response by the states' systems as well as by non-governmental actors to the regulatory gap between the territorial logic of the political space and the functional logic of the economic space. In doing so, the chapter will not only draw on some of the recent literature in legal sociology but will also review the contributions to the present volume. Finally, the chapter will draw some conclusions from this journey into an interdisciplinary understanding of changes in the OECD system.

12 This contribution distinguishes between "cross-border", "transnational" and "international" interaction. Cross-border interaction denotes a type of interaction which crosses borders without necessarily involving states as actors. Transnational interaction denotes a type of interaction, exclusivly conducted between non-governmental actors, and international interaction is analogously reserved for the interaction of states.

Territoriality and Functionality in the OECD System

One might wonder why the review which this chapter is going to undertake restricts itself to international relations theory and international political economy. To be sure, there can be little doubt that a variety of other disciplines, such as intercultural studies or comparative social sciences, have also made important contributions in this regard.[13] There are mainly two reasons for this restriction. First, politics and economics may be viewed as being the two most important dimensions for regulatory politics in each society and therefore legitimize a special concern. As this body of literature also makes clear, the capacity of the state to satisfy the demand for regulation depends on a variety of conditions which are negatively affected by the globalization process. Second, both discourses point to the fact that the recent regulatory deficits of the OECD system can only be understood by approaching the state system as a historically specific type of social organization. Therefore the state-centredness of the OECD polity may reflect more elements of institutional inertia than functional usefulness. The task of regulating cross-border interaction is in fact delegated to the states not only because they command the resources and the necessary administrative capacity for coping with the difficulties involved, but maybe even more so because they were able in the past to use their domestic political authority to monopolize the job. In such a historical perspective we can read both approaches rather easily as different analyses of an identical problem, namely the ability of public authorities to deal with the problems arising from cross-border interaction and the need for national institutions to deal with risk and uncertainty.

The Territorial Logic of International Politics

There can be little doubt that by far the most important analytical category of cross-border politics is the territorial nation-state. Not only do realists maintain that states are by far the most important actors in cross-border politics and that most cross-border political processes can be understood by focusing on their interaction[14] but also liberals most often take the state as a starting-

13 For an approach which also integrates security and cultural issues, see Chapter 9 of the present volume.

14 Some of the classical texts realists refer to are Kenneth Waltz, *Theory of World Politics* (New York: McGraw-Hill, 1979); Robert

point for their analyses. To underline this argument we will briefly discuss the different approaches.

Realists argue that the anarchic nature of the international system[15] forces states to be mainly concerned, not with enhancing the economic well-being of their citizens, but simply with surviving in a dangerous and anarchic environment, or, to put it in economists' terms, to maximize their external survival. Therefore it is further argued that states are to be understood as independent 'survival-maximizers' which feel constantly threatened by their neighbours. Realism's main concern in explaining political processes is with power and interest. It is argued that a certain international policy is ultimately a result of the interest of the most powerful actors. Power, however, is in realists' terms mainly the ability to use force, which means the ability to influence actors to behave in a different way than they would have done on their own. The enforcement of a certain policy, however, is a domain of the state. Non-governmental actors can therefore only to a rather low degree be powerful. As far as they are living in an anarchical environment, it is no big step to argue that they are relatively helpless in dealing with foreign states when it comes to conflicting interests. Therefore cross-border interaction of non-governmental actors is always accompanied by uncertainty and risk and has to rely on the goodwill of the states. Furthermore, it is argued that the activities of non-governmental actors have to be conducted under the legal authority of states. Thus they can only be a shaping force of cross-border politics insofar as the security of their home states is not reduced and their activities are allowed by the states. Private interests therefore act under a kind of veto power of their home state. In this kind of reasoning, the perspective of a globalizing world in which non-governmental interests become a shaping force of cross-border politics is understandably viewed with strong scepticism.

Whereas the realists' discourse focuses on the role of the state in the international system, liberals[16] are far more concerned with the

Gilpin, *War and Change in World Politics* (Cambridge: Cambridge University Press, 1979); and Hedley Bull, *The Anarchical Society. A Study of Order in World Politics* (London: Macmillan, 1979).

15 For the purpose of this chapter, anarchy can be understood as the absence of a central government which can enforce certain international policies. Cf. Waltz, 'Theory of World Politics', n. 15.

16 A classical textbook is provided by Richard Rosecrance, *Der neue Handelsstaat: Herausforderungen für Politik und Wirtschaft*

growing political, economic and judicial relevancy of societal actors in the international system. Liberal scholars argue that the global political environment is far less dangerous than realists maintain and that the assumption of states as being unitary actors who are functionally identical is a gross oversimplification of the reality. Liberals start with the assumption that states are neither functionally identical nor part of an international anarchy. As opposed to realists' assumptions, liberals regard the conduct of foreign policy as being heavily influenced by dominant domestic interests and the function of international institutions which reduce cross-border uncertainty and risk. Furthermore, an important assumption is added by their pointing to the fact that all countries of the OECD area are by definition democracies whose governments try to win elections and need popular consent. Only under very restricted conditions, however, is investment in military security an appropriate tool for facilitating this consent. In most cases it is rather economic performance and the perception of social stability which sets the frame for voters' decisions.

Therefore the governments of states have a strong incentive to institutionalize their interaction with other states for further reduction of cross-border risk and uncertainty, and a strong disincentive to focus on security issues. This general interest of states, it is argued, has been the main driving force in the postwar establishment of the United Nations, the International Monetary Fund and other international institutions. These institutions have provided the interaction of states with a high degree of principles, norms, rules and decision-making procedures (international regimes[17]) which have gradually transformed an international anarchy dominated by uncertainty and risk into an international society in which few areas are still lacking regulation.

In this civilized world of international relations, liberals argue not only that states behave otherwise than realism assumes, but that also societal actors gain new importance in cross-border af-

(Frankfurt/M.: Campus, 1987). For a debate between liberalism and realism, cf. David Baldwin, *Neorealism and Neoliberalism. The Contemporary Debate* (New York: Columbia University Press, 1993).

17 The classical definition of international regimes has been provided by Stephen D. Krasner, "Structural Causes and Regime Consequences: Regimes as Intervening Variables", in *International Regimes*, ed. Stephen D. Krasner (Ithaca: Cornell University Press, 1983), 1–22.

fairs. They are no longer bound to their national territory by the restrictions of international anarchy, but have a high incentive to exploit the opportunities of global markets and a debordering system. The growth in cross-border trade, traffic and communication in the postwar era is explained by liberal institutionalists as a function of the growing density of international institutions and the improving relationship between costs and benefits of cross-border interaction. Growing cross-border interaction, however, is viewed not only as a result of the civilization of international relations but at the same time as an independent variable. The argument goes that the more interdependent the relation between two countries becomes, the higher are the costs to one of the countries to break this relationship by political means and the lesser is the probability that this will happen. International institutionalization therefore leads to intensified cross-border interaction and increased importance of societal actors for cross-border political outcomes.

From the liberals' perspective, conceptualizing cross-border interaction may no longer mean focusing on the interaction of states but involves integrating a variety of non-governmental actors. However, they are not a homogeneous group but may be divided into a huge variety of different groups: they can be either profit-maximizing private corporations or persons with an individual cross-border interest (for example, cross-border refugees or couples living in two different countries) or non-profit humanitarian organizations like the Red Cross, Amnesty International or Greenpeace (to name just a few). Their activities may be directly oriented towards challenging the dominant position of states in cross-border affairs and may be motivated by political reasons (regions, cities or organizations like Greenpeace) or their cross-border activities may only respond to economic reasons without any political intentions (corporations, individuals).

In all cases, however, their commonality is that they are composed of non-governmental actors whose interests are different from states' interests. They do not represent a territorially defined political constituency, but are the emanation of particular subnational or transnational political or economic interests of a social group or a collective of particular social groups. Recent estimations are for about 18,000 transnational non-profit organizations[18] which influence

18 Cf. John Smith, Richard Pagnucco and Walter Romeril, "Transnational Social Movement Organisations in the Global Political Arena", *Voluntas* 5, no. 2 (1994), 123.

cross-border political processes. Their integration into the global polity is partly due to the scientific and technical expertise which they command. As the confrontation between Greenpeace and Shell in the case of Brent Spar has shown, however, equally important is their ability to use national media to focus public awareness on certain issues and thereby exert political pressure on states' governments.

The general impact of the political influence of non-profit organizations on the behaviour of states' governments is difficult to qualify. It may be rather the exception than the rule that states change preferences as the result of direct political pressure originating from transnational non-governmental organizations. Furthermore, inasmuch as the global media industry is still predominantly of a national character (which, of course, might change in the future), the importance of the impact of transnational interests on cross-border affairs may be attributed primarily to indirect agenda setting by relying on support from the national media and mobilizing the critical awareness of a national public. Owing to their insufficient administrative and technical resources, they therefore have to rely on national audiences and their support in influencing national governments. The autonomous ontological status of transnational interest groups for conceptualizing the OECD system therefore seems to be rather weak. To further their interests they always have to compete with other interests for access to public decision makers.

The same holds true for the liberals' argument of the growing importance of subnational groups in shaping the politics of nation-states. In having access to international decision making they need to pass through the bottleneck of national administrative structures and therefore have no great opportunity to escape the principle of territoriality of international politics. A truly transnational system or even a transnational society is therefore hardly imaginable. At least in the world of today it has to rely on some degree of benevolent support by the states' systems.

The Functional Logic of the Global Economy

Insofar as the main concern of scholars in international political economy is not with the tension between anarchy and order but with that between markets and states, we may distinguish analogously two opposed perspectives, namely a state-centred discourse and a market-centred discourse. Whereas the state-centred discourse highlights the negative consequences of intensifying cross-border interaction for the regulatory capabilities of the nation-state,[19] the market-centred discourse focuses on the new opportunities for microeconomic actors which flow from technological progress and national as well as international liberalization.[20] However, they share a fairly common understanding not only of the empirical aspects of intensifying cross-border interaction, namely the transnationalization of production, capital and services,[21] but also of its driving forces. There is wide consensus among scholars that these must be attributed, not primarily to international trade (conducted by states), but to the functional logic of a liberalizing world economy in which private actors seek new opportunities and therefore transcend the borders of national markets.

The rather consensual assessment of the empirical aspects of major changes in economic cross-border interaction, however, does not lead the community of international political economy scholars to derive a coherent set of political and economic implications. Market-centred approaches argue that any intervention of the state in the economy leads to a disruption of markets and an inefficient allocation of resources. The state should therefore restrict itself to providing a legal framework which guarantees private property and sets the basic rules. The story these scholars tell starts most often with the recession in the 1970s and argues that the slowing down of economic activity in the OECD area was largely a result of the dominance of national regulations over national economies.[22] As a

19 For an analysis along these lines, cf. Stephen Gill and David Law, "Global Hegemony and the Structural Power of Capital", in *Gramsci, Historical Materialism and International Relations*, ed. Stephen Gill (Cambridge: Cambridge University Press), 93–124; and Phillip G. Cerny, "Globalization and the Changing Logic of Collective Action", *International Organization* 49, no. 4 (1995), 595–625.

20 This approach can be found in Dunning, "Multinational Enterprises" or in Walter Wriston, *The Twilight of Sovereignty* (New York: Macmillan, 1992).

21 A much more detailed analysis of structural changes in the global political economy than we can provide here is to be found in Neyer, "Spiel ohne Grenzen"; cf. also Ulrich Menzel, Mathias Albert, Lothar Brock, Stephan Hessler and Jürgen Neyer, *Die postmoderne Weltwirtschaft. Entstofflichung und Entgrenzung der Ökonomie* (Frankfurt/M.: Suhrkamp, 1997).

22 For a very influential analysis along these lines, cf. Mancur Olson, *The Rise and Decline of Nations. Economic Growth, Stagflation, and Social Rigidities* (New Haven: Yale University Press, 1982).

result of the strong position of the unions and states' (successful) efforts to regulate domestic labour markets, the costs of labour rose in nearly all OECD countries (apart from Japan) above their productivity level. This not only led to a dislocation of resources which favoured macroeconomic consumption over microeconomic investment, but also resulted in inflation and competitive disadvantages as compared with Japan and the newly industrialising countries. Furthermore, in order not to lose their ability to remain competitive, microeconomic actors were forced to invest in countries with lower labour costs than at home and started to export employment. The result of this process, it is argued, was inflation, recession and unemployment.

This became even more serious as states started to react to the recession by opposing further international liberalization and erecting new non-tariff barriers to trade (neoprotectionism). The re-emergence of neoclassical economics in the 1970s and early 1980s, the liberalization of cross-border trade and the deregulation of cross-border capital flows are from this perspective to be understood as the result of a learning process of societal actors in the OECD societies from policy failure in the past. This failure was, from the neoclassical perspective, primarily one of the dominance of national regulatory politics over transnational private interests. Correspondingly, the resurgence of the OECD economy in the 1980s is understood as a response of market forces to the liberalization of economic cross-border exchanges and therefore the increasing opportunities for private interest in shaping cross-border affairs.

Whereas the liberalization of market forces since the late 1970s may have had an important impact on the efficiency of the OECD economy and therefore the furthering of economic growth, there can be little doubt that efficiency has had its price. Since Keynes wrote his famous 'General Theory on Employment, Interest and Money',[23] a growing number of economists are rather sceptical about the performances and side-effects of unregulated markets.[24] This scepticism results not only from the experiences of the Great Depression but also from a theoretical argument which holds that

23 John Maynard Keynes, *Allgemeine Theory der Beschäftigung, des Zinses und des Geldes* (Berlin: Duncker & Humblodt, 1955).

24 The classical text is Karl Polany, *The Great Transformation: The Political and Economic Origins of Our Time* (Boston: Beacon Press, 1957). For a more recent contribution along these lines, cf. Cerny, "The Changing Logic", (fn. 20).

market failures and unacceptable social costs are a structural feature of unregulated markets. One of the main reasons for the need of markets for a helping hand, it has been pointed out, is that they are composed of microeconomic actors who are independent utility maximizers who may sometimes find themselves in a dilemma over collective action. Such a situation happened in the 1930s, when it was individually rational for enterprises to disinvest but collectively irrational to bear the macroeconomic losses of the Great Depression. The fashionable argument put forward by authors like Ohmae,[25] that the importance of the nation-state in a globalizing economy is rapidly diminishing and that its competencies may be restricted to providing locally the public services that the global economy requires of them, therefore needs to be viewed sceptically. The underlying assumption of this argument, that firms become truly global players and loose their ties to their former home economies, is contradicted by more balanced accounts. Kapstein, for example, points out that US firms have very real benefits in remaining distinctly American firms, which stem directly from the power and functions of the national state: among these benefits are the ability to have access to regulatory and standard-setting bodies like the Federal Aviation Administration (FAA) and the Food and Drug Administration (FDA), to subsidies provided by the American government for research and development (R&D) and, last but not least, having protection when it comes to conflict with foreign governments.[26]

Private economic actors therefore need the state not only for guaranteeing private property and enforcing contracts but also for providing macroeconomic investment in situations of economic depression and high unemployment. Even more important for our context, interaction and exchange of goods, services and capital need rules which not only satisfy the requirements of dominant actors but provide for a level playing ground. However, the ability of the state to provide these regulatory devices depends on a variety

25 Cf. Ohmae, "The Rise of the Region State".

26 Ethan B. Kapstein, "We are Us: The Myth of the Multi-National", *The National Interest*, Winter (1991), 55–62; Cf., for similar arguments, Paul Hirst and Grahame Thompson, *Globalization in Question – The International Economy and the Possibilities of Governance* (Cambridge: Polity Press, 1996), and Laura Tyson, "They are not us: Why American ownership still matters", *The American Prospect* (Winter, 1991), 37–49.

of conditions which are critically affected by processes of economic transnationalization. Philipp Cerny points to this relation by arguing:

> the more that the scale of goods and assets produced, exchanged, and/or used in a particular economic sector or activity diverges from the structural scale of the national state ... and the more that those divergences feed back into each other ... then the more that the authority, legitimacy, policymaking capacity, and policy-implementing effectiveness of states will be challenged from both without and within.[27]

Some scholars even argue that states need to respond to their reduced regulatory capacity by giving up their postwar function as intermediaries between the global economy and domestic social interests. Robert Cox argues that the effect of the transnationalization of private interests is to 'convert the state into an agency for adjusting national economic practices and policies to the perceived exigencies of the global economy. The state becomes a transmission belt from the global to the national economy, where heretofore it had acted as the bulwark defending domestic welfare from external disturbances.[28] Not surprisingly, state-centred scholars take a critical view on the long-term prospects of the structuring power of private interests in the OECD economy. As Polanyi has pointed out in his study on the 'Great Transformation', a liberalized world economy which functions according to the logic of private interests can quickly run into deep conflict with domestic political regimes based on the principle of democratic representation. The ordering potential of private interests in the OECD economy not only poses a serious danger to the social homogeneity of national societies but also stimulates demands for a politically motivated protectionist backslash.

In the light of our discussions above, the intensifying of cross-border interaction conducted by private actors can be understood as supporting a bifurcation of economic and political structures and weakening the regulatory links between the two: whereas the economic structures of the OECD system are in a process of debordering,

27 Cerny, "The Changing Logic", p. 597.

28 Robert W. Cox, "Global Restructuring. Making Sense of the Changing International Political Economy", in *Political Economy and the Changing Global Order*, ed. Richard Stubbs and Geoffrey R.D. Underhill (Toronto: Macmillan, 1994), 45–59.

the polity of the OECD system remains fixed to the principle of territoriality. Therefore it can be argued that states are losing capacity to regulate microeconomic actors, which may not lead directly to a new depression but at least increases the probability of market failures and high transaction costs which may be of a prohibitive nature for cross-border interaction.

Bridging the Gap between Territoriality and Functionality?

The preceding paragraphs have focused on delineating the two different organizing principles in the political and the economic realm of the OECD system. It was argued that the functionality of the OECD polity in coping with the regulatory demands of a transnationalizing system is hampered by its still dominant territorial structure, which again leads to regulatory gaps in terms of rising transaction costs and socially unacceptable outcomes. Legal approaches show a high awareness not only of the negative implications of the gap between territoriality and functionality but also of international structures dealing with overcoming them. Lawyers point to efforts at making national legal provisions uniform and to private international law· which applies to transactions extending over more than one legal system and determines in an individual case the law applicable to the dispute between the parties and the jurisdiction of the courts that have to adjudicate the issue. Ferid,[29] for example, points out that the issue of providing cross-border legal certainty to private actors has been dealt with since the Middle Ages by Italian cities. Furthermore, a variety of international agreements such as the Brussels Convention on Recognition and Enforcement of Judgements in Civil and Commercial Matters or the New York Convention on the Recognition and Enforcement of Arbitral Awards are securing the cross-border enforcement of law. Even foreign child maintenance claims are no longer unenforceable but are legally ordered.[30]

Critics of the efficiency of private international law, however, argue that in a variety of cases private international law contributes little to reducing risk and uncertainty. Schmidtchen, for example, argues, 'whereas for domestic trade the legal foundation appears

29 Murad Ferid, *Internationales Privatrecht. Das neue Recht* (Frankfurt/Main: Metzner, 1987).

30 Cf. Chapter 6 of the present volume.

unequivocal, and the "protective state" fulfils the necessary task of enforcement, international transactions make contact with a multitude of legal systems and with the power monopoly claimed by each state within its borders'.[31] Therefore collisions of norms and gaps between different norm systems are ubiquitous and the parties subject to courts' rulings are in a state of 'constitutional uncertainty' which may lead to situations where private actors have to submit the case to a foreign legal order unknown to him or – even worse – where different legal systems may contradict each other.

Another important aspect of practical difficulties is provided by the fact that the application of international conventions and uniform law by national judges often follows the patterns of domestic legal reasoning and therefore involves the risk that uniform interpretation and application will be the exception rather than the rule.[32] Last but not least, it has to be mentioned that, in applying foreign law, judges may sometimes have problems in understanding its meaning or even have difficulties accepting it (for example, applying legal provisions of Islamic countries). In all three cases, the barriers to cross-border interaction may not in theory be of a prohibitive nature but may prove to be so in fact, owing to the costliness of overcoming them. Not surprisingly, international commerce does not only rely on private international law but has also developed its own mechanisms for resolving business disputes.

One important matter arising in this context is the need to ask for necessary institutional devices to bridge the growing gap between territoriality and functionality or, to put it in simpler terms, for mechanisms being able to cope with the practical difficulties which accompany legal cross-border interaction. In this context, a number of studies in sociology of law have pointed out that not only do private actors have high incentives for overcoming this unsatisfactory state of cross-border interaction but that this has led in the past to the emergence of a 'separate legal culture of international transactions with autonomous rules and its own infrastructure

31 Dieter Schmidtchen, "Territorialität des Rechts, Internationales Privatrecht und die privatautonome Regelung internationaler Sachverhalte", *Rabels Zeitschrift für ausländisches und internationales Privatrecht* 59 (1995), 111.

32 Volkmar Gessner, "The Institutional Framework of Cross-Border Interaction", in *Foreign Courts – Civil Litigation in Foreign Legal Cultures*, ed. Volkmar Gessner (Aldershot: Dartmouth, 1996), 33.

for advice and decision-making'.[33] This legal culture can be understood as a 'decentralised network of self-elected and customised rules'[34] between economic actors, which accompanies the more traditional forms of nation-state-produced law applicable to cross-border legal interaction. Slaughter describes the (re-)emergence of this 'new merchant law' accordingly as a body of law which has no more formal status than voluntary norms but nevertheless proves to provide important devices for guiding the interaction of transnational actors. Similarly, Shapiro identifies 'some movement toward a relatively uniform global contract and commercial law'[35] which is based on an international effort propelled, not by states, but by private lawmaking. Furthermore, private ordering[36] has led to the rise of a variety of non-governmental institutions for safeguarding private contracts, such as the International Chamber of Commerce (ICC) in Paris. The ICC is merely a private institution (although it has a consultative status at the United Nations) for providing information, undertaking arbitration and proposing standardized rules for economic interaction. Owing to its nature as a non-governmental institution, it has no formal power to enforce contracts and property rights. However, insofar as business relationships are often characterized by iteration and the need of contracting parties for high reputation, private actors have strong incentives to comply with its decisions.[37]

Whereas the empirical investigation into the mechanisms and difficulties of legal cross-border interaction promises to provide

33 Ibid., 34.

34 Anne-Marie Slaughter, "International Law in a World of Liberal States", *European Journal of International Law* 6 (1995), 518.

35 Martin Shapiro, "The Globalization of Law", *Indiana Journal of Global Legal Studies* 1, no. 1 (1993), 38.

36 Private ordering means a certain kind of formal or informal rules that non-governmental parties bring into existence by mutual agreement.

37 This is elaborated more fully by Stewart Macaulay, "Contract Law Among American Businessmen", in *The Social Organisation of Law*, ed. Donald Black and Maureen Mileski (New York, London: Seminar Papers, 1973), 75–94: "Not only do the particular units in a given exchange want to deal with each other again, they also want to deal with other business units in the future. And the way one behaves in a particular transaction, or a series of transactions, will color his general business reputation."

important insights into the question of how private actors deal with legal uncertainty, the already existing literature has not attributed too much importance to formal and informal support structures for establishing legal certainty.[38] The most important contribution of this volume is therefore to shed some light onto this comparatively unknown field of research by providing detailed studies of selected cases. In the following pages, this chapter undertakes to review the different contributions to this volume by asking how far we can gain insights into the importance of public and private formal or rather informal support structures in establishing legal certainty in cross-border interaction. In the context of the debates on international relations and international political economy, two questions in particular seem to be especially important: first, under what circumstances are private actors autonomously able to cope with legal uncertainty; and, secondly, under what circumstances can we expect 'small people' to participate successfully in cross-border legal interaction? Whereas the first question concerns the legitimacy of the emerging transnational legal order, the second question seeks to identify the necessary role of the state in reducing transaction costs and thereby facilitating cross-border interaction.

Formal and Informal Support Structures

Especially in the cross-border interaction of big business, formal support structures for cross-border legal claims seem to be no big issue. Stammel supports this point in Chapter 3 of this volume by arguing that in reinsurance business legal battles were until the end of the 1980s very rare and actors were strongly interested in finding private solutions to their disputes. Arbitration and informal modes of self-regulation were far more common than reliance on formal conflict settlement by courts. The same holds true for cross-border payments through banks where formal legal uncertainty is obviously high but situations in which one of the parties defects barely exist. As Frick argues in Chapter 4, it is not primarily the shadow of the law which forces banks to stick to their contracts but rather the expected benefits of high reputation and iterated business relationships. Not surprisingly, nearly all of the contributions in the first part of the present volume underline the smooth working of mechanisms of private ordering based on rather informal modes of compliance enforcement. Moreover, the fact that

38 For a discussion of the term "legal certainty", cf. Chapter 12 of the present volume.

cross-border interaction takes place at all is, from the perspective of these contributions, not so much owing to private international law and the cooperation of governments in unifying national legal systems as to autonomous support structures created by the self-regulatory activities of private actors or by mechanisms of social control. Support structures therefore do not in all cases have to be of a formal nature: in the case of cross-border payments through banks, as well as in the reinsurance market, both Stammel and Frick argue that informal mechanisms of social control, reputation and the 'shadow of the future' seem to be more important devices than the shadow of the law.

However, the study by Stammel also underlines that informal support structures are dependent on a variety of conditions for their smooth functioning. The fundamental change in coping with dispute settlement she observes at the close of the 1980s may be attributed not least to the significantly increasing number of actors involved and a change in the business attitude of these actors, as well as intensifying costs of compliance with informal support structures. Both factors have undermined the functionality of social control and rebalanced the incentives for actors in the reinsurance game by making it increasingly attractive to defect from informal modes of conflict settlement. Not least as a consequence of these changed circumstances, the regulatory task became far more difficult and implied a new demand on public power and ordinary courts.

While the first part of the present volume deals with business claims and emphasizes the smooth working of informal support structures, the second part points to the practical difficulties 'small people' face in coping with the enforcement of cross-border claims. In the cases of legal problems arising from migration and the enforcement of cross-border maintenance claims of children, the functionality of legal provisions depends crucially on their support by public institutions. In this regard, Guibentif points to the importance of networks composed of informal personal relations between officials from different countries which have been a necessary condition not only for providing citizens with the formal right to migrate but also for enabling them to actively use it. Without the helping hand of interadministrative networks, migrants would in most cases be unable to overcome the practical problems accompanying cross-border matters. For having the chance to use their rights, they need to be 'enabled' by the state.

A similar argument is made by Grotheer in Chapter 6: without the support provided by the German Institute for Guardianship, the practical difficulties of applying multilateral or bilateral conventions would easily prove prohibitive. With an empirical focus on the mechanisms of recovering cross-border debts between Turkey and Germany, Budak underlines this point (in Chapter 1) by arguing that the number of practical difficulties which the creditor has to overcome (such as locating the address of the foreign resident debtor and communicating in a foreign language) leads him or her to refrain from the enforcement of judgments rather than to pay its costs. However, the fact that cross-border interaction takes place even under conditions of legal uncertainty is in this case again not only because of the existence of private (non-state) enforcement mechanisms (for example, factoring and forfaiting firms and commercial debt collection agencies) but maybe even more so because of informal mechanisms of compliance enforcement, such as reputation and the weighing of the benefits of defection against the benefits of iterated interaction.

Therefore the usefulness of either private international law or merchant law without the state being involved, or relying on other formalized mechanisms of compliance enforcement, is in fact restricted to those sets of games in which players interact who either put high value on their reputation or are economically powerful enough to be able to afford the costs of hiring specialized lawyers and translators as well as undertaking the necessary investigations. For the cross-border interactions of ordinary individuals, these conditions on most occasions do not apply. Iterated interaction happens only rarely and the costs of formal enforcement are very often far too high for the effort to be worthwhile. Furthermore, and sometimes this is even more important, these people very often even lack the necessary information about their rights and possibilities.[39]

Legitimacy and Local Polities

There are few topics in recent social science approaches to the study of globalization which receive more attraction from scholars than the question of legitimacy. To be sure, the question of legitimacy is a classical one which can be traced back to the very early beginnings of social theory. However, the growing consciousness of the regulatory deficits of territorial states has added new emphasis to this topic. In the world of today it is only to a lessening degree elected officials of governments who shape the externalities under which individuals and firms conduct their living, and increasingly it is forced beyond their control. Debordered structures of interac-

39 Cf. Guibentif in Chapter 7 of this volume.

tions do not comply with democratic rules but are constituted under the influence of a variety of other factors, such as market processes or decisions taken by foreign governments. Obvious examples of such influences are the decision of the French government in 1995 to undertake nuclear testing and the decisions by some investors to force a currency to devaluate.

In this context, the approach of Banakar in this volume to questioning the legitimacy of international arbitration and the *lex mercatoria* is highly interesting. In Chapter 10, Banakar directs our attention to one of the essential dilemmas of the globalization process: how can legitimacy of rules be provided when there is no single authority responsible for rule making and subject to control by democratic constituencies? Banakar tries to find an answer to this dilemma by explaining arbitration as a self-regulatory device of a restricted set of actors. His notion of 'reflexive legitimacy' puts forward the idea that legitimacy of rules can be provided if they are only flexible enough to fulfil the needs of the contracting parties while having few negative side-effects for third parties.

There can be little said against such an argument, which is surely appropriate if one restricts the focus to arbitration. However, the question of how to provide legitimacy to debordered interactions goes far beyond arbitration. While we are interested in learning how contracting parties deal with their problems, we are perhaps even more concerned with the question of how to ensure that the side-effects of the decisions of private actors are negligible to third parties. In most cases there will be little need for such a guarantee because of the restricted character of most private contracts. Inasmuch as recent trends in the OECD economy point not only to increasing interdependence of different national economies but also to a centralization of economic power under the control of transnational corporations, investment funds and the like, however, the number of cases in which the externalities of private decisions have an important impact on third parties will surely rise. And here it cannot at all suffice to restrict the question of legitimacy in cross-border interaction to its usefulness for contracting parties. Much more, we have to ask more generally how non-hierarchical postnational structures without an identifiable locus of clear authority can be organized not only to serve the interests of strong participants but also to be open to diffuse interests[40] and the legitimate concerns of individuals.

40 Cf. Norbert Reich, *Förderung und Schutz diffuser Interessen durch die Europäischen Gemeinschaften* (Baden-Baden: Nomos, 1987).

This is certainly not the place for an in-depth discussion of different concepts of legitimacy and their appropriateness for cross-border legal interaction.[41] As this chapter aims to review the contributions gathered in this volume, we will instead consider how far these contributions may help us to identify the circumstances under which diffuse interests will not only be subject to the externalities of the decisions taken by strong actors in cross-border affairs but may be able to act successfully on their own. By considering the contributions of Grotheer and Guibentif we have learned so far that individuals are, in rather rare cases, autonomously able to overcome the costs which accompany cross-border legal interaction but generally need to be enabled by public support.

Yet, as Olgiati makes clear in Chapter 5, it is not only public power which is needed to enable rather small private actors, but sometimes even more important is a specific local institutional setting in which these actors are embedded. Olgiati argues that the Chamber of Commerce in Milan may be understood as an institutional response of local actors to the challenges of a globalizing world. In being confronted with the ever-increasing need to compete in a debordered world economy, the Chamber not only provides microeconomic actors with necessary information, expertise and administrative resources but also cooperates in shaping the economic identity of the whole region. In touching upon the importance of local levels of political and economic governance, Olgiati reverses the common understanding of the global economy as a one-way street, in which the global level dominates the local level, and points to the fact that local institutions are of great importance as regards the opportunities private actors have in dealing with this new environment.[42]

This argument follows closely a rather new strand of theoretical research on world society. A growing number of researchers point to the fact that the regulatory deficits of modern states are leading to a growing demand for local levels of governance to provide functional substitutes.[43] And, indeed, the relevance of cities and

41 For an introduction to this topic, cf. Banakar in Chapter 10 of this volume and, more extensively, Giovanni Sartori, *Demokratietheorie* (Darmstadt: Wissenschaftliche Buchgesellschaft, 1992).

42 Similar approaches can be found in this volume in the contributions by Stammel and Guibentif.

43 For a debate on overlapping levels of governance, see Chapter 9 in this volume.

micro-regions has since the middle of this century increased significantly in comparison to the territorial state. Today, global cities and large urban conglomerations are not only important sites and centres of the world economy; they are gaining importance as part of an emerging linkage between local politics and world affairs, therefore exceeding their traditional role as passive reflections of statist policies. Not surprisingly, there has been since the mid-1980s an intensifying debate on the 'new regionalism'. It is no longer only states but increasingly also regions which are the most relevant units of economic activity and the loci of interest for business firms.[44] Whereas local levels of governance have for a long time been subordinated to the central bureaucracies of the territorial state,[45] this hierarchical relationship today needs some qualification. James Rosenau even argues in this regard that cities and micro-regions are likely to be major control centres in the world politics of the twenty-first century: 'They seem destined to emerge as either partners or adversaries of states as their crucial role becomes more widely recognised and they thereby move from an objective to an intersubjective existence.'[46]

Building on the contributions of this volume we surely can make no final judgment on these rather long-term perspectives for the importance of local levels of governance. However, as the contributions of Guibentif and Olgiati show, local institutions can provide important devices for managing the articulation between the economic space of flows and the social space of places, between economic functions and social experience.[47] Therefore

44 Cf. Ohmae, "The Rise of the Region State".

45 Cf. Peter J. Taylor, "World Cities and Territorial States: the Rise and Fall of their Mutuality", in *World Cities in a World-System*, ed. Paul L. Knox and Peter J. Taylor (Cambridge: Cambridge University Press, 1995), 51: "Rather than mutuality between state and city, states seemed bent on destroying cities either physically or economically."

46 James N. Rosenau, "Governance in the Twenty-First Century", *Global Governance* 1, no. 1 (1995), 27.

47 An even more visionary perspective has been formulated by William Drodziak, who interprets the recent dynamic in intercommunal networking as indicating a "resurrection of city-states", which will not only reshape but revolutionize the political landscape of Europe. He identifies a "new historical dynamism that will ultimately transform the political structure of Europe by creating a new kind

the globalization of the economy does not reduce the political importance of support structures provided by the state or by local levels of governance, but rather invests both of them with new importance by emphasizing the task of enabling private actors to cope with a debordering and therefore increasingly complex world.

Debordering the State

Investigating the problematics of establishing cross-border legal certainty in a debordering OECD system, we are witnessing a variety of challenges to the nation-state which point to the growing inadequacy of a purely territorial understanding of its functions in coping with non-territorial interactions. In summarizing the argument of this chapter we can build on three theoretical discourses and at least two important theoretical insights from the contributions to this volume. All three approaches we have reviewed were arguing that major changes are propelled by the growing importance of non-governmental actors and international as well as transnational organizations. Legal approaches therefore share with social–scientific approaches the emphasis put on the transnationalization of private interests. They also highlight the fact that non-governmental rules and institutions react to a demand by transnational private actors and provide important devices for overcoming regulatory deficiencies of the principle of territoriality by being able to guide the behaviour of transnational actors even when there is no authority to enforce them.

It has been pointed out that these transnational rules and institutions do not follow a state-centred logic but are supplied by transnational actors themselves according to their interest-specific needs. The contributions to this volume underline this argument by questioning the usefulness of an exclusive focus on the state as the main provider of regulation in cross-border interactions and argue for a widening of the analytical scope, not only by integrating private actors into the analysis, but also by pointing to the smooth working of mechanisms of private ordering. Furthermore, they challenge the dominant perspective of a 'top down' approach (from the global to the local) by giving weight to the impact of local structures on cross-border processes. The 'elitist flavour in the famous

of 'Hanseatic' League that consists of thriving city-states" (William Drodziak, "Revving up Europe's 'Four Motors'", *Washington Post*, 27 March 1994, C3).

lex mercatoria' (Gessner), however, emphasizes the fact that transnational non-governmental actors in legal affairs are primarily corporations, banks and their agents, whereas small actors face serious difficulties in dealing with the practical problems of enforcing cross-border legal claims.

In looking for the implications of this argument, we can further argue that the legal provisions of the modern welfare state will only be able to maintain the postwar level of support and protection to its citizens insofar as the understanding of its adequate functions adapt to the changing circumstances of a debordering world. Public institutions need, not only to transcend national boundaries by developing cross-border support structures for 'small people', but also to provide mechanisms for coping with the externalities of the decisions taken by transnational private actors. In analysing the role of the state in a debordering OECD system, however, one needs to accept that its historically rooted claim as being the only provider of rules in cross-border affairs is a phenomenon of the past. This is due not only to its limited resources, which cannot cope with everything, but also to the expertise provided by local levels of governance as well as by transnational non-governmental actors (including non-profit organizations as well as firms) which may be needed to help the territorial state to bridge the gap between territoriality and functionality. To be sure, the state and the international system will remain important institutions, not only for guaranteeing property rights, but also for setting the guidelines for cross-border interaction and providing diffuse interests with the necessary support for participating in national and cross-border affairs. The growing importance of mechanisms of private ordering, however, implies that the principle of territoriality, in the OECD system of today, is no longer the only ordering principle but has to compete for influence with more specific and non-territorial forms of representations of interest.

References

Baldwin, David. 1993. *Neorealism and Neoliberalism. The Contemporary Debate*. New York: Columbia University Press.

Brock, Lothar and Mathias Albert. 1995. Entgrenzung der Staatenwelt. Zur Analyse weltgesellschaftlicher Entwicklungstendenzen. *Zeitschrift für Internationale Beziehungen* 2, no. 2.

Bull, Hedley. 1979. *The Anarchical Society. A Study of Order in World Politics*. London: Macmillan.

Cammilleri, Joseph A. and Jim Falk. 1992. *The End of Sovereignty? The Politics of a Shrinking and Fragmenting World.* Aldershot: Edward Elgar.

Cerny, Phillip G. 1995. Globalization and the Changing Logic of Collective Action. *International Organization* 49, no. 4.

Cox, Robert W. 1994. Global Restructuring. Making Sense of the Changing International Political Economy. In *Political Economy and the Changing Global Order*, edited by Richard Stubbs and Geoffrey R.D. Underhill. Toronto: Macmillan.

Drodziak, William. 1994. Revving up Europe's Four Motors. *Washington Post*, 27 March.

Dunning, John H. 1993. *Multinational Enterprises and the Global Economy.* Reading, Massachusetts: Addison-Wesley.

Ferid, Murad. 1987. *Internationales Privatrecht. Das neue Recht.* Frankfurt/M.: Metzner.

Gessner, Volkmar. 1996. The Institutional Framework of Cross-Border Interaction. In *Foreign Courts – Civil Litigation in Foreign Legal Cultures*, edited by Volkmar Gessner. Aldershot: Dartmouth.

Gill, Stephen and David Law. 1993. Global Hegemony and the Structural Power of Capital. In *Gramsci, Historical Materialism and International Relations*, edited by Stephen Gill. Cambridge: Cambridge University Press.

Gilpin, Robert. 1979. *War and Change in World Politics.* Cambridge: Cambridge University Press.

Hein, Wolfgang. 1990. Die neue Weltordnung und das Ende des Nationalstaates. *Nord-Süd aktuell* 1.

Hirst, Paul and Grahame Thompson. 1996. *Globalization in Question – The International Economy and the Possibilities of Governance.* Cambridge: Polity Press.

Kapstein, Ethan B. 1991. We are Us: The Myth of the Multi-National. *The National Interest.* Winter.

Keynes, John Maynard. 1955. *Allgemeine Theory der Beschäftigung, des Zinses und des Geldes.* Berlin: Duncker & Humblot.

Krasner, Stephen D. 1983. Structural Causes and Regime Consequences: Regimes as Intervening Variables. In *International Regimes*, edited by Stephen D. Krasner. Ithaca: Cornell University Press.

Lipschutz, Ronnie D. 1992. Reconstructing World Politics: The Emergence of a Global Civil Society. *Millennium* 21, no. 3.

Macaulay, Stewart. 1973. Contract Law Among American Businessmen. In *The Social Organisation of Law,* edited by Donald Black and Maureen Mileski. New York, London: Seminar Papers.

Mann, Michael, ed. 1990. *The Rise and Decline of the Nation State*. Oxford: Basil Blackwell.

Menzel, Ulrich, Mathias Albert, Lothar Brock, Stephan Hessler and Jürgen Neyer. 1997. *Die postmoderne Weltwirtschaft. Entstofflichung und Entgrenzung der Ökonomie*. Frankfurt/M.: Surkamp.

Neyer, Jürgen. 1996. *Spiel ohne Grenzen. Weltwirtschaftliche Strukturveränderungen und das Ende des sozial kompetenten Staates*. Marburg: Tectum Verlag.

Ohmae, Kenichi. 1993. The Rise of the Region State. *Foreign Affairs* 72, no. 2.

Olson, Mancur. 1982. *The Rise and Decline of Nations. Economic Growth, Stagflation and Social Rigidities*. New Haven: Yale University Press.

Polany, Karl. 1957. *The Great Transformation: The Political and Economic Origins of Our Time*. Boston: Beacon Press.

Reich, Norbert. 1987. *Förderung und Schutz diffuser Interessen durch die Europäischen Gemeinschaften*. Baden-Baden: Nomos.

Rosecrance, Richard. 1987. *Der neue Handelsstaat: Herausforderungen für Politik und Wirtschaft*. Frankfurt/M.: Campus.

Rosenau, James N. 1990. *Turbulence in World Politics*. Brighton: Harvester Wheatsheaf.

Rosenau, James N. 1995. Governance in the Twenty-First Century. *Global Governance* 1, no. 1.

Ruggie, John. 1993. Territoriality and Beyond: Problematizing Modernity in International Relations. *International Organization* 41, no. 1.

Sartori, Giovanni. 1992. *Demokratietheorie*. Darmstadt: Wissenschaftliche Buchgesellschaft.

Schmidtchen, Dieter. 1995. Territorialität des Rechts, Internationales Privatrecht und die privatautonome Regelung internationaler Sachverhalte. *Rabels Zeitschrift für ausländisches und internationales Privatrecht* 59.

Shapiro, Martin. 1993. The Globalization of Law. *Indiana Journal of Global Legal Studies* 1, no. 1.

Slaughter, Anne-Marie. 1995. International Law in a World of Liberal States. *European Journal of International Law* 6.

Smith, John, Richard Pagnucco and Walter Romeril. 1994. Transnational Social Movement Organisations in the Global Political Arena. *Voluntas* 5, no. 2.

Taylor, Peter J. 1995. World Cities and Territorial States: the Rise and Fall of their Mutuality. In *World Cities in a World-System*, edited by Paul L. Knox and Peter J. Taylor. Cambridge: Cambridge University Press.

Tyson, Laura. 1991. They Are Not Us: Why American Ownership Still Matters. *The American Prospect*. Winter.

Waltz, Kenneth. 1979. *Theory of World Politics*. New York: McGraw-Hill.

Wriston, Walter. 1992. *The Twilight of Sovereignty*. New York: Macmillan.

Zacher, Mark W. 1992. The Decaying Pillars of the Westphalian Temple: Implications for International Order and Governance. In *Governance Without Government: Order and Change in World Politics*, edited by James N. Rosenau and Ernst-Otto Czempiel. Cambridge: Cambridge University Press.

The Author

Jürgen Neyer is a political scientist. He works as a research associate at the Zentrum für Europäische Rechtspolitik (ZERP) at the University of Bremen, Germany.

Address: ZERP, Universitätsallee GW1, 28359 Bremen, Germany.
E-mail: jneyer@zerp.uni-bremen.de

Abstract

Globalization may be understood as a socioeconomic process that gives demand to a new mixture of parallel transnational private and national public legal regulations. In order to maintain the postwar level of support and offer the same protection to its citizens, the territorial state needs to adopt an understanding of its transnational functions and to develop not only cross-border support structures for 'small people', but also mechanisms for coping with the externalities of the decisions taken by transnational private actors. In making this argument, the chapter brings together some of the theoretical findings of recent research in international relations theory, international political economy and – last but not least – the empirical studies collected in the present volume.

12 Globalization and Legal Certainty

VOLKMAR GESSNER

Transnational Infrastructures in Cross-border Legal Interaction

When legal sociology became interested in globalization processes, other disciplines had already accumulated important knowledge on what is sometimes called the 'world society'. This is true for cultural as well as for structural, for micro as well as for macro aspects. The literature relevant also for law is – on the microcultural level – the debate on intercultural communication and – on the macrostructural level – the contributions to institutional economics and to a political economy of 'the changing global order'. Legal sociological insights might fruitfully complement what has so far been produced in these disciplines because legal sociological approaches point to structural elements without which neither intercultural communication nor economic exchanges can be realized effectively. Similar to other societal contexts, the world society patterns of action develop social institutions which provide orientation and security.

Our empirical research for this project has discovered a colourful patchwork of structures which help people in their legal dealing across borders. Creditors of business claims use the court system as well as private collection agencies for the enforcement of foreign debts. They use credit reference agencies and credit insurance, but they may also get some legal assistance and practical information from consulates in foreign countries. Creditors of maintenance claims do not have this choice and depend on state support which is organized in a complex and costly way in order to bridge the institutional gap between legal cultures. Only in Germany is a semi-private institution available which complements and mostly replaces bureaucratic procedures. Migrants are highly dependent again on state structures for obtaining social security benefits from their former host countries and find their individual case reduced to a form which is filled in the same way all over Europe. Italian business was able to develop the chambers of commerce into a multifunctional agency for support in the European and global markets, compensating for weak and clientelistic government administration. Banking institutions have created their own transnational structures and do everything to avoid state interference. Insurance and reinsurance companies, on the other hand, are in the process of giving up their traditional autonomy and settle their global reinsurance deals and their more frequent disputes in law offices and the London Commercial Court.

Our theoretical discussions mainly focused on the role of the state and state law in organizing cross-border affairs. We recognized a changing role of the state but could not share the opinion of those authors who tend to disregard state-created structures in the new and rapidly developing global environment. Independently of whether the new world order is organized by nation-states or other global actors, further questions were asked concerning the legitimacy of rules and dispute settlement institutions and also concerning their efficiency in providing behavioural orientation and security. In the case of legally relevant behaviour, we speak of legal certainty.

Theoretical Approaches to Explain Legal Certainty

The term 'legal certainty' needs some explanation before we examine what psychological and economic approaches contribute to our understanding of the dilemma of legal (un)certainty in the context of global legal interaction.

First, it seems useful to distinguish between efficiency of law and legal certainty in order to separate the fields of vertical and horizontal legal relations. Interactions between state institutions and citizens are (in western democracies) defined by *Rechtsstaat* or rule of law principles and are to a certain degree independent of characteristics on the actors' levels. The law attempts to define the situation with more or less success; that is, it is more or less efficient. Horizontal relations between citizens (or business undertakings and corporations) on the other hand are very much defined by the actors. They create themselves and, eventually, with the help of support structures, the necessary degree of legal certainty. In the previous chapters of the book, as well as in the following discussion, we are mainly focusing on this latter situation.[1]

1 Hence we are not dealing with problems of governance (by nation-states, international regimes or international institutions) but rather

Whereas Theodor Geiger was for a long time influential in emphasizing the sanctioning power of law for the achievement of legal certainty (*Realisierungssicherheit*),[2] Niklas Luhmann points to mental processes which create legal certainty by establishing stable structures of expectations, or rather expectations of expectations.[3] Law is primarily not effective by coercion but by orientation of human beings.[4] Generally, normative orientation is achieved on different levels of abstraction: expectations can be integrated (kept coherent) either on the level of persons or on the more abstract levels of roles, of programmes or of values. Legal orientation can mainly be achieved on the levels of roles and programmes, that is intermediate levels of abstraction which permit both sufficient generalization and adequate differentiation of expectations, and which can be stabilized by the creation of institutions. But this model for institutionalizing normative expectations has cultural and structural prerequisites not to be found in every society. It has even been suggested that modernization processes, instead of fostering the strength of legal institutions, lead rather to what is called *normerosion*.[5] The more

with support structures provided or not by state or non-state institutions. A certain overlap of vertical and horizontal legal relations must nevertheless be admitted.

2 Theodor Geiger, *Vorstudien zu einer Soziologie des Rechts* (Neuwied: Luchterhand, 1964), 102–3. Legal certainty is based on knowledge of law (*Orientierungssicherheit*) and probability of sanctions against deviant behaviour (*Realisierungssicherheit*).

3 Niklas Luhmann, *Rechtssoziologie* (Reinbek: Rowohlt, 1972), 38, 54. Luhmann's distinction of four levels of expectations is an elaboration of Parsons' and Shils' pattern variables, universalism and particularism: cf. Talcott Parsons and Edward A. Shils, "Values, Motives, and Systems of Action", in *Toward a General Theory of Action*, ed. ibid (New York: Harper & Row, 1962), 45–243, at 82); and Talcott Parsons, *The Social System*, 4th edn (New York: The Free Press, 1968), 101–12 and *passim*.

4 Parsons, 1968, 100. German legal philosophy has a more narrow focus when it mainly deals with normative orientations of judges. Legal certainty is then the predictability of court decisions. Cf. Arthur Kaufmann and Winfried Hassemer, *Einführung in die Rechtsphilosophie der Gegenwart* (Heidelberg: Müller, 1977), 73–7.

5 Volkmar Gessner, "Kognitive Elemente sozialer Ordnung", in *Normenerosion*, ed. Monika Frommel and Volkmar Gessner (Baden-Baden: Nomos, 1996), 207–24.

societal processes are differentiated – and globalized – the less they may get integrated on the levels of roles and programmes. Cognitive mechanisms (negotiations and renegotiations, legal scientific and legal political discourses, flexible contracts, mediation) then prevail over legal certainty.

This more recent view in legal sociology seems to be overemphasized in intercultural communication research and underemphasized in institutional economics. The former only conceives uncertainty as a cognitive problem, the latter only as an institutional failure.

Intercultural communication theory deals with uncertainty as one of its main assumtions: 'Interacting with strangers is characterized by anxiety and uncertainty... Uncertainty is a cognitive phenomenon ... An increase in our ability to gather appropriate information about strangers will produce an increase in our ability to accurately predict their behavior.'[6] In Luhmann's terms, this approach explains only expectations on the lowest level of abstraction, namely the level of the person (the stranger) and neglects all three other levels where expectations may become defined (roles, programmes, values). Intercultural communication theory is a psychological approach and therefore tends to neglect structural variables. This is also true for, at face value, a very suggestive distinction between 'low uncertainty avoidance' and 'high uncertainty avoidance' cultures.[7] This focus on cultural values which either tolerate or avoid ambiguity in interpersonal interactions again isolates one of the four levels where expectations may become defined, and is based on the problematic assumption that cultural values determine structural developments of a society. Indian society, as a 'low uncertainty avoidance' culture, obviously has structural elements like the castes (role level) and the Hindu and Moslem religions (programme level) where uncertainties are eliminated to an extreme degree.The Indian tolerance of uncertainties is confined to those few areas which are not directly defined by those roles and

6 William B. Gudykunst, "Anxiety/Uncertainty Management (AUM) Theory – Current Status", in *Intercultural Communication Theory*, ed. Richard L. Wiseman (Thousand Oaks/London/New Delhi: Sage, 1995), 8–58, at 10, 41.

7 Geert Hofstede, *Culture's Consequences: International differences in work-related values*: Beverly Hills, CA: Sage, 1980); idem, "National Cultures in Four Dimensions: A Research-based Theory of Cultural Differences Among Nations", *International Studies of Management and Organizations* 13 (1983), 46–74.

programmes. Disregarding these limitations, intercultural communication theory contributes to our discussion on legal (un)certainty in global legal communication important cognitive and cultural aspects which are certainly overlooked in legal discourses.

The process of 'structuration' of the world order is made the object of analysis of important empirical studies mainly in political sciences, international relations research and peace research. Of particular interest in our context is the concept of international regimes, because it points to structural elements which in most cases have a legal character: regimes are 'principles, norms, rules and decision-making procedures around which actor expectations converge in a given issue area'.[8] This concept is used mainly for explaining cooperation among nation-states. It replaces more and more in political science the focus on international organizations and describes the networks which in some areas have been established in the international arena. The same idea of conceptualizing cross-border networks could also be adopted by legal sociology which deals with individual behaviour rather than state actors. In order to distinguish between the two levels of action – the individual and the state levels – we prefer to use another more traditional term, namely '"Third cultures" learned by men of different societies who are in the process of relating their societies, or sections thereof, to each other'.[9] But the idea behind both terms is quite the same.

Insofar as global exchanges are economic exchanges, and this is certainly true for most cross-border interactions, there is a strong emphasis on institutions in the recent work of Douglass C. North, whose merit lies in making use of established sociological knowledge for classical economic theory.[10] He criticizes the explanation of economic success only by rational choice in classical economic theory by pointing to incomplete information of the actor: 'The costliness of information is the key to the costs of transacting,

8 S.D. Krasner (ed.), *International Regimes*, quoted in John Vogler, "Regimes and Global Commons: Space, Atmosphere and Oceans", in *Global Politics*, ed. Anthony G. McGrew, Paul G. Lewins *et al.* (Cambridge: Polity Press, 1992), 122.

9 John Useem, Ruth Useem and John Donoghue, "Men in the Middle of the Third Culture: The Roles of American and Non-Western People in Cross-Cultural Administration", *Human Organisation* 22 (1963), 169–79.

10 Douglass C. North, *Institutions, Institutional Change and Economic Performance* (Cambridge: Cambridge University Press, 1990).

which consist of the costs of measuring the valuable attributes of what is being exchanged and the costs of protecting rights and policing and enforcing agreements.'[11] These transaction costs are a function of the institutional framework of legal rules, support structures, judicial enforcement and informal patterns of behaviour. In our context, it is important to note how much importance North attributes to effective third party enforcement in the historically most advanced form of exchange, the impersonal exchange. Third party enforcement reduces transaction costs and hence contributes to economic growth.

The problem of transaction costs in cross-border economic exchanges has become a major issue in discussions of the World Trade Organization, the World Bank, the OECD and the European Union. The debates become more and more aware of legal certainty as a key factor in reducing transaction costs and in the weakness of the institutional framework so far created for world trade, consumption in foreign countries and global financial deals. Among the empirical studies attempting to describe and even quantify the negative effects of legal uncertainties caused by weak legal institutions is one carried out (for the Commission of the European Union) by the Bremen research group on 'Global Legal Interaction'. The study qualifies domestic institutions in Europe as mostly ill-adapted for international legal matters and estimates the annual loss for economic wealth in the Single Market, caused only by legal uncertainty for European consumers, at between ECU7 billion and ECU73 billion.[12]

Political science and institutional economics both complement cognitive and cultural conceptions of global uncertainties developed in intercultural communication theories but overemphasize the structural prerequisites of the world society. They have always to be read against the background of their disciplines, where utilitarian approaches prevailed for more than two centuries and still dominate analyses of political and economic behaviour. Institutions in transaction cost approaches are to be understood only as complementary to market (cognitive) elements of economic choices.

11 Ibid., 27.

12 Hanno von Freyhold, Volkmar Gessner, Enzo Vial and Helmut Wagner, eds, *Cost of Judicial Barriers for Consumers in the Single Market*, Report for the European Commission (Consumer Policy Service) (Bremen: Zentrum für Europäische Rechtspolitik an der Universität Bremen (ZERP), 1995).

Global exchanges require more and more complex devices which sociology describes on the level of (national) societies as 'social institutions'; that is, relatively stable action patterns which reduce the uncertainties with respect to the behaviour of other individuals in the process of human interaction. Social institutions mainly help the actor making choices without necessarily executing formal and informal sanctions against deviant behaviour. They are considered as indispensable coordination mechanisms even by those approaches in sociology which are critical of systems-theoretical and functional approaches.

Social institutions are relatively stable patterns of behavioural expectations on the levels of roles and programmes. They do not necessarily have an organizational structure, but may derive their relative stability also from customs and – as the case of the *lex mercatoria* demonstrates – from commercial practice.

A sociology of the world society and particularly a legal sociology of the world society will have to deal primarily with social institutions in the above-mentioned sense. These institutions have a Janus quality: they are part of a societal structure but develop their own culture in implementing rules and programmes. The following discussion on global institutions as support structures for cross-border interactions attempts to relate some of our empirical observations to the problem of legal (un)certainty in the global arena.

Institutions Providing Global Legal Certainty

The social institutions providing (or not) stable action patterns in legally relevant situations (on the horizontal level) are rules, courts, legal professions and support structures. Institutions created in order to foster legal certainty for cross-border legal interaction can then be distinguished as those located on the programme level and those on the role level (see Table 12.1).

Legal Rules

In our previous study[13] the role of state law (private international law and international conventions) and of state courts in reducing insecurity of cross-border exchanges has been discussed and – as regards international cases in domestic courts – made the

13 Volkmar Gessner, ed., *Foreign Courts – Civil Litigation in Foreign Legal Cultures* (Aldershot: Dartmouth, 1996).

Table 12.1: Social Institutions for Cross-border Legal Interaction

	Programs	Roles
State	International private law	Judges in international cases
	International conventions	Central authorities in the fields of international legal assistance Consulates
Non-State	Law merchant	Institutions of third cultures
	Rules of third cultures	Chambers of commerce Commercial associations Non-commercial institutions Law firms Arbitrators Brokers Debt collection agencies

object of empirical research. The system of state conventions appeared to be very weak in guiding global legal interactions because of its lacking universality and its being frequently disregarded in legal practice. It was found that courts handled international cases like domestic cases, unable to consider foreign elements of the cases and uninformed as regards foreign law. Legal certainty may only be provided to those parties whose law is applied. Owing to the fact that domestic courts do not take much notice of court opinions in other countries, we also observed hardly any international legal developments initiated by case law. The globalization of law is still mainly an exercise of legal science and international organisations and has not as yet reached far into judicial practice.

This is also true of the *lex mercatoria*. The law merchant is spoken of under a number of names, including international, transnational or supranational commercial law; international customs or usages; general principles of international commercial law; and *lex mercatoria*. Regardless of the label, the same phenomenon, a set of rules encompassing the trading practices of the international merchant community, is being described. The ambit of the *lex mercatoria* is determined by the object of its constituent elements, but also by its origin and its customary, and thus spontaneous, nature.[14] Elements of this legal order are the following:

- general principles of law recognized by the commercial nations;
- universal rules like the Uniform Customs and Practices for Documentary Credits;
- universally used contract clauses like the INCOTERMS;
- universally used standard form contracts;
- codes of conduct;
- arbitral awards.

This normative order is far from being comprehensive and may therefore in many cases lead to insecurity and uncertainty about the legal situation. One must often seek guidance from sources other than the law merchant, in particular from state law, or must invent a new solution. In addition, most state courts refuse to apply the *lex mercatoria* and even refuse to enforce arbitration awards based on these autonomous rules. Hence arbitrators are also reluctant to refer to this set of rules.

It appears from these discussions that legal certainty cannot be achieved globally on the level of programmes. Programmes are a relatively abstract form of integrating expectations which requires a minimum of homogeneity of its legal subjects. Because of differences in their economic position, highly industrialized and developing societies will not integrate their expectations easily. Negative examples of unified (civil) law conventions which were signed and ratified by only a few countries are abundant. The positive exceptions of numerous ratifications are to be found mainly in procedural law (such as the UNCITRAL Arbitration Conventions and the Hague Conventions) and – as regards substantive law – in transport law. Ole Lando perceives many situations in which the application of the *lex mercatoria* provides legal certainty. This is certainly true for some of the *lex mercatoria* rules which are universally recognized and applied in legal practice, such as the Uniform Customs and Practices for Documentary Credit and the INCOTERMS. Equally, a number of trade norms and standard conditions help to secure cross-border commercial transactions. Export trade could not be

14 Michael T. Medwig, "The New Law Merchant: Legal Rhetoric and Commercial Reality", *Law and Policy in International Business* 24 (1993), 589–616.

imagined without these autonomously created legal instruments. But even these *lex mercatoria* rules are universal only in part because some areas of commercial activities are far from being homogeneous globally. In particular, Third World legal actors complain of a bias in favour of the interests of industrialized nations.

Other failures of integration on the level of programmes are based on cultural differences which already hinder the ratification of many international conventions and certainly influence the implementation of global legal programmes. Unlike the European Union, where the European Court of Justice effectively directs the application and interpretation of European law, there is no such court with a global jurisdiction. The implementation of international conventions is left to the judicial styles of courts and the claim consciousness of parties of different legal cultures in the world. Last but not least, geographical aspects are responsible for unsurmountable differences. For example, standards for environmental protection are more relevant for some parts of the world because of their geographical location and relative economic wealth and therefore do not lead to universal integration of expectations.

Our empirical studies observed the weaknesses of programmes like the (Brussels) Convention on the Recognition and Enforcement of Foreign Judgments, the (Vienna) Convention on the International Sale of Goods, the (Hague) Legal Assistance Conventions and domestic international private law as regards state programmes. *Lex mercatoria* rules were hardly found at all in fields of legal practice observed in the course of our empirical and comparative research.

Legal science and international institutions active in the production of globalized law are very aware of the weakness of their programmes but generally do not question the programme level of global regulation as such. Notwithstanding this programme optimism, they have also been active at the roles level, creating and fostering the autonomous creation of global legal institutions.

Professions

Expectations which are integrated by roles are placed on a lower level of abstraction and may therefore be more suited to the global type of interaction. They are more specific to areas of action such as those of the customs officer, the stewardess or the hotel receptionist. Travellers know their expectations and expect them to be realized in quite a similar way all around the world. Some legal roles like those of lawyers, brokers, notaries, arbitrators and law professors are likewise relatively well defined globally and are able to create and support universal legal orientations. These orientations are legal not because they are supported by law (which is the programme level) but by legal roles. As regards arbitrators, this was well demonstrated by Dezalay and Garth: members of the international arbitration 'club' have a common understanding of legal principles and legal procedures. Parties who opt for arbitration know perfectly well the (international commercial) principles for the decisions and the basic ideas of the arbitrators. The circle of international arbitrators consists of only some 200–300 people from whom the parties choose those they know from previous arbitration procedures or published awards or legal practice.[15] In this highly personalized situation, their expectations as to the outcome of the dispute seem to be more secure than when anonymous state courts decide the cases.

This view is strongly supported by Ole Lando, who asserts that 'arbitrators of different nationalities who have applied the *lex mercatoria* in collegiate arbitral tribunals have not experienced great difficulties in reaching consensus ... Most arbitrators have common ethics and common notions of how business should be conducted that lead them in the same direction.'[16]

As regards the legal professions all around the world, first one has to state that, in general, lawyers get little to no training in international or foreign aspects of law and are mostly unable to handle cross-border cases. Private individuals therefore get no legal advice on the international matters with which they are more and more confronted: in family affairs, consumer affairs and tourism.[17] Only larger business actors find legal advice in international law firms (mostly of US-American provenance) who draft their contracts in such a way as to protect them against any state law influence. These complex contracts are indeed able to provide a high degree of legal certainty. The lawyers' role is to provide legal

15 Yves Dezalay and Bryant Garth, *Dealing in Virtue: International Commercial Arbitration and the Construction of a Transnational Legal Order* (Chicago: University of Chicago Press, 1996).

16 Ole Lando, "The Lex Mercatoria in International Commercial Arbitration", *International and Comparative Law Quarterly* 34 (1985), 747–68.

17 Cf. Hanno von Freyhold, Volkmar Gessner, Enzo Vial and Helmut Wagner, eds, *The Cost of Civil Litigation for Consumers in the Single Market*, Report to the EU-Kommission (Bremen, 1995).

information on domestic and on foreign law, to develop new financial instruments and sophisticated drafting, negotiating and deal making techniques, to resolve disputes out of court[18] and to bridge the gap between legal cultures.[19] To that extent, their situation is comparable to that of the 'arbitration club': because the number of players is limited, their role is defined by a set of global behavioural patterns which is often maintained by frequent contacts (there exist only a few centres in the world where most of these law firms are located) and exchanges in networks, journals and the Internet mailboxes. International lawyers may not yet have formed an autonomous community comparable to the 'arbitration club', but, as legal representatives in negotiations, litigators or in-house councils, they are of considerable economic and legal influence and have the power to create a certain degree of legal certainty simply by the fact that they monopolize legal interactions of all important global actors. It seems to be a common situation that Chinese, Egyptian, German and Malaysian firms are internationally represented in contract negotiations by US-American law firms just like their US commercial partners. There is no 'third culture' of law firms around the world, but US law firms clearly have been able to define the roles an international lawyer has to play if he or she wishes to succeed in the global market of legal services.

It is true that even experienced US-American law firms report frequent interaction problems in their global dealings, in contract negotiation and conflict resolution.[20] But they are in the process of creating a surprising variety of networks, training centres and courses, international libraries and international associations which will enable them soon to feel almost at home in the global legal market – at least as long as the US and common law domination prevails.

Rather than focusing on arbitrators and international law firms (an area in which we have not carried out much empirical research)

18 Our court file analyses in Bremen, Hamburg, Milan and New York support the assumption that disputes over complex contracts are never taken to court. Cf. Volkmar Gessner (ed.), *Foreign Courts*.

19 Roger J. Goebel, "Professional Qualification and Educational Requirements for Law Practice in a Foreign Country: Bridging the Cultural Gap", *Tulane L.Rev* 63 (1989), 443–523.

20 Sunwolf, "Communication between Legal Cultures: Strategies, Perceptions and Beliefs of American Lawyers Who Practice International Litigation", in *Interaction of Legal Cultures*, ed. Johannes Feest and Volkmar Gessner (Oñati: Oñati Pre-Publications, 1998).

we will proceed with a discussion on the possible contribution to legal certainty of other types of support structures which can be observed in the world society: institutions of the law merchant, in particular institutions of global 'third cultures', as well as other support structures whether created by state initiative or by non-state actors.

Third Cultures

These structures, like the aforementioned professional communities, do have a set of rules common to all members but in the main integrate expectations on a much lower level than the programme level. They develop well defined roles and expect their 'clients' also to observe very specific behavioural patterns. Global differentiation of social fields, rather than creating anomic situations, shapes secure expectation structures, the only problem being how to get into the subsystem.

Third cultures as conceived above are regular phenomena of the *lex mercatoria* as well as of global non-business communities. They develop in the world society just as semi-autonomous fields develop in national societies, are defined by a limited number of actors who share (economic or idealist) interests, have common ethics and follow the same patterns and customs. Worldwide third cultures are the scientific communities, the mafias, the religious communities and above all those commercial branches which were able to a large degree to monopolize the area of their activities. The example of the diamond industry as well as those studies elaborated in the course of our own project (the banking sector and the London reinsurance market) may illustrate their characteristic way of creating autonomous behavioural patterns and the high degree of 'legal' certainty all members can rely on.

The diamond industry, that internationally active and economically important branch of business, has been carefully studied by Lisa Bernstein.[21] In the market of rough diamonds, 80–85 per cent of the world's supply is controlled by the De Beers cartel, which distributes the rough diamonds through four brokers. The brokers sell presorted boxes of diamonds to some 150–200 dealers, known as sight-holders, during 10 viewing sessions, held in London each year. Sight-holders together with manufacturers, wholesalers and

21 Lisa Bernstein, "Opting Out of the Legal System: Extralegal Contractual Relations in the Diamond Industry", *Journal of Legal Studies* 21 (1992), 115–57.

brokers, are members of the worldwide 20 diamond dealers clubs which secure the steady supply of goods. Although it is possible to buy stones on the 'open market', a dealer who does not have access to the trading clubs – essential links with the worldwide diamond distribution network, the 'World Federation of Diamond Bourses' – will be at a competitive disadvantage. The clubs or bourses therefore can exercise a strict control over their local or foreign members and impose their own rules and dispute resolution mechanism. Non-compliance means loss of reputation (the name of the rule-breaker is circulated to all of the bourses in the world federation) and in practice exclusion from the diamond business. The system remains completely apart from state penal law, contract law and bankruptcy law, and state courts are replaced by arbitration or on occasion by proceedings in Jewish rabbinical courts.

The diamond cartel is not so much integrated on the programme level but has developed specific roles like sight-holders, brokers, club members, arbitrators and the rabbi within which expectations are defined and implemented. It seems irrelevant to which legal culture the actors belong, because the diamond dealers' culture is a global culture independent of national legal or legal cultural influences.

Recent information in the media seems to indicate that the De Beers cartel will come under pressure from diamond producers so far not active in the cartel (such as the countries of the former Soviet Union). New global actors might destroy cultural patterns of global interaction and quickly reduce successful structures of legal certainty.

In Klaus Frick's research project,[22] the international activities of the banks are in a similar way described as a 'third culture' where all actors have 'opted out of the legal system'. As in the diamond trade, there is only a limited number of actors and strong control over compliance with usages, contracts, verbal commitments and standard forms. Despite the enormous number of transactions and the gigantic amounts of money transferred worldwide, disputes hardly ever arise. Some few cases go to arbitration and hardly any to state courts. The system has been rationalized for centuries and has recently been computerized in order to avoid errors and misunderstandings. The personnel have well-defined roles and are trained carefully to comply with global behavioural standards. No elaborated programme is integrating mutual expectations all over the world, but roles are clearly defined up to the pinstripe suit of

22 Chapter 4 of the present volume.

higher-ranking executives. And the institutions do everything to negotiate problems that arise and will rather write losses off than go to third party dispute resolution – to say nothing of litigation.

As far as state law exists (letters of credit, documentary credit, cheques) it has been prepared with the strong participation of the banking sector. Recent attempts of the European Union to gain some control (for example, over the costs of money transfer in the Union or over money laundering) have so far been successfully held back in order to allow for autonomous solutions of the problems. Regulatory interventions might in this specific case be successful on the programme level owing to the homogeneous structure of the European banking sector. But this is true only for the European Union, where the programme level is used frequently and with not completely unrealistic chances of implementation. Universally, the banking sector is integrated on the role level rather than on the programme level.

Christine Stammel's research project concerns the 'third culture' of the reinsurance business.[23] This business is to a very high degree dominated by international actors who participate in global exchange. A major market-place is the City of London, where a number of brokers bring the reinsurers and their clients, the ceding offices (the primary insurers who are seeking insurance cover) together. The contractual practices in use are extremely informal. The broker drafts a 'slip' which is nothing but a paper which documents the contract conditions in a short form. He will also collect the premium from the ceding office and deduct his share before he passes the money on to the reinsurer. His task is, furthermore, to collect the claims arising under the reinsurance contract and he will sustain the communication between reinsurer and ceding office. This picture of informal contracts and relationships based on trust rather than on law is very much akin to Stanley's description of the subcultural code of ethics in the City of London.[24] Disputes until recently were resolved only by arbitration. In the last few years a series of catastrophes started which hit the market hard. The fact that documentation of reinsurance contracts had been treated as a 'stepchild' in the past was an

23 Chapter 3 of the present volume. Her doctoral dissertation on the same subject will be published soon (Christine Stammel, *Waving the Gentlemen's Business Good-Bye*, Frankfurt/Main: Peter Lang Verlag, 1998).

24 Christopher Stanley, "Serious Money: Legitimation of Deviancy in the Financial Markets", *International Journal of the Sociology of Law* 20 (1992), 43–60.

invitation at least to try to avoid payments under the policy. Under economic pressure and the growing number of actors, the autonomy of this 'third culture' apparently breaks down. Disputes lead more frequently to litigation before the London Commercial Court where highly specialized judges (possibly experienced in the reinsurance business in their previous role as barristers) seem to have gained the confidence of the reinsurance business. This is probably not a shift to the programme level but rather a development on the level of roles: insiders are replaced by external experts who are able to deal with the rising complexity of reinsurance issues. The community of experts involved in these issues remains small: it consists of some 30 London City law firms and a handful of High Court judges.

Support Structures

Most state support structures for cross-border legal interaction work on the basis of a programme, a municipal law or an international convention. Consulates execute the consular law, central authorities mostly execute a legal assistance convention, domestic judges are guided by private international law or some unified law. But there is empirical evidence that, if these structures offer legal certainty at all, this is due to specific roles: a judge specializing in commercial cases or a member of a chamber for international matters,[25] a civil servant experienced in cross-border matters such as social security of migrants,[26] a consul with a legal background able to understand the law and the legal culture of the host country.[27] If

25 Cf. Christine Stammel regarding the judges in the London Commercial Court, in the present volume; and Volkmar Gessner, International Cases in German First Instance Courts, in idem (ed.), *Foreign Courts*, pp. 149–207, at 181–5 with regard to the judges in the Hamburg international chambers.

26 Cf. Pierre Guibentif (Chapter 7 of the present volume) who found that cross-border social security rights are protected in Portugal thanks only to an administrative network of contacts otherwise atypical in the context of Portuguese administrative culture. This network creates a special relationship between officials all of whom are particularly concerned with the problems of Portuguese emigrants abroad.

27 Cf. Andreas Petzold (Chapter 8 of the present volume). The overall picture of the quality of legal advice given by consulates is one of a few thoughtful, creative responses, and a few dreadfully ignorant and useless replies. The great majority provide some of the infor-

the programmes determined the practice of these support structures, the latter would show similar patterns of behaviour. This is not the case, neither in an international comparison (for example, German and New York and Spanish judges) nor even in a national comparison (German consuls in the Netherlands and German consuls in Kuala Lumpur).

The focus on roles is equally justified in regard to non-state support structures. Lawyers and arbitrators have already been mentioned in their well-defined international business for well-defined groups of global actors. Whereas most lawyers and most arbitrators are unfamiliar with international matters, a small number of those professionals are highly experienced but only accessible to important business enterprises who act in the main outside state-provided patterns. Neither commercial institutions (like the national chambers of commerce, the foreign chambers of commerce or the International Chamber of Commerce in Paris) nor the headquarters of commercial branches or commercial services (like the debt collection agencies[28] or the brokers in insurance business[29]) nor non-commercial institutions (like those supporting child support claims[30]) are executing a universal or in some way general

mation that is required and obtainable, but remain below the potential the existing sources allow.

28 Ali Cem Budak, in Chapter 1 of the present volume. According to this study, debt collection agencies have developed a bundle of strategies for collecting foreign debts and are highly successful whenever they use renegotiation instead of law enforcement.

29 Christine Stammel, in Chapter 3 of this volume. Brokers handle reinsurance contracts in a surprisingly informal way and often only write down on a "slip" what seem to be the essentials of the insurance cover. Neither legal nor law merchant rules define this situation. Recently, more and more lawyers are becoming involved in contract drafting and conflict resolution, which may lead to some reinsurance contract law; that is, to the development of expectations on the level of programmes.

30 Cf. Kirstin Grotheer (Chapter 6 of this volume). This study gives the impression of a legal "overkill" of legal assistance and law enforcement conventions, leading to extraordinary bureaucratic efforts, costs and delays. Some small institutions with a modest budget seem to handle cross-border maintenance claims much better. As Grotheer suggests, they provide on the basis of experience and contacts a feeling of legal certainty in an otherwise rather anomic situation.

programme. They render (or not) legal certainty to very specific clients by complying (or not) with very specific expectations, making use of complex devices of which an international convention might be a part. A good example is the Milan Chamber of Commerce,[31] which serves the local industry by providing assistance in its domestic and international dealings without referring to programmes or state rules and even without using *lex mercatoria* rules or arbitration.

Winners and Losers of Global Legal Uncertainty

Legal certainty is a complex phenomenon which consists of shared normative expectations and of trust in compliance. Studies in comparative law show the different ways this goal can be achieved in national legal systems. A sociolegal comparison in addition demonstrates that not only legal structures but also social structures with autonomous rules and sanction mechanisms succeed in providing legal certainty. Globally, legal and social structures compete in offering better solutions. Our brief overview has compared the contributions of state law (including international conventions), law merchant and third cultures to securing stable expectations and predictable behaviour. All in all, the picture we have offered suggests little success in achieving legal certainty on the programme level. Legal certainty increases from transactions governed by state law, over transactions governed by the law merchant, to transactions governed by third cultural mechanisms. The non-state mechanisms, in spite of the relative security which they offer to their 'clients', seem fragile and may break down whenever the number of actors increases (this may be the case already in some international transactions, such as consumer transactions), whenever the transaction costs of third party decision making surpass the transaction costs avoided by the creation of third party intervention (this may be the case with arbitration) or whenever economic interests prevail over group solidarity (this is the situation in the

31 Cf. Vittorio Olgiati on the Milan Chamber of Commerce in Chapter 5 of this volume. He describes this institution as being based in the Mussolini era on Fascist corporatism. During that period the chambers of commerce in Italy were conceived in legal terms as a sort of economic prefecture. Since 1993, they have constituted a system of autonomous institutions performing functions of general interest as well as providing private support, assistance and advice.

reinsurance market). In spite of interesting global developments in favour of securing economic exchanges, legal certainty is accomplished successfully and in a stable way neither by state legal devices nor by *lex mercatoria*, nor by norms and behavioural patterns created autonomously within third cultures. Some specific roles create legal certainty for some specific groups, but most global actors, such as small and medium-sized enterprises, consumers, members of binational families, migrants and victims of accidents in foreign countries, gain no access to these groups and cannot make use of qualified support structures.

This leads us to a step across the borders of our own discipline which we would like to discuss briefly. If global exchanges remain for the time being to a large degree insecure, it would be interesting to observe whether cultural, in addition to structural, elements contribute to defining the chances of legal certainty. Intercultural communication theory tells us that some societies socialize their members into accepting the uncertainty of the future and not become upset by it. People of such 'weak uncertainty avoidance societies' will readily take risks and do not develop support structures for risk avoidance. Other societies socialize their people into trying to 'beat' the future. Because the future remains essentially unpredictable, in those societies there will be a higher level of anxiety in people. Such 'strong uncertainty avoidance societies' have institutions that try to create security and avoid risk, among others legal institutions, public law and private contracts.[32] It follows that those actors socialized in uncertainty avoidance societies will suffer more from the uncertainty of global exchanges than their counterparts to whom uncertainty is familiar and who have experience in coping with unstructured situations.

According to Hofstede, Germany is among those uncertainty avoidance societies. This explains why Germany has not only developed highly efficient domestic structures which organize and secure daily life, but is also particularly active in legalizing and institutionalizing cross-border exchanges. But if these institutions do not accomplish their goals, German actors may easily get lost in the global arena. They are not used to being confronted with ambiguous or anomic situations and therefore experience them as chaos,

32 Geert Hofstede, "The Cultural Relativity of Organizational Practices and Theories", *Journal of International Business Studies* 14 (1983), 1–91; Volkmar Gessner, "Global Legal Interaction and Legal Cultures", *Ratio Juris* 7 (1994), 132–45.

disorder and fraud. Other cultures may feel almost at home in the world society. This could already be true for Italians who experience weak and inefficient state structures at home but have become accustomed to coping with failing institutions by – in Luhmann's terms – integrating expectations on the level of the person. They may therefore be able to handle unstructured cross-border situations equally well. The fifth place in international trade of Italy, which is only in its northern part a highly industrialized country, would support this hypothesis. The best examples of success with a particularistic approach on the global market are certainly Asian legal cultures which prefer to base their contractual relations on interpersonal loyalties. The Chinese business culture is widely believed to rest on values that denigrate formal law in favour of personal relations and networks termed *guanxi*, networks which link mainland China with ethnic Chinese all over the world and fully secure exchanges in global operations.[33] Western businessmen are generally advised to take this informal approach into account in their dealings with Asia. They might even have to completely renounce their legalistic approaches if the next century is largely shaped by Asian expansion and, in particular, China's economic growth.

Another distinction, which might be added to the previous one, could be made between global *legal* actors in particular. Those legal actors trained in the civil law tradition are used to dealing with programmes (and not roles or persons). They need statutes in order to have a feeling of security. International cases have to be subsumed under written law – if possible with the help of huge commentaries. In the phase of contract drafting, they need institutional support where legal information and advice are provided. This, as we have seen, is definitely not the situation in global legal affairs. Common law lawyers might be much better equipped to cope with this strange mix of inefficient international conventions, soft law and case law which is typical of the global legal arena. They are used to relying much more on their own research, on creative drafting of contracts and on autonomously established global networks. They are more 'professional', which again means they are role- and not programme-oriented. If this distinction is

33 Richard P. Appelbaum, *Business as Bribery: The Future of Law in a Global Economy*, paper presented at the workshop on Interaction of Legal Cultures (Oñati: Oñati Pre-Publications 1998).

true, continental legal education systematically produces global losers.

The question remains, what follows from our observation that the world society provides such a different form of behavioural (and legal) certainty? National societies integrate legal expectations on the levels of programmes and roles, whereas the world society seems to integrate them on the lower levels of roles and persons. Obviously, one consequence is the absence – compared to the national political field – of democratic participation (which is mainly focused on the legislative process, that is the programme level). Another aspect is the further differentiation of societal structures into a myriad of global subsystems.[34] Not only political science,[35] but also legal sociology, are challenged to develop new paradigms of 'social order'. Normative expectations can be maintained only in regard to very specific 'life worlds': a firm or a business branch, but not the consumer or the foreign state; a law firm, but not the foreign court. This means that for a global sociology of law many established concepts such as rules, legal consciousness, access to law and legitimacy have to be newly defined. The last aspect of the global construction of legitimacy[36] has been elaborated by Reza Banakar in the context of international commercial arbitration and could be generalized in areas such as European law and international conventions. New structural devices for the creation of legal certainty have to be taken into account. As regards contract law, cognitive processes of drafting, negotiating or contract adaptation have to be taken much more seriously in law and legal education than is actually to be observed at the end of an era dominated by state law and national legal cultures.

References

Appelbaum, Richard P. 1997. Business as Bribery: The Future of Law in a Global Economy. Paper presented at the workshop on Changing Legal Cultures II. Oñati: Oñati Pre-Publications 1998.

Bernstein, Lisa. 1992. Opting Out of the Legal System: Extralegal

34 Niklas Luhmann, "The World Society as a Social System", *International Journal of General Systems* 8 (1982), 131–8.

35 Cf. the contributions of Anthony McGrew and Jürgen Neyer in Chapters 9 and 11 of this volume.

36 Cf. Reza Banakar in Chapter 10 of this volume.

Contractual Relations in the Diamond Industry. *Journal of Legal Studies* 21.

Dezalay, Yves and Bryant Garth. 1996. *Dealing In Virtue: International Commercial Arbitration and the Construction of a Transnational Legal Order*. Chicago: University of Chicago Press.

Freyhold, Hanno von, Volkmar Gessner, Enzo Vial and Helmut Wagner, eds. 1995. *Cost of Judicial Barriers for Consumers in the Single Market*. Report for the European Commission (Consumer Policy Service). Bremen: Zentrum für Europäische Rechtspolitik an der Universität Bremen.

Geiger, Theodor. 1964. *Vorstudien zu einer Soziologie des Rechts*. Neuwied: Luchterhand.

Gessner, Volkmar. 1994. Global Legal Interaction and Legal Cultures. *Ratio Juris* 7.

Gessner, Volkmar, ed. 1996. *Foreign Courts – Civil Litigation in Foreign Legal Cultures*. Aldershot: Dartmouth.

Gessner, Volkmar. 1996. Kognitive Elemente sozialer Ordnung. In *Normenerosion*, edited by Monika Frommel and Volkmar Gessner. Baden-Baden: Nomos.

Goebel, Roger J. 1989. Professional Qualification and Educational Requirements for Law Practice in a Foreign Country: Bridging the Cultural Gap. *Tulane Law Review* 63.

Gudykunst, William B. 1995. Anxiety/Uncertainty Management AUM Theory – Current Status. In *Intercultural Communication Theory*, edited by Richard L. Wiseman. Thousand Oaks, London, New Delhi: Sage.

Hofstede, Geert. 1980. *Culture's Consequences: International differences in work-related values*. Beverly Hills, California: Sage.

Hofstede, Geert. 1983. National Cultures in Four Dimensions: A Research-based Theory of Cultural Differences Among Nations. *International Studies of Management and Organizations* 13.

Hofstede, Geert. 1983. The Cultural Relativity of Organizational Practices and Theories. *Journal of International Business Studies* 14.

Kaufmann, Arthur and Winfried Hassemer. 1977. *Einführung in die Rechtsphilosophie der Gegenwart*. Heidelberg: Müller.

Lando, Ole. 1985. The Lex Mercatoria in International Commercial Arbitration. *International and Comparative Law Quarterly* 34.

Luhmann, Niklas. 1972. *Rechtssoziologie*. Reinbek: Rowohlt.

Luhmann, Niklas. 1982. The World Society as a Social System. *International Journal of General Systems* 8.

Medwig, Michael T. 1993. The New Law Merchant: Legal Rhetoric and Commercial Reality. *Law and Policy in International Business* 24.

North, Douglass C. 1990. *Institutions, Institutional Change and Economic Performance.* Cambridge: Cambridge University Press.

Parsons, Talcott. 1968. *The Social System.* 4th edn. New York: The Free Press.

Parsons, Talcott and Edward A. Shils. 1962. Values, Motives and Systems of Action. In *Toward a General Theory of Action*, edited by Talcott Parsons and Edward A. Shils. New York: Harper & Row.

Stammel, Christine. Forthcoming. *Waving the Gentlemen's Business Good-Bye.*

Stanley, Christopher. 1992. Serious Money: Legitimation of Deviancy in the Financial Markets. *International Journal of the Sociology of Law* 20.

Sunwolf. 1998. Communication between Legal Cultures: Strategies, Perceptions and Beliefs of American Lawyers Who Practice International Litigation. In *Interaction of Legal Cultures*, ed. Johannes Feest and Volkmar Gessner. Oñati: Oñati Pre-Publications.

Useem, John, Ruth Useem and John Donoghue. 1963. Men in the Middle of the Third Culture: The Roles of American and Non-Western People in Cross-Cultural Administration. *Human Organisation* 22.

Vogler, John. 1992. Regimes and Global Commons: Space, Atmosphere and Oceans. In *Global Politics*, edited by Anthony G. McGrew, Paul G. Lewins *et al.* Cambridge: Polity Press.

The Author

Volkmar Gessner is Professor of Comparative Law and Sociology of Law at the University of Bremen and, from 1997 to 1999, Visiting Professor at the University of California, Santa Barbara. Since 1992, he has directed the Bremen research group on 'Global Legal Interaction'.

Address: Law Faculty, University of Bremen, 28359 Bremen, Germany.

E-mail: Bremen: vgessner@barkhof.uni-bremen.de.; California: gessner@alishaw.sscf.ucsb.edu.

Abstract

This concluding chapter attempts to go beyond the empirical evidence of state versus autonomous regulation in specific fields of global legal interaction. If regulation is at issue, the debate always refers to the problems of societal order, that is to social control and/or behavioural orientation. In horizontal relations which are the object of the civil law rules, this latter aspect is predominant. Behavioural orientation, in legal and legal sociological debates described by the term 'legal certainty', is achieved depending on structural or cultural variables on one of the following four levels: values, programmes, roles and persons. The levels of values and programmes are (in Talcott Parsons' terms) universalistic patterns of orientation; the levels of roles and persons belong to the particularistic forms of expectations. Both state and non-state legal orders produce universalistic as well as particularistic normative orders. The chapter draws a preliminary conclusion from the contributions to this book: universalistic norms are largely ineffective in providing legal certainty for global legal interaction. Specific institutions shaped to the needs of international actors, such as the London Commercial Court or the German Institute for Guardianship or international debt collection firms are much more successful. Some legal cultures completely renounce generalizing expectations and reduce legal certainty to personal relationships. This pattern might even become predominant with the further growth of Asian business cultures in the world economy which rely on networks rather than law.

Index